Alexander Patterson

The greater life and work of Christ : as revealed in Scripture, man, and nature

Alexander Patterson

The greater life and work of Christ : as revealed in Scripture, man, and nature

ISBN/EAN: 9783337263621

Printed in Europe, USA, Canada, Australia, Japan

Cover: Foto ©Lupo / pixelio.de

More available books at **www.hansebooks.com**

THE GREATER LIFE AND WORK OF CHRIST

AS REVEALED IN SCRIPTURE,

MAN, AND NATURE

BY

ALEXANDER PATTERSON

FLEMING H. REVELL COMPANY

CHICAGO   NEW YORK   TORONTO

Publishers of Evangelical Literature

Entered according to Act of Congress, in the year 1896, by

FLEMING H. REVELL COMPANY,

In the Office of the Librarian of Congress at Washington, D. C.

THIS BOOK IS INSCRIBED IN
REMEMBRANCE OF

REV. ROBERT PATTERSON, D. D.,

BY HIS SON, THE AUTHOR,

IN LOVING TESTIMONY TO HIS TRUE PIETY AND CHRISTIAN MANHOOD, HIS FAITH IN, UNDERSTANDING OF, AND FIDELITY TO, THE WORD OF GOD, AND HIS UNWAVERING HOPE IN THE KINGDOM AND COMING OF OUR LORD JESUS CHRIST.

PREFACE.

It will be seen at a glance that this is not a life of Christ in the usual sense. It is not a review of the events of the earthly existence of our Lord. There is a greater life and a larger work of Christ of which his life on earth is but a single chapter. While no apology is needed for any publication of the great theme of the gospel, it may be stated that there is a special reason for such a book as this. The author has examined many works on Christ and lists of hundreds more, and has conferred with competent literary authorities, and has learned of few works, if any, covering this greater life and work of Christ. Such a study of Christ should be available. The author presents this, hoping it may in some measure supply the need, and lead to further presentation of this great theme by more competent students.

There are still greater and more vital reasons for such a review of Christ. The Eternal Christ is the theme of Scripture, and not the Christ of the gospels simply. Until this is seen, the Bible will be an enigma. The study of the Bible should therefore begin with him who is its Alpha as well as its Omega. This book is a study of Scripture from this standpoint. It covers the whole Bible narrative, not in an attempt to mention all details, but only the great personages, events, and crises in which the person and work of Christ are seen.

It follows from Christ's place in Scripture that he is also the center of all Christian doctrine. Every truth radiates from him. A discussion of the work of the Eternal Christ necessarily involves a consideration of collateral truths. This book therefore contains an outline of the Christian doctrines studied from the historical base line of the eternal life of Christ, and running concurrent with his work from the development of which they spring.

A right conception of Christ is necessary to a right view of every doctrine of the Christian faith. Wrong or defective views of Christ will affect every other truth. Heresy begins with, or is based upon, such wrong ideas of Christ. Not only all Christian belief but all the philosophy of life is involved in the question, "What think ye of Christ?" Every problem and question arising among men may and should be studied from the Christological standpoint.

A more vital because a more personal reason calls for a study of the Eternal Christ. The believer's personal welfare and growth are in proportion to his knowledge of Christ. The spiritual nature may be stunted by being kept in a narrow range of truth as surely as poisoned by error. The soul must be fed by continually advancing study. The common evangelical presentation of the rudiments of the gospel is not intended as the only or sufficient subject of the Christian's consideration. We are therefore exhorted, "Let us cease to speak of the first principles of Christ, and press on unto perfection." The gospel is robbed of its power and attractiveness by being narrowed down to a few themes and aspects.

The great stimulant, corrective, and sustenance of the spiritual nature is the knowledge of Christ. To this the apostles continually urge, intending as we more fully apprehend Christ, we shall personally appropriate him, and so attain to the "measure of the stature of the fulness of Christ." It will be found that this intellectual apprehension of Christ will minister to the emotional reception and manifestation of him. The final goal of the Christian's faith, hope, and love is God the Father. To bring us to the Father was Christ's work. He does this by the revelation of God in himself. But it is himself in all the many phases of his character, of which the gospel narrative is but one. Christ there was "God manifest in the flesh," but in the flesh only, and only so far as flesh can manifest God. But there are revelations of Christ, and hence of God, which flesh cannot make by reason of its limitations. These are seen only in the Eternal Christ.

The great defect in the study of Christ is to consider him in but a single chapter of his life and work. It has been a great mistake to rest the proof and teaching of the nature and work of Christ upon this one revelation of himself, precious as it is. A defective conception of Christ is almost as dangerous as a false one. Indeed, all the heresies, fanaticisms, and dwarfed experiences may be traced to partial rather than false views of Christ. The great cure for all the errors of doctrine and defects of experience will be found to be the full presentation, knowledge, and reception of the Eternal Christ in all the many phases of his work and nature.

While this does not profess to be a critical work, it has been prepared with care. Every passage of Scripture quoted has been closely examined with the aid of approved critical authorities, and no view adopted without good outside warrant. Over seventy authors and works have been quoted and many more consulted. The author rests, however, upon Scripture alone for all final conclusions, feeling that this is the court of last resort in all revealed truth. The Revised Version has been exclusively used and quoted. This is a comparatively small book for so great and extended a theme. It is purposely made so. The author's desire is to show, if possible, in a comparatively brief review, the entire course of the great Life as far as it has been revealed, and as the author has apprehended it.

CONTENTS.

	Page.
PREFACE....................................	5
INTRODUCTION.............................	13

Christ a development in Scripture — The many views possible — Outline of the Eternal Life.

CHAPTER I.

CHRIST IN THE ETERNAL PAST.................... 17

Mystery of the Eternal Past — First light upon it — Christ "in the bosom of the Father " — " Before the foundation of the world "— " Framing the ages "— " First-born of all creation " — " The Word."

CHAPTER II.

THE WORD.

CHRIST IN CREATION........................... 27

Creation, the work of the threefold Godhead — Christ's part — " The Master Workman " — The Six Days' work — Evolution not Christ's method in either the natural or spiritual world — Objections to it — Scriptural narratives literal — Testimony of Christ and New Testament writers — The Bible a scientific book — Creation of man and woman — Plan of creation was Christ — Christ and the gospel are revealed in nature.

CHAPTER III.

JEHOVAH.

CHRIST IN THE OLD TESTAMENT AGE.............. 69

Jehovah was Christ — Fellowship with Adam — Adam's gospel the same as ours — Some reasons why God permitted the Fall — The greater Fall in Heaven — Preparation for the Fall in Adam and Eve — What the serpent was — Why Adam did not die — Christ and the Antediluvian World — The religion of Babel — Christ and Abraham — Beginning of the church — The Father of the Church — The beginning of grace — Christ's purpose and plan with Israel — The ideal social state — Christ in David — Christ in the prophets — World mission of Israel — Christ's work for the heathen in the Old Testament age — Results of that age.

CHAPTER IV.

JESUS.

CHRIST IN HIS EARTHLY LIFE. 128

The four Old Testament gospels — Humiliation of Christ in heaven — Descent of Christ to the lowest level — Birth of Christ as seen from heaven and earth — The Virgin Mary; her cross — The first "Christopher" — Jesus' silent years, growth, education, trade, as seen by neighbors; struggles, and temptations — Coming to consciousness of himself — Meaning of his baptism — The temptation — Breaking home ties — How Jesus lived, acted, looked; manner, disposition — Mission to Israel — Jesus and the Old Testament — Argument of probabilities — Jesus and the Church — The world's gospel — Testimony of unbelievers to Jesus — His claims for himself — How Jesus revealed God — Subordination to God — Gethsemane, its three temptations, spiritual, psychical, and physical — Jesus and Judas — The crucifixion — Meaning of his death to Jesus personally — Jesus between the death and resurrection — The scene of the resurrection — The three resurrection gifts to the apostles — Many acts and appearances of Jesus in the forty days — Ascension view of Jerusalem, Israel, and the world — Christ's visit to the spirits in prison — Christ's reception in heaven — His work there affecting man, heaven, and Satan — Christ's Pentecostal gifts to the Church.

CHAPTER V.

JESUS CHRIST.

CHRIST IN HIS PRESENT STATE AND WORK. 213

The three revelations of the New Testament — Titles of Christ in the Epistles — Difference between the gospel to Israel, the world, and the church — Apostles' omission of earthly life and words of Jesus — Disregard of Mosaic Law — Meaning of death of Christ for the world — Christ's resurrection the corner stone of Christianity — Why apostles disregarded social reforms — Is the Sermon on the Mount the gospel? — Christ as preached by apostles to the Church — Peculiar relationship to the Church — Christ's work for the believer — The living Christ — Intercession — Christ's work in the believer — Christ's work with the Church — The Kingdom as portrayed by Christ — Why the world has not been converted — Net results of this age — Christ's purpose in our age.

CHAPTER VI.

THE KING OF KINGS AND LORD OF LORDS.

CHRIST IN THE DAY OF THE LORD.................. 285

> The Day of the Lord the theme of all Scripture — The Christ of the future as preached by the apostles — Why neglected now — John the prophet of the Day of the Lord — The Apocalypse — Names and titles of Christ in the Apocalypse — Christ of the Apocalypse — Premonitory signs of the Day of the Lord — Longer than a day and more than judgment — Christ himself the great event — Christ and the resurrection and translation of the Church — Christ's judgment of the Church — Judgment of Christendom — Respites, gospel, conversions, and apostasies in the Day of the Lord — Rise of Antichrist — Rise and fall of the false church — Enthronement of the true — The overthrow of Antichrist — Judgment of the nations — The Millennium ; its rise, nature, and close; only a transition period — The final conflict — Christ in the judgment of the Great White Throne — Destruction of the world by fire — Problem of the lost.

CHAPTER VII.

CHRIST IN THE ETERNAL FUTURE 370

> Scriptures upon the eternal state — Christ's gain — His unknown Name — Arrangement of the spiritual temple — A material heaven — The new earth this planet — Restored humanity — Will the place of the new earth in the heavens be changed ? — Christ giving up the kingdom to God — Christ's continued work in eternity — Peopling the stars — The eternal, universal Fatherhoods — The varying ages of eternity — Christ's eternal office — Terms applied to residents of new earth — Race increasing in the eternal ages — Vast system of worlds — Earth the center of the universe — God all in all — Space is limitless — Earth the seed-bed from which God will people the heavens — The Church still patriarchal — Music of the spheres — Fate of other worlds hung in the balance. CONCLUSION : All have part in the future blessedness — "The Spirit and the Bride say, Come."

INTRODUCTION.

The purpose of Scripture is the glory of God in the welfare of all created things by the revelation of himself and his will to them concerning them. The means of this revelation is Christ. He is not only the conveyor of the revelation but the revelation itself. Christ is then the theme of Scripture.

The history of Christ in Scripture is a development. His picture is seen to grow from point to outline, from outline to feature, from feature to a living, moving, speaking form. We can see in the opening chapters of Genesis by the plural forms of names and pronouns applied to God that there are more than one present. As the narrative advances, a second person becomes clearly discernible. He assumes a name, and is seen and heard. After a time he appears in human form and is handled and felt, and in this form lives among men. He afterward reveals himself to individuals in a still more intimate way, so that each can say, "I know him." So also we see him revealed to enlarging circles of observers. He is at first seen with God alone; then he is observed by the heavenly intelligences, and finally by all creatures in heaven and earth. To mankind he is also so revealed. First to a few occasional individuals, then to a single nation, later to many of all nations, and at last every eye sees him, and in eternity he is known to a great multitude whom no man can number.

Christ is also presented in Scripture from various standpoints. He may be studied as seen by God the

Father, by saints, by enemies, and even by devils. He is seen to be connected with every created thing, animate and inanimate. We must observe him in many different activities and conditions. We are permitted to gaze upon him in the solitude and glory of eternal existence with God. We are told to watch him in the work of creation, and to follow him in his dealings with unfallen man in Eden, and as he afterward follows the wayward race in the long, sad journey through a world of sin and sorrow. We are even allowed to enter heaven and witness his reception as he returns victor over the enemies of God and man; and when he comes to restore all things, we may accompany him and witness the great restoration, and even watch his course as he disappears from our vision down the long vista of the eternal future. And longing to know him in some closer and more familiar relationship, we may turn our eyes inward and in ourselves each see Christ in himself.

The successive periods in which Christ is revealed to us in Scripture are seven: The Eternal Past, Creation, the Old Testament Age, his Earthly Life, his Present State, in the Day of the Lord, and in the Eternal Future. These form a continuous narrative running through Scripture. Each of them is a distinct epoch; and each succeeding era grows out of the preceding, the whole forming one great plan directed by uniform principles and tending to a prearranged and glorious goal. Christ is seen in these successive manifestations in extending displays of grace, each of them an addition to the preceding, and covering greater areas of blessing. The whole history displays a continually advancing and enlarging work of grace, until the spreading circles are lost in the eternal future.

The key-note of these chapters is "Jesus Christ, the same yesterday, to-day, and forever." We will endeavor to show that He who commanded the destruction of the Canaanites was the same who said,

"Father, forgive them, they know not what they do;" that he who said, "Come unto me all ye that labor and are heavy laden," afterward said, "Depart ye cursed into everlasting fire." We will see that the same hand planted the garden of Eden, opened the fountains of the great deep, blessed the little children, and draws the sword of Har-Magedon.

We shall endeavor to discover the principles upon which Christ works, and above all, the will of God for our lives, that we may so come into relations to himself as to one day be able to see and know him as we are known.

THE GREATER LIFE AND WORK OF CHRIST.

CHAPTER I.

CHRIST IN THE ETERNAL PAST.

The eternal past is an incomprehensible mystery. It is more so than the eternal future; for the latter is an extension of the present and has much in common with it, and therefore we may understand something of it. But that "before all things," before man or earth or any material thing or being—what then? We face a dark, silent, empty, and endless universe. The opening words of Scripture give us the first ray of light: "In the beginning GOD." This is the first fact known or knowable to man. But this adds to the perplexity. God is incomprehensible at any time—but in the eternal past, in an empty universe? Question after question arises in the mind. We find ourselves involved in a labyrinth of mysteries. The very superiority of God to duration and space perplexes us the more.

John, in the opening of his gospel, adds a second fact to the first: "In the beginning was the Word, and the Word was with God, and the Word was God." This brings us to the remotest point revealed to man. Genesis takes us back to creation, but John leads us to the Creator before creation began. At this remotest point, we see, side by side with God, a second Person, and One we know. Here, where the lines of the perspective meet, stands Christ. He is "with God," and the inference is clear that he was always "with God." There never was a time when Christ was not, as there never was a time when God was not.

In his epistle John adds a further statement of the eternity of Christ: "The Life was manifested, and we have seen, and bear witness, and declare unto you the life, the eternal life, which was with the Father, and was manifested unto us."[1] Other Scriptures also declare the eternal existence of Christ. The following identifies the Eternal Christ with Jesus: "But thou Bethlehem Ephratah, which art little to be among the thousands of Judah, out of thee shall one come forth unto me that is to be a ruler in Israel: whose goings forth are from of old, from everlasting."[2] Under the figure or name of Wisdom, which corresponds to "the Word," Christ himself thus speaks of this eternal state: "The Lord possessed me in the beginning of his way, before his works of old. I was set up from everlasting, from the beginning, or ever the earth was." With these all the statements of Jesus and the apostles agree. This truth is a great rest for the mind, wearied in its efforts to penetrate the boundless past, and baffled by the infinity of the three thoughts, — God, and duration, and space. It is the person of Christ which illuminates the eternal past, as it is the presence of Christ which is the glory of the eternal future. We can judge of the former by the latter, and both by the present; for he is the same in this, his "yesterday," and in the still greater "forever," as he is in his great "to-day."

Christ's relationship to God is described during this great past by this expression: "In the bosom of the Father."[3] The attitude is the familiar one of John who rested his head on Jesus' bosom, and that of the beggar who reclined on Abraham's bosom. It is a comment on the statement — "The Word was

[1] 1 John i. 2.   [2] Micah v. 2.   [3] John i. 18.

with God." It declares how he was with God and his relationship to God. This was to Christ a state of infinite beatitude. To this he looked back from the gathering shadows of Calvary, and in his prayer he referred to it in these words: " O Father, glorify thou me with thine own self with the glory which I had with thee before the world was."[1] It was a peculiar and exclusive relationship for Christ. After that, his glory and fellowship with God were shared with others; and although for Christ to share his glory is to increase it, yet this undivided communion with the Father was something which nothing could replace. We must not exalt ourselves and our concerns on our world and race by supposing that any or all of these are necessary to the happiness or the glory of the Godhead. Here is infinite glory and bliss before any created being or thing existed. The fellowship of infinite beings we cannot know; equal natures only can understand it. It is the full flow on the level of perfect equality, of perfect appreciation, comprehension, and affection. There went out from each to the other the wealth of infinite love.

We may reverently inquire, What was the subject of the divine conference in this remote point in the eternal past? We are encouraged to seek to know, for it has been revealed to us in some measure. In the mind of God the whole future lay in a perfected plan awaiting execution. It was undoubtedly the subject of divine contemplation. We afterward read of instances of this mutual conference. "Let us make man," was the expression used in conference over the creation of man. This reveals to us that there was a conference, as well as the subject of that particular one. We have a right to judge divine matters in some degree by our own ways, for we are made in the image of God. A Father and a Son looking forward to an undertaking in which both were

[1] John xvii. 5.

mutually interested would confer as to the whole plan and as to each part of it. When we remember that that plan was to be the beginning of what was to last forever after, and in which Christ was to have such a place, we can see that it was worthy of such conference.

The expression, "Before the foundation of the world," which occurs in Scripture, refers undoubtedly to this remote period. A study of the passages where this phrase occurs will give light upon this subject. They are as follows: "Blessed be the God and Father of our Lord Jesus Christ, who hath blessed us with every spiritual blessing in the heavenly places in Christ; even as he chose us in him before the foundation of the world, that we should be holy and without blemish before him in love; having foreordained us unto adoption as sons through Jesus Christ unto himself."[1] "Ye were redeemed, not with corruptible things, with silver or gold, from your vain manner of life, handed down from your fathers; but with precious blood, as of a lamb without blemish and without spot, even the blood of Christ: who was foreknown indeed before the foundation of the world, but was manifested at the end of the times for your sake who through him are believers in God."[2] "Father, that which thou hast given me, I will that, where I am, they also may be with me; that they may behold my glory, which thou hast given me; for thou lovedst me before the foundation of the world."[3] The latter passage identifies "before the foundation of the world" with the eternal past.

We see clearly from these passages that the whole plan of redemption was in the mind of God in that distant past. "The blood of Jesus; foreknown before the foundation of the world,"—here was all that was implied in redemption and its work. It was no after-consideration; no remedy to correct a mistake.

[1] Eph. i. 3-5.   [2] 1 Peter i. 18-20.   [3] John xvii. 24.

It was part of the great original plan. While we cannot fathom the purposes of Omniscience, it is profound satisfaction to see that all was known to God. The whole history of the future in all its details, the place of every person, the effect of every act, the course of all the ages, the final outcome of all, were known, considered, and arranged. This is as sure as that God is God. God has left no gaps; there are to be no surprises, nor any mistakes to be rectified. Every contingency was provided for.

We are now to contemplate Christ at this point of his history. He has a part in this great future. He is to be a subject of the plan, a beneficiary of it, and above all, its great executive. He therefore must have regarded it with the most intense interest and expectancy. He looks forward to activity, to struggle, to accomplishment, to victory, to the joy which shall come to himself, and infinite blessing which shall come to myriads of created beings; and more than all, to the glory which shall come to God his Father. For Christ, personally, it is a new life into which he is to enter. He is to have a new companionship. A company of beings are to be his for a peculiar possession. They are to be his bride. They are to take his nature, and he is to take theirs. Herein lies the grandeur of the believer's position. It is to this Paul refers in this passage: "Who saved us, and called us with a holy calling, not according to our works, but according to his own purpose and grace, which was given us in Christ Jesus before times eternal."[1]

It is also to this period this Scripture applies: "Through whom also he made the worlds [margin, ages]."[2] The ages were framed by the word of the great Architect of the universe. The duration of each period of the coming time and its character were established by him. The æons necessary for the forma-

[1] 2 Tim. i. 9.   [2] Heb. i. 2.

tion of earth and the old world of monstrous life, and the after world of the present creation, and the era of the antediluvians, and the Israelitish age, and our own, and that to follow, and down to the last temporal world or age, and beyond into eternity,—all were then "framed" by Christ on the plan of God. These are so framed together that they constitute one harmonious whole, each part contributing to the other and dependent upon it. The successive ages grow out of the previous age, as plant from seed, flower from plant, and fruit from flower, and yield each its harvest of results as God has purposed from the beginning, and Christ has appointed.

It is to Christ's preexistent state that the words, "The first-born of all creation" refer.[1] The expressions "born" or "begotten" refer to three manifestations of Christ: His resurrection — "the first-born from [or of] the dead;"[2] his birth of Mary — "There is born to you this day in the city of David, a Saviour which is Christ the Lord;"[3] and to his preexistent state — "The first-born of all creation." In the resurrection he became the first-born from the dead, and was manifested in a glorified body. In his birth of Mary he revealed himself in a human nature or soul with all its properties. This first manifestation of Christ we can scarcely understand. But judging from the subsequent experiences to which the same expression is applied, and the connection of the term with the coming creation, it was a definite revelation of himself, purely spiritual, in which he prepared himself for the execution of the great plan which lay before him. All these revelations were peculiar to Christ. He was in each "The only-begotten Son of God." In a sense, also, in each he was "the first-born among many brethren." It is the same difference and similarity which exists in all things between Christ and his people. He lived our life, and we live his.

[1] Col. i. 15.   [2] Rev. i. 5; Col. i. 18.   [3] Luke ii. 11.

By primogeniture in all these respects, but especially in the primordial manifestation, Christ entered a position of sanctity, dignity, privilege, responsibility, and infinite possibilities. The first-born was holy unto the Lord [1]— God's especial property and servant. So Christ became God's great servant in a sense, perhaps, impossible in his original divine, personal equality with the Father. Christ is also by primogeniture Lord of all. He is by his resurrection the head of all glorified saints, by his birth the first of all humanity, and by his primordial manifestation, first and Lord of all intelligences in earth or heaven. By these successive manifestations Christ, by the divinely acknowledged law of primogeniture, received the birthright also. He became thereby successively Prophet, Priest, and King to all succeeding things, beings, and ages. He is Prophet by his primordial manifestation; Priest by his incarnation, and King by the resurrection from the dead. These offices far transcend the relationships to Israel and the church. They are the great universal offices to all creation.

Especially was this true of his prophetic office. It was as Prophet he acted from this on, as will be seen, until redemption. The spiritual manifestation of Christ was his special fitting for this office which is peculiarly a spiritual one. It is the spirit of the prophet which receives the message, and it is in the spirit he does his work. The Holy Spirit had in Christ, then, a perfect spirit to which and through which he could and did communicate, and speak, and act. Christ also assumed in this spiritual manifestation vast responsibilities. He stands to all coming creation and beings as Adam stood to the human race. From him all proceed; on him all depend. Their loss is his loss. Whatever consequences befall the coming creation, Christ must bear the whole responsibility and guilt and fate. The destroyer attacks

[1] Ex. ii. 15.

the first-born.¹ So also the deliverance depends on Christ. Their ruin is his to remedy. We see here the ground plan of redemption. It is inwoven in the very nature of Christ. "He is before all things, and in him all things consist."² In this, Christ entered upon the great plan of the ages and fully committed himself to the great undertaking. In this primordial manifestation Christ ever after revealed himself until his incarnation. In this he was Creator and Jehovah. In this he was the Angel of the Covenant. In this he is regarded as subservient to God. It was the first of the steps by which the eternal and infinite God in the person of his Son descended to, and entered into, connection and fellowship with finite and created things.

The title applied to Christ in this manifestation is "The Word." It is the designation of his prophetical office. Cremer writes on this as follows:—

"When St. John calls Christ according to his eternal being 'The Word,' this must not be regarded as the expression and designation of his inner, divine relationship. . . . Christ is called the Word because of what he always is for the world, and on account of what he is for the New Testament church, as thus designated; viz., the representation and expression of what God says to the world,—he in whom and by whom God's mind and purposes toward the world find their true and full expression. . . . His relationship to the world and to mankind rests upon this."³

This title, then, is the designation of Christ after entering the relationship spoken of, in the first manifestation of himself, and refers not to the eternal relationship of Christ to God the Father, but his subsequent relationship as the manifestation of God, contemplating and conducting the great plan now being entered upon.

"THE WORD" declares Christ's relationship to God in this first manifestation of himself. As a word

¹ Heb. ii. 28. ² Col. i. 17.
³ Biblico-Theological Lexicon, Edinburgh, 1872, p. 406.

is to the thought, as a perfectly expressive word declares the very thought, so Christ manifests the mind of God. The whole wisdom of God is shown in Christ. Therefore this title "Wisdom," is also applied to Christ.[1] It is also to Christ in this character that the scripture refers which reads, "In him were all things created." He was God's plan of creation as will be seen. He is the embodiment of God's purposes from first to last in all ages. There is more than wisdom or plan in this title. God's word is equal to his act. It is clothed with the plenitude of energy. The prophet works as well as speaks. Indeed, looking at the earthly office, it is by the prophet alone that not only all God's words were spoken, but all his acts were performed up to the time of redemption. In this office, then, and in this title were expressed and effected all that was said and done by Christ up to the assumption of the succeeding offices of Priest and King. It was as the Word he acted not only in creation ("all things were made by him"), but it was as the Word he acted all through the Old Testament age. "In him was life, and the life was the light of men."[2] All his dealings with all mankind as well as Israel were as the Word of God. Even in the time of the assumption of his kingly office, before taking to himself openly the kingdom, but in the preparatory conflict, leading the victorious hosts of heaven, the name he then assumes is this his first title. It is recorded: "His name is called The Word of God."[3]

This title however does not express all of Christ's nature or work. It is expressive of intellectual rather than affectional nature. But more than intellectual or even dynamic display is necessary for redemption. Christ must become man; and man is more than intellect. This title, then, expresses Christ's work and nature up to his incarnation, when we read: "And

[1] Proverbs viii.   [2] John i. 3, 4.   [3] Rev. xix. 13.

the Word became flesh and dwelt among us (and we beheld his glory, glory as of the only begotten from the Father), full of grace and truth."[1] Christ, then, under this title must be regarded, as the Scripture indicates, as manifesting himself in his first and partial revelation. It is the Christ of wisdom and power, the qualities necessary in the work of creation, and also seen in the Old Testament where these qualities characterize the divine actings.

In this title and power Christ advances to the execution of the great plan which lay before him. We can judge his thoughts in a limited way by our own. As man is in the divine image and reflects the divine nature even in his ruined state, we with the Spirit of God may enter into some apprehension of the mind of Christ in this his first revealed acting. We see him looking out into an empty universe and down the long vista of the eternal ages, with feelings infinite yet comprehensible. Infinity is not absence of all such feelings as we know, but rather intensity and infinity of them. So Christ, we may believe, looked forward with expectancy, confidence, and triumph. He well knows all which is involved in bringing into existence created beings with all their frailty and indeed certainty of erring and failing. He sees the final outcome, and it is infinitely glorious. It is all one great plan in which everything has its place and works out its intended purpose, and all to display the glory of God in the grace he is to show to the coming universe and all its beings.

[1] John i. 14.

CHAPTER II.

THE WORD.

CHRIST IN CREATION.

CREATION was the work of God the Father, Son, and Holy Spirit. This is not only intimated by the plural forms of the names and pronouns applied to God in the account of creation in Genesis, but can also be inferred from the spiritual work of regeneration of which it is a type and the specific statements as to the part of each person of the Godhead. Over against the three divine persons in creation we see three distinct parts, — the production of Life, Matter, and Arrangement.

"A threefold unity; namely, a unity of power, a unity of form, or family, and unity of substantial composition does pervade the whole living world." [1]

We are instinctively led to ask if there was not an allotment of these parts in creation to the several Persons of the Godhead. We find it is so in the spiritual sphere.

God the Father is the Great First Cause. From him came all existences; he is the Father of Spirits. To God the Father we must attribute also the creation of elementary matter. Whatever view may be taken of the subsequent process, this is essential to every system of science and philosophy. No theory has ever been even proposed to account for the origin of existences. This is the statement of the first verse of Genesis which is literally, "In the beginning God

[1] Huxley, "Lay Sermons." New York, 1871, p. 122.

created the substance of the heavens and the substance of the earth."

The Holy Spirit is expressly declared in many scriptures as the author of life. We know well this is true of spiritual life; but it is also true of all other forms of life. His sphere as the Lifegiver extends over all forms of life. He is the author of all psychical and even organic life. Each living thing can say, "The Spirit of God hath made me and the breath of the Almighty hath given me life."[1] Not only so, but that strange form of life which resides in inorganic things, which we call Force, comes from the great Life- and Force-giver. "The Spirit of God moved upon the face of the waters."[2] "By the word of the Lord were the heavens made; and all the host of them by the breath of his mouth."[3] "By his Spirit the heavens are garnished."[4]

This leaves as the sphere of the special work of Christ, arrangement, or formation of all things.

This is Christ's own account of his work. "Then was I by him as a master workman."[5]

We have seen that Christ was the embodiment of the divine wisdom. All God's workings also are through him. He was and is God's great Executive. He takes that which God has created, and from it forms all things, material, psychical, and spiritual. This threefold work of the Godhead is seen in the creation of man: "And the Lord God formed man of the dust of the ground, and breathed into his nostrils the breath of life."[6] Christ took the substance already created and "formed" man; then into this formed body through him the Holy Spirit "breathed the breath of life." So in the spiritual work of Christ; he takes "the men whom thou hast given me," forms them into followers, disciples, and apostles, and into these afterward the Holy Spirit, on the day of Pen-

---

[1] Job xxxiii. 4. [2] Gen. i. 2. [3] Ps. xxxiii. 6.
[4] Job xxvi. 13. [5] Prov. viii. 30. [6] Gen. ii. 7.

tecost, breathes life. The work of God and Christ is so spoken of by the apostle : " There is one God, the Father, of whom are all things, and we unto him ; and one Lord, Jesus Christ, through whom are all things, and we through him."[1]

We should clearly distinguish between three great stages in the creation of the universe and our world. The first was the formation of the material universe, of which our world is a part, and doubtless formed at the same time and in the same way. The second great stage was the creation of the primeval order of life which geology reveals to us. The third stage was the six days' work spoken of in Genesis. The first stage was the formation of the material, inorganic universe. Of this Scripture says : " In the beginning God created the heaven and the earth." How God made the universe we are not told. It was no doubt a long series of ages. Christ labored by what we call natural processes. The description of the workings of Christ in the forming of the universe of primeval matter is given in many places. " By the word of the Lord were the heavens made and all the host of them by the breath of his mouth."[2] " Who hath measured the waters in the hollow of his hand, and meted out heaven with the span, and comprehended the dust of the earth in a measure, and weighed the mountains in scales, and the hills in a balance."[3] The whole of this description conveys the idea of careful, systematic execution. It is the work of the builder constructing a great edifice, and this is the figure everywhere applied to the construction of the earth. " It is he that buildeth his chambers in the heaven, and founded his vault upon the earth."[4] Job, the oldest book of Scripture, is particularly rich in accounts of the cosmical work of Christ.

[1] 1 Cor. viii. 6.
[2] Ps. xxxiii. 6.
[3] Isa. xl. 12.
[4] Amos ix. 6.

It is implied in Scripture, if not directly stated, that angels were created before other things or beings. Christ first surrounded himself with assistants. It is taught in Scripture that angels are used in all realms of divine operations. They assist in the administering of the affairs of divine government, and are ministering spirits to God's people. They are also used in the operations of nature. "And of the angels he saith: He maketh his angels winds and his ministers a flame of fire."[1] The passage in the creation psalm, from which this is a quotation, is thus rendered there: "Who maketh winds his messengers: his ministers a flaming fire."[2] Here, then, is a great revelation of personal, supernatural, intelligent beings operating the forces we call natural. All this agrees with the discoveries of science. We see that our globe, which is undoubtedly a specimen of the universe, was formed by the operation of the great forces of nature, especially fire, all in an intelligent manner working to the great end we see displayed in the perfect adaptation of the earth to its purpose. This makes creation comprehensible. Here is a succession of sufficient causes. First, God by a certain act producing the elements of all substance, force, and life; second, Christ forming these, by means of intelligent subordinates, working through these great natural agencies, into the manifold forms we see in earth and air and sea and sky.

Olshausen writes on this:—

"The agency of angels has reference principally to the physical part of existence. They are the living supports and springs of motion to the world for which the modern mechanical view of the world has substituted what are called powers of nature."[3]

There occurs in the record various expressions describing the divine operation, such as, "And God

---

[1] Heb. i. 7.   [2] Ps. civ. 4.
[3] "Gospels," 5 Vols., Edinburgh, 1855; Vol. 1, p. 46.

said;" "And God created;" "And God made." These are not synonymous. They imply varying forms of operation; sometimes creative fiat; again, by gradual formation; at times, by the operation of powers by us as yet undiscovered, and again, by such forces as fire, to us well known.

Having finished the earth to a condition capable of supporting life, Christ begins the second great part of storing the earth with necessary materials and provisions for the comfort of the race during the ages to come. We see in this old world a vast population of plants and animals. They were monstrous races. They were evidently not made for beauty or admiring contemplation, as is nature to-day. Nor were they fit for the association of human beings. Looked at for themselves, there appears to be no reason for their existence. But they lived, not for themselves, but for the race and world to come. Their mission was to accumulate wealth and leave it to others. To them we owe our vast supplies of coal, oil, gas, and other products, some of which are doubtless not yet discovered. Here was Christ in prevenient grace. He toils ages to build the house, and ages longer to fill its treasure vaults with precious metal, and still more ages to fill its cellars with fuel for winters which have not yet commenced their icy rounds, and illuminating substances for darkness not yet existing, and all for a race not yet created, but on which he has set his heart with the love of infinite desire. The work of the monstrous fauna and flora being done, they are overwhelmed in world-wide overthrows, and their remains hermetically sealed for the use of those who shall need them.

The state of the earth at the close of this old age is described in the Revised Version as "waste and void."[1] This conveys a very different idea from that given in the Authorised Version. The expression

[1] Gen. i. 2.

there is, "without form and void." The latter describes an unformed world, while the former an earth formed, but in ruins. As we have seen, the earth was formed and had been used for many ages.

The state described by the words in the Revised Version, quoted above, is the true one. It is that of a world in ruins. The earth was a globe as it is to-day before the six days' work began. The geologic strata were as we see them, save for subsequent upheavals in the formation of continents and islands. It was however covered with water and enswathed in clouds and darkness. It was the same state in which the prophet saw the earth after the desolating judgments of the last day: "I beheld the earth, and, lo, it was waste, and void; and the heavens, and they had no light."[1] It is important to remember this as we now come to consider the subsequent work of creation. The six days' work, then, was commenced on an earth finished as to its form and internal contents long before this period began.

The word "day" is used in the first two chapters of Genesis in four different meanings: the time of daylight, twenty-four hours, each of the six days, and the whole creation age. Examining the six days' work from this point of view, we see that while we cannot tell how long each "day" was, no long periods were necessary, under any view of creation, to effect all described in the record. Why should a long age be required to produce light? The world is flooded with light every morning in less than an hour. It was doubtless some special kind of light, for it is recorded, "God saw the light that it was good." The conditions were different and the operation also; yet whether by those operations we call natural, or those we call supernatural, the lifting or dissipation of the surrounding vapors to permit the entrance of light sufficient for the growth of the lower forms of plants

[1] Jer. iv. 23.

does not seem such an incredible event as to lead to incredulity upon the part of any one believing in God. The second day's work was the production of atmospheric air by the combination of its constituent gases or its diffusion by the lifting of the clouds of vapors which rested upon the waters. We see this done upon a lesser scale at the breaking up of every storm.

The third day's work was the separation of a portion of land by its elevation above the surrounding waters, and the infusion of the germs of plant life. The beginnings of life were no doubt small, as is the beginning of all life still. All this calls for no very extended period. Upheavals of great portions of the earth's surface have often occurred in a short time, while the sproutings of a spring day are a greater exhibit than this first and probably limited growth.

The work of the fourth day related to the sun and planets. These globes are formed of the same constituents as the spectroscope tells us, and therefore of the same origin as the earth. This was not therefore the creation of the solar bodies. The record tells us what the work of the fourth day, which related to them, was: "Let there be lights in the firmament of heaven to divide the day from the night, and let them be for signs and for seasons, and for days and for years; and let them be for lights in the firmament of the heaven, and it was so."[1] The word "light" is literally, light-bearer. The latest deliverance of science as to the sun is that it is a dark body surrounded by a luminous photosphere or flame; or in the language of Scripture, a "light-bearer." Whether this photosphere was then produced or its rays were then permitted to penetrate the atmosphere of earth still further is immaterial, it was then established for light.

[1] Gen. i. 14.

Sufficient attention has not been given to the remainder of the record, wherein it is declared they were appointed for signs, seasons, days, and years. The varying seasons and the years are produced by the inclination of the earth's axis, as is well known, but there was a time, science tells us, when there was no varying in the seasons. There were at the poles regions of perpetual winter as now, and at the equator a region of perpetual heat as now, and between these, regions of different but unvarying temperature, but there were no annual changes anywhere. This indicates a position of the earth's axis parallel to that of the sun. The time came when, so science tells us, the earth's axis was suddenly changed, the climatic zones were therefore modified and became as they are to-day, or nearly so. There is no want of harmony here between science and the Bible. If this was the work of the fourth day, and there is much reason to think so, it too could have occurred in a comparatively short time. The creation of the higher forms of plants and animals in land and sea suitable to such a a changed climatic condition was the work of the fifth and sixth days, ending in the creation of man.

It is interesting to notice that the six days' work lies in two corresponding periods of three days each, the last three corresponding to the first three. In the first day, light is created; in the fourth, the heavenly luminaries are adjusted to their office. In the second day the waters and air are produced or rather gathered into their respective spheres; in the fifth day fish and birds are created. The third day land is separated; and in the sixth, the land animals and man are created.

If we could see creation in actual operation, we would probably see all being done as naturally as the operations of nature about us every day. There are forces, of which we know but little, whereby mind acts upon matter in what is to us a mysterious manner. We realize in our own bodies this strange acting of the psychical upon the physical, and even stranger operations of mind upon outside matter. The great Mind which pervades all the universe could act on the surrounding substance in entire harmony with laws to us unseen and unknown. When the Creator said, "Let there be light," "Let the waters bring forth," "Let the earth bring forth," there accompanied these commands an energy which carried them into effect. The uniformity of nature shows one great whole produced by one great Mind. Life is the seed and nucleus of the physical surrounding substance. Given this germ of life, and all things are possible. Here we may study the type by the antitype. The in-breathing of the Holy Spirit is the beginning of that new life which develops into the babe in Christ, grows into the youth, and finally reaches the measure of the stature of the full-grown man in Christ. At Pentecost we see a spiritual work parallel to that of creation. There are the same phenomena,—the light, the wind, the earthquake,—all referring us to the old creation as a type of the new. By that one great in-breathing there were imparted to the subjects of the divine power the germs of all divine gifts and graces. So in creation there was by the same breath or word the infusion into air and earth and sea the germs of the countless forms of life, each coming to maturity under the divine law of its being which has governed it ever since. There is an added clause to all the fiats of creation—"And it was so." This means more than the taking place of the events commanded.

"The particle (or the adjective rather) never loses the primary idea of fixedness, establishment, order. And it was so,— rather, 'and it became forever fixed, established.'"[1]

The fact that creation is one of the types of the spiritual work of Christ, makes it important and ab-

[1] Lange, "Commentary on Genesis;" New York.

solutely necessary to notice what it was. It is thus defined in Scripture: "By faith we understand that the worlds have been framed by the word of God, so that what is seen hath not been made out of things which do appear."[1] There is no preceding life from which the new creation comes. In the earth's former state there was a monstrous order of things utterly unfit for the use of man. It was suddenly and completely destroyed as Scripture and geology agree in showing. So in the spiritual work of Christ there is a killing before a making alive, "mortification before vivification." Both these divine works are from above. It is as true of a world as it is of a man, each must be born again. Regeneration is distinctly stated in Scripture as a creation. "If any man is in Christ, there is a new creation."[2] The regenerate are "created in Christ" "after the image of him that created him," "created in righteousness."[3]

Seeing, then, that creation is a type and illustration of the spiritual work of Christ in the soul and in the world, it makes a radical difference what the work of the six days was. Indeed, this is the great line of division and conflict to-day between the adherents of the Biblical account and those who reject it. This line of division extends, as is inevitable, to spiritual truth, and therefore is the line between evangelical and heterodox views. It affects all philosophy and sociology as well as all theology. Indeed, there is scarcely a range of human thinking which is not vitally affected by the view taken of the work described in the first chapters of Genesis. It is for this reason that space is given here to the most prevalent and unscriptural opposing theories.

The theory which confronts the Scriptural narrative and the spiritual process alike is evolution. If this was the method of creation, it is also the spir-

---

[1] Heb. xi. 2.   [2] 2 Cor. v. 17, margin.
[3] Eph. ii. x; iv. 24; Col. iii. 10.

itual method, for the one is the Scriptural type of the other. If this is the case, then man is not guilty, he is simply imperfect. Human nature is not in ruins, it is in process of formation. Both man and world contain within themselves the "power and potency of every form of life." All that is needed are the proper conditions, and the world and mankind by development will attain to the kingdom of God. Religion itself was a development which came because man found it necessary. All religions are good, Christianity being the best so far reached by man; but he still advances, and other and better faiths are to come. Christianity, or much of it, may be laid aside as we have laid aside paganism. The ultimate man will by his own unaided efforts banish evils from life. Poverty will cease; disease will be almost annihilated by the advance of medical and sanitary science; life will be vastly lengthened and made pleasant by inventions and improvements, and this will be the kingdom of God on earth. From all of which it will be seen that the death of Christ on the cross was unnecessary for man's salvation, and in fact was only a beautiful example of self-sacrifice. As to those who die without reaching this lovely state of life and earth, there is no provision for them. From this it will be seen that evolution is not only a theory of science, but a religion also, and has obtained as such a wide acceptance. What is called "liberalism" derives its strength from it. Development is the liberalist's Saviour.

This theory is formidable because it originated in the domains of science. The vast and deserved respect in which we hold the deliverances of science has won for this, its favorite theory to-day, wide acceptance. Evolution has not, however, met the unanimous approval of scholars in the various fields of natural science.

Agassiz wrote: —

"I shall therefore consider the transmutation theory as a scientific mistake, untrue in its facts, unscientific in its methods, and mischievous in its tendency."[1]

Dr. Dawson, principal of McGill University, Montreal, writes: —

"The evolutionist doctrine is itself one of the strangest phenomena of humanity. It is destitute of shadow of proof, and is supported merely by vague analogies and figures of speech, and by the arbitrary and artificial coherence of its own parts."[2]

The Duke of Argyle writes: —

"These hypotheses are indeed destitute of proof, and in the form which they have as yet assumed, it may be said that they make such violation of, or departure from, all that we know of the existing order of things, as to deprive them of all scientific base."[3]

Sir Roderick Murchison writes: —

"I know as much of nature in her geologic era as any living man, and I fearlessly say that our geologic record does not afford one syllable of evidence in support of Darwin's theory."

We are met by the assertion that no one is capable of passing upon the merits of this theory or discussing it unless he is schooled in the various fields it explores, and technically skilled in its methods of study and experiment. This claim we cannot acknowledge, especially in view of its inroads on Scriptural and evangelical faith. We claim that ordinary intelligence is capable of considering its main lines of argument and the objections to them. One may be fully competent to pass upon the merits of money and detect the counterfeit, who knows nothing of the production of bills good or bad. On the other hand, the technical knowledge required to study in such fields as biology is not necessarily accompanied with the

---

[1] *American Journal*, July, 1880.
[2] "The Story of Earth and Man;" New York, 1874, p. 317.
[3] "The Reign of Law;" New York, 5th ed., p. 29.

higher order of wisdom which accurately discovers final conclusions. Indeed, it is often the case that the wider outlook is obscured and sometimes perverted by the immediate objects and themes of study which are no true guide to the general and accurate results.

Evolution is confessedly unproven. Its actual operation has never been seen or known. Certain facts are presented, and from these the inference is drawn that development was the process by which all things came and that there could have been no other way. This is a philosophically false position. Its firmest advocates admit its weakness. Tyndall said in a lecture before the Royal Institute in London, in 1887: —

"From the beginning to the end of the inquiry there is not, as you have seen, a shadow of evidence in favor of the doctrine of spontaneous generation. I am inexorably led to the conclusion that no such evidence exists, and that in the lowest as in the highest of organized creatures the method of life is that life shall be the issue of antecedent life."

In his Belfast address he said: —

"Those who hold the doctrine of evolution are by no means ignorant of the uncertainty of their data, and they only yield to it a provisional assent."

Mr. Huxley wrote as follows: —

"After much consideration and assuredly no bias against Mr. Darwin's views, it is our clear conviction that, as the evidence stands, it is not absolutely proven that a group of animals having all the characters exhibited by species in nature, has ever been originated by selection, whether artificial or natural." — "*Lay Sermons,*" *New York, 1871, p. 295.*

Dr. Rudolph Schmid, of Würtemberg, an advocate of evolution writes: —

"All these three theories [descent, selection, and development] have not yet passed beyond the rank of hypotheses." — "*Theories of Darwin,*" *Translation, Chicago, 1885, p. 61.*

Yet the whole school of this system are building upon these unproven theories as if they were facts ascertained beyond the shadow of a doubt, and advancing into every sphere of thought and activity, and demanding universal acceptance.

The nature of the facts adduced and the style of argument used in support of this theory and its conclusions, are well illustrated by the following summing up of general conclusions of evolution by Prof. Drummond:—

> "Take away the theory that man has evolved from a lower animal condition, and there is no explanation whatever of any one of these phenomena. With such facts before us, it is mocking human intelligence to assume that man has not some connection with the rest of the animal creation or that the processes of development stand unrelated to the other ways of nature. That Providence in making a new being should deliberately have inserted these eccentricities without their having any real connection with the things they so well imitate, or any working relation to the rest of his body, is with our present knowledge simply irreverence." [1]

The unscientific and unphilosophical assertion that "there is no explanation whatever of any one of these phenomena" except by evolution, is the foundation-stone of the whole theory. It is a negative assertion and not a proven fact. The facts alluded to by Prof. Drummond are these: The alleged power of new-born babies to hold by a cane or finger so as to permit of being lifted thereby, meanwhile keeping their limbs drawn up. The infant monkey does so also. Of this, Prof. Drummond says "there is no explanation whatever" save that man came from the monkey. Another of these facts is the presence of hair on the human body, especially on the fore-arms where it grows in reverse direction to the rest of the body, and long hairs occasionally found in the eyebrows. This also resembles the ape, and is therefore another irresistible proof, to doubt which is "irreverence," whether to the ape or man he does not say. The power some persons have of twitching the ears and

[1] "Ascent of Man," New York, 1895, p. 87.

moving the scalp is a further proof of animal origin, to doubt which is "insulting human intelligence." There is found in some instances in the neck peculiar marks called "gill slits," especially in the embryo. These resemble in position and in some other respects the gills of fish, and thus prove that man is descended from the fish. To doubt this is also "irreverence" and "insulting to human intelligence." These are specimens of basal facts, arguments, and conclusions of the development theory as stated by one of its most recent and able advocates. We answer the whole by an extract from one of the fathers of evolution more modest in his claims than his disciples. Huxley wrote: —

"No amount of purely morphological evidence can suffice to prove that forms of life have come into existence in one way rather than in another."[1]

Evolution is opposed by vital facts far greater in their force and vastly more fundamental in their character than the correspondences which it rests its claims upon. Some of the facts which resist the assertions of this theory are as follows: —

1. Geologic remains often show a reverse order of production to that demanded by this theory. New and great forms appear suddenly and without any intermediate links. Evolution presupposes development inevitably upward. But facts often show the reverse. Most of the forms of life in the geologic ages appear at the first at their best. To-day there is no fact better recognized than a tendency to degeneration.

2. The extreme length of time demanded by this theory is utterly inconsistent with the age of the earth as evidenced by the action of tides, the heat of the earth and of the sun. The comparatively recent period of time within which man has appeared on earth, as shown by all the evidences of geology, ethnology,

[1] "Study of Zoology," New York, p. 286.

archaeology, chronology, as well as history, is inconsistent with the long period necessary for his development according to this theory.

3. Nature shows fixed limits, or barriers, in organic life. Hybrids are sterile. Artificial varieties produced by man disappear when allowed to revert to a state of nature. In a state of nature each thing seeks its own proper food and environment, and failing to find it, perishes. Each propagates after its own kind and develops unvaryingly on its own lines.

4. No such changes or modifications of species as presupposed by this theory are found or observed in thousands of years of human observation. The forms pictured on the monuments of Egypt and Assyria are precisely such as we have to-day; while if this theory was true, these forms would in thousands of years have been pushed up so far at least as to permit of measurement or recognition.

5. Other fatal objections are thus stated by Dr. Robert Patterson : —

"Natural Selection is not a productive force: it cannot create, but only preserve, and therefore could not populate the world. . . . Natural selection cannot account for organs made or strengthened in opposition to the physical force of the animal. . . . Many variations are positively injurious to their owners. . . . Variations are not generally profitable at first, and therefore according to this theory could not be preserved. . . . Anticipatory organs cannot be accounted for by Natural Selection. . . . The improved types do not crowd out the simple forms as this theory requires. The accidental occurrence of profitable variations at long intervals of time could not possibly have produced the beautiful adaptations of nature. . . . It attributes the elevation of man and of all animals to an agency [the struggle for existence] which cannot possibly have elevated these higher races, since it always has a degrading agency."[1]

6. This theory confounds two things which differ, — the development of species and of the individual. The facts of the latter it adduces in support of the

[1] "Errors of Evolution ," Boston, 1885, pp. 238-267.

former. Such are the facts of embriology and the finding of rudimentary organs or parts or habits of the lower forms in the higher. These only prove the development, as will be seen later, of the individual, and the formation of all on a general plan.

7. History and archæological discovery condemn by positive facts. Savage races are races in a state of decay from former higher conditions and not in process of development. There is no evidence of advance among such races to-day, save as effected by outside influence. The Chinese have made no progress in thousands of years. The Hindus, save as affected by European civilization, have retrograded. The pigmies of Central Africa are just what they were pictured on the tombs of Egypt three thousand years ago. The ancient civilizations of Egypt and Assyria and Mexico appear at their best at first. They have no preparatory stages. The more ancient peoples such as the Babylonians and Persians were more true and reverent than the later Greeks. The earlier Greeks and Romans were more advanced in all moral traits than their descendants in the time of Christ. Decline marked the course of all up to the Christian era.

8. There are seven great fundamental facts which evolution has not accounted for, and makes no pretense of doing so. These are Matter, Motion, Life, Consciousness, Christ, Christian Experience, and the Future Life.

The demands of evolution upon credulity are far beyond those which Scripture asks of faith, and are extravagant and absurd. An organ as complex and perfect as the eye was, it claims, the product of repeated, chance, and favorable happenings continued persistently, and operating on that particular spot during long ages by which it was gradually developed and became the delicate and complex organ it is. The process is thus described: There was a thin spot in the skin of the animal's head; under this was a cell containing liquid, in which was a nerve. The light falling upon this thin place in the skin produced a gratifying sensation and caused the animal to turn that side of its head to the sun. Its progeny inherited the same habit, and their progeny also, and so on indefinitely. By this use, that part became sensitive to the light and more and more so, as thus used, and so the sense of sight was aroused or produced, and, with it, the organ by which sight was exercised was finally and fully developed. There came from this sense of sight ideas of things, as fear at the appearance of enemies and desire at the sight of food, and reasonings accordingly, and all that makes up mind in animals or what corresponds to it, and the full-formed mental power of man, with all his hopes and aims, aspirations, education, civilization, religion, and moral and spiritual character. All this came from the animal turning that thin spot in its head to the sun. We are asked to believe this, and to call it science, and for it to reject the simple and sufficient and noble account of the Scriptures.

Evolution is wholly unchristian in its spirit. It is a harsh and cruel theory. It sacrifices the individual to the class. It destroys or neglects myriads of creatures to advance one. It looks to the race and takes no account of the individual. It bids him look for his consolation to the advance of the race, ages after he is dead and gone. It teaches the fierce struggle for existence and "the survival of the fittest," that is, the strongest. These are the principles of the brute, pure and simple. It tells man he came from the brute and then leads him back to the brute. It is diametrically opposed to the divine principle as seen in Christ and his work, which is the welfare of others and not self.

Evolution is a relic of heathenism revived and expanded.

"In the systems of Greek and Scandinavian mythology, spirit is evolved from matter; matter up to spirit works. They begin with the lowest form of being,— night, chaos, a mundane egg,— and evolve the higher gods therefrom."[1]

Evolution in its radical, and only consistent form is absolutely atheistic. It needs no God either at the beginning or end of human existence. The basis of it is the fixedness of the natural and its sufficiency to account for all things. Matter is the cause and mind the effect. There was no preconceived plan. All we see is the result of a multitude of chance happenings operating through a vast period of time.

There is a modified view of evolution held by many believers in the Scriptures, that man's body was derived from some animal, but his soul imparted by a divine act. This renders the first half of the Scripture account figuratively and the second part of the same verse literally. This system of exegesis is vicious in the extreme and violates all rules of literary and Scriptural interpretation. By this any scripture may be made to mean anything. Nor, if evolution is true at all, is there any logical reason why the soul should not be developed as the body was? This is the position of the radical evolutionist and is consistent. Equal evidences can be given for the one as for the other. This half-way acceptance of evolution does by no means relieve the narrative of difficulty. Let any one try to imagine man being created in this half and half style. Since the evolutionist is instructing us, we have a right to more definite information than generalizing statements, such as that man was created out of "organic dust." This long, intricate, and incredible account can by no means be drawn from these words: "And God made man in his own image and breathed into his nostrils the breath of life." Here are two parts in the process. It was the first

---

[1] "Ten Great Religions," James Freeman Clarke; Boston and New York, 1892, p. 231.

which was in the image of God. A beast is not the image of God no matter what life is imparted to him. The modified view of evolution is exposed to even greater objection than the radical view. The believer in it is on a side hill. He must go up or down. To accept as a "method of creation" an unproven theory is unsafe in the extreme. It is simply a "refuge of lies" which time and investigation and the word of God, and above all the judgments of God, will inevitably sweep away.

This theory not only is not taught in Scripture but cannot by any means be inferred from it. A totally different method of creation is there taught. The two accounts are wholly irreconcilable as those who are consistent believers in either Bible or evolution admit. In fact, a Scripture argument for evolution is never presented. Its consistent follower recognizes Scripture as vitally antagonistic. No one need hesitate when he is offered the choice between the speculations of a confessedly unproven, disjointed, and absurd theory and the plain statements of a book which has witnessed the rise and fall of hundreds of conflicting theories, sixty of which it is said the French Academy of sciences disposed of in the last hundred years.

Why should man turn from the Scriptural account of his origin? What is there in it so incredible? Given an Almighty God,—the necessary predicate of all belief,—and all is possible. Nor is there anything demeaning or ignoble in this origin or the account of it. Better trace our origin to the skies than to the slime of the shore. Better, more noble and more credible, to believe that we are the result of a carefully designed plan and supernatural act, than to believe that there came by "a fortuitous concourse of atoms" and along the operation of accidental and scarcely perceptible happenings, either body or mind of man, and all his faculties and powers with all education and art and religion. Which is the most credible? which is the most worthy of man and God? which furnishes the safest basis for hope here and hereafter? To follow science, falsely so called, into this theory, even in a partial acceptance of it, is to be led by it through labyrinthine wanderings and into absurd and ruinous predicaments, and in its logical and final analysis into loss of all faith and hope.

The claim that the narratives of Scripture are allegorical is a twin theory to evolution. They are generally held by the same persons. A set of phrases has been adopted to describe and account for the Scripture narratives. They are styled "idealized history." They are called allegories and poetry. To these terms is attached the modern literary meaning of fiction, a thing unknown in Scripture. Nor have they any of the well known characteristics of the fable, myth, or parable. Neither in the accounts themselves nor in any other places are they so spoken of; but on the contrary, they are set forth as veritable narratives, and wherever Scripture elsewhere refers to them, it speaks of them so. The silence of the writers of Scripture as to there being any doubt of the literal truthfulness of these accounts would of itself be sufficient to give us the warrant of their authority. Surely Moses, Solomon, and Paul must have known the truth, yet they never intimated the slightest doubt as to the literalness of any of their narratives. It is the first rule of literary criticism that a writer is to be understood as he intends to be understood, and there is not the first scrap of evidence that they intended to be understood otherwise than literally.

But there is greater authority still. We must add to this testimony the witness of Him who spake as never man spake, and who said of the future, "If it were not so, I would have told you." It is inconceivable that Christ would have left us in error as to these facts, knowing as he did that we should have to meet them in these latter days. We will examine what he did say about the truth of the Old Testament narratives. Christ spoke of "the creation which God created."[1] He specifically mentions the creation of man, the story of the murder of Abel, the account of the flood. He mentions Abraham; he certifies to the narrative of the destruction of Sodom and Gomorrah; the giving of the manna as narrated; the story of the brazen serpent; David, Elijah, and Elisha, and their miracles, particularly the healing of Naaman, and the story of "Jonah and the whale." All of these he verifies as literally true events. We can claim, also, Christ's testimony for the events not specifically mentioned. It is inconceivable that Christ would have verified parts of these books and remained silent as to parts not true or real. He taught from it, and drew his teachings from it, and lived the life there predicted for him, and obeyed its precepts. In all this he affirms its truth. He quoted from nearly half the books of the Scriptures. He mentions several by name as we have them. He refers to the whole in a single statement, "All things must be fulfilled which are written in the law of Moses and the prophets and the Psalms concerning me."[2] These were the three parts into which the Jews divided the Scriptures, and include what we have to-day. He never once intimates that any of these were other than they claim to be. Jesus stands by the Old Testament Scriptures and holds himself responsible for their historical accuracy and divine origin. The apostles follow in the same regard for the Scriptures. They everywhere affirm their truth and rest their doctrines upon it.

Further: seldom is there any argument or reason advanced for rejecting the literal interpretation of these narratives. It seems to be merely a matter of taste and prejudice. The rejected narratives are those which deal with ignoble, or at least familiar

[1] Mark xiii. 19.   [2] Luke xxiv. 44.

things, such as the serpent in the fall; the "whale" part of Jonah's history; the swine in the miracle of Gadara. It is a characteristic of ignorance to doubt exceptional occurrences in matters of every-day life, while accepting others far more incredible but beyond the range of observation. We expect this in ignorant people, but we do not expect it in the class advancing these objections. Yet this is the basis on which rests this whole position. Any one who can believe Jesus Christ rose from the dead ought logically to have no hesitation in accepting any other narrative in Scripture. Yet some who profess to believe this stupendous occurrence, hesitate at these comparatively simple narratives. This is illogical and inconsistent. There are but two consistent courses — accept all or reject all.

The religion of the Bible rests on a foundation of historical facts. Overthrow these and its doctrines are rendered uncertain. To take the miracles out of the Bible is not only to take away its evidences and the basis of all its truth, but it is to destroy the very structure of the Bible itself, leaving a mass of uncertain, unsanctioned teaching, to which no one need give heed except so far as his own interests in this life are concerned. The body cannot live long after its bones are removed.

It is sometimes stated as an excuse for the Bible by those who do not accept the narratives of Scripture, and yet cling to its moral teachings, that it is not a scientific book, that it does not pretend to teach science. This account of the Bible does not agree with the character of its writers as capable and honest, and least of all as an inspired book claiming to be from God. Nor does this agree with the contents of the book itself.

The Bible is a scientific book, if teaching science correctly is a mark of its being such a book. The Bible is a standard book on jurisprudence, and its teachings are the basis of all civilized law. It is supreme in ethics. It contains the model form of government which is more or less copied by all modern constitutional governments to-day. It is a standard work in literature. It is full of political and commercial wisdom. Its rules for personal and family life have, when followed, led to the highest and best results. It contains sound hygienic principles. Now, it would be strange if a book so full of all other wisdom should fail when it comes to speak of matters touching cosmogony and natural science. It would be more than strange that a book able to tell about the life to come should be mistaken as to the affairs of this life and world. If we cannot believe a man's statements, we are not likely to take his advice. So with the Bible.

The Bible does not undertake to give a full account of every branch of science; but wherever it touches the field of any science, it does so with precision. The geological, botanical, zoological, and archæological discoveries of recent years, *where they have proved to be facts*, are in accord with the statements of Scripture. A few illustrations will show this. Job refers to the creation of the earth as follows: "He stretcheth out the north over the empty place and hangeth the earth upon nothing."[1] Long before the discovery of the sphericity and suspension of the earth and the inclination of its axis were these facts inscribed in Scripture. In the prophecy of Amos occurs this statement, scientifically accurate as to the production of rain: "He calleth for the waters of the sea and poureth them out upon the face of the earth."[2] The nature of the sun as a dark substance surrounded by a luminous flame has been already referred to. This is the title of it in Scripture — "light bearer." The great orbit of the sun has been spoken of in this text: "He rejoiceth as a strong man to run his

---
[1] Job xxvi. 7.   [2] Amos v. 8.

course." In the promise to Abraham the stars are spoken of as the sand of the sea. It is one of the most recent revelations of our perfected telescopes that the stars are absolutely innumerable. The figure of the sand is the very one used to express this amazing fact by astronomical writers. In Job again it is written, "To make a weight for the winds."[1] Here is stated a fact science did not discover until the seventeenth century. The atmosphere presses with the weight of fifteen pounds to the square inch. In motion air presses as wind according to velocity.

Lieut. M. F. Maury, superintendent of the United States Observatory and Hydrographical Office, thus writes: —

> "'Canst thou bind the sweet influences of the Pleiades?' It has been recently settled that the earth and sun with their splendid retinue of comets, satellites, and planets are all in motion around some point of attraction inconceivably remote, and that point is in the direction of the star Alcyone, one of the Pleiades. As for the general system of atmospheric circulation which I have been so long endeavoring to describe, the Bible tells it all in a single sentence: 'The wind goeth toward the south and turneth about unto the north: it turneth about continually in its course, and the wind returneth again to its circuits.' Eccl. 1:6. Wherever the Bible speaks clearly on natural phenomena, it affords a valuable clue to the scientific observer."[2]

It may be remarked here that the list of objections to the Bible is growing less every year, as the exact readings, meanings, and references of Scripture are being ascertained, and experiment and discovery bring to us the actual facts. Those who are doubting this Book which has stood so many centuries, for these puerile objections, will yet have cause to be greatly mortified at having given way in their faith.

---

[1] Job xxviii. 25.
[2] "Wind and Current Charts," Washington, 1859; Vol. I, p. 17.

When the Creator comes to the formation of man, there is a solemn pause and consultation! "Let us make man in our own image, after our likeness, and let them have dominion over the fish of the sea, and over the fowl of the air, and over the cattle, and over all the earth, and over every creeping thing that creepeth upon the earth."[1] The creation of man is described as a definite event. There is no room in the narrative for any long process of development. It is interesting to note that recent archæological discoveries confirm the Biblical narratives by the earliest traditions of the human race. Professor Sayce writes of the deciphering of an Assyrian inscription (Academy, July 23, 1893): "The text I have just translated shows that the first man so created was Adepa. But in the Sumerian the character *pa* might also be read *ma*. So that the name of the hero of the legend would in this case be Adema, the Biblical Adam."

We are to consider Christ as he contemplates this great work of making man. Let it be remembered that he was now to form a being with which he himself was to be associated from this on and forever. That he was himself afterward to enter the life he was now to create, and share all its nature and whatever changes and vicissitudes might come to it. We see from this that Christ had a personal interest in the formation of that being called man; further, that the being now to be made was to be not only the summit of all created things but was to be a partaker in the nature of God himself. "In our image" was the plan of the Godhead for man. He was to be like God in being a spirit, infinite in his possibilities, eternal in his existence, and eventually unchangeable in his destiny and character, and to possess wisdom, power, holiness, justice, goodness, and truth. He was to be like God the Father in supremacy over all created things. He was to be like Christ in created

[1] Gen. i. 26.

mediatorship between all lower beings and their Creator. He was to be like the Holy Spirit in being a life-giver to others.

The creation of man is illustrated to us under a figure of mechanical operation, that of the potter and the clay: "And the Lord God formed man of the dust of the ground."[1] The inspired account presents a figure everywhere understood, even by the lowest tribes; for the molding of vessels of clay is perhaps the most universal art. In civilized lands it is applied to the representation of the internal organs as well as the full and perfect human figure. Every sinew and organ and gland have been represented by the plastic art. And that which the potter and anatomist has done the Creator of the potter and anatomist could surely do. But the same figure is also used of all subsequent human beings coming by natural birth. Elihu said, "I also am formed out of the clay."[2] Paul, quoting Isaiah, uses the same figure: "O man, who art thou that repliest against God? Shall the thing formed say to him that formed it, Why didst thou make me thus? Or hath not the potter a right over the clay, from the same lump to make one part a vessel unto honor, and another unto dishonor?"[3] Even the evolutionist, Prof. Drummond,[4] uses the same figure: "By a magic which has never yet been fathomed the hidden Potter shapes and reshapes the clay."

It was or will be easily conceived to be a kind of art altogether different from that of man. Lange thus writes:—

"The process presented in Scripture, however difficult to be understood, conceptually, is the opposite of mechanical formation. It is the distinction between human and divine art. God does not stand on the outside, like a human artist, and by means of tools and shaping processes introduce his idea into the work. It is the word and idea working from

[1] Gen. ii. 7. [2] Job xxviii. 6. [3] Rom. ix. 20, 21.
[4] "Ascent of Man," New York, 1895, p. 71.

within. The outward material organization is its product instead of its cause."¹

Mr. Huxley describes both the same figure and the process in the beautiful description he gives of the hatching of the salamander's egg : —

> "It is as if a delicate finger traced out the lines to be occupied by a spinal column and molded the contour of the body ; pinching up the head at one end, the tail at the other; fashioning flank and limb to due salamandrine proportions in so artistic a way, that, after watching the process hour by hour, one is almost involuntarily possessed by the notion that some more subtle aid to vision than an achromatic would show the hidden artist with his plan before him, striving with skilful manipulation to perfect his work."²

The Psalmist in describing his own formation, has also followed the same process as to himself: "Thine eyes did see mine unperfect substance, and in thy book were all my members written, which day by day were fashioned, when as yet there was none of them."³ There is substantial agreement between the statements of Scripture and the revelations of science as to two of the three great facts of the problem. The material was earthy, the formation a process corresponding to natural embryonic growth. The point of disagreement is that the Scripture speaks of a *de-novo* creation. He who believes in God can believe he could produce a human being under conditions unknown to us, and yet as naturally as the formation of all subsequently born. The absence of the matrix is not an insuperable difficulty to an omnipotent God.

The Scripture narrative of the creation of Adam's psychical and spiritual natures is as follows: God "breathed into his nostrils the breath of life, and man became a living soul."⁴ Here is the work of the Holy Spirit seen afterward when Christ "breathed upon them, and said, Receive ye the Holy Ghost,"⁵

---
¹ "Commentary on Genesis;" New York, 1869, p. 146.
² "Lay Sermons," New York, 1871, p. 261.
³ Ps. cxxxix. 16.   ⁴ Gen. ii. 7.   ⁵ John xx. 22.

and so imparted spiritual life to the disciples he had formed. When this spiritual illustration of the creation of Adam is added to the divine plan of the first man — "Let us make man in our image, after our likeness" — and the actual work, — "And God created man in his own image, in the image of God created he him,"[1] — we see that by no possible allowance can original man have been a savage or a "caveman." Lange thus writes upon this: —

> "The primitive divine impulse in the first man and in the first race, makes them something very different from what is now called the savage state, and which is everywhere found to be the dregs of a once higher condition, the setting instead of the rising sun, the dying embers fast going out instead of the kindling and glowing flame. All past and present history may be confidently challenged to present the contrary case. Among human tribes, *wholly left to themselves*, the higher man never comes out of the lower. Apparent exceptions do even, on closer examinations, confirm the universality of the rule in regard to particular peoples, while the claim as made for the world's general progress can only be urged in opposition by ignoring the supernal aids of revelation, that have ever shown somewhere, directly or collaterally, on the human path."[2]

The creation of woman followed that of man. This agrees with the facts. Physiologically, woman is a fairer and finer creature than man. She is more refined in texture of skin and bone and hair, more delicate in form and nerves, more beautiful in face, more quick in intuitions, more sensitive in feelings. All this testifies that she came after man and was made of more refined material. This is the account of Scripture: "And the Lord God caused a deep sleep to fall upon the man, and he slept; and he took one of his ribs and closed up the flesh instead thereof: and the rib which the Lord God had taken from the man made he a woman, and brought her unto the man. And the man said, This is now bone of my

---
[1] Gen. i. 26, 27.
[2] "Commentary on Genesis," New York, 1869, p. 355.

bones and flesh of my flesh."[1] There are four witnesses to the truth of this narrative. First, the Scripture writer, who records it; second, Adam, who affirms the account; and, third, the Holy Spirit, who inspires both. In addition to these we have the testimony of Christ himself in these words: "Have ye not read, that he which made them from the beginning made them male and female."[2] Here Christ verifies both the authenticity and truth of the narrative and also the facts as related. Delitzsch thus writes upon this: —

> "What thus became independently existent in the woman, had existed previously in Adam. We say it was in him, not, it was his; for a glance at Scriptural passages such as Luke xx. 35; 1 Cor. vi. 13, which point to the abolition of bodily distinction of sex in future life, instructs us that, as the end is the fulfilment of the beginning, Adam was externally sexless. But being externally sexless, the distinguishing of the sexes was effected by a separation of opposites, which up to that time had been united, not outwardly, as pertaining to Adam, but inwardly in him; and the bodily distinctions of sex are only the external manifestation of the bodily organism transformed in conformity with that inward separation."[3]

This agrees with the original account, "In the image of God created he him; male and female created he them," and also with physiological facts.

Woman's nature and sphere are here declared. She is not self-derived nor independently created. "The head of the woman is the man;" "The woman is the glory of the man;" "The man is not of the woman but the woman of the man: for neither was the man created for the woman but the woman for the man."[4]

In all this Eve was a type of the church, to which Christ was to occupy a similar relationship. In her creation is seen a forecast of the broken body and

---

[1] Gen. ii. 21-23.   [2] Matt. xix. 4.
[3] "System of Biblical Psychology," Edinburgh, 1869, p. 123.
[4] 1 Cor. ii. 3, 7-9

pierced side of Him who was to so bring to himself his eternal companion. Adam himself was a type of his Lord. He stood at the head of the race as Christ does of his race spiritually. So also the process of formation is the same as in the church, — building. Everywhere the church is spoken of as formed upon the foundation of Christ by building. The purpose is also the same, — fellowship and increase. The figure of the woman is always used in Scripture to represent the church, and the mission and place of the church is best understood when so looked upon.

In the description of man's primeval home there is every evidence of a literal account. The names of rivers and places are given, and we can identify them, and locate them approximately. Here are none of the characteristics of the fable or myth. It agrees with what we know from secular sources of the beginning place of the human race. Nearly every nation has traditions corresponding more or less to this account. It was the right center from which to effect the distribution of the race. From this spot radiate the three great continents and great seas. Eden was to be the center of the earth. From this they were to disperse, and to this they were to return as their center of worship and of government. Eden was to have spread over the earth. Civilization was also contemplated; for here was gold, the essential and peculiarity of civilization. Without a standard of value no great commerce is possible. The precious stones represent luxury and adornment, another essential or accompaniment of a civilized state. There is here contemplated, not a race of savages, but cultivated, educated, sinless beings — a civilization without sin or shame.

The verdict pronounced on all by the Creator was, "All very good." It is to-day, although sharing in the results of sin, a beautiful world, and displays its Creator's purpose for man and love to him. But as it came fresh from its Maker's hand, it was a radiant jewel. It was at this point, doubtless, that heaven's hallelujah was heard: "The morning stars sang together and all the sons of God shouted for joy."[1] It presented such glory as no other sphere could exhibit. Its brightness was less than that of many others, but no other could show such perfection of finish and infinity of detail. Seen from a distance, as John saw the New Jerusalem, it was a jewel of green and blue, tipped at either end with burnished silver. It was curtained in fleecy clouds, which by partly concealing, enhanced its beauty. Closer examination revealed it swarming with an infinity of living things in endless variety of form and color and motion. There is no shape or combination of form or color which can not be duplicated in nature. Examining still more closely and critically, it is seen to present everything that can please the sight, gratify the palate, or delight the hearing, not only for the simple needs of the first pair, but for countless generations yet unborn, and ages to come, and conditions which had not yet appeared. The need of clothing, fuel, and light had been foreseen and provided for. The use of animal food, material for building, metals for money, and tools and materials for means of transportation, — all are there. When Christ built this world, he stored it with all necessaries to last it throughout its endless journey.

We cannot conceive, after reading this verdict: "All very good," that there was anything but peace and happiness in this creation. Whatever might have been the case in the former world, this was a blessed place. The animals as well as man were vegetarians.[2] Here, then, is the absence of that ravaging and tearing with tooth and claw by greater creatures of lesser ones. The reconstructed earth tells us what that world was: "The wolf shall dwell

[1] Job xxxviii. 7. [2] Gen. i. 29, 30.

with the lamb, and the leopard shall lie down with the kid, and the calf and the young lion and the fatling together, and a little child shall lead them. And the cow and the bear shall feed, and their young ones shall lie down together, and the lion shall eat straw like the ox. And the sucking child shall play on the hole of the asp, and the weaned child shall put his hand on the basilisk's den. They shall not hurt nor destroy in all my holy mountain."[1] This, then, was the state of earth when God said, "It was all very good." This was and is God's purpose for earth and all that it contains. This state in which we live is an interregnum. Suffering is an interloper; tears and sighs are abnormal; graves are excrescences. None of these are inseparable from earth and man.

We can now review the plan on which Christ formed all things, and their purpose. The following scripture declares all this: "In him were all things created, in the heavens and upon the earth, things visible and things invisible, whether thrones or principalities or powers; all things have been created through him, and unto him; and he is before all things and in him all things consist."[2]

The one thing clearly seen in nature is design. A great operation is seen advancing on the lines of a pre-arranged plan. To this every change conforms. From this no creature ever deviates. In this every organism has a place, and fills it. All work harmoniously together in air and earth and sea to carry on the purpose of the common design, as if one supervising intelligence was directing each individual thing and class, here pushing that one on and there holding another back, and animating all and leading all to the completion of a great and supreme purpose. In the inspired account we see the production of life during

[1] Isa. xi. 6–9. [2] Col. i. 16, 17.

successive periods by well-defined stages, from lower to higher forms, culminating in man. The Scriptural order is the scientific order of complexity, perfection of organism, and historical appearance. The same accuracy is discerned in the enumeration of the plants.

The order is the botanical one — "grass, herb, tree." In all this is also seen the adaptation of the lower to the use of the higher as is seen in their prior creation. The Master Workman planned and made a full unbroken assortment. Species and varieties have been from time to time dropped out, but the original plan shows no gaps, no unfilled places either in the design or sphere of nature. The Creator began at the lowest type and worked up, each succeeding type being an improvement upon that which preceded it. This beautiful order of created things shows a working up to some great plan, which is to be the culmination of all and the embodiment of all.

The plan of creation is also seen advancing upon interior lines in the individual organism. Embriology shows that all living things start life alike. The germ of all plants and animals is the same. Neither chemical analysis nor microscopic examination can discern any difference. In its growth each organism passes up through all those lower forms until it comes to the level of its own predetermined existence, when it stops and emerges into its life. The next higher beginning its journey at the same point, advances through the same stages, but goes on a stage further, so also with the next and each succeeding creature. Each is laid out upon the same plan, and is perfect so far as it goes.

Both these courses of development — the external advance of all from lower to higher organisms and the internal advance of the individual — are aiming at the same point of perfection, and find at last their goal to be the same. Both meet in the same ideal organism — man, which was the plan on which all these were formed. Man is the ideal of all lower forms. They are created "unto him." They are laid out on the human outline, and fill out the form to a greater or less degree. The Creator had man in mind when he made them, and he had them in mind when he made man. Creation is thus seen to be one plan and organism. Man has often been called a microcosm of the universe. In his body are found all the constituent parts of the inorganic world. Every sun, no matter however great, every star, however distant, is represented in the physical composition of the human body. In a closer and more vital way he represents all living things. In the growth of the embryo he passes up through every phase of organic life. He lives for a little time the life of each lower kind of being, and arrives at the end of his journey, having reached that which all others failed of attaining. Man fills out the full plan of the lower creation.

But man was not the ultimate plan. He was made in the "likeness of God," and this scripture we are considering tells us the special meaning of this likeness. It was in the image of Christ man was made. Christ was the special ideal to which man was measured. As all things of the lower forms of life look to man as their ideal, so man looks to Christ as his ideal. Christ was before all things, and looking to him as the ultimate plan, "in him were all things created." He represents the full wisdom of God, of which every other thing is but a part. God saw in Christ his ideal, and in creation worked it out. Creation is a manifestation of Christ. Every part and thing in creation is a reproduction of the divine nature as seen in Christ. Christ worked himself into creation as he does spiritually into those who are the subjects of the new creation. The converse of this is true,— "In him all things consist." In Christ is everything represented — the material universe in all its elements, life in all its forms, from the lowest organism in the ascending scale to man; and from man up through the higher forms which inhabit the, as yet to us, unseen world; and to God himself — all are represented "in him." They are created "unto him," and are found "in him" in all their constituents. Christ is the bond of the universe, for "in him all things consist." He is that which holds it together. He not only unites God and man, but all creation is united together in him. Creation is a unity, and Christ is its bond and center. Creation is therefore holy. It is the house of God, that larger house of which Christ spake when he said, "In my Father's house are many mansions."

Further: "In him all things consist." Creation depends on Christ. The correlation of forces is a well-known fact. They are interconvertible. Light can be changed into chemical action, and that into heat, and that into motion, and that again into light. And this order can be reversed. The conclusion is inevitable that these are forms of one and the same force, or are various operations of some common central force. Scripture shows this to be the emanation of the divine energy, which is the power of the Holy Spirit operating in force, organic life, psychical activity, and spiritual power. We know the Holy Spirit proceeds from God through Christ. Christ therefore is the immediate source of all life. That which we call gravity, and its compensatory force which we call centrifugal, all forms of chemical action, all organic life of plants and animals, all that varied animation which throbs in man and lifts him above all creation, that higher form of life which expresses itself in prayer and piety and self-sacrifice, all that further power by which immortal beings live and exercise their mighty powers,— every one of these forms of life depends on Him "in whom all things consist." In him all things live and move and have their being.

In a still higher sense, "In him all things consist." He is "the firstborn of all creation." He is, as has been seen, the great universal Prophet, Priest, and King. Mediatorial work was and is needed for creation as well as for sinful man. Together they came, and together they fell. But in another sense and a broader sense Christ is the great Mediator between all things and God. Sin and death came long before man. Leaves faded, animals died, angels sinned, before man had a being. All these needed a mediator. We must ever bear in mind that we are not all of creation, and that the work of Christ extends far beyond the bounds of man. Creation needed a Saviour as well as a Creator. We can distinguish between Christ's work as universal Mediator and as man's Redeemer. The former is much older and wider than the latter. It is in this wide sense all things consist in him.

"Unto Him" were all things created. Christ is the owner and heir of all creation. He is so by the three rights of Primogeniture, Redemption, and Victory. But we are now considering the first only. This has been referred to as coming from his being the "first-born of all creation." Every foot of land on earth is Christ's. The silver and the gold are his. Every living thing is his. He has the original deed, and has never conveyed title to any, save those who are to be joint heirs with him, in final ownership and occupancy. Sin is a trespasser, and Satan a robber. God has by this original right given Christ the fee to all creation. "The earth is the Lord's and the fulness thereof."

If Christ is so personally and intimate.y connected with nature, it should reveal him, and reveal him in his peculiar personality and offices. It has been seen that there was a plan on which creation was constructed, and that plan was Christ, and that Christ worked himself into creation. Therefore creation should show all of Christ and all of the gospel; and it does. The argument for the existence of God from design seen in nature is presented in many places in Scripture, and has never been answered. But we are now to look for Christ himself in nature. It was man's first Bible, and for centuries it was his only Bible. Whoever shuts his eyes to this older Scripture is not wise. To it Christ turned for texts and parables; to it he betook himself for comfort as he fled from the haunts of man, for rest and strength in the wilderness and mountain-top. It was to the Creator the apostles directed their prayer when seeking the Holy Spirit, and to him the greatest of the apostles appealed, to bring careless man's thoughts to God.

The incarnation of Christ in nature has been shown. He lives in every living thing. The double relationship of the Christian is true of all Christ's holy world of created things. They are in him and he is in them. The earthly life of Christ is seen in nature's processes. Every living thing is born as he was. In solitude and silence everything that hath life is born of God. Every plant and animal has its time of waiting until its hour is come, and it receives its baptism for service of fruit-bearing.

The ministry of Christ is being repeated every day. The Son of man is still on earth. Miracles have not ceased. The only healing natural man can effect is nature's healing. Every harvest is a table spread in the wilderness. Every storm is stilled as that on Galilee. And if we would only listen, we would hear sermons from lilies and sparrows and fields of grain as in days of old.

The cross is the great principle of nature's action. "Except a grain of wheat fall into the earth and die, it abideth by itself alone: but if it die, it beareth much fruit."[1] The story of the cross is told whenever a grain of seed falls into the ground and dying gives life to others. Vicarious suffering is the law of nature. By it come fruitful harvests and filled granaries. The struggle for existence is not the great effort of living things. There is a greater struggle than that. The aim of every organic thing is not self-preservation but propagation. For this it lives and eats and toils, and at last, having accomplished that for which it came, it dies. The mother animal struggles most fiercely, not for her own life, but for that of her young. The plant strives to lift its head up through the surrounding mass to reach the light and blossom and bear its fruit.

We have seen that the law of entrance into the kingdom of God is this: "Ye must be born from above." The clod cannot enter the plant sphere nor the plant into that of the upper animal kingdom, except it be born from above. The power of the upper kingdom must come upon it, and by its own strength incorporate it and make it part of itself. The six days' creation teaches this lesson and is set before us as a type of the necessary change. The first chapter of the Bible is a proof and type and illustration of the law, "Ye must be born again." There the steps of the change are shown. First, in the creation and regeneration is the Spirit of God moving in the darkness. Light is the first gift to the soul as to the dark world. The breath of the Spirit, the formation of a new heart in which the seeds of all life can grow, and the culmination of the work in the new man are the steps of the work of Christ in the soul and the earth. A Sabbath rest and a life in Eden follows each.

There is faith, too, in nature. All things live there by faith. There is no distrust there. Each plant and animal lives by the day. The seed sprouts, and trusts that showers will come and sun will shine.

[1] John xii. 24.

The ground sparrow builds her nest beside a clod, and trusts that no foot will crush it, and that her small family will be provided for. The little ant goes forth on its daily ramble amid untold and awful dangers, and doubts not it will return safely to its home.

For entire consecration we must look to nature. There everything is wholly devoted to the will of Him who made it, and asks for nothing more than to do his will. There is no sin in nature. Every plant and bird and animal is perfectly holy. The little insect fluttering in the sunshine for a day, perfectly fulfils its Maker's will.

Nature tells us of another life and world. Resurrection is taught by Paul in the great resurrection chapter[1] in the language and processes and forms of nature. The whole plan of Christ, the plan of the ages, has been disclosed in every field sown and reaped. Creation is a prophecy. The stars tell of other worlds than ours. The sunset is an open door into heaven through which every devout soul may look and see an apocalyptic vision. It comes to us silently in the evening of the day when weary man needs to be helped to his rest; and as the rising shadows of the earth veil it from our sight, it sends to us through the twilight a parting message,—"I will come again." Summer is nature's account of heaven. We instinctively describe our heaven so. We love to picture it a land of green fields and crystal streams, of fruits and flowers. We ask where heaven is, and looking up, the heavens declare to us the coming glory of God.

Nor is the truth of the other and sterner side left untold. Nature visits awful penalties on all violators of her laws, even to death. She punishes the rebel and abuser of the natural laws of God. The fate that smites the glutton and drunkard and de-

---

[1] 1 Cor. xv.

bauchee, the pestilence that walks through the haunts of filth and vice, are nature's penalties. The thunder and earthquake warn man of a coming day of doom. The fires of the volcano tell of the possible fate of earth, and the bottomless lake of fire living in earth's center verifies Scripture which says, Such is hell. Nature tells us some are lost. Every belated stalk moans in its wintry fate, "The harvest is passed and the summer is ended; and I am not saved."

It is in view of all this that the apostle writes: "The invisible things of Him since the creation of the world are clearly seen, being perceived through the things that are made, even his everlasting power and divinity; that they may be without excuse."[1] At the last great accounting, if any voice shall say, "I did not know," nature will answer by ten thousand voices, "I told you all." Impiety is unnatural; unbelief is insanity; atheism is a crime against nature. Nature's gospel is despised of man as her Master's gospel was and is. She, like her Master, is sad over man's neglect. All her voices are in the minor key. Nature's aspects are strangely solemnizing. Not only the undevout astronomer is mad, but all are worse than mad who in Nature's temple forget to worship Him who made and sustains it all. It was this Christ had in mind when he said, "If these should hold their peace, the very stones would cry out." Nature is indignant at man's impiety and rebellion against their common Maker and Ruler.

There is great comfort to the people of Christ, as they look out on it all, to know it is his and therefore holy. We are in his temple wherever we are. Every stone is sacred, every foot of earth is consecrated. All its many voices are sounds of praise. All its creatures are worshipers. As surely as from around the throne there rises a pure and full anthem of glory to God, so from all in air and earth and sea

[1] Rom. i. 20.

there rises an answering volume of praise. Science tells us all things are in motion ; nature is constantly vibrating with sensation ; that even stones are not lifeless things. Their atoms are constantly moving. From the lowest depths of earth to the highest and most distant star, creation praises God. The Psalmist describes it in these words — nature's song of praise : "Praise the Lord from the earth, ye dragons and all deeps : fire and hail, snow and vapor ; stormy wind, fulfilling his word ; mountains and all hills ; fruitful trees and all cedars ; beasts, and all cattle ; creeping things and flying fowl."[1] There is great peace for the believer in the knowledge of the world he lives in. He is in his Father's house ; and looking forward to the new earth, knowing whose it was and is, can say, "I shall dwell in the house of the Lord forever." Death is only passing from the outer to the inner sanctuary.

[1] Psalm cxlviii.

CHAPTER III.

JEHOVAH.

CHRIST IN THE OLD TESTAMENT AGE.

WITH the advent of man, the work of Christ changed. Creation gave place to providence. Christ now began that long course of varied experiences with man which was to continue thenceforward forever. He then identified himself with a race from which he was never to be separated.

There is a change in the name applied to Deity when man comes into view. The name previous to this event is the general name, "God." In Christ's special dealing with man it is the "LORD God." This is Jehovah, the name by which Christ was to be known to his own people, and in the special relationships he held to them. Jehovah of the Old Testament was Christ. The Scriptural argument is briefly as follows: Jehovah was often seen, while "no man hath seen God at any time." Jehovah was the God of Abraham, and the body of believers is one from Abraham down,[1] and Christ is the head of the church. There are also distinct statements of Scripture to this effect: "He was in the world, and the world was made by him, and the world knew him not;"[2] "They drank of a spiritual rock that followed them, and that rock was Christ."[3] The vision which Jesus said Isaiah saw of Jehovah was himself.[4] The prophecy, "Prepare ye the way of the LORD — Jehovah —" was fulfilled for Christ by his forerunner.

[1] Rom. iv. 11.
[2] John i. 10.
[3] 1 Cor. x. 4.
[4] Isa. vi. 1; John xii. 41.

It was Christ, then, who was so intimately connected with the Old Testament saints and known by them as Jehovah. Yet this identity is closely veiled both in the Old Testament and in the New. The above are about all the direct statements to this effect. The reasons will be more fully considered hereafter. It may be stated here briefly that he wished to be recognized by other means.

The name Jehovah is one of divine origin. It occurs seven thousand times in the Bible. Its meaning is most comprehensive. It is an epitome of the whole nature, history, and work of Christ. It means first, "The Living One," in this expressing the work of creation. There is also in it the idea of "the Ever-present One," and hence the character of Christ as Providence. It means further, "Covenant-keeper;" and in this we see the special relation of Christ to the church. All that is meant by "Jesus" is in this older name. He was the Saviour of the church always. It also looks into the future; for it is interpreted by himself as meaning "Him who was, and is, and is to come, the Almighty." By this heaven-born name, first of all, Christ revealed himself to man. Dr. Newberry[1] gives its origin as from parts of three words meaning, "He who was and is, and is to come," the title Christ applies to himself in the Apocalypse.

Christ's dealings with men are seen to be with them as individuals, families, nations, the church, and the race as a whole. Adam represented each and all of these. He was the head of the race by being first, by divine appointment and by fitness. The dealings of Christ with him therefore are illustrative of his attitude toward the whole. The relationship of Jehovah to Adam will be seen by recalling the purpose for which man was created. He was intended for divine companionship. The actual enjoyment of

[1] "Newberry Bible," London, 1893, p. 22.

this is seen by a single hint in the record, "And they heard the voice of the LORD God walking in the garden in the cool of the day."[1] The whole expression is very suggestive, "the cool of the day," the time for leisure and for friendly intercourse. Jehovah is walking, looking, and calling for his companion as if it was a common practice and the usual time to meet him. It is a single glance, but it reveals the daily intercourse of Eden.

After the day's occupation is over, the divine Son seeks his human brother for loving intercourse. It reminds us of the same Christ on the Mount of Olives or in the home at Bethany, where loving friends listened to his words. It was for Christ, as well as the happy recipient of his confidence, a foretaste of the fellowship of eternity. He spoke of this time afterward in these words, "My delight was with the sons of men."[2] It was not for Christ the fellowship of an equal being as was the fellowship with the Father; but it was with one who like himself was in the image of God and therefore could hold intercourse with him as no angel could. Each, although in a vastly different way, was a son of God. Each had a place in the great plan, each looked forward to the realization of it as the consummation to be longed for.

Adam was as yet not suited for the exalted privilege of fellowship eternally with God the Father. He was holy, but untrained; and therefore as to experience, immature. The first attitude, therefore, of Christ toward man was that of instructor. The Great Teacher began with his first pupil. Adam had this advantage over all his children in this beginning of his education, in that he had all his faculties in primeval perfection. The volumes out of which the Great Teacher instructed his first pupil, were Experience, Nature, and Revelation. They are the means of the instruction of his descendants from that

[1] Gen. iii. 8. [2] Prov. viii. 31.

day to this. They seem to have been given to him in the order named.

The first lesson was obedience. The Lord put him in the garden to dress it and keep it.[1] It is the first necessary lesson of youth. Obedience is the law of the family, the foundation of society; and as will be seen, one thing the whole story of man's experiences is designed to teach. This was joined to responsibility. The keeping of the garden was his charge. Work was the first thing given to man. It was not the penalty of sin, nor is it a penalty at all. It is the condition of life, and always has been, and always will be. However high the creature rises in the scale of being or the plane of privilege in this world or any other, the law of his welfare will be work. When any living thing stops working, it begins to die. Work is the law of life. Christ gives his own example and that of his Father when he said, "My Father worketh hitherto, and I work." But in neither case was it toil. For man that came later.

A lesson in the book of nature is related: The birds and the animals were brought unto the man "to see what he would call them, and whatsoever the man called every living creature, that was the name thereof."[2] The inference is plain that there was a knowledge of the nature of these creatures on Adam's part, and this came either from previous instruction, or experience, or both. It is a fair inference that Christ did not stop with the creatures, but that plants and the stars and all the many chapters of nature were opened and perused by this quickest scholar who ever lived. It is inconceivable that with such a mind in its virgin power and with such a teacher there should have been any hesitation in desiring on the one hand, or any unwillingness to impart on the other. Undoubtedly all the sciences in

[1] Gen. ii. 15   [2] Gen. ii. 19.

all their length and depth were unrolled before that ready learner. With perfect wisdom as teacher and faultless faculties in the pupil, learning advanced with such progress as is unknown to us. We have been trying to regain a little of that which our great ancestor had in all its fulness. It is certain that the first man was the greatest in natural ability and the best educated in all scientific truth that the world has ever had. Only by the same divine teacher can we regain his level of intellectual attainment.

It was especially by what we call revelation that Christ instructed Adam. Here was one capable of receiving the most exalted truths. All his faculties were in divine perfection. The body was unclogged by gross food or deadening drink or stupefying lust. The mental powers were in all the strength in which they were created. He was "in the image of God." In the closeness of this loving fellowship, truth flowed unimpaired from mind to mind. The story of creation was then no doubt revealed to Adam as we have it recorded in Genesis. The account is so orderly and so correct as compared with science in all particulars, it is withal so simple and so dignified that it bears all the marks of a divine hand. We may feel sure that the first chapter of Genesis was spoken by the same mouth as the last chapter of Revelation. Christ was the Alpha and the Omega of Scripture. No doubt the future was also then made known to Adam. There was surely given to him also, some intimation of his own place in the great plan of the ages, and the responsibility which rested upon him as leader of the great company who were to come.

But this was more than a state of training for Adam. It was one of probation also. He was not yet fit by nature for the exalted place God designed him for. His nature is thus described by the apostle: "The first man is of the earth, earthy."[1] Adam was

[1] I Cor. xv. 45-48.

not a spiritual being yet. The same change had to take place for Adam as for all his descendants since. His was not an immortal body. "Dust thou art" was true of him from his creation. It is interesting to consider what would have been the change which would have fitted Adam for his eternal state. Of one thing we are sure,— it would not have come by death. Death was no part of God's plan for man. He would probably have been translated as Enoch was, at the close of his appointed life-time, probably a thousand years, of which all afterward fell a little short. It is not necessary to suppose that he would have been on probation all that time. There was placed within his reach a means by which he could attain to the certainty of that happy state at any time. We often wonder what would have been the state of man on earth if sin had not entered. One thing is certain, Christ would have always been with man in visible and daily fellowship. Every blessing would have flowed from the presence of Christ on earth. Eden would long since have covered the earth. Millions of happy creatures would have been translated to heaven.

The question is often asked, Why did God permit the fall. Looking back as we do through the history of redemption, and having looked forward from the view we took from the eternal past, we see that the fall was foreseen from the beginning. Indeed, knowing human nature as we do, each one must feel that created beings left to their own choice will fall sooner or later. This only makes the question more difficult. Why, knowing this to be the certainty, or at least the possibility, did Christ create them, give them free will, and expose them to temptation? He knew it would result as it did. He foresaw that it would devastate Eden and plant earth with misery.

From that awful issue then opened would flow a stream of evils which would call for all his own mighty power to stay and overcome, and cause him shame, agony, and death. It is enough for the believer to know it was the will of God. God's will needs no defense. It is the standard of righteousness. This is to be fully demonstrated before all the universe, but now we must believe it to be so by faith.

We are not left wholly in the dark, however, as to the purposes of God, and he invites our inquiry that we may see and learn and believe. We say, and in a sense correctly, that God does all things for his own glory. But to think of this glory apart from the welfare of the beings of his creation, is not the Scriptural idea of the glory of God. To say that God allowed man to fall that he might in his recovery display his power and grace, is to attribute to God purposes and actions which do not give him glory, but the reverse. For a father to allow a child to become sick and suffer in order that he may show his skill in the methods for his recovery, is cruelty. God did not and does not so seek glory. Nor was the first purpose of God the salvation of the lost. Had this been all, he could have saved all by preventing the fall of any. The only satisfaction to the mind, aside from the attitude of simple faith, is the discovery of a reason or reasons great enough to justify the permission of sin and suffering. While we cannot solve this greatest of questions which has perplexed the wisest, we may inquire into it and find some light upon it, or at least see that there can and must exist sufficient reasons, although to us unknown.

Recalling the view taken of the eternal past, we discovered that the distant view reveals the existence of a great plan in the mind of God for this world and man and all ages and beings to come. Part of this plan, as we have seen, is the securing of a race of beings who shall be fit for use by him, and cooperation with him in his great, eternal purposes. They are to be with God as children with their father. They are to live with Christ as a wife with her husband. It is evident that there must be on both sides not only love but perfect confidence. They must trust God fully, and God must be able to fully trust them also. They must have an established reliability which will stand true under any test, and be absolutely devoted to God's interests, and perfectly and whole-heartedly and gladly submissive to his will. They must accept and believe without a shadow of doubt that God's will is best and right, and be immovably fixed in this conviction. This faith is the only ground from which can spring that love which is the bond of the union God desires.

God could have made beings so from the first, infallible and unchangeable. But the character of such beings would be fixed by decree as is the character of brutes or rocks. They would be holy because they could not be otherwise. They would remain faithful to him by the same kind of law which keeps a stone in its place. It is evident that such beings would not be suitable for the companionship of God and the high destiny he has in mind for them. God could have kept Adam in a state of unconscious and untempted innocence by allowing no means of temptation. But to give a being free will and then no possibility of alternative choice would be farcical. Such a state would be little different from the last described.

None of these conditions, then, nor any other conceivable one, could be the permanent state of such beings as God created. We can see from all the past history of God's dealings with his people as well as our own experience, what this character must be and how obtained. There is a character which can only be obtained by choice of right, struggle against sin and for right, and victory. Even Christ submitted to this process. He was "tempted in all points as we are." He was "made perfect by suffering." There is for us a necessity in this. Only by falling can we learn the value of standing; only by sickness do we appreciate health; only by failure do we learn the worth of success.

For the production of such beings there must be capacity of choice, and opportunity of choosing. They must have an alternative choice. They must know both sides, and by turning from wrong to right, exercise purpose and will. There must follow this choice a proof of it by struggle against sin and victory over it. From this there comes a knowledge of the awful nature and effects of sin and a detestation of it, and a full and hearty committal to right and God. They must learn by full and repeated trial that the will of God is best and right, and that for them there must be no other way. But there must be more than this. They must be led by hope, and see in God the future bright with promise for them and all. Still further, they must be bound to God by love, and this from a deep sense of his goodness to them.

There is to be one lesson such beings must once for all learn. The evidence of God's faithfulness will be forever established. The severest temptation which besets the believer now is when by distress or by apparent failure in answer to prayer, it seems as if God either did not hear or did not care for him. To doubt God's love, or at least his care, was the first and has been the constant temptation of the Christian. Faith in God will always be the bond of the soul to God and the source of power. This will be established by the repeated trials and proofs of life. It will appear that there has been no neglect by God of the smallest of his creatures, that every prayer was answered, that with all our mistakes and sins, all things worked together for good to each believer.

All this will give deep and immovable faith in God which cannot be shaken.

There was more involved in the demonstration begun in Eden than the welfare of those who heard and acted, or even their race. This world is only the beginning of other ages and worlds. For them, as well as this, the test was made. This is expressly declared to be the purpose of this display of grace, "to the intent that now unto the principalities and the powers in the heavenly places might be made known through the church the manifold wisdom of God, according to the eternal purpose which he purposed in Christ Jesus our Lord."[1] There is no doubt that this purpose extends to the whole demonstration and for the benefit of all intelligences and ages to come. We are "compassed about by so great cloud of witnesses."[2] "Which things the angels desire to look into."[3] All this tells us that not unto ourselves but to coming ages we are living and unfolding the purposes of God.

The purpose undoubtedly was to settle eternal problems. In some world, if not in this, in some time, if not at this time, the question was sure to arise whether the will of God was best and right. People will think, and in eternity harder than ever. Given the essentials of free moral beings, and questioning is inevitable. It is no harm to think or to question provided one is open to the truth. The question would have to be met and settled. God could have met it by a display of power and might and silenced all opposition, but that would not be an answer but a supression. It would not be worthy of the plan which God had before him as seen in the ages. To silence by authority is not to settle the question. It would not answer the questions which would arise. These beings would be under a continual reign of force which would be no such state as

[1] Eph. iii. 10, 11.   [2] Heb. xii. 1.   [3] I Peter i. 12.

God desired, and as was best for the permanent happiness of all. Better this issue fully and fairly met now, and the questions answered at once, than that it should be left open, a constant danger ever threatening the universe, hanging like an avalanche over the future, to break forth perhaps when the universe was filled with holy, happy beings; and, instead of affecting one small world, to involve the universe in an overthrow compared with which the sin and sorrow and suffering of earth and hell would be as the dust of the balance.

There seems to have been but one way — to permit an actual experiment and demonstration of the whole question. To this end sin must be allowed to present itself in all its hideous nature and effects; suffering must follow, and sorrow deep and widespread must be felt and endured. When this great experiment is over, every question will be forever settled. Every alternative opposed to the will of God will have been tried on this earth. Every problem will have been solved. It will be apparent as the noon-day sun to all intelligences that all has been passed through the crucible of actual demonstration. The verdict from this will be that there is but one standard of right, but one way of happiness, but one way of holiness, and that is the will of God. The participants in this struggle are to be rewarded for their part in this sad stage of suffering by correspondingly and vastly increased benefits hereafter. They are to have the highest state in that kingdom to come. They are to be the closest to God in all the universe. They are to bear responsibility and power for which their long training has fitted them.

The age of sin came at the very beginning of the long eternal plan. It was to be but a short era. What are a few thousand years in comparison with eternity? This earth is to be the only one stained by sin. It is but a small one and rightly so chosen. It is large enough for the scene of sin and suffering. The record of this world's history is being kept above. It will possibly be to the church in heaven as the Bible is to us. To this record of the great demonstration, reference can be made on any debated question. For we may be sure that questions will arise even in eternity, and perhaps emergencies and crises come where the wisdom gathered from the past will be used. As we look back to the little land of Israel, so worlds may regard this small earth and its eventful history.

In the execution of the great plan there was for Christ also a great reward. Christ already had universal dominion as Creator, but this is a rule by right and might. He longed for the rule by the free acquiesence of grateful and loving beings. He sees in the future a sphere far greater than the reign of law. He sees the reign of love. He has the crown of creation and providence; he covets the crown of redemption. He created a world of wondrous wisdom and beauty, but he sees in the cross a way by which he can produce a creation which shall far transcend this in every element of greatness. He will give an example of perfect obedience to the will of God. He will by the cross show what the nature of sin is in such a way as to make it hideous. He will thereby so show the awful penalty of transgression as to fill with holy fear of sin all beings forever. He will by his sacrifice thereon show the love of God in his death so as to hold by the bonds of love forever those whom he has won from sin to God. There is to appear by reason of the presence of sin, and as its great antidote, that matchless attribute of God in Christ — grace. "Where sin abounded grace did abound more exceedingly."[1] In spite of the mighty influences sweeping about poor, swaying man, he was to be irresistibly drawn away from all, and to be fixed in the love of God.

[1] Rom. v. 20.

The tree of life was Adam's gospel. By eating of it, he could attain to the same condition as one who is in Christ now. The tree of life contained symbolically the gospel of Christ as we have it to-day, save that it was a bloodless gospel. It was for a sinless race, and therefore no shedding of blood was needed. Adam's salvation was to be had as ours is. The believer is saved by faith in Christ. Faith implies repentance. The latter is a turning away from sin, and the former is a turning to Christ. There was before Adam the tree of the knowledge of good and evil and the tree of life. His salvation was to be by turning away from the one and turning to the other. In short, Adam was to be saved just as we all are, by repentance from sin, and faith in Christ. There was no different covenant or salvation from that which has existed ever since. For even with Israel faith was the condition, and obedience its test. Adam, Abraham, Israel, the believer, and the world have all the same gospel.

The strangest thing in all this narrative was the fact that Adam did not eat of the tree of life. This is apparent from the divine message at his expulsion from the garden: "And now, lest he put forth his hand and take also of the tree and eat and live forever, therefore the Lord God sent him forth from the garden of Eden."[1] We can scarcely understand how he should so neglect the greatest thing in the garden. This indicates something wrong and deep seated. He doubtless felt secure in the possession of such abilities and privileges.

Perhaps he did not feel his need of the means of grace and life. Under all was either pride in his own sufficiency, or doubt as to the efficiency of the tree, or unbelief in the certainty of the consequences. There was pride in some form doubtless. Whatever it was, we see clearly that the fall was no suddenly sprung attack from without. It is according to the method

[1] Gen. iii. 22, 23.

of the tempter that there should be a preparation for temptation. The readiness with which Eve and Adam yielded shows a weakening of resisting power. As to the tree of knowledge of good and evil, there was commanded him, "Of the tree of knowledge of good and evil, thou shalt not eat of it, for in the day thou eatest of it thou shalt surely die."[1] This called for simple obedience. It was a test of the main question as to the will of God. There was no explanation of why the knowledge of good and evil was not good for them. They were left with the will of God as their only guide, and expected to obey in simple faith.

The fall began in heaven. Sin entered God's house before it invaded man's. Christ felt its sting before man felt its stab. All Scripture agrees that sin began with Satan. He was an angel of great power and glory. It was doubtless Satan who was meant in the following words applied to one of his earthly agents: "Thou sealest up the sum, full of wisdom, and perfect in beauty. Thou wast in Eden the garden of God; every precious stone was thy covering. . . . Thou wast the anointed cherub that covereth: and I set thee, so that thou wast upon the holy mountain of God; thou hast walked up and down in the midst of the stones of fire. Thou wast perfect in thy ways from the day that thou wast created, till unrighteousness was found in thee. . . . Thou hast sinned; therefore I cast thee as profane out of the mountain of God: and I have destroyed thee, O covering cherub, from the midst of the stones of fire. Thy heart was lifted up because of thy beauty, thou hast corrupted thy wisdom by reason of thy brightness."[2]

There is evidently more than a mere earthly prince meant here. There is a strange correspondence drawn in Scripture between the seen and unseen, as though the one was the counterpart of the other. "The

[1] Gen. ii. 17.   [2] Ezek. xxviii. 12–17.

prince of the kindgom of Persia" and "the prince of Grecia" are earthly princes, and are declared to be evil spirits also. So with the "prince of Tyre," to whom this is applied. There seems to have been a close relationship between the glorious being who afterward became Satan, and his Lord and Master, Christ. Perhaps he was one of a heavenly apostleship who became a Judas, and fell by the same unholy coveting and pride. The story of that greater fall will be read by us when we read the Genesis of heaven. Christ saw the rise of the evil thought in the heart of the first Judas as he did in the later one, and no doubt gave him the repeated warnings he gave the latter. He is allowed liberty and even access to heaven. He sees the forming of the new world and race. Whether it was envy of Christ or coveting of lordship over his beautiful world, we do not know; but the evil purpose of effecting their ruin comes into his mind, and he proceeds to its execution. Satan's own sin and ruin long antedated this, we feel sure.

The form Satan assumes is described as "the serpent." The name is evidently taken from the subsequently degraded form, and does not describe the original state of the creature whose personality he assumed or used, and which the record intimates was far different, the serpent shape being the punishment afterward visited upon him. The whole impression left by the account is that it was a creature of a beautiful or at least attractive form, certainly not a repulsive thing such as the serpent now is. It was "more subtle than any other beast of the field which the Lord God had made." This is far above the reptile we call the serpent. It was a creature Eve was familiar with. She had no surprise at its accosting her or having the power of speech. Perhaps it was the link between man and the lower animals. All these are now dumb, but there is no anatomical reason why they should be, and doubtless some of them had the power of speech. Whatever this creature was, it does not now exist, and was no doubt destroyed, perhaps perishing in the flood.

Satan does not approach Adam directly, but through his wife. Adam is a type of Christ. Even in his fall he represents the second Adam in many particulars. It is through and for the church Christ goes down into the valley of sin. Satan first attacks the faith of Eve. To undermine faith in God has ever been his purpose. "Yea, hath God said, Ye shall not eat of any tree of the garden?"[1] The insinuation is against God's goodness. "Is he so unkind as to forbid to eat of any tree of the garden?" It is the temptation which assails every believer from that day to this, to doubt the goodness or wisdom of God in his dealings with ourselves. When we think prayer is not answered, or we do not get our share of the good things of life, or are hardly treated or forgotten by God; when suspicion of want of love in God enters the heart, enmity to God is not far off. It was a direct meeting of the issue for which the whole history of man was initiated,— whether the will of God was best and right.

Eve's reply, "Of the fruit of the trees of the garden we may eat," would have been the sufficient answer of a loyal friend of God. The presence of discontent is plainly seen in the rest of the answer, "But of the fruit of the tree which is in the midst of the garden, God hath said, Ye shall not eat of it, neither shall ye touch it, lest ye die."[2] Discontent is seen in the added words, "neither shall ye touch it." Unbelief is seen in the change of the direct threat of death into a peradventure — "lest ye die." Neither Satan nor Eve uses the name of Jehovah, but the ordinary name for God. Here is the ignoring of Christ from hatred on Satan's part, and forgetfulness

[1] Gen. iii. 1.   [2] Gen. iii. 3.

or something worse on Eve's part. It was, all told, want of faith in Christ by which the first sinner fell. Then came the positive side of Satan's temptation: "Ye shall not surely die: for God doth know that in the day ye eat thereof then your eyes shall be opened, and ye shall be as God, knowing good and evil." In the former words, Satan assaults by insinuation as to God's goodness, in this he directly denies the truth of God's word. Discontent is a certain precursor of, and preparation for, unbelief. The rest of the account shows human nature as it was and is: "And when the woman saw that the tree was good for food, and that it was a delight to the eyes, and that the tree was to be desired to make one wise, she took of the fruit thereof, and did eat, and she gave also unto her husband with her and he did eat."[1] The threefold nature of man is appealed to in the threefold temptation — the lust of the flesh and the lust of the eye and the pride of life. The spiritual course of the fall seems to have been first, pride in their state and superiority; second, discontent with their surroundings; third, coveting; fourth, unbelief in God's word; fifth, disobedience; sixth, shame and fear; seventh, deception. If the progress is continued, hatred of God ensues, and this is the Satanic state.

Adam's first part in the guilt of the fall is the fact that he heard and saw all and could have prevented all. He was "with her." He doubly sinned by allowing one to fall who was committed to his keeping. After the sin, shame begins its work. "And the eyes of them both were opened and they knew that they were naked, and they sewed fig leaves together and made themselves aprons." There was a horrible jest in Satan's promise, "Ye shall know good and evil." They did know it as a child knows fire after it is burned. They realized it first in this,

[1] Gen. iii. 6.

"They knew that they were naked." Self-consciousness, "the bane and malady of man," had come. It is the torment of humanity. In its keener work it is conscience, and in the end unspeakable remorse and agony.

The hour comes for the daily meeting with their loving, gracious Lord. They hide themselves. Hitherto they have gladly come to meet him. For the first time they shrink and hide and are silent. Christ knew all and foreknew also, but yet the actual occurrence was a blow to the great heart of Christ, as is every sin of his people still. This was the first of the bitter cup put to his lips to be drained to the dregs in Gethsemane. We must not, in the conception of the infinite nature of Christ, clothe him with impassiveness. Infinity is infinity of all right feelings. Christ felt in infinite degree all we would feel when a loved and trusted friend doubts and sins against us. The record is silent, and this silence is more eloquent than words. He who wept over the unbelief of Mary and Martha at the grave of Lazarus, could not be impassive at the first manifestation of unbelief which brought sin and misery in its course.

With the change in man the attitude of Christ toward man also changes. He approaches the guilty pair, not as the approving friend and teacher, but with the reserved aspect of the Judge. He has full understanding of the nature of the act of sin which man has committed, and full appreciation of the dreadful consequences of the apostasy, but he has infinite pity for the wretched couple who are coming slowly toward him in answer to his call. A gentle but searching question brings out the facts of the case in a faltering confession. Christ leaves them to their thoughts while he administers judgment upon the tempter. The wicked being is not to be allowed to rejoice over the condemnation of his victims or be a witness to their shame. Satan's case is disposed of first. A curse is pronounced upon him. There is no saving clause for Satan. Even the creature is degraded who has been his medium. He is reduced to the level of the reptile where he will do no more harm of that kind.

The curse upon Satan is as follows: "I will put enmity between thee and the woman, and between thy seed and her seed; it shall bruise thy head and thou shalt bruise his heel." The purpose of Satan is declared by Christ in the parable of the tares, sown among the good seed. Satan's purpose evidently was to mingle his own progeny among the people of God. It has been his one great plan ever since. The force of the curse is in the fact that Christ unmasks the purpose of Satan to mix his children among the people of God, and establishes a radical distinction between them in the enmity which shall ever exist between the two sides. There is irreconcilable antagonism between the flesh and the spirit, truth and error, the church and the world. This leads us to see the entrance into the world of a new order of beings who are averse to Christ and his people, and who shall war with them until the end. This double line has existed and shall exist until the final victory over sin and Satan.

Christ now turns to his once happy, now wretched children. We can see that his tone, and no doubt his looks also, change. There is no trace of anger in the words, and we cannot believe there was in the voice. He is in the judge's place, but the heart is that of him who wept over Jerusalem as he pronounced its doom. The penalty threatened was, "In the day thou eatest thereof thou shalt surely die." But that did not happen. Adam did not die that day nor for many centuries after. Nor did he die spiritually for we read that he was a son of God.[1] The penalty visited upon them was very far from being a fulfilment of the threatened death. Eve

[1] Luke iii. 38.

is given an increase of the burden and pain of childbearing, and placed in subordination to her husband, and Adam is sent to earn his bread by the sweat of his brow.

We need to enquire why Christ did not visit upon them the penalty, "In the day that thou eatest thereof thou shalt surely die." Immediate execution of the penalty of death was the essence of this warning. There is a difference between man's sin and Satan's. Adam's sin differs from Satan's. Man showed shame, but we read of none, and have every evidence of there being none, in Satan. Satan's sin had a self-hardening effect at once. This effect in man is gradual. Satan's sin brought no forgiveness. It was that spiritual sin for which Scripture tells us there is no forgiveness. Satan's sin was the summit of his wrong doing; Adam's, the beginning. In the worst state of man there may be rebellion and hatred of God, but envy and ambition is only possible to a being of Satan's high place. Man's sin is mainly self-destruction; Satan's is mainly destruction of others. Hence for man there is redemption; for Satan, none. There is no direct disclosure in the record of the means of Adam's salvation from immediate death, for the time had not come for the revealing of the gospel of redemption. Yet there is some intimation of the gospel having been revealed to him.

Christ closes his interview with a loving act of great significance — "And the Lord God made for Adam and his wife coats of skins, and clothed them." Their bodies needed protection in the rough life of the outer jungle through which they were now to hew their way. The sense of shame was seen also in every act and look. Christ will not send them out in shame and nakedness. Clothing is a badge of shame, and therefore guilt. They were not only humbled by the garb of the lower animals, but they were put on a level of exposure with them. As these animals had suffered and died, so were they to suffer and die. They were to share the lot of creation. Henceforth nature and man were one, they were to suffer together storm and heat and hunger, thirst, disease, and death. Nature was involved with them, and they were made to suffer with all creation.

But something more than clothing and physical protection was needed. What was needed for man now and at once was a stay of proceedings; for the edict of death had gone out against him, and hung suspended over him. Something or some one must intervene, or death in all its forms must fall upon the guilty couple. Some one must appear, and in his behalf present a sufficient plea for man's immunity from instant death. This Christ did. He did what we well know he did and does for every one since, who comes to him in confession of sin and acceptance of the plea he offers. Christ stepped into man's place. He took upon himself the guilt of the first as he did of all subsequent sins of all the race from that day to this. No doubt the animals slain were in sacrifice as symbols to man of the nature of the salvation Christ obtained for him.

The sacrificial idea is clearly presented here. The skins were no doubt those of the first of the long line of offerings slain for man. There is substitution in the death of these for man. The animals were probably lambs. These were no doubt included in the reference to "the lamb slain from the foundation of the world." They typified Christ as did all the long line of sacrifices from that day on. Here the first and universal Priest began his office. Development will no longer do for man. To develop a sinner is only to develop sin, and that when it is developed, is death. Sin must be recognized and accounted for and punished. This is the inviolable law of all right rule. The very throne of God rests upon this idea of justice. It is because redemption recognizes this primal law that it is so reasonable and safe. All thinking persons must see that what is right is safe. The competency of Christ to take man's place is not questioned, nor his right to do so. The fact that he did so is stated in clear terms. It was the first step on the path which led to the cross. That and every intervention of Christ was a forfeit Christ was pledged to redeem by the offering of himself at an appointed time. By this pledge, given and accepted by infinite justice, and planned by infinite love, the doom of man was stayed. But on Christ rested the burden of the fulfilment and redemption of the pledge until he could by one offering once for all fulfil and redeem all. Here, and not in the prohibition, is seen Christ's covenant with Adam. It was a covenant of redemption and not of condemnation. Grace was on the ground as soon as sin, and Christ's sheltering covenant extended over the first sinner.

By the intervention of Christ was this first sinner saved as all have been ever since. But relationship to God is one thing, and fellowship with God is another. This latter Adam lost. The consequence of the fall was the loss of Eden. Adam went out to toil and delve and struggle with the creatures for food. They find some sheltered spot and erect a hut and earn a scant subsistence by toil and pain. At the close of the weary days they throw themselves on the earth for rest. But it is not rest. All creation seems against them. They are stung by insects and alarmed by the roar of wild beasts. Malaria fills their system. They have aching backs and throbbing heads. But the worst of all is the loss of that fellowship which was the joy as it was the life of Eden. They turn sad, longing eyes to the brightness which tells them where Eden is. We can hear their sobs and bewailings for the departed blessings, and bitter self-reproaches for their awful apostasy from Christ. Above all, they long for the tree of life. To have one taste of its fruit with its life-giving power seemed to them now the summit of bliss. It was the first of man's sad "might-have-beens." We read little more of Adam. There was nothing good worth recording in his life. He had sorrow in the murder of one son by another, and lived to see vice spread through his descendants, and at last tasted the results of his sin in death — a blessing to such as he. Eternal life in sin would have been eternal misery.

Adam was not the only sufferer by the fall. It is not detracting from the divinity of Christ to say that he lost by Adam's fall. Christ feels all we do of human feelings which are not sin. Christ lost the sweet fellowship of Eden. In taking up the office of Redeemer, Christ incurred for the first time the actual burden of man's sins and guilt. The travail of his soul includes suffering. Every separation of a soul from Christ causes him pain; what, then, must have been the separation of the race!

The plan of Christ in the age which followed the fall was to permit the planting of that crop to bring forth its harvest. Man was given perfect liberty to put into practice "the knowledge of good and evil" which he had gained. Satan said he would thereby be "as gods." It was now to be demonstrated whether Satan's way or God's was best. The hard lesson of experience was to be learned. In the work of saving man it was necessary to let man eat to the full of the tree of knowledge of good and evil. This is the divine way with either individuals or worlds. The prodigal must be allowed to wander, lose all, and come to himself before he thinks of the father's house.

In this case the visible result seemed to be all that Satan had promised. We read of great advances of every kind. "There were giants in the earth in those days" and "mighty men of renown." With such extended age and primeval vigor of body and mind, with Satan to help them prove he was right, there seemed plausibility in the assertion that they would become "as gods." It was an age of great attainment in every element of civilization. We read of the establishment in the seventh generation of the three departments of progress,— agriculture, art, and mechanical invention. That they understood the art of shipbuilding we see from the construction of Noah's ark. Although this was divinely commanded and planned, it was constructed by uninspired workmen showing ability and appliances for such construction. The Great Pyramid was erected soon after the flood by the immediate descendants of this age. This is in some respects still the greatest of human edifices. It is said to bear on its stones the mark of the tubular and diamond drill, cutting the tenth of an inch in the hardest rock, with no signs of wear in the tools. Their conception of and attempt to construct a building whose top should reach "to heaven" shows ability to erect great edifices. Here are all the indications of a great civilization. Christ describes the state of the world at that time: "They were eating and drinking, marrying and giving in marriage."[1] The outline is scant, but it reveals a merry age. This is the human ideal. That great civilization was all of Satan. It sprang from his act, and was nurtured by his spirit, and was the product mainly of the family of Cain.

We read of few who obeyed God. In the days of Seth, the third son of Adam, some began calling themselves by the name of the Lord. This was the

[1] Matt. xxiv. 38.

first of the long line of revivals which has blessed earth and man. But like all revivals it ran its course, and was followed by the age of unbelief. The friends of Christ are seen during this time running in a certain line of descent of which Seth is the head. There is a second line running along side of this, the line of Cain. It is in this line that all the material and social progress appears. Before the flood these two lines merge by marriage and otherwise, and both become one in merriment, sin, and unbelief.

Morally, it was the age of license. There was little law and less religion. "The earth was filled with violence."[1] Human nature absolutely unrestrained was permitted to show what it could do, and to what it could attain. Even guilty Cain was unpunished, and Lamech boasted of still greater immunity from punishment for the murder he committed. The moral state which came from such a condition was thus described: "The wickedness of man was great in the earth, and every imagination of the thoughts of his heart was only evil continually. . . . All flesh had corrupted his way upon the earth."[2]

Persecution of God's people is plainly intimated: "The earth was filled with violence." We may be sure this extended to the saints. The example of their ancestor, Cain, in killing Abel, and his immunity from penalty would undoubtedly encourage others to do likewise. Out of that civilized, prosperous, and merry world but one man was right with God. The race was corrupt beyond endurance.

We now come to a new phase of the character and dealings of Christ. "And the Lord saw that the wickedness of man was great upon the earth, and that every imagination of the thoughts of his heart was only evil continually. And it repented the Lord that he had made man on the earth, and it grieved

---
[1] Gen. vi. 11. [2] Gen. vi. 5, 12.

him at his heart. And the Lord said, I will destroy man whom I have created from the face of the ground; both man, and beast, and creeping thing, and fowl of the air: for it repenteth me that I have made them."[1] Here are feelings and purpose equally and plainly declared. There is no gain or right treatment of Scripture in trying to explain away this statement. Jehovah did feel and act as here stated. The difficulty arises partly from a wrong idea of Deity. We have imported into our conception of God the heathen idea of impassivity. As seen, infinity is not absence of all feelings but infinity of all feelings. Further, Jehovah is the same as he who wept over the grave of Lazarus, and at other times was troubled and amazed and surprised. He is speaking as then in his self-limiting way, comprehensible to man. Further, he is speaking from the standpoint of man's deservings wholly, and not divine interests or necessities. Man had forfeited any rights; by his conduct he had not justified his creation. Jehovah was justified in repenting of making him. The treatment of man by Jehovah in his destruction by the flood is here justified. This is Jehovah taking a local and temporary view of man and his state, and feeling and judging accordingly, and doing so for the sake of all who were to come, that they may see reflected in his feeling the true nature and guilt of sin and deservings of sinners.

In this we see also Christ enter upon another new character and office. He becomes the minister of justice. He comes with the purpose to sweep the earth clean and to begin again. In all that great civilization he sees nothing worth saving. He cares nothing for all that intellectual and material greatness. All that world of beauty and grace and merriment he determines to drown out of existence. This he determined, and this he did. Let those who see

[1] Gen. vi. 5-7.

nothing in God but a sentimental love try to account for this. Christ did destroy that world with all its millions. The deluge is recorded as a historical fact in the records and monuments of all nations. God's great providential acts need no defense from man. "He doeth according to his will in the army of heaven, and among the inhabitants of earth: and none can stay his hand, or say unto him, What doest thou?"[1]

In that awful outpouring of justice we see mercy. It would be cruelty to allow such a world to continue. "My spirit shall not strive with man forever, for that he also is flesh"[2] is a message of mercy and pity as well as of judgment. The world's state was violence, and the certain end, universal misery. Christ's mercy is seen in his ministers of warning. Enoch, the first of the prophets, was God's messenger, the ark was the gospel to that old world. Every nail driven in it was a call to salvation. Its open door was a constant offer of mercy, and Noah's hundred and twenty years of preaching were one long call of Christ to man to come and be saved. The ark did not so much symbolize Christ personally as the godly life for the believer and his family, which will bring the household safe through to a new world and life.[3]

Christ begins the new world with a covenant to which he gives the rainbow as a seal. A great and favorable change occurs in the outward lot of man. The regular recurrence of the seasons is assured him, and the curse is removed from the earth. At the same time his age on earth is reduced to a seventh of the former time. The reign of law is introduced, and the special blessing of God pronounced on the new progenitor of the race. Man begins the long climb up the ascent back again to God, holiness, and happiness.

[1] Dan. iv. 35.   [2] Gen. vi. 3.   [3] Heb. xi. 7.

The work of Christ and Satan is seen in strange parallels and contrasts. Christ made the man in the image of God, and Satan proposes a way by which they shall be as gods. Christ gives them an Eden, and Satan tries his way of producing a state of universal merriment. Christ gave man liberty, and Satan gives him license. God gives them a covenant of security that there shall be no more flood, and Satan suggests a tower whose top shall reach to heaven. This is evidently more than a mere building for safety. It is to be the center of the government and religion of the earth. The experiment of the age of license was seen by all to be disastrous. Henceforth man has ever had government and religion. Babel was the original of Babylon, and this is the type of the false religion of the world. The Tower of Babel, the city of Babylon, and the Babylon of the Apocalypse are three representatives of the attempts of Satan to establish a universal religion on earth. Satan has always inspired a love of tower building. To gather great bodies and parties, to build vast edifices, to gather great churches, to found great institutions, to compile enormous figures, and then to fall down and worship these things, and say, "Is not this great Babylon which I have builded?" this is the devil's idea of religion. Christ ever frustrates all this as he did at Babel. The confounding of the false is followed by the founding of the true. In the place where Satan obtained his following, Christ finds a single man, with whom he began his church.

Genesis is the history of three great families,—those of Adam, of Noah, and of Abraham. Each of these brought to earth a new and divine institution,—the family, the state, and the church. These represent respectively man's physical, social, and spiritual needs, and by these they are presented. In Abraham Christ begins the church, and by the church the restoration of the world. In the development of the church Christ follows the same order, the natural order, as in the other two institutions. He begins with an individual. From him comes a family, and then a nation, and later, a world-wide institution which finally is to be universal. It is one of the objections to the Old Testament that it confined its religion to a single family and people. We will see later that the care of Christ was not confined to this people, and that there was a reason why the work of Christ in the restoration of the race should begin with a single man, family, and nation. This built into the holding power of the true faith the strength of the family and the nation. These three divine institutions buttressed each other. There was further reason for the choice of a single man as the beginning, rather than a world-wide propaganda of religion.

The plan of divine action in spiritual things as seen in the Scriptures may be described alliteratively as Selection, Sanctification, and Service; or to follow the order of nature, Christ sows the seed, allows it to ripen, selects the best, and sows again, and repeats the process. Adam was the first sowing; from his family he selected Noah and sowed the earth again. From Noah's family he selects Abraham. Down through his family there is seen the same process of selection of Isaac as against Ishmael, Jacob as against Esau, and out of the twelve tribes, Judah, from whom came Jesus. In this, as well as in a higher sense, Christ was "the Seed." He represents the final result of this long course of sowings. The perfect Seed has been found. The plan of Christ was then to find a single man whom he could so impress, and through him his descendants, that he could separate them to himself, and from them produce a nation also so separated as to be thoroughly devoted to himself and be by him used to bless the world. It was not therefore for himself Abraham was chosen, nor for themselves Israel were chosen, but for the purpose of world-wide blessing.

The man chosen for this high honor was one who, in the very seat of the false worship of Baal, remained true to God and kept himself from the idolatry around him, and restrained his family so also. He was one so true to God that on the command, "Get thee out of thy country and from thy kindred," he obeyed without question, not knowing where he went; giving up a settled home for the life of a wanderer, and leaving home, native land, and friends for strangers and dangers unknown. The subsequent tests applied to him showed that God knew the man he chose to be the human head of the church, "the father of all them that believe," in the only sense in which any one can be pope or primus in the church of Christ. Abraham's true piety and strong character are seen in the fact that he was able to take his family with him, his father being influenced also to go with him. The great fact is recorded as to Abraham that God said of him, "I have known him." For two thousand years Christ had waited for such a man.

The appearances of Christ to Abraham were in Ur, in Haran, and in Canaan. It was not until he reached the latter that the covenant was given him. The covenant was revealed to Abraham in successive sections. He was promised successively that he should become a nation and be blessed, that he should have the land he journeyed through, that he should have a special seed, and that through him all the nations of the earth should be blessed, and finally, that his seed should be as the stars of heaven and as the sand of the seashore for multitude. But this great covenant was not easily gotten. We read of those who through faith "obtained promises."[1] Every

[1] Heb. xi. 33.

section of this great instrument was won by a step of mighty faith. Every stage of the covenant was marked by a special seal from God. First, there was the covenant made by fire, when between the pieces of the bleeding sacrifice, Christ in the symbol of fire, and Abraham, passed in sign of the given and accepted faith. Again, later, he is given the seal of circumcision; and last, he has the oath of God given to him. It was the same threefold witness given to all believers still. "There are three that bear witness, the Spirit, and the water, and the blood."[1] It was by repeated steps of faith shown by corresponding steps of self-denial, that he won the repeated and enlarged blessings. In the offering of Isaac we see the last idol laid on the altar and the fulness of blessing poured out upon him.

The pure gospel was given to Abraham, and it was the whole gospel also. It was a coming Christ in whom he believed, "Your father Abraham rejoiced to see my day, and he saw it and was glad."[2] So said Jesus of his faith. He saw in Isaac the promise of the coming Son of God. In his sacrifice on Mount Moriah he saw Calvary; and in his restoration to him alive after the offering, he saw the resurrection of Christ. In the stars to which God pointed him, he saw the coming glory, and "he looked for the city which hath the foundations, whose builder and whose maker is God."[3] Abraham's faith is the standard faith. All other faith must be measured by his. It was faith in a simple promise of grace. There was no law nor any threat. "Abraham believed God and it was imputed unto him for righteousness" is four times recorded in the Scripture. Paul declares it was the pure gospel given four hundred years before the law. James refers to Abraham's faith as living, because it endured the divine test. Abraham was the church in embryo. His life in the promised

[1] 1 John v. 8.   [2] John viii. 56.   [3] Heb. xi. 10.

land is a type of the believer's life on earth. He receives the bread and wine of the sacramental feast at the hands of Melchizedek, who is a type of Christ in his priesthood.

In Abraham Christ found a friend. He had had since Eden few of human kind. Abraham was one with whom he could walk and talk. So he calls him "Friend." Among the people of that land to-day Abraham is called "the Friend of God." There existed on both sides the basis of true friendship — faith. Abraham had faith in God, and God said of Abraham, "I know him." Christ treats Abraham as a confidential friend. "Shall I hide from Abraham what I do?" and so he tells him all. The great separation between Christ and man was partly healed in this established friendship. Heretofore the appearances of Christ to man were few, now they are to be numerous. The chasm was closed from the Christ side. There is always reestablished communication between heaven and earth when Christ can find a man who will fully trust and obey him. Abraham towers up in simple faith above all who have come since. No apostasy follows the faith of Abraham.

The reward of Abraham was not seen by himself in his life. But we have seen it as the centuries roll by. No other man has so blessed the world. From no other one man has flowed or can flow such a stream of influences as from Abraham. The great Israelitish nation and all its vast influences for good are his. The Scriptures are the continuation of the revelation first given to him, and came to us through his race. And, as has been seen, the church had its rise in him. He is its father and human head, and there never can be another. From him all its blessings came as a human source. All the widening circles of Christian civilization which have blessed man are the result of the religion which rose with

Abraham. Not only the blessings of the past but the blessings of the future are to flow in the same channel. Everything good which shall come to man is to come from the church and the revelation and the religion which came from this one godly man. Even eternity is to share in his blessing. All we call heaven is the result of the grace which came in response to the faith of Abraham. The God-head even is a partaker of the same, for Christ wears forever the form of a son of Abraham.

The appearance of Christ to, and dealings with, Isaac and Jacob are merely continuations of those with their father Abraham. There is nothing in either of special grace or faith. Isaac is a silent and passive character. Jacob is the subject of pure grace. All who had been favored so far had some merit or some reason for favor. Adam had but one trial, and was the first exposed to the assault of Satan without experience. Cain had no law. Abel was righteous. Enoch walked with God. Noah was righteous in an ungodly world. Abraham had faith, and Isaac, sweet submission. But Jacob had none of all this. He did not have the common manliness of Esau. He showed unbrotherly selfishness. He cheats his brother and deceives his father and robs his uncle. He is wanting in all right instincts and virtues. He is withal a craven coward, and tries to bribe his way to safety. He forgets God and vows and favors innumerable. But Jacob is blessed as few have been. He is protected from the justly-deserved consequences of his own sin. He is blessed in property and family. He is given a name from heaven. He is given visions of God as have never since been surpassed. He is permitted to confer blessings on his descendants and to give his name to the coming people; and last and most wonderful, he is called a prince of God, and is made a type of the coming Messiah, and God declares, "Jacob have I loved."

He deserves none of all this. It is not just nor justice. It is more. It is grace.

Now begins that stream of free, unmerited favor which has flowed ever since, and has blessed the church and the world, and of which each of us has partaken. He is blessed for the father's sake. Jacob lived under the covenant made with Abraham. Under that covenant Christ now deals henceforth with all who come under its provisions by faith in him. To the sinner it is as it was to Jacob, free, sovereign, unmerited favor. The basis of all is the covenant made with Abraham. The source of that was the love of God in Christ. There were not wanting displays of grace to those outside of the covenant. Ishmael was not included in it, but was blessed notwithstanding. The covenant was not exclusive. It did not shut out the rest of mankind from blessing as we shall see later. The world, aside from the blessing to flow from the people of the covenant, were also to be participators in the work of Christ directly and indirectly. But the record of Christ's work is from this on for two thousand years to be with the people of Abraham, Isaac, and Jacob.

During the next four hundred years there is little to record. The family are in Egypt, where they are sent to grow into a nation. Jehovah goes before them in prevenient grace, and by the strange eventful career of Joseph brings them into the place best suited by abundance of food for increase. They are kept separated by the operation of racial, religious, and social traits, as well as by the location of their residence and their occupation. The purpose of Christ was to make a homogeneous nation, to increase them to large proportions, and to give them the benefit of the learning and civilization of Egypt. At the close of the period of formation we find them a nation strong in numbers and wealth; welded into one by a common and honored ancestry, a common hope, and peculiar customs, and above all, a faith diverse from Egypt. They further needed to have given them a knowledge of God, and love for him as their God, and desire for the land and life God intended them to enjoy. Their natural desire would have been to settle down in Egypt, that land of plenty and luxury. But that was not their rest. A better place Christ had prepared for them. To this end the dealings of Jehovah were now directed. They were permitted to feel the hatred and oppression of the powers of Egypt, and this to such an extent as to "make their lives bitter with hard service, in mortar and in brick, and in all manner of service in the field, all their service, wherein they made them to serve with rigor."[1] The hatred of Egypt inbred by this was such that it was ever after "the land of bondage" to them. The command of Pharaoh to destroy their little new-born children intensified this feeling, and made them long for deliverance and Canaan.

Whenever Christ had a great blessing or deliverance for his people, he raised up a great human instrument with which to work. Moses was the second great leader he chose for Israel. He was fitted for his work by birth, traits, and by training. The latter consisted of forty years each in Egypt and in Midian, by which he was fitted for his third forty years with Israel. The first gave him all the learning, statesmanship, and military knowledge and experience of the foremost land on earth. The second gave him the spiritual training which can only be gotten by prayer, meditation, and fellowship with God. Christ revealed himself to Moses as he did to Abraham, and as he did and does to all, before sending him on his mission. Moses was Christ's first apostle "sent" to save man, the first of that long line of ministry by which the church has been blessed. He was the embodiment of the prophetic spirit of Christ. He differed, and

[1] Ex. i. 14.

Christ's revelation to Moses differed from all who were before him in that it was for others rather than for himself the revelations were made.

In the vision of the burning bush Christ revealed himself as the coming Jesus. The union of the human and divine is clearly displayed. But there was a present Christ also revealed. Moses was to be sent on an unparalleled mission. He was to face the monarch of the mightiest empire on earth and demand single-handed the granting of an unheard-of request,—the release of the people who were multiplying the wealth of the land. In the burning bush Moses was shown not only Jehovah, but also himself as he would be, and as any one is who is filled with the Spirit of God. He is given his commission and the signs of the power he was to use. The rod changed into the dragon, and back into the rod again; the hand covered with leprosy and cleansed again were to him signs of the power of Christ over Satan and sin, and seals to him of divine cooperation in the overthrow of the power of Satan over the people, and the power of Christ to cleanse them from the sins and contamination of Egypt. Moses well knew who the people were whom he had to deliver. He had made an attempt to arouse their patriotism and desire for freedom by an attack on one who was oppressing an Israelite, and to mediate between them, expecting they would recognize him as their deliverer, but was sadly disappointed to find they had little real desire for deliverance. By the time of his return, forty years after this attempt, they had tasted deeply the bondage of Egypt, and were ready for the deliverer.

The first step was to win their confidence as a God-sent man, which he did by repeating the signs. The next step was to reveal to them Jehovah. There seems to have been little development of religion in Egypt. The patriarchal religion was simple in doctrines, forms, and life. They knew of God and his dealings with Abraham, and promises to him. They knew of his strange coming out of Chaldea, and of the covenant of the land of Canaan to him and them. All this remained with them and cheered them in their stay and latter hard life in Egypt. They kept also the sacrifices and the patriarchal forms of the eldership in their tribes; but apart from this there was little knowledge of God. They knew him in a distant way as the one true God. They must now be made to know him as their own God. Hence the revelations of Christ to Israel were as their own national God. He was Israel's Jehovah as distinguished from the gods of all other peoples. Christ so revealed himself to win their attachment and love to himself, and so that he could instruct and bless them, and through them bless the world.

The message of Christ to Israel by Moses was as follows: "I am Jehovah: and I appeared unto Abraham, and unto Isaac, and unto Jacob, as God Almighty; but by my name Jehovah I was not known to them. And I have also established my covenant with them, to give them the land of Canaan, the land of their sojournings, wherein they sojourned. And moreover I have heard the groaning of the children of Israel, whom the Egyptians keep in bondage; and I have remembered my covenant. Wherefore say unto the children of Israel, I am Jehovah, and I will bring you out from under the burdens of the Egyptians, and I will rid you out of their bondage, and I will redeem you with a stretched out arm, and with great judgments; and I will take you to me for a people, and I will be to you a God; and ye shall know that I am Jehovah your God, which bringeth you out from under the burdens of the Egyptians. And I will bring you in unto the land, concerning which I lifted up my hand to give it to Abraham, to Isaac, and to Jacob; and I will give it you for an heritage : I am Jehovah."[1] It will be seen how this was calculated to draw the hearts of the people to their Jehovah.

The next step was to show the superiority of their Jehovah to all the gods of Egypt. This was effected not only by the signs given before Pharaoh but by all the plagues of Egypt which were expressly declared to be directed "against all the gods of Egypt." The plagues were a contest between the Jehovah of Israel and the gods of Egypt. This is clearly seen by the fact that after each of the opening plagues, it is recorded that the magicians "did in like manner with their enchantments." Each plague was directed also against one of the divinities of the land or their worship. The first was against the Nile which they worshiped. It was polluted by turning its waters into blood, and in the second emitting swarms of frogs. The priests were rendered unfit for worship by being defiled by the lice in the third plague. The fly god was shown to be helpless to protect from the plague of flies. The sacred bull was dethroned by the plague on the cattle. The ashes scattered were a parody on a sacred custom in the worship of Typhon. Isis and Osiris, the gods of sun and moon, were defeated by the darkness. The plague of locusts was a direct defeat of Serapis, the god who was to protect from that infliction.

It does not detract from the supernatural character of the plagues of Egypt that each of them had a natural basis. There were evils of a natural kind which existed, such as the emission of frogs from the Nile, the locusts, and the darkness which sometimes comes in that land from the dreaded sand-storms. The divinity of all was in the directing of these natural evils to do the will of Christ at the place and at the time he commanded. In the plagues of Egypt we see Christ in a new character. The previous acts of

[1] Ex. vi. 3-8

judgment on his part were, after the fall, against guilty man. In the plagues we see Christ stretch his hand against the powers of Satan. The whole story is a forecast of the Day of Judgment, and the song of Moses is the song by the victorious church in that day.

The passover was the Old Testament sacrament. It meant all to them that the Lord's supper does to us. The bread and the wine were both there. It was another forfeit given and accepted for the fulfilment by Christ at a later day in his own person, by his own flesh and blood. Jehovah meant thereby not only that he was their deliverer, that they now knew, but that the very strength of body by which they marched out came from him. It was the lesson we learn in these words: "He that eateth my flesh and drinketh my blood hath eternal life; and I will raise him up at the last day."[1] By this formal deliverance Jehovah won the gratitude of Israel. He was to them and is to-day the God who brought them "out of the land of Egypt and out of the house of bondage."

It is recorded directly of Jehovah that it was thus he dealt with Israel: "He compassed him about, he cared for him, he kept him as the apple of his eye. As an eagle that stirreth up her nest, that fluttereth over her young, he spread abroad his wings, he took thee, he bare them on his pinions."[2] The reference is primarily to the pillar of cloud which covered the camp as a canopy, shielding them as with sheltering wings from the burning sun by day, and illuminating the camp by night. The loving care of Jehovah is seen in the daily supplies of manna and the flowing stream of which they drank. They had given them a year of absolute rest after the long hard bondage of Egypt. There was little work and no toil in the life in the wilderness. Their every want was foreseen and met. They learned here the goodness of their Jehovah.

[1] John vi. 54.   [2] Deut. xxxii. 10, 11.

There were times of trial when at the edge of want they were called to trust, and here they learned the great lesson of faith.

Sanctification was the next process with Israel. This was begun by giving them a sense of reverence for Jehovah. The thunders of Sinai left them prostrate and trembling at the mountain's base, and filled with a deep sense of God's holiness. The giving of the law and the requirements of personal cleanliness in food and clothing, in person and house, and in every act down to the smallest doings of every-day life, taught them the necessity of holiness in the service of such a God. In the law they saw the holiness of God manifested. In the sacredness of the tabernacle and its holy rites they read the need of reverence in approaching their Jehovah. In every ceremony, in all the washings and cleansings after any defilement, they saw what Jehovah expected of them. The nature and need and practice of holiness was the great lesson of the wilderness. Their frequent and certain chastisements enforced the lessons of sanctity, and the blessings of obedience incited them to purity of life. The whole Levitical law may be summed up in three alliterative words, which are an outline of the book itself — Sacrifice, Separation, and Satisfaction. First, the sacrifices, then the acts and ceremonies of cleansing, and then the feasts. The whole first year was a school of religion.

The purpose and the history of the forty years is given in the words of Moses: "Thou shalt remember all the way which the Lord thy God hath led thee these forty years in the wilderness, that he might humble thee, to prove thee, to know what was in thine heart, whether thou wouldest keep his commandments, or no. And he humbled thee, and suffered thee to hunger, and fed thee with manna, which thou knewest not, neither did thy fathers know: that he might make thee to know that man doth not live by bread alone, but by every word which proceedeth out of the mouth of the Lord thy God doth man live. Thy raiment waxed not old upon thee, neither did thy foot swell these forty years. And thou shalt consider in thy heart, that, as a man chasteneth his son, so the Lord thy God chasteneth thee."[1]

They were to consider themselves as a specially holy people, and to hold aloof from all others, and to have no intimate connections with them. Their land was chosen for this. It was separated from all about them by deserts and mountains and the sea. Christ strove to shut Israel up to himself. This is the only state for sanctification still. The form of the separation has changed, but the essential condition remains.

Moses was a reflection of Christ. We can see in him the work and nature of his Master. He was a type of Christ in his prophetic office. He was the great teacher and wonder-worker. He was the guardian of the family, the shepherd of the flock. We see an exhibition of the heart of Jehovah in the attitude of Moses when Israel committed deadly sin, "Oh, this people have sinned a great sin, and have made them gods of gold. Yet now if thou wilt forgive their sin — and if not, blot me I pray thee out of thy book which thou hast written."[2] This is the same spirit which showed itself afterward when Christ cried, "Father forgive them, they know not what they do." In this Moses shows the spirit of Christ as the substitute for sin. This attitude is further seen in the exclusion of Moses from the promised land. Personally it was wholly undeserved by Moses. God charges him with unbelief, yet nowhere does he show this. He acted at Meribah exactly as he did on other similar occasions. He himself afterward declares, "The Lord was angry with me for your sakes, saying, Thou shalt not go in thither."[3] It was as the representative of Israel he was held accountable for

[1] Deut. viii. 2, 3.   [2] Ex. xxxii. 31, 32.   [3] Deut. i. 37 ; iii. 26.

the unbelief and rebellion of Israel and punished in their place, and fell as they did, and was buried as they were outside the promised land. As the giver of the law, he was held to it, as Christ by his being born under the law became liable to it and its curse.

We are to look at the cost of all this to Christ. He had taken upon him the burden of their guilt as well as their care. Every one of the innumerable sacrifices meant another pledge given by Christ for future redemption. He was to be called to make good each pledge and answer for each guilty sinner in himself and by the offering of himself as their substitute. Not only as a nation in a general way, but individually the whole vast accumulation of sin was laid at his door. The sacrifice meant immediate forgiveness for the sinner, but it was by Christ's assuming their obligations in the offering so made and accepted, to be by him made good in his person.

The history of Israel is one constant record of apostasies. Unbelief and stiffneckedness were their besetting sins. They lost the promised land at its very door, and were sent back to perish in the wilderness where they wandered and wasted away. Ten times they sinned so in the forty years of the wilderness. More than once they were at the brink of destruction. When the promised land was reached at the end of the years of wandering, but two of the multitude who left Egypt remained. Here, again, is a new feature of the character and work of Christ. Jehovah punished his people even to the loss of Canaan and life itself. He was as faithful in dealing with the sins of his own as he was fierce against the malice of Satan. They were taught the evil of sin by sad experience. One by one they learned the ways of God.

Jehovah's purpose for Israel is seen in their entrance into Canaan. The one who led them in and gave them the land, was he whose name Christ afterward chose in his earthly life, for Jesus is the Greek for Joshua. Here then is one who will reveal the character both of Jehovah and Jesus. Joshua represents Christ in sharing the lot of Israel in the wilderness during the forty years. He with Caleb had not turned away from the promised land at Kadish as did all the others, yet he shared the penalty with them. Joshua differs from Moses in being a soldier, and his work was leading the victorious hosts of Israel in war. The manifestation of Jehovah in Joshua as well as to him was as captain. He appeared thus to him; "And it came to pass when Joshua was by Jericho, that he lifted up his eyes and looked, and, behold, there stood a man over against him with his sword drawn in his hand; and Joshua went unto him and said unto him, Art thou for us, or for our adversaries? And he said, Nay, but as captain of the host of the Lord am I now come. And Joshua fell on his face and did worship, and said unto him, What saith my Lord unto his servant?"[1]

What Moses was not permitted to do, Joshua did. Moses is the law. The law cannot bring the soul into rest. It can bring it out of Egypt, and that is a great work and place, but it is not the full and perfect work of Christ, as the wilderness was not the perfect work of Jehovah. Israel is seen in three states, in Egypt, in the Wilderness, and in the Promised Land. The whole story, aside from its historical truth and meanings, is also an allegory, and the apostle tells us is written for our instruction. Here are three states of spiritual experience. We see the soul under sin, under law, and under grace. Every soul on earth is in one or other of these states. We learn the bitterness of sin by feeling its bondage. We realize the nature of holiness by hearing the terrors of the law and feeling the pangs of conscience. We are led into a state of rest by entering with full faith and consecration into Christ.

[1] Josh. iv. 13, 14.

One of the most difficult parts of the Bible to understand is that which tells of the destruction of the Canaanites. They were exterminated, and by command of Jehovah. The slaughter was practically universal. This seems to present Jehovah in an awful light. It does. It was an awful dispensation of divine wrath. Here is Jehovah, and therefore Jesus, and God, in another of the acts of judicial wrath seen before in the flood; only that was world-wide, and this was local; that was by water, and this was by sword. There is no defense of this or of any such doings in the Bible. God gives no accounting of his acts to man. His own people will trust him in this, and believe all will one day be made clear; and those who turn away from him in impenitence would not be changed by any explanation. Christ stands here in the light of an apparently almost censurable act, and takes the responsibility. It is hard to bear the censure of creatures who are living in rebellion against him and in fellowship with the enemy of God and man; but he does so silently until the end shall come. The question of life and death God holds in his own power. He gives life and takes it away. Neither for the taking away nor the manner of it, does he hold himself amenable to man. Millions die each year by disease and accident, sword, and awful calamities. The whole is one great question of the reason of suffering and evil, and we are not given all the facts in the case with which to judge. No system of philosophy satisfactorily accounts for it.

A close study of the account and subsequent conditions and events shows there was reason for the destruction of the Canaanites, and that mercy and grace were not wanting. Sodom was the typical city of the land. It was, as its name still testifies, the scene of unmentionable crimes. Licentiousness was

CHRIST IN THE OLD TESTAMENT AGE. 113

the religion of Canaan, and to a more or less extent of the surrounding countries. Their religious gatherings were orgies of unspeakable vice. Chastity was unknown. The apostle describes thus the state in which those who fall under such inflictions of divine wrath are in. He doubtless has in mind these very people or such as they were. "They exchanged the truth of God for a lie, and worshiped and served the creature rather than the Creator, who is blessed for ever. Amen. For this cause God gave them up unto vile passions: for their women changed the natural use into that which is against nature: and likewise also the men, leaving the natural use of the women, burned in their lust one toward another, men with men working unseemliness, and receiving in themselves that recompense of their error which was due.[1] The whole land and population were physically corrupt. Venereal disease was in the blood of all. The whole population was physically and morally rotten beyond any hope of restoration. It was the plague-spot of earth. No traveler was safe from their attacks for the gratification of their beastly desires. This is seen in the attack on the house of Lot where the angels were, whom they would have violated if they could. It is a picture of their daily state and life. The safety of mankind demanded their extermination, root and branch. It was either that or let the earth come to the same state. God still destroys such, but by the slower operation of natural results of vice. Millions so perish yearly.

Nor was mercy wanting to that people. Jehovah had made every effort to save them. Abraham was sent pilgriming through the land, showing the example of a godly life. After him came also Isaac and Jacob, each by their lives so far above that of the people about them, reproving their sins. Righteous Lot lived in their very midst, and was vexed by their unholy deeds, and no doubt showed his vexation.

8 [1] Rom. i. 25–27.

But more than all these there lived among them the greatest being who ever filled the office of the priesthood, Melchizedek was their princely priest. Surely with such ministry they had no reason to complain of want of efforts for their salvation. In sending Abraham's children down into Egypt, one reason given by God to him was that " the iniquity of the Amorites is not yet full." They were given that four hundred years to repent. They heard all the story of the plagues of Egypt and the deliverance of Israel, and that they were on the way to their land, yet there is no sign of repentance. In the year of Israel's journey to Canaan they might have sued for mercy, but we hear of the contrary.

Forty years are given them to repent while Israel wanders in the wilderness. Probably like Pharaoh they hardened their hearts because of the respite. They well knew the fate which threatened them. At the very border of the land Israel waits three days, but there is no suing for mercy, or sign of repentance. Jericho is compassed seven days, and every day is a day of mercy. Rahab and her house are saved, and thereby is proven the possibility of salvation for all. Those who come asking mercy are saved. The saved Gibeonites were God's witnesses to his mercy. In all the record of the war this is the only case of anything like a desire for mercy or friendship with the people of God. Their fate came in spite of all a merciful God could do to save them. Mercy rejected is judgment invited.

The national life of Israel lasted fifteen hundred years. It may be divided roughly into three periods of equal length,— the Commonwealth, the Kingdom, and the Captivity; for after the return from Babylon they were free from foreign interference but for brief intervals.

The state of Israel under the commonwealth in Canaan reflects the character of Jehovah in his love and purposes for that people and all mankind. It was an ideal condition. The land was all that could be wished. It was situated between the extremes of heat and cold. It was a land of plenty, "flowing with milk and honey." The government was the least oppressive possible. The individual had the greatest liberty consistent with the common interest. It was the ideal social state. There was the maximum of rest and enjoyment with the minimum of labor. Three feasts in the year gave them recreation as well as rest and worship, for the feasts were such.

Every seventh year was one of absolute rest, and every fiftieth year there were two years of rest in succession. In the seventh year all debts were canceled, and in the fiftieth year every bondman went out free, and every homestead was restored to its owner. Thus every one was given a fair chance once in his lifetime, no matter how unfortunate he had been. This system prevented the accumulation of vast fortunes; where debts were canceled and lands restored, monopolies were impossible. There was no excessive wealth and no poverty. There was the ideal life of the country with the advantages of the town; for the country was so fertile that it supported a dense population, and towns were close together. Indeed the most lived in town and went out to their daily labor. This was a sample Christ gave the world of what he could do and would do for mankind if they would obey him. Israel was a great object lesson of temporal prosperity flowing from godliness. All this reflects the heart of Jehovah. It was man back again in Eden, as nearly as Eden was possible with fallen human nature.

It was under such conditions Israel grew into a nation geographically. It was not uninterrupted advance; for there were six apostasies, from each of which they were reclaimed by the chastisement of a foreign invasion and oppression. Their Jehovah was faithful to their best interests. They were by these made to abhor the heathen nations about them, the worship of whose gods was the cause of each apostasy. Israel was being taught to hate idolatry and to cleave to the one true God. They did not during this time advance much beyond their original borders, but grew, and gradually filled the land.

The Kingdom was the divinely intended state for Israel. The enlarged nation needed the strength and orderly administration of the more powerful form of government. The world purposes of Jehovah required this also. All so far was preparatory as to this. The great principle of service had as yet been but little displayed in the history of Israel. They had lived for themselves. Now they were ready to begin the fulfilment of the divine promise to Abraham — "In thee shall all the families of the earth be blessed." The preparation for this is seen in the development of a people physically and morally pure, and having the true faith. Their location was all that was desired for such a purpose. They were at the center of the earth. It was needed that they should expand to the borders promised Abraham, "from the river of Egypt unto the great river, the river Euphrates."[1] This would give them eastern as well as western seaports, and enable them to control the highways of the world. All this required a leader and armies — in short, a kingdom. Their demand for a king was only wrong in being premature, in the motive for it, and the kind of king they wanted. It was Jehovah's purpose from the beginning to form them into a kingdom. But they, as the whole world also, *must* learn the value of God's King by sad experiences with their own kings.

Under David and Solomon, who must be regarded as a continuation of the Davidic reign and principles,

[1] Gen. xv. 18.

the nation was greatly enlarged, and made a military power of great wealth. To some extent they began the world mission of disseminating the true faith. The surrounding nations learned of the one true God. The visit of the Queen of Sheba was an instance of many such visits of lesser note. It is no wild declaration to say that the continuation of the Davidic reign, or equally strong and godly reigns, would have in a few centuries extended the influence of the true faith all over the world. But he who said, "My kingdom is not of this world, else would my servants fight," did not intend by the sword to evangelize the world. Israel was a preparation of the world for Christ, in a better way. But there was a temporary purpose served in the world's evangelization by Israel in this time, as we will see later. Aside from the errors of Israel, the state under the Davidic kingdom was all that it was under the Commonwealth with the added splendor and power nationally, and a vast increase of individual wealth. "And the king made silver to be in Jerusalem as stones, and cedars made he to be as the sycamore trees that are in the lowlands for abundance."[1] The reign of Christ on earth has ever been so, wherever it has, even for a short time and a limited area, been permitted.

With David, Christ makes a new covenant. It is the covenant of kingship. Hitherto Christ had not so revealed himself. He was Prophet and Priest, now he declares himself King. The chief clause of the covenant is as follows: "Thine house and thy kingdom shall be made sure for ever before thee; thy throne shall be established for ever."[2] This has so far not been fulfilled as to the throne and kingdom of Israel and David. There is a spiritual fulfilment in Christ, but the covenant with David, as the covenant with Abraham, awaits its fulfilment. It occupies a large place in the prophecies of both Old and New Testaments. Israel is the people of David, Jerusalem the

[1] 1 Kings x. 27.   [2] 2 Sam. vii. 16.

city of David. The kingdom which is to come is the kingdom of the Son of David. It is the Son of David who is to rule forever and ever. Here, then, is the full type of Christ as King. All relating to Christ as king must be studied from the standpoint of the throne of David, or a correct conception cannot be had.

Here is the identification of the throne of Christ and David and its nature: "Unto us a child is born, unto us a son is given: and the government shall be upon his shoulder: and his name shall be called Wonderful, Counselor, Mighty God, Everlasting Father, Prince of Peace. Of the increase of his government there shall be no end, upon the throne of David and his kingdom to establish it, and to uphold it with judgment and with righteousness from henceforth and forever."[1] This covenant is henceforth the hope of Israel as a nation. All the prophecies speak of it and point forward to it. It is a new starting point for the nation. The throne of David is the mountain peak of the coming glory for Israel. It is the hope after Jesus came, and is referred to by the apostles as "the hope of Israel," "the sure mercies of David." It is identical with "the kingdom." Israel, the church, and the world, alike look to the establishing of the throne of David as their hope.

David gave Israel spiritual truth as Abraham and Moses gave them respectively physical and social being. Through David, Christ manifested himself spiritually. David saw few if any visions, nor did he work miracles or have any wrought for him. His fellowship with Christ was different in this respect from those who had gone before. Christ spoke in him rather than to him. This is a great advance of the work of Christ with man. David lived the life of Christ from cradle to throne. He is the great Messianic character of Scripture. He had the same ancestry, was born in the same place, and came to his place by the same course of obscurity and adversity.

[1] Isa. ix. 6, 7.

He was betrayed by his own, was received by few at first, then by more, and at last by all Israel; and in Solomon attained to a measure of world-wide supremacy. He was inspired to speak for Christ. In no other way can we explain the Messianic psalms. He uses words and figures which in no way were true of himself. "They pierced my hands and my side" was not literally true of David, and was of Jesus. Hence it was he who spoke. We see in him the spirit of Christ.

No Old Testament writer attains to the spiritual conceptions of David. The Psalms read more like New Testament writings than those of the Old. They not only describe the experiences of David and Christ but of the believer. We go to them instinctively for help. We travel a well-known path when we read them. We feel we are following one who has been over the same experiences as ourselves. We read in them not only the experiences and feelings of David but of Christ. Only so can the Psalms be understood. David's grief and David's ecstacies were those of Christ. So was the love for the Scriptures and for the people of God which David shows. Christ is best revealed in the Psalms. They are the climax of the spiritual revelation of Jehovah. Hence we see the reason of the love of Jesus for them.

There are among the Psalms some whose spirit seems far from that of Jesus. These are usually termed the "Imprecatory Psalms," such as the seventh, thirty-fifth, sixty-ninth, and one hundred and ninth. Yet it is noticeable that some of them, the sixty-ninth especially, are Messianic. From the latter are taken the quotations applied to Christ: "The zeal of thine house hath eaten me up;" "They gave me also gall for my meat, and in my thirst they gave me vinegar to drink." In those psalms, then, we are also to see Christ speaking. The persons against whom these imprecations are launched are indicated by Peter's quotation of them as applying to Judas Iscariot, whom Christ said was a devil. These psalms, then, refer to those like Judas, who by surrender to Satan, become part of that awfully sinful and accursed combination whose head is Satan, and who with all his host is doomed to suffer the outpouring of the wrath of God. There is such an awful guilt in sin, especially in its fountainhead, which we cannot understand, but which Christ did fully see and feel in all its venom. This, as represented in persons wilfully given up to it in face of light and warning, is the object against which is launched the maledictions of these psalms.

The history of Israel in its entirety may be represented by an ascending line to David and Solomon, and a descending line from that down to their final overthrow as a nation. Their climax was reached in the Davidic kingdom. They existed for a thousand years longer, and enjoyed much blessing every way, but in all fell short increasingly every way from that on. After this we see the beginnings of disaster. For the first time we see the people of God divided. Idolatry comes in. Apostasies come one after another, led by their kings. Irreligion increases with luxury. Amos describes their "summer and winter houses," "houses of ivory," "great houses," "houses of hewn stone." Here is a picture of their state: "Ye that put away the evil day and cause the seat of violence to come near: that lie upon beds of ivory, and stretch themselves upon their couches, and eat the lambs out of the flock, and the calves out of the midst of the stall; that sing idle songs to the sound of the viol; that devise for themselves instruments of music, like David; that drink wine in bowls, and anoint themselves with the chief ointments, but they are not grieved for the affliction of Joseph."[1] Religion was turned into a means of gain and luxury. Their religious times and ceremonies become abhorrent to

[1] Amos vi : 4-7.

their Jehovah, and they themselves sink lower in impiety. Jehovah follows them in a double line of dealing, — afflictions and prophetic warnings. Defeats in war, and foreign invasion become frequent to the invincible armies of the kingdom of David. Their holy city is entered, defiled, and robbed. Internecine strife weakens and disgraces them; insect plagues devour their crops; famines waste them; earthquakes terrify them, and at last the end comes in overthrow. Israel is driven from their land and scattered over the earth, and their holy city burned, and their land left desolate.

All this did not happen in a short time. It covered five hundred years. Nor did it come on them without warning, nor without efforts of their Jehovah to save them. There began with the decline of Israel the long line of prophets whose words occupy the last quarter of the Old Testament. We must not suppose that these books were all the messages given to the apostatizing nation. Israel swarmed with prophets during the centuries of her decline. All these breathed the messages of their Jehovah. Every prophet was a block thrown under the wheels of the chariot of Israel in its mad rush down the declivity of national apostasy. There are no more tender tones of love and pity than the beseeching of their Jehovah through the prophets to backsliding Israel. It is the same Christ who in Jesus wept over them on the Mount of Olives. In the prophets the figure of woman and wife is first applied to Israel, the people of God. Christ assumes the close relation of husband to his people in their decline. He represents Israel as an adulterous wife, and yet loves her and follows and entreats her return to his house. In order that Hosea may feel his grief, he gives him for wife an abandoned woman. That Ezekiel may feel some of Jehovah's loss, he lets his wife die. Every prophet carries some of Jehovah's burden. "The burden of the Lord" was the burden the Lord himself bore first before being laid on the prophet. Jeremiah's tears were Jehovah's. In every prophet must be read not only the words but the heart of his Master. They were the constant attendants of Israel in all their vicissitudes. They went with them into captivity and dispersion. They hung their harp on the willows of the Euphrates, and returned with them to the ruins of their city and cheered them as they began the toil of rebuilding, surrounded by scoffing enemies, and when Jerusalem was rebuilt, instructed and guided them.

Each prophecy, or more properly, message, may be divided into three parts,—warning, exhortation, and promise. The warnings are plain and definite. Their fate is exactly foretold. So also is the future of blessing after the affliction. Every sad message ends in a bright and hopeful outlook. The valley of Achor is a door of hope. Although their fate at last becomes inevitable and cannot be averted, even by repentance, and all the prophet can do is, like Jesus, to give his message and weep over them, yet even then there is hope beyond. Jehovah will not and does not cast down his people into the gulf of despair. The further shore of blessing is always discernible over every sea of sorrow. The dark clouds of prophetic doom have an edge of silver cheer. It is so Israel went down. Not as those who have no hope did the nation die. They rest in the grave of national death, the penalty of violated vows and law and loss of faith in God, but in the certainty of a national resurrection. Their Jehovah has not forgotten his triple covenant given through Abraham, Moses, and David. Israel is not lost, but still lives as a people, awaiting the call of their Jehovah to national life and activity. The great purpose for which they were chosen has not yet been fulfilled. They are to be a blessing to the whole earth.

Israel is left fixed forever in the faith of the one true and living God. Idolatry has been utterly eradicated. Whatever else they may be or become, Israel will never be worshipers of any but the God of Israel. They are bound to each other and to their nation by the most honorable history, and lineage the purest on earth. Their literature is the purest and oldest in the world; their hold on life, their mental and physical vitality, the strongest. They compete successfully with every race and wrest the prizes of life from all. They have all the abilities for the formation of a great nation, if settled under circumstances where their powers could operate in national autonomy toward enlargement and progress. They wait as a people prepared by this long course of training for some great purpose. Their schooling seems complete. They are fit for some great mission. Jehovah's people await Jehovah's time and purpose.

A recent Jewish writer has said: "If the history of Israel which touches all recorded time has no dynamic significance, supplies no hint as to the destiny of humanity, then is life indeed a walking shadow, and history 'a tale told by an idiot, full of sound and fury and signifying nothing.' It is a story that has chapters in every country on earth, and which has borne the impress of every period. All ages pass through in marching procession Israel's army. To the Jew the world owes its vision of God." Another has said: "Israel is among the nations as the heart among the limbs." Renan says, "Jerusalem is still the house of prayer for all nations."

In considering the work of Christ in the Old Testament age, we must not forget that he had a relationship to the whole race as well as to Israel. The children of his first human friend were not forgotten in all this time. What he did for the world through

Israel was all the time in his mind. He was not neglecting the world outside of Israel. The Bible is a history of Israel mainly, therefore it records little of God's doings outside of that nation. But there are glimpses of a wider sphere of divine working, and world-wide acts of evangelizing grace in that Old Testament age. The call and departure of Abraham was not without its effect on the land he left as well as on the land to which he went. Abimelech, king of Egypt, received a divine message. We have seen the exalted privilege the citizens of Canaan enjoyed in the ministry of Melchizedek.

The sojourn of Israel in Egypt was a protest then against idolatry and a mission of the truth. The display of power in the plagues of Egypt surely must have had effect on some in turning them from error. Israel in the wilderness was an astonishing evidence to the whole world of the reality, power, and goodness of God. In Canaan the nation was, as we have seen, a witness for God as a nation of the Lord. On the highway of the world Israel was the observed of all nations. The temple and its services attracted seekers after truth from all the world. Israel was a national missionary. Solomon was the greatest preacher the world has ever had. His sermons were, and are still given a world-wide circulation. In Babylon Israel testified for God and not without effect. Nebuchadnezzar was converted by the power of their testimony and the hand of God upon him, and issued to the world a proclamation confessing the truth of the God of Israel and his acceptance of him, and commanding all people everywhere to worship him and him only. It is inconceivable that this royal evangel should not have led the effort in bringing many to know God.

Jonah was sent to Nineveh with a gospel message of repentance. There followed the greatest revival the world has ever seen in the same length of time.

In three days a city of at least a million was turned from its sins and brought to repentance. We have a right to see in this a sample of what God was constantly doing. Nineveh was no exceptional case in any way. We may believe that the prophets of Israel went everywhere, and that many a city and land in that time had a visitation from the messenger of God. In fact we may safely conclude that in one way or another Israel did in a measure fulfil her mission and become in some degree a blessing to all the families of the earth.

In reviewing the history of Christ's dealings with the ages of the Old Testament, we discover that some things were thereby settled, some facts demonstrated. We have seen that man proved a failure under license. So far from their becoming "as gods" as Satan promised, they became as devils, and brought upon themselves swift destruction. It was further shown by actual demonstration that man was also a failure under law. This is the testimony of the history of Israel. The whole religious system of Moses was as perfect as divine wisdom could produce with any hope of its success. It was a race specially chosen and prepared. The law fitted close to every act of life. "Thou shalt" and "Thou shalt not" hedged in the Israelite on every side. He was commanded what to eat and wear, and how to cook and speak and wash, and down to the minutest and most private acts.

All his worship was prescribed, what was wrong was specifically named, so he could not fail to know right and wrong. For every sin there was a sacrifice; for every act of ceremonial uncleanness, there was a ceremony of purification. There were countless priests and Levites to instruct him in carrying it out. The service of the tabernacle and temple was most perfect in ceremony and significance. The adornments were all that precious materials and skill could produce. The feasts were continuous, weekly, monthly, and three times a year, and the great seven- and fifty-year feasts added. Yet all failed to make or keep Israel holy. It failed because of the weakness of human nature. It was scarcely inaugurated until, as Paul says, and even the Talmud shows, it began to "vanish away," and little by little its provisions were dropped, and those which were retained became mere forms, covering lives and natures still unchanged. It has been demonstrated that heredity, environment, and development cannot save man, because they do not touch the heart. The law was therefore swept away, and the apostles forbade and condemned it as a means of salvation or Christian living.

In view of all this, the inquiry arises, Why did Christ give the law? It was and is the greatest blessing this world ever had next to Christ. It has made the world endurable. But for this it would long ago have sunk into total corruption. It has given to man the best system of ethics the world has ever had. The world's jurisprudence is founded on the national code of Israel. Man could not have lived without law, as was seen in the case of the old world and Sodom and the Canaanites. The law was Israel's criminal and civil code. Further, the law was educational. It was Israel's text-book. It was their literature, probably all they had. It was above all a revelation to them of the holiness of God. It lifted their idea of holiness and the character of God in Israel and throughout the world to this day. The sacrifices were a stay of proceedings of judgment against guilty man. It has been shown that every sin deserves swift punishment. God has so declared. Christ interfered by his first sacrifice in Eden in behalf of man, and has interfered in behalf of every sinner who comes to him. The sacrifices of the law were the Old Testament way of coming to Christ. Still further, the law was the path which Christ himself was to walk. All was demanded of him. He was called upon to fulfil all righteousness. Every sacrifice was a forfeit he was called upon to redeem. He fulfilled the law in all its righteousness for himself, and for those whose guilt he assumed, paid the penalty with his life.

For Israel Paul wrote: "The law hath been our tutor to bring us unto Christ."[1] Regarding the church then and now as one, it kept us in control and together until Christ came, to whom it turned us over, its work being ended. It serves a spiritual purpose as showing the legal state into which some come by not understanding Christ or coming fully to him. It convicts of sin, and shows the soul its need of Christ.

Concurrent with all this, millions of the people of God have been individually schooled for eternity. The precious grain has been gathered into the garner. Another stage of the great demonstration has been conducted. It has been shown what man is and will be under law, as it was shown what he is and will be under license. The results are recorded for the use of the eternal ages. Further, and most of all, Christ has been more fully manifested, and in Jehovah, God was brought still nearer to man. We begin to see the features of a well-known face and to hear a well-known voice.

[1] Gal. iii. 24.

CHAPTER IV.

JESUS.

CHRIST IN HIS EARTHLY LIFE.

THERE are four gospels in the Old Testament as in the New, and they also tell the story of the earthly life of Christ. They run parallel with the history of Christ as Jehovah. Creation was the first gospel, its life of Christ has been examined. The second gospel was written in flesh and blood. There are certain specifically named persons who are appointed to represent Christ as types. Adam was the first, representing Christ as the head of the race.[1] Melchizedek was the type of the priesthood of Christ,[2] Moses with Joshua a type of his prophetic office,[3] David with Solomon types of Christ in his kingship as Son of David to Israel. In the wider kingship of universal dominion Nebuchadnezzar is the one whose title " king of kings " he assumes.[4] Ezekiel is the one from whom Christ takes his favorite title, " Son of Man," and Jonah was a type of his burial. Israel as a nation, as has been said, was a Messiah among the nations, and is as a nation a type of Christ.[5] Every one of the Old Testament saints had some features of the coming Christ. In one respect they differ from those of the New. The latter have each an undivided part of the whole Christ, "Of his fulness have we all received and grace for grace." This helps us to understand the fragmentary character of the experiences and lives of Old Testament saints. They were in-

---

[1] 1 Cor. xv. 22, 45.
[2] Heb. v. 10.
[3] Deut. xviii. 15 ; Heb. iv. 8.
[4] Dan. ii. 37.
[5] Hosea xi. 1.

complete in their understanding of Christ and their reception of his grace. The third gospel was written in symbols. These are seen from the tree of life down through the long line of appointed types of things natural or artificial, all the articles and ceremonies of the tabernacle and the temple, and the entire ritual of worship. The fourth gospel consists of the written prediction beginning with the first in Eden down to the last as to his forerunner in Malachi.

While Jehovah as a second person was but dimly known to Israel, the coming Christ was fully revealed. It is evident he did not wish to be known in the future as Jehovah but as Christ. Israel seemed to gradually come to understand the truth as to the coming Christ. A few at first comprehended, though in a limited degree. Before his coming it was generally understood. But it was then as now; those who did not desire him did not learn much about him or look for him. The heart want must precede the head belief. To each longing soul the coming Messiah was revealed according to his needs. We must distinguish then .as now, between Christ revealed in us, and to us. As types each showed the former; as individuals they realized the latter according to their desires and effort to do so, and this was according to their circumstances. To Abraham the coming Christ was the longed-for Seed; to Jacob a deliverer; to Moses a revelation of glory; to David an heir; and so to each believer however humble. Yet Christ was not fully foreseen even by the utterers of the prophecies. There were two points they failed to perceive, — the preexistence of the coming Messiah and his afflictions. They did not understand that the coming Messiah was to be Jehovah. Most of the predictions of Messiah came in their declining days, and they saw what they most desired, a Deliverer coming in glory.

Israel was not the only people looking for or desiring a Coming One. The Magians from the East represented many to whom God revealed him or in whom a sense of need created a desire for the Deliverer. The prophecies had been carried far and wide wherever scattered Israel went, and were read by seekers after truth, such as the Ethiopian eunuch. Christ was in a limited measure "the desire of all nations." Plato said, "It is necessary that a lawgiver be sent from heaven to instruct us. O how greatly do I desire to see that man, and who he is! He must be more than man." The Sibylline oracles predicted and described fairly well Christ as he was prophesied, evidently drawing on the prophecies for their forecast. But in all, whether in Israel or the world, the desire or knowledge of the coming Messiah was at best limited and indifferent. There was no deep, world-wide expectancy as might have been expected with such repeated and detailed predictions, well understood too, as is seen by the conduct of the chief priests in telling Herod where Christ should be born. We would suppose that Israel at least would be awaiting in preparation and intense expectancy the advent of Christ. It was, as has been seen, a prepared people to whom Christ came. Centuries had been spent in their schooling for this great event. The land to which Christ came was Israel's. It was chiefly for the purposes of this advent of Christ that it was selected. It was on this platform of the world that Christ came to display the glory of divine grace. It was at the center of the earth he began his work.

But there was one vast and interested circle of intense observers. We must remember that all this display of the work of Christ is for all worlds and ages. We are actors and observers, but we are not the only ones nor the largest number nor those seeing all or most. Angels are to be instructed as well as man — "Which things angels desire to look into."[1] They had followed their Lord in his creative and providen-

[1] 1 Peter i. 12.

tial work, and had assisted in it as we are told. They had heard, and doubtless studied, the meaning of the prophecies. They knew more than man, but it is not probable they knew all. It was to be a revelation to them as to man. So when the time came to see the great event, we can well believe there was the most intense expectancy among the beings of the other world.

It was, perhaps, the occasion of a great assembly. There are such in heaven. There was one when creation was finished and "the sons of God shouted for joy." There certainly was when Christ was born. There is reference to some such gathering, perhaps this, in the words heard by Isaiah: "And I heard the voice of the Lord saying, Whom shall I send, and who will go for us?"[1] This was the prophet's call to service, but each prophet walked the path of his Master. Here, then, was a call for some one to go on some great mission. We can well believe that in answer to a call for some one to go to earth and save man, there would be many responses; but this was more than an errand of mere mercy. If this were all Christ had had before him, any angel could and would have done the work, even to die for man. Men have died for each other and for loved ones, and why not angels? Surely they are neither less willing nor capable. But this call involved far more, as will be seen when we come to consider the details of the great descent of Christ.

Christ had made himself personally responsible for the sin and state of man. As the "First-born of all creation," as Creator, and in the relations he has assumed toward the race, by the countless sacrifices and types, by his own express declarations, by every solemn act, Christ made himself the sole possible Saviour of man and creation and heaven. And now the time had come to fulfil all the vast obligation. The call, if such there was, could only have been to

[1] Isa. vi. 8.

draw attention to the vastness and urgency of the task for the instruction of all. The fate of the whole race depended on the step Christ was now called on to take. The salvation of all believers past was not complete until sin was atoned for, and Satan conquered and salvation secured. If there was any objection to the redemptive work of Christ, that was the time to declare it. True, there were no human beings present. But if there were any reasonable or unreasonable objection or arguments of any force to present, Satan was competent to present them. Doubtless he also was present, for we read in the account of such an assembly: "Now there was a day when the sons of God came to present themselves before the Lord, and Satan came also among them."[1] We come to the conclusion that the devil did not know of any such objection, and that those who object now either know more or less than Satan.

To Christ this was the great step in the execution of the plan of the ages. The life he was now to enter he well knew. He had lived it in type and person of his people. It was written in creation and by the pens of holy men of God who spake as they were moved by the Holy Ghost. But now the life was to be lived in person. The reply of Christ to the call of the Father is given to us: "Wherefore when he cometh into the world, he saith, Sacrifice and offering thou wouldest not, but a body didst thou prepare for me; in whole burnt offerings and *sacrifices* for sin thou hadst no pleasure: Then said I, Lo, I am come (in the roll of the book it is written of me) to do thy will, O God."[2]

The entire humiliation of Christ is given in the following passage: "Being in the form of God, counted it not a prize to be on an equality with God, but emptied himself, taking the form of a servant, being made in the likeness of men; and being found in fashion as a man, he humbled himself, becoming

---

[1] Job. i. 6. [2] Heb. x. 5-7.

obedient even unto death, yea, the death of the cross."[1] This shows the parts in the humiliation of Christ,— what he relinquished, what he became, and what he did. This describes his state before he began his great descent. He had the form of God. He had equality with God. This he might have retained. But he counted it not a thing to be grasped and held. Christ's humiliation began in heaven. The first part of Christ's humiliation, that which was seen by heaven alone, is described in these words: "He emptied himself, taking the form of a servant." He first "emptied himself." The verb rendered "emptied" occurs in four other places, and is rendered "made void."[2]

That of which he "emptied himself," is stated in the previous sentence,— "Being in the form of God," "on an equality with God." Of these, then, he emptied himself. He laid aside the form of God, he relinquished equality with God. He rises like a monarch, relinquishing royal power and office for a time, lays aside his crown and robes, and descends from the throne.

We have noted his eternal place "in the bosom of the Father," with its nearness, fellowship, and honor. We must not suppose that because Christ was an infinite being, it was not a sacrifice to relinquish this. He afterward looked back to the glory he then relinquished in these words, "O Father: glorify me with thine own self with the glory which I had with thee before the world was."[3] It was dearer to Christ than all else save to do the will of God and save man. "He emptied himself of his divine glory, and laid his divine attributes, omnipotence, omniscience, omnipresence, under temporary voluntary limitations."[4] He laid aside his administrative power over the affairs of earth and heaven. None of this he

[1] Phil. ii. 6-8.
[2] Rom. iv. 14; 1 Cor. i. 17; ix. 15; 2 Cor. ix. 3.
[3] John xvii. 5.
[4] Dr. A. T. Pierson, "Many Infallible Proofs," p. 286; Chicago, 1891.

claimed during his earthly life. Nor did he resume it until he said, "All authority hath been given unto me in heaven and on earth."[1]

He also laid aside his creative power. None of his miracles were creative. The healings were remedial only. The miracle of the loaves was increase of existing food and not creation. Jesus limited himself in his knowledge. He said, "Of that day and hour knoweth no one, not even the angels of heaven, neither the Son, but the Father only."[2] There is no gain, but on the other hand great loss in making this step of self-emptying in Christ less than it was. By so doing we minimize the humiliation of Christ and so rob him of his glory and ourselves of the comfort in knowing how he was made like unto us. This mistaken interpretation comes from a timid fear lest Christ be made less in his divinity, and this comes from resting the argument for his divinity and nature on this one chapter of his life. Christ's humanity is seen in his humiliation, his divinity in his exaltation.

The second step—"taking the form of a servant"—was also an act in the presence of the heavenly assembly. We are reminded of a corresponding act on earth, when laying aside his garments, he took a basin of water and towel and washed the disciples' feet. He took the form of a servant. So in the presence of the greater discipleship of heaven, by some act of infinite condescension, he, having laid aside his divine glory and power, stepped down among the lowliest of the serving, waiting host, and took the form of a servant.

But Christ was destined to become "lower than the angels." He was "made in the likeness of men" and "found in fashion as a man." He was to enter human life and nature as though a man could and should lay aside his human form and nature and take upon himself the form and nature of a worm and live

[1] Matt. xxviii. 18.   [2] Matt. xxiv. 36.

its life in all its conditions. This is but a feeble comparison to the descent from deity to humanity, from heaven to fallen earth. He was to begin where every human being begins, and to travel the whole journey. Through the Psalmist he speaks of himself thus: "I was cast upon thee from the womb."[1] This then was as truly Christ as he who hung on the cross. It is no more strange that Christ should enter life so, than that he should enter life at all. We are not asked to understand this but to believe it on the statement of the word of God. All attempts to explain by abstruse terms and reasonings the time and manner of the union of the two natures of Christ are unsatisfying; and unsatisfying explanations breed unbelief. We must leave it therefore where God has left it,— unexplained.

In this beginning Christ descends to the lowest level of existence. We have heretofore seen that the beginnings of life are all alike. In plant, animal, insect, or man there is no discernible difference. We have seen that man passes up through all the lower forms of life; he exists as each for a time, and passes on to his own state. Christ did all this. He not only traveled the path of human life but also the path of all life. He tasted the life of every living thing. He thus became incarnated not only for man but for all creation, that he might redeem everything that hath life. Christ embodied all heavenly intelligences in his spiritual nature, all mankind in his psychical nature, and all organic and inorganic creation in his physical nature. Christ therefore summed up all things in his redemptive work.

A greater contrast could not be conceived of than the advent of Christ as celebrated by heaven and received on earth. It is the occasion of another great call for the adoration of the heavenly beings. "When he again bringeth in the first-born into the world, he

[1] Ps. xxii. 10.

saith, And let all the angels of God worship him."[1] Heaven was undoubtedly absorbed in its joyful celebration. It was the beginning of the fulfilment of the four-fold gospel of the Scripture. All they knew of nature, all they had seen of the gradual revelation of the coming Christ in his people, in the countless types and ceremonies; all they heard of the spoken predictions of Scripture which they so desired to look into, was now to be fulfilled. The first step in the overthrow of the enemy of Christ was now taken. The beginning of the end of sin had come. The opening of the path back to Eden was now begun. They had sung anthems of joy over earth's creation. If creation filled them with joy and praise, what must have been the effect on these spiritual and holy beings of the commencement of redemption? It was to them as to us the central point from which all events were to be hereafter measured. To heaven as to earth it was to be the reckoning point of all time, and more, for B. C. and A. D. are to be the extensions of eternity.

The world was asleep, and so was the church when Christ was born. Of all that city full of ecclesiastical dignitaries, but one was apprized of the great event. They might have known of its imminence. Indeed, they did know and directed Herod to the very place. But they were not watching or waiting or even ready. We read of no exultation on the news being received, nor even a tardy reception. They were wrapped up in acquisition of property, in formal and splendid liturgical worship. They were divided into bitter sects and were engaged in endless discussions, and worst of all were immersed in lives of secret or open sin, all the while looking for the establishment on earth of a state of power and glory for themselves by the coming kingdom.

To a few poor shepherds was given the great honor of welcoming the Son of God in his advent to

[1] Heb. i. 6.

earth. They were watching over their flocks. We must believe they were also waiting and watching for the coming Messiah. Perhaps they were that very moment talking of the great hope of Israel, and expressing the longing that they might be living when he came and be permitted to see and hear him, and above all to receive a share in the blessing he was to bring to Israel. Perhaps, like David, one of their own occupation long ago, they were singing their hopes in sacred song. The inspired account is as follows: "And an angel of the Lord stood by them, and the glory of the Lord shone round about them: and they were sore afraid. And the angel said unto them, Be not afraid; for behold, I bring you good tidings of great joy which shall be to all the people: for there is born to you this day in the city of David a Saviour, which is Christ the Lord. And this is the sign unto you; Ye shall find a babe wrapped in swaddling clothes, and lying in a manger. And suddenly there was with the angel a multitude of the heavenly host praising God and saying, Glory to God in the highest, and on earth peace among men in whom he is well pleased. And it came to pass, when the angels went away from them into heaven, the shepherds said one to another, Let us now go even unto Bethlehem, and see this thing that is come to pass, which the Lord hath made known unto us. And they came with haste, and found both Mary and Joseph, and the babe lying in the manger."[1] Jesus was probably born in a cave, for such were the stables for cattle in such humble communities. No lowlier place could be imagined. He entered the lowest condition of man, for even savages have better accommodations.

There could be no higher honor awarded woman than to be the medium of the earthly advent of the Son of God. By woman came sin, but by woman came Christ. In this was more than compensated

[1] Luke ii. 9-17.

her share in the fall. Women were the constant friends of Jesus. No woman's hand was ever lifted to smite him; no woman's voice was ever raised against him. In his hour of trial a woman only of all earth's multitude spoke in his defense, and on his way to the cross only woman's words were spoken in sympathy. The woman God selected of all the thousands of Israel was a chosen vessel for the high honor. We have no record of her life, but there are intimations which give us some glimpses into the history and character of the woman so signally honored.

In her song she speaks of her "low estate." Hers was a life of poverty and toil. The position of Joseph tells us that. She lived in a humble home, with little to make life vain or idle. She speaks of "the proud" in her song: "He hath scattered the proud in the imagination of their heart." Here is reference to some personal enmity against her or the contempt of some such people, as well as spiritual meaning; whether for her lowly position or for her piety we do not know, probably the latter. She was, as all are who share Christ's cross or crown, schooled in the ways of adversity. It is related of her afterward in connection with the strange things done and said at the birth of her Son, that she "kept all these sayings, pondering them in her heart."[1] Here is a glimpse of a reserved, meditative disposition. She is seen directing the servants at the marriage of Cana, and seems to be in charge there of the preparations for the feast. She has the confidence of others and the ability to direct, in short, a womanly strength of character. She was probably far from the appearance of the madonnas of art, as was her divine Son from the same artistic ideals.

Her piety is seen in connection with the great event of her life. She accepts the announcement in perfect faith and in glad submission. It was to bring upon her suspicion and obloquy. It proved so. Even

[1] Luke ii. 19.

Joseph did not believe her, and was preparing to put her away. If the one she loved doubted her, what must have been the feelings and conduct of the cynical, sneering world about her? A shameful stigma was attached to her name. It was an awful burden which Mary so joyfully accepted. On her first of all fell the shadow of the cross. Alone she bore the burden and reproach, knowing herself that she was true, and that God knew so also. The most painful of all was to be suspected by the one she loved. A worse fate, all in all, could scarcely befall woman. The stigma doubtless followed both her and Jesus, who thus began life among the most despised.

The manliness of Joseph, as well as his piety, is seen in his prompt acknowledgment of Mary as his wife at the divine command. He thereby took her reproach and bore it with her, silently accepting the odium as his own. Together this simple, loving couple stepped into the shadows which were to cover their lives. No greater task or trust was ever committed to man than to be the custodian of the Son of God in his helpless infancy. Joseph was the true "Christopher" or Christ-bearer. He accepted the burden as cheerfully as Mary. It was a burden. It sent him from home to a strange land for two years, and made him the possible object of suspicion to watchful civil and ecclesiastical powers. Joseph sings no "Magnificat." He seems to have been a simple, silent, faithful man. He toils at the bench and fills his allotted place, and passes out of the narrative without record, probably dying, as tradition tells, early in Jesus' life.

The rite of circumcision placed the receiver under obligation, as the apostle tells us, to keep the whole law. Christ entered on that obligation. It was the first act of the life of "righteousness" he was to live. In that one act he was committed to the keeping of the whole law in all its spiritual as well as all its literal ceremonies. The name "Jesus," given by God's command, was a common one. It has become an uncommon one to us by his adoption of it; but at that day there were many of the name of Jesus. It was, as has been mentioned, the name of Israel's victorious leader who brought them into the promised land. For this and its meaning, "Saviour," it was chosen.

The unrecorded thirty years of the life of Jesus were not particularly different from the life of others at that time. The record of his childhood gives all we need to know: "The child grew and waxed strong, filled with wisdom: and the grace of God was upon him."[1] Here is natural growth of every kind. He came to recognize his mother and other members of the household. He learned to crawl and to walk, holding his mother's hand. He took his first step alone. He learned to speak a few small words and names. He played with other children, and learned to run errands, and helped about the humble home. He became an apprentice to Joseph's trade, and learned the use of tools, and how to make yokes and pails and plows. He was taught to say prayers and verses of Scripture, and was taken to the synagogue, and at twelve to the temple. He learned to read and write.

If, as we believe, Joseph died early in the life of Jesus, he was left with the burden of the support of the family upon him as the eldest son. He toiled early and late; he bought materials and sold the articles of his handiwork. He was "in favor with God and man." He was a good, obliging neighbor, a kind brother, an honest tradesman, a dutiful son. As the oldest son and the support of the family, he would or should have had some authority. No doubt this would be disputed, and there would arise occasions for the display of all forbearance and wisdom. He lived these years in Nazareth. It was a poor place, and the family were poor, and it was a daily struggle

[1] Luke ii. 40.

for food and clothing. Jesus was always poor. Doubtless he often went hungry that others might have enough, and helped those still poorer than himself.

Spiritually his teacher was the Holy Spirit. The text-books were Nature, Man, and Scripture. He was a close observer of nature. What he afterward spoke of lilies and sparrows and growing crops, was doubtless learned in these early years. So also of the panorama of human life passing before him. The parables were doubtless all actual events of which he knew. He observed men sowing and shepherds going after lost sheep and a woman looking for a lost coin and the joy she felt at its recovery. He heard of a younger son who went into a far country and came back the poorer for his trip. He watched wedding feasts. He learned of debtors and creditors and their doings. But his great text-book was the Scriptures, especially the Pentateuch and the Psalms. His mind penetrated its meaning with lightning-like rapidity and accuracy; yet it was learning by the process of reading and thinking over its meaning and comparing scripture with scripture. It was doubtless his early proficiency which made him the reader in the synagogue.

His inner life was lived alone. His brothers did not appreciate his spiritual desires. He soon got beyond his mother in thoughts. Nazareth was the most uncongenial place in the land for him. It was a rude, coarse, and godless place. He was as much alone as his forerunner in the deserts. There is no natural or divine requirement to think that the human nature of Jesus was any departure from the laws of heredity. He was like his mother in his human disposition as far as we can read hers and know his. He was serious and meditative, yet capable of great outbursts of expression. We judge from Scripture that his voice was low and his manners quiet. He was not strong physically, but could on an emergency put forth great and long-continued efforts, leaving him utterly exhausted. He was never jovial but extraordinarily sympathetic. He could be ironical and even severe. He could and did show anger, and could terrify by his looks. Strong men felt they were in the presence of a master before that plain Galilean. The personal appearance of Jesus is not made a matter of particular mention in Scripture. There are few personal allusions of any kind. Evidently the person of the earthly Jesus is not to be the subject of contemplation or of picture. We have this, however, about him: "He hath no form or comeliness, and when we see him, there is no beauty that we should desire him." "His visage was so marred more than any man, and his form more than the sons of men."[1] The conventional pictures are probably very far from his actual appearance. They are all Grecian in face, and Jesus was a Jew.

We must not suppose the spiritual life of Jesus at this time was one of unruffled peace. It was a life of struggle every way. It was the same as the life of a believer. "Since the children are sharers in flesh and blood, he also in like manner partook of the same. . . . It behooved him in all things to be made like unto his brethren. . . . He himself hath suffered being tempted."[2] He had a daily battle against the common temptations of man. If we can judge from ancestry, he had in his physical nature that which made temptation a terrible thing to him. We must not in our conception of the divinity of Jesus, remove him beyond the power of temptation. He had a fair, full trial of human life. He was tempted or tried in all points as we are, and each of us knows what that is. It is temptation from within as well as from without, and from the beginning to the close of life.

Jesus had to pray and resist and struggle and turn away from temptation. It was not temptation

[1] Isa. lii. 14; liii. 2.   [2] Heb. ii. 14, 17, 18.

hurling its shafts against a stone wall but against flesh and blood. He was "the Word made flesh." He was "in the likeness of sinful flesh." His was a body derived from a weak, sinful woman. "He took upon him man's nature with the essential properties and common infirmities."[2] His sinlessness was not the result of unimpressibility, but of constant and perfect victory over sin. Temptation may be met in several ways. It may be felt and yielded to. It may be met, considered, struggled against, and finally yielded to; it may be felt, considered, struggled against, and rejected; or it may be felt and instantly rejected and struggled against. This latter was we think the way with Jesus. He felt it all in all its forms, and resisted and came through stainless, the first in human form who so did. Those thirty silent years of his life were years of struggle.

The life of Jesus was a development from the manger to the ascension. In this also he traveled our path. "For it became him, for whom are all things, and through whom are all things, in bringing many sons unto glory, to make the author of their salvation perfect through sufferings. For both he that sanctifieth and they that are sanctified are all of one: for which cause he is not ashamed to call them brethren."[2] There is more in the believer's life than resisting temptation. That is negative; there is a positive side also. He was developed and "made perfect." All which implies increase of gifts and graces and development of all spiritual parts. The waiting until thirty years of age before beginning his mission, means more than simply waiting until he was at the priestly age. It meant waiting until maturity. He was gathering the strength which was to be poured out in the few short years of his ministry. They were to be years of expenditure of all the forces he had, as we shall see. He needed all the strength he could accumulate.

[1] Westminster Confession, chap. vii. sec. 2.   [2] Heb. ii. 10.

We do not know when Jesus came to the consciousness of his divinity and mission. He " grew in wisdom," and so probably came gradually to the knowledge of who and what he was. At the age of twelve he had a knowledge of God as his Father, but it is not certain that this was the knowledge of his divinity. Whether his mother ever told him of his divine origin is very doubtful. It would not be according to the ways of God that the knowledge of his Sonship should rest in ever so slight a measure on the word of any save himself. Jesus followed our experiences. We are not without light as to how he came to know his Sonship. Certainly there was a time when he did not know, and the time came when he did come to know. We come to faith in God and his mercy by the Word. On this we rest in simple faith. There follows the witness of the Spirit, witnessing with our spirits that we are the sons of God; there follows this the experiences of the believer, such as love for the brethren, which also tell him he is a child of God. It is according to the analogy to believe Jesus came to see himself *a* son of God before he came to know himself as *the* Son of God. We may believe the time came to Jesus in childhood when he knew of God, and when he desired to be a child of God, and, led by this desire, to yield himself up to God to be his, and perhaps later a desire to serve God in some special way and to present his body a living sacrifice, holy, acceptable unto God. All the spiritual experiences the Christian has gone through, we may be sure Jesus also experienced. By the Scripture he came to know of a coming Messiah and the time and place and events of his coming. By the Holy Spirit's still small voice he was told he himself was the Messiah, and by the subsequent experiences he was further certified of his Messiahship. Doubtless one of the marks he saw in himself was the Messiah feeling for Israel. They were as sheep without a shepherd. His whole heart went out to them to save them.

After Jesus' commencement of his office, there was a difference, if not before, in the manner of receiving or knowing the truth. It was certainly different from that of any prophet. John the Baptist makes this clear: "What he hath seen and heard, of that he beareth witness."[1] How he saw and heard, Jesus tells in these words: "The Son can do nothing of himself, but what he seeth the Father doing: for what things soever he doeth, these the Son also doeth in like manner."[2] He refers again to his learning in these words: "I do nothing of myself, but as the Father taught me, I speak these things. . . . I speak the things which I have seen with my Father."[3] He here refers undoubtedly to his pre-existence, but his knowledge was continuous also: "The words that I say unto you I speak not from myself; but the Father abiding in me doeth his works. Believe me that I am in the Father and the Father in me."[4]

Jesus was in constant communication with his Father. The unseen world was constantly open to his vision. "Ye shall see the heaven opened and the angels of God ascending and descending upon the Son of man,"[5] refers not to an occasional or future experience of Jesus, but to a necessary condition to be given the disciples by which they would be able to see as Elisha's servant saw the angels who were there before.

In this secret assurance he goes to the baptism of John at Jordan. He gazes on the scene. He well knows what it means to the people and to himself. He quietly waits until all have been baptized, and steps forward to offer himself for the rite. John recognizes him and expostulates. This draws from

---

[1] John iii. 32. [2] John. v. 19. [3] John viii. 28, 38.
[4] John xiv. 10, 11. [5] John i. 51.

Jesus that which gives us the meaning of his baptism — "Thus it becometh us to fulfil all righteousness." It was confession of sin and an act of repentance as to the law. All John did was to make reformed Jews of his converts. He brought them back again to the law. So Jesus, in submitting to baptism, took his place as a sinner who needed repenting. He identified himself with that guilty, conscience-stricken throng. It was his first act of personal substitution. It meant more to Jesus. The Jordan was the boundary over which Israel crossed into the promised land. Crossing the Jordan fully committed them to all the risks and all the gains of the future. And entering the land, as they did and were commanded, they passed between Mounts Ebal and Gerizim and between the blessings and the cursings. All this Jesus knew. It was therefore to him a full committal, first to his own personal obligation to keep the law; and by identifying himself with Israel in baptism he thereby made himself liable for all the consequences of violated law on their part. It was a formal act by which Jesus accepted the whole mission before him, and fully committed himself to it.

Three divine manifestations follow the baptism, — the Open Heaven, the Descending Spirit, the Voice of God saying, "Thou art my beloved Son. In thee I am well pleased."[1] These three had each a special meaning to Jesus. The Open Heaven was the attestation of God to his sinlessness. Never since the withdrawal of the divine, visible presence had heaven and earth been united, for heaven must be shut to a guilty world, but here was one over whom heaven could open. The Voice of God was the open acknowledgment of his Sonship. The third was the Descent of the Holy Ghost. It was the *anointing*. It was this which gave him his name — the Christ. Anointing was performed on the sick to give health

[1] Luke iii. 22.

and strength, and upon guests as a mark of honor, and upon persons set apart for special service or office, as prophets, priests, and kings. In all these meanings, it may be considered. It was God's strength given Jesus. It was earth's guest so honored. It was, chief of all, the setting apart of Jesus to his life work.

The anointing of Jesus was also that of power for service. It was in the power of the Spirit he henceforth did and spake, suffered, died, and rose again. He had laid aside his primeval glory and power as we have seen. This was not his assumption of these again, for that did not occur until he ascended. This is the filling of the Holy Spirit. Now he receives that energy and power by which he wrought all his miracles and all he did up to his taking his place at God's right hand. It is expressly stated that by the Spirit he was led up into the wilderness to be tempted of the devil; by the Spirit he preached; by the Spirit he cast out devils, and wrought all his miracles; by the Spirit he knew all things. It was by the Spirit he knew the hearts of men and the future. All was given him by the anointing of the Holy Spirit.

There is a difference between the Holy Spirit in Christ and the believer. In the believer the Holy Spirit divides gifts to each severally as he wills.[1] In Christ abode the entire personality of the Holy Spirit. "In him dwelleth all the fulness of the Godhead bodily."[2] We receive of Christ's fulness, — "Of his fulness we all received, and grace for grace."[3] The Church as one body has now the Holy Spirit in all his fulness, but no one person has such a measure. The believer may be filled with the Spirit, but it is according to his measure. "Unto each one of us was the grace given according to the measure of the gift of Christ."[4] While of Christ it is said: "He whom God

---

[1] 1 Cor. xii. 11.
[2] Col. ii. 9.
[3] John i. 16.
[4] Eph. iv. 7.

hath sent speaketh the words of God; for he giveth not the Spirit by measure."[1] It was in the similarity of the power and not in the measure of it that Jesus was made like unto his brethren. Hence we see all the Old Testament prophets did, Jesus afterward did. On the other hand every miracle of Jesus can be paralleled by one from the records of the prophets and apostles. So the apostles knew what was in the hearts of men. Peter read Ananias and Simon the sorcerer, and Paul again and again did likewise. So also they spake. Indeed Jesus said, "Greater works than these shall he do."[2] There is great strength to the believer in thinking he has the same power as his Lord. All that Jesus was and did and endured the believer may also enjoy according to the measure of the gift of grace given him.

The anointing was also Jesus' preparation for temptation. There were several purposes in his being "led up of the Spirit to be tempted of the devil." As a man he needed that which comes from the struggle. As a Saviour he was to be tested for his work, and as the head of the church he was to be tempted in all points as his brethren are. As the Redeemer he had to meet the great enemy of souls. Satan is the prince of this world. He was not the being to sit still and see his kingdom invaded and his supremacy imperiled. This was to Satan the crisis of his existence. There was in his mind that unbelief which he holds to all the people of God. He believed in God and trembled, but he neither believed in Christ nor trembled at his presence. He certainly acted as if there was a possibility of success in the attempt. He saw one in human form and nature under actual human conditions. He had never failed to overcome such. In this spirit and confidence Satan approaches the object of his hatred. He probably appeared at first in the person of a holy

[1] John iii. 34. [2] John xiv. 12.

pilgrim or recluse, of which the wilderness had many living in solitude for the gain of purity or piety or as a relief from the vain world about them. In the subsequent temptation, however, Satan disclosed his personality, seeing it useless to try to deceive Jesus. The time was opportune for the temptation. Jesus was in the wilderness. He was weakened by the fast of the forty days. He was exposed to the peculiar dangers of solitude.

The temptation of Jesus was a repetition of that of Adam. It appealed to the threefold nature of man,— "the lust of the flesh, the lust of the eyes, and the vain glory of life."[1] It was an epitome of all temptation from that day to this. The second Adam entered the struggle where the first Adam failed. The first Adam and the second Adam were representatives of mankind appointed of God. These respective trials were therefore world-wide in their scope. Satan begins with the lowest nature — the flesh. He always does with man. If he can tempt by the flesh, he need not try any higher form. Christ is hungry, and he tempts him by offer of food.

A distinction must be discerned between the sin to which Jesus was tempted and the appeal by which he was attacked: "If thou art the Son of God, command this stone that it become bread."[2] It implied a doubt of his Sonship, and this implied doubt of God who had a little before said, "Thou art my beloved Son; in thee I am well pleased." It was the same attack as that of Eden — a doubt of God. This was directed also against his claims as Creator. It also questioned his claim as the Jehovah who fed Israel in the wilderness with manna. The test covered the whole past of the life of Christ as born of God, as Creator, as Jehovah. The act proposed was right enough in itself. He was hungry. He must eat or starve. "Why not take care of yourself; you have

[1] 1 John ii. 16. [2] Luke iv. 3.

the power and the right. Here, take this stone, command it to be made bread." It is significant that in all his after miracles Jesus never did turn stones into bread. The temptation by want is the most common to-day. Men struggle most fiercely for the means of living, and for this most wrong-doing is committed. It represents all demands of the flesh.

The second temptation was an offer of universal dominion. Rome ruled the world, and Satan ruled Rome. To make this one or that one emperor was to him a small thing. He could have made Jesus so as well as any other. So this was his offer: " Bow down and worship me, and all shall be thine. It will give you the opportunity you want. You can be thus a world ruler and reformer." It is so still. "Get wealth, power, and so you can do good." The third temptation was more subtle still. Seeing the spiritual nature of Jesus, he proposes a spiritual temptation, the performance of a mighty deed of faith in God. Probably there was a purpose to further his Messiahship. The Jews expected a Messiah who would give them a sign. "What better sign than this? Descend from the pinnacle of the temple; you need fear no evil, for he will give his angel charge over thee; and as you alight in the midst of the wondering throng, and they see your power, they will accept you at once as the Messiah." The attitude of Jesus in these three temptations was that of passive resistance. He simply declines the conflict as he declines the offers. It will not be thus Satan is to be defeated. He refuses to discuss with him the question of his relationship to God, the world, or the church, which the three temptations respectively question. With a few words of Scripture he replies to Satan, and he retires. Satan attacks Jesus hereafter through others rather than directly. He speaks through Peter; he raises storms; he afflicts poor creatures, and excites opposition among the people;

and finally inspires Judas and the Jews to destroy him. But he meets him again after a season.

Jesus returns and enters his work. He has been tested in all the ways of trial and found true. Yet there is no restless looking for work. Jesus always waited his time. So now we see him with the power of the Spirit upon him, and a nation to bring back to God, and he is at a wedding feast and by his miracle assisting to promote the enjoyment of the occasion. He seems to have returned from the baptism to his home, and we read of him with his family. But soon he leaves Nazareth and goes to Capernaum, where he resides, probably with one of his disciples. The family soon after follow him.

But there are hints of trouble in his family relationship. His brethren do not believe in him. They all, mother as well, think him beside himself, and seek to divert him from his work or at least restrain him. He openly and formally renounces all family ties and declares, "Who is my mother? and who are my brethren? and he stretched his hand toward his disciples, and said, Behold my mother and my brethren."[1] This seems to have been the final separation from the home and ties of his youth. The breaking of home ties was no light effort for Jesus. We must not extinguish natural affection in our conception of him. He was complete man as well as God. He had all the tender feelings of a son and brother and friend and neighbor. But these came between him and his work, his duty to God and man, so he lays on the altar the dearest affection of the human heart and says farewell to the earthly mother whom he never after recognizes in that relationship. For this he was no doubt censured. This was hard to bear, but was one of the burdens of the Christ, and is so still to some of his people.

He was, as to his after life from this on, wholly dependent. Jesus was poor. He was literally penni-

[1] Matt. xii. 48, 49.

less. When he wanted a penny for an illustration, he was obliged to borrow one. He took what was given him. He accepted invitations to meals or lodging. But he was often hungry, and is seen seeking for a few over-looked figs on a tree and raw grain from the fields to satisfy his hunger. He slept often in the open air. It was a poor living the Creator got on his own earth.

Jesus was wholly natural and unassuming. He was neither in manner nor voice peculiar. It was foretold of him, "He shall not strive, nor cry aloud; neither shall any one hear his voice in the streets."[1] It was neither outward looks nor sensational conduct which made Jesus famous. He did not seek notoriety but often avoided the crowd. He did not run after people, but waited for them to come to him. But he made himself accessible; he went everywhere. He was footloose to go anywhere. He mingled with the people; and, in the first year, was not especially observed. He was to those who saw him simply the carpenter of Nazareth. He went to marriages and feasts and through the market-places. He was always on duty, however. He was Christ as much at a wedding as on the cross. He met all kinds of people. When he became famous, he was invited to the tables of the rich, and he went. He was the most approachable man who ever walked the earth. Women and the poor and the outcast accosted him and feared not to be repulsed. He was at home and self-possessed in every circle. He was regarded by fishermen as one of themselves, and Pharisees saw that he was equal to all their questionings. He was scarcely ever alone; indeed the hours of necessary devotion were hard to get. People were attracted to him, and this aside from his miracles. He had no stiff, ecclesiastical mannerisms; he had no assumed dignity. He was not afraid people would take advantage of him

[1] Matt. xii. 19.

or impose upon him. Jesus was "the Son of man" in a whole-hearted devotion to every human being who needed or wanted his help. He talked with an outcast woman, and ate with publicans and sinners, and shocked the proper and churchly people by his so doing.

That feature of the character of Jesus which most drew people then and now to him was his compassion. Again and again is it said, "He had compassion on them." That which drew out his compassion most was the spiritually deserted condition of the common people. He described them as sheep not having a shepherd. It was a very religious age. There were hosts of religious teachers of all kinds, and the most splendid services imaginable, costing vast sums; but the common people got little out of it all. To them Jesus went. They responded by crowds. "The common people heard him gladly." It is written: "The people wondered at the gracious words which proceeded out of his mouth."

But the attitude of Jesus was not all that of unvarying graciousness. He was sometimes severe and on some occasions angry. With hypocrisy he had no patience. The most scathing words which ever came from prophet's lips he addressed to them: "Ye serpents, ye offspring of vipers! How shall ye escape the judgment of hell?"[1] He was especially grieved at the blindness of the people to their Messiah and the unbelief of his disciples. Nothing seemed to give him such pleasure as to find one in whom was full faith. He eulogizes it wherever he finds it. He never hesitates to rebuke any, even his loved disciples for a wrong spirit, and calls Peter "Satan," as he tries to dissuade him from the cross. In his cleansing of the temple, there was evidently a departure from his usual calm bearing. There is every indication of intense energy not unmingled with anger.

[1] Matt. xxiii. 33.

He drives out the herds of cattle and sheep, lashing them with the whip of cords. He orders in stern tones the removal of the cages of doves, and indignantly hurls out of his way the stands of the money-changers.

Jesus had in coming a threefold mission—to Israel, the church, and the world. The mission of Jesus was first of all to Israel. He came as their Messiah. In his early ministry he sought Israel exclusively. "I was not sent but unto the lost sheep of the house of Israel"[1] was his own declaration as to his mission. Jesus was Israel's prophet. He came as the fulfilment of the priestly types of Israel's worship. He was emphatically the King of Israel, born of the royal line and in the royal city. The words and work of Jesus must be looked at in this exclusive light first of all, if we would understand their meaning. It was the Jehovah coming to be recognized and received by his own. To this end the whole life of Jesus was lived on a prearranged and predicted plan, all for the purpose of identification.

So, too, the teachings of Jesus were all evidence of his claims. The Old Testament was his great text-book. He emphasized the law and upheld it. He showed his authority over it by amending it when he saw necessary, saying, "Ye have heard that it hath been said by them of old time, An eye for an eye and a tooth for a tooth: but I say unto you, Resist not him that is evil."[2] This is no disannulling but an addition to the law. He claimed to be Lord of the Sabbath. He by all this treatment of the law showed he was the Author of it. All his miracles were also adapted to this end. They were repetitions of those of the Old Testament. The power over the sea was the same as that of Moses; the miracle of the loaves also was as the work of Jehovah in the wilderness. In

[1] Matt. xv. 24.   [2] Matt. v. 38, 39.

the healing of the leper, they could see the God of Elisha. Jesus wondered that they could not see in him their Jehovah. It was this he meant when he said, "The works that I do they testify of me." It was to Jesus as Israel's Jehovah that his life teachings and words testified.

The force of this argument for the divinity of Jesus, not only to Israel then, but to all in every age, will be seen by reviewing the Messianic predictions. They number hundreds, and are remarkable for particularity and novelty of detail. They refer to his coming ; the design of his mission ; his divinity ; his nation, tribe, and family ; the year he was to come ; the place of his birth ; the messenger who was to precede him ; his virgin mother ; the worship by the wise men ; the massacre of the babes at Bethlehem ; his Egyptian sojourn ; his grace, and the gift of the Holy Spirit ; that he should preach and how and what he should preach ; that he should work miracles and cleanse the temple ; his triumphal entry into Jerusalem ; that he should be hated, persecuted, betrayed by one of his own, and sold for thirty pieces of silver ; his disciples to forsake him ; false witnesses to testify against him ; his silence under all this ; the smiting and plucking out of the hair of his face; the scourging and his death by their unusual way of nailing to the cross ; the piercing of his hands and his side; the offer of gall and vinegar ; the parting of his raiment and casting lots for his vesture ; the mocking, his patience under all this ; praying for his enemies ; that not a bone should be broken ; that malefactors were to be associated with him in his death ; that he was to die in the midst of his life and be buried with the rich.

Many of these are events which appear to be wholly incompatible with each other and with the circumstances of the time, place, character, and work of the Messiah ; and are such as would never occur to any one attempting to foist a series of predictions upon the world. No such person would attempt to make the Messiah appear in two such apparently incongruous positions as his state of humiliation and dignity. Indeed this was the point the Israelites could not understand. They therefore supposed there must be two Messiahs, one of humble state and the other coming in glory. They could not see how he could be of royal descent, have a forerunner, be worshiped by the wise men, ride in triumph into Jerusalem, be buried with the rich, and, at the same time, be poor, persecuted, scourged, mocked, and crucified. By the law of probabilities the simultaneous occurrence of these many and diverse details, with all their possible combinations, would not be one in a million million. This would be the chance a putter-forth of such a series of predictions would run of having his prophecies come to pass. When it is remembered that these predictions were in existence hundreds of years before Jesus came, as is evidenced by the Septuagint version of the Scriptures; and that Jesus' life corresponded thereto as acknowledged by all; we see all the marks of a divine prediction and fulfilment which testify unanswerably that Jesus was the predicted Messiah of Israel and God's Son for the world.

Yet Jesus did not openly and publicly announce himself as the Christ. The partly concealing and partly revealing is seen in the titles applied by himself. He is called "Son of David" by others, but he does not openly and formally so speak of himself. His favorite title is "The Son of Man." This occurs frequently in the Old Testament especially in Ezekiel; to whom it is applied nearly one hundred times. It is always applied with disparagement. It is applied to Christ but once in the old Testament. The Jews evidently did not understand it as referring to the Christ, and so ask him, "Who is this Son of Man?" It was a peculiar way of presenting himself. We ask why he did not openly say, "I am the Christ;" but he did not, save to a few individuals, and at his trial when asked plainly, "Art thou the Christ?" when he replied affirmatively. This peculiar way of presenting himself was for the purpose of securing the truehearted ones. Those who were looking for him or seeking truth or were willing to receive it when presented, would recognize it and receive him. All others would not, or seeing him would hate him the more. It is the divine way to-day and always. The evidence for Christianity is enough for those who wish to know the truth and are willing to do the right. Others cannot be convinced or will not act accordingly if convinced. To such there are difficulties in the Bible and Christianity and, above all, in Christians, enough to turn them away.

Israel rejected their Jehovah, and by that act lost the place as the favored people in the plan of God as the evangelizing nation of the earth, until they turn again to Christ. It was no oversight or surprise to God. His purposes and plans are always capable of adjustment to the various possible outcomes of any event. Indeed we have seen that from the beginning all was foreseen and provided for. We ask with propriety, What would have been the outcome if Israel had accepted Jesus as their Messiah?—He would have undoubtedly accepted their allegiance, and become their spiritual Leader. He would have reformed their ways and worship. He would have sent missions to the scattered ten tribes and called them also to the truth. All this would have brought upon him the animosity of the Roman power, who would in time have arrested him. He would have been betrayed by some of his own and crucified. Of this Israel as a nation would have been guiltless. They would have escaped the long ages of trouble. The end of the age of sin would have come sooner, and the establishment of the kingdom greatly hastened. The rejection of the Messiah by Israel was followed by their overthrow as a nation, the destruction of their city, and all that made up the old economy. We must recognize the unity and continuity of the divine plan in the ages. The overthrow of that age leaves a remnant as each of the previous ages did. Of this remnant Jesus gathered the nucleus before his ascension. The Israelitish age yielded a chosen company with which once more to sow the earth.

In the formation of the Christian church, Jesus uses the order of the Israelitish church. It is one body as to all true believers who follow in the faith of Abraham, the great founder of the church. The number of the apostles and of the seventy are both those of the tribes and eldership of Israel. So the sacraments of the Israelitish church are perpetuated in the sacraments of the Christian church. Circumcision and the passover still exist in baptism and the Lord's supper. We have in the Lord's day the Sabbath. Our churches are the synagogues little changed; our church officers those of Israel little modified. We read and believe their Scriptures. Their hope is ours.

To the institution of the church Jesus gave the last year of his life. The increasing opposition made intercourse with the public less frequent. He was much alone with his disciples. The followers of Jesus appear to have gathered about him in concentric circles. Inside the number of those who believed in him there were the seventy. The twelve were a closer circle. Within this circle were the three who accompanied him on three, and doubtless many other special occasions. There was one out of these who was not content until he leaned his head on Jesus' bosom. We are reminded of David's similar surroundings. Out of the tribes Judah was nearest; his chosen band still nearer, and among these the thirty mighty ones, and out of these the "three mightiest," one of whom was the superior of all. When Jesus left, there were not probably more than five hundred, a band about as large as that which was faithful to David. These Jesus left as the beginning of the great structure of the church.

On the disciples gathered by Jesus, he so impressed himself that they went out repetitions of himself. He wrote no books, but what he said was recorded with perfect accuracy, as seen by the gospels of four widely different persons. His words and acts were imprinted upon their memories and by them recorded without bias or opinion. There is in the Gospels the absence of the usual laudatory expressions and general comment of biographers. The Gospels are perfect photographs of the life and words of Jesus. The special love of Jesus for his own is seen in his intercourse with his disciples, particularly the twelve. To these he addressed words of great tenderness such as, "Your Father careth for you;" "The very hairs of your head are all numbered;" "Fear not little flock; it is your Father's good pleasure to give you the kingdom."

The teachings of Jesus are the constitution of the church, to which he expects all his people to conform. Again and again he urges them in such words as these, "Why call ye me, Lord, Lord, and do not the things which I say;" "If ye love me, keep my commandments." His blessings are conditioned on obedience, and the one who hears and does not is like a man who builds on the sand. His last command to the world outside, after making disciples and receiving them into the church, was, "Teaching them to observe all things whatsoever I commanded you." The life and teachings of Jesus furnish the picture of the possibilities of a regenerate life. His own words were, "Follow me." To live after the teachings of Christ is possible to every believer. What the Holy Spirit did in Jesus, he will do in degree for any and every one

[1] Matt. xxviii. 20.

who will follow Jesus. The branches are partakers with the vine of its life, beauty, fragrance, and usefulness. The teachings of Jesus describe the character of those who attain to the kindgom. They are the standard of citizenship. By his words will all be judged. The Sermon on the Mount is the spiritual exposition of the law. It is designed for conviction, and is the most searching message which can be addressed to those who believe in Christ.

The gospels contain the model of Christian work. When Jesus said, "Follow me, and I will make you fishers of men," he gave the secret of success. In preaching, in working, in life, the great example is He who spake as never man spake. The work of Jesus was threefold. He saved bodies, souls, and spirits. His was a mission to sickness, sorrow, and sin. He contemplated the whole man. The church has in a measure followed his example. The hospital, the school, and the church have sprung up together, or rather the two former from the latter.

The mission of Jesus was larger than Israel or even the church. It was world-wide and universal. This is seen in himself. Jesus is not to be thought of as a Jew although he was one. He was the "Son of man." He was the universal man. He was in the highest sense a cosmopolitan, a world man. He is felt to be a brother to every man and in every age. Black and white, rich and poor, see in Jesus their brother. He rises above all rank and race. He is an inhabitant of every land. There is no other personage, real or imaginary, who is so universally received by men of every age, race, and rank. All others are local, and belong to their time and partake of their nation. Jesus belongs to mankind.

John is the chronicler of the gospel for the world. The word "world" occurs in his writings more often than in all the other New Testament books. To John, Jesus is the Saviour of the world. He is presented by him in great world-wide figures — Light, Water, Bread, Shepherd, Door, and others understood everywhere. John alone notes that the world was made by Christ, and that God so loved the world that he gave his only begotten Son; that he was the Lamb of God that taketh away the sin of the world; that God sent not his Son into the world to condemn the world, but that the world through him might be saved; the remark of the Samaritan that Christ was the Saviour of the world; and Christ's own remark that he gave life unto the world, and gave his flesh for the life of the world; that he said, "I am the light of the world," that his earthly mission was not to judge the world but to save it. It is John who notes the saying of Jesus, "That the world may know that I love the Father, and as the Father gave commandment even so I do." And again it is John alone who writes of the convicting work of the Spirit for the world and his petitions in his prayer that the world may believe and know that God had sent him.

In John's Gospel the way of faith is clearly set forth. The word "believe" also occurs more in his Gospel than in all others. He states distinctly the purpose of his writing it. "Many other signs therefore did Jesus in the presence of the disciples, which are not written in this book: but these are written, that ye may believe that Jesus is the Christ, the Son of God; and that believing ye may have life in his name."[1] All this shows the purpose of the whole life and work of Jesus as he has expressed it in his prayer,— "that the world may believe that thou didst send me."

To the world Jesus presented himself to be believed, first as to himself, and then as to his teachings, and to be received. Jesus established himself as a witness, competent and reliable. The world has accepted him as such. That such a man once lived is fully admitted by the world. That the Gospels are

[1] John xx. 30, 31.

the record of his character and words is also fully admitted. That he reached the summit of perfection of character is another accepted fact. Some well-known testimonies to these statements may be repeated here.

Renan, who denied the divinity of Jesus as Christians accept it, writes as follows: —

"It is more inconceivable that a number of persons should agree to write such a history, than that one should furnish the subject of it. The Jewish writers were incapable of the diction, and strangers to the morality contained in the Gospels. The marks of its truth are so striking and inimitable that the inventor would be more astonishing than the hero. Whatever may be the manifold phenomena of the future, Jesus will not be surpassed. All ages will proclaim that among the sons of men there is none born greater than Jesus."

The Unitarian Theodore Parker wrote: —

"Shall we be told such a man never lived? the whole story is a lie? Suppose that Plato or Newton never lived: who did their works and thought their thoughts? It takes a Newton to forge a Newton. What man could have fabricated Jesus?—None but a Jesus."

Jean Paul Richter thus writes of Jesus: —

"The holiest among the mighty, the mightiest among the holy, lifted with his pierced hands empires off their hinges, and turned the stream of centuries out of its channel, and still governs the ages."

The infidel Rousseau said: —

"How petty the book of the philosophers with all pomp compared with the Gospels. Can it be that writings at once so sublime and so simple are the work of men? Is there anything in his character of the enthusiast or the ambitious sectary? What sweetness, what purity in his ways, what touching grace in his teachings; what a loftiness in his maxims, what profound wisdom in his words; what presence of mind, what delicacy and aptness in his replies; what an empire over his passions! Where is the man, where is the sage who knows how to act, to suffer, to die without weakness and without display? My friend, men do not invent like this; and the facts respecting Socrates, which no one doubts, are not so well attested as those about Jesus Christ. If the death of Socrates be that of a sage, the life and death of Jesus are those of a god."

The testimony of all agrees with these. No enemy has ever pointed to a flaw in the life, character, or words of Jesus. His challenge, "Which of you convinceth me of sin," has never been met.

The testimony of Jesus is first of all as to himself. In his life he did not rely upon the testimony of himself, but on that of others. His life was incomplete, and they did not have, as we have, the full Christ. He pointed Israel to the testimony of John the Baptist, the predictions of Scripture fulfilled, his miracles, the voice of God heard. There is also the testimony of his enemies and of such as Pilate and the centurion who crucified him, angels and devils, and others. It must be borne in mind that all this was to Israel. It was evidence for them particularly. It was testimony to those who accepted the Scriptures and God and the hereafter and a future life and the possibility of miracles, and, in fact, all we believe up to Christ. The validity of all this depends on the New Testament, which must be accepted first. All this, then, is testimony for the believer to confirm his faith. To quote any of the above evidences to one who does not accept the truth of either the New or the Old Testament is useless. It is reversing the Scripture argument which makes Christ himself the foundation of all faith.

The world is presented with the testimony of Jesus, that unimpeachable and accepted witness, as to himself. The claims of Jesus as to himself are the most conspicuous part of his teachings. They are utterly inconsistent with any theory except their truth. Since no one else can account for him, his own account is our only resource. He claimed to be the Son of God and equal to God in such passages as these: "I and the Father are one."[1] "He that hath seen me hath

[1] John x. 30.

seen the Father."[1] "The high priest said unto him, I adjure thee by the living God that thou tell us whether thou be the Christ the Son of God. Jesus saith unto him, Thou hast said."[2] On this statement he was condemned to death. Jesus also claimed to have preexisted, and to be the final Judge of the living and the dead. Jesus also ever declares himself as the sole way of salvation: "I am the way and the truth and the life; no one cometh unto the Father, but by me."[3] He uses such figures as, "I am the Door;" "I am the Bread of heaven;" "I am the Light of the World," to express this truth. He declared, "He that climbeth up some other way the same is a thief and a robber." He claimed to be the only Saviour for lost man.

There is no escape from one of three positions: Either Jesus was all he claimed, or he was mistaken, or a wilful deceiver. The first is in accord with his universally admitted character, the others are utterly inconsistent therewith. It is inconceivable that one so holy and wise could be deceived as to himself or would deceive others. Jesus must be accepted on his own claims as the Son of God. Any other conclusion would violate all the rules of evidence. In view of the spotless character and matchless wisdom of Jesus, there is no escape from the conclusion — "Truly this was the Son of God."

The testimony of Jesus to the Scriptures has already been mentioned. He declared of the law and the prophets: "I came not to destroy, but to fulfil."[4] Contrast this statement with the word and utterances of destructive criticism. The same authority he gave his disciples for the New Testament, saying, "He that heareth you heareth me; and he that rejecteth you rejecteth me; and he that rejecteth me rejecteth him that sent me."[5] So that the greatest proof of the Bible is the testimony of Jesus. The surest as

---

[1] John xiv. 9.   [2] Matt. xxvi. 63, 64.   [3] John xiv. 6.
[4] Matt. v. 17.   [5] Luke x. 16.

well as briefest argument that the Bible is authentic, true, and inspired is — Jesus said so.

Jesus came as a witness for God. He came to reveal God to man. He revealed God by his teachings, and by himself, his life and acts. In his teachings he revealed God in nature, in man, and, chief of all, in Scripture. The Israelite of that day was a neglecter of the great natural volume of divine wisdom. Jesus opened and expounded it and brought therefrom lessons of God's love and wisdom; as in the well-known passages: "Behold the birds of heaven;" "consider the lilies of the field." He called attention to the imminence of God in nature in the words, "Not a sparrow falleth to the ground without your Father." He declares the plan of God in nature and in providence in these words: "The earth beareth fruit of herself; first the blade, then the ear, then the full corn in the ear."[1] The scoffers who came asking a sign, he points to the sky, and bids them learn therefrom. A very large part of the teachings of Jesus are illustrated by, or wholly taken from, the natural works of God.

Jesus also revealed God in man. He saw in the original nature of man and in every natural relationship the work of God and the impress of God himself. He saw God in the good Samaritan and the merciful creditor and the prodigal's father. His favorite name for God— "Father"— was taken from a human relationship. He appealed to their own natural parental instincts as showing the feelings of God: "If ye then, being evil, know how to give good gifts unto your children, how much more shall your heavenly Father give the Holy Spirit to them that ask him?"[2] The parables of Jesus were taken wholly from the books of nature and humanity.

But the great revelation which Jesus brought to earth was that which he taught of God from the Scriptures, which were to him a revelation of the will

[1] Mark iv. 28.   [2] Luke xi. 13.

of God, and as such he taught them. But he brought out what had been long hidden and almost lost,— the spiritual sense and the real desire of God in the law. The scope of the Sermon on the Mount was to bring out the spirituality of the law. This is the sense of the words, "I desire mercy and not sacrifice."[1] Their whole idea of God had been perverted. The Jehovah they saw was a being of rites and ceremonies who cared for a special class and, like themselves, despised or ignored all others. The law they thought was a machine of value in itself and for itself. He showed them its meaning in the words, "The Sabbath was made for man and not man for the Sabbath." In all this Jesus sought to reveal God in the Scriptures.

The chief revelation of God which Jesus brought to man was that which he exhibited in his own nature, person, and life. Jesus was himself a revelation of God, he was "God manifest in the flesh." What Jesus was God is. All the great compassion and tenderness of Jesus is but a reflection of the nature of God. Jesus shows fully what Nature and Man reveals partially of God. The evils of nature and the imperfection of human life conceal the love of God. Looking at life from some standpoints it seems all sadness, and nature all wrath. This picture is relieved by considering Jesus. As he felt and acted toward man, so God feels, and so would be his dealings if man would receive his Son as their Saviour and King. To see the love of God for man, Jesus must be known and studied. He fully exhibits God's holiness also. Jesus was God's idea of perfection. Jesus was God's ideal man. He was not simply sinless; that is not righteousness, still less holiness. Jesus was the embodiment of God's idea of perfection.

Nor was the justice of God lacking in Jesus, although he came, as he expressly said, not to judge

---
[1] Hosea vi. 6 ; Matt ix. 13.

the world nor to condemn it. But there was a class to which Jesus showed no forbearance. The hypocrite was the object of his unmeasured severity. Jesus seemed willing to stand anything but self-righteousness and hypocrisy. To those who had the light and refused to receive it, he declared the certain consequences. He upbraided the cities where his mighty works were done because they believed not in him. All his exposition of the law in the Sermon on the Mount was a vindication of the righteousness of God.

The great hereafter is by Jesus set forth in all its grandeur and certainty. In the parable of the rich man and Lazarus, he lifts the curtain and shows us the course of two souls passing out into the eternity, and their respective fates. Jesus knew the future and declared it. The great fact of hell is distinctly taught by Jesus. The passage above is only one of many. He warns against it in these words: "And be not afraid of them which kill the body, but are not able to kill the soul: but rather fear him which is able to destroy both soul and body in hell."[1]

The great heart motive of Jesus and the greatest lesson he came to teach not only this world but all worlds and all ages, is seen in the passages such as the following which were continually upon his lips: "I am come down from heaven, not to do mine own will but the will of him that sent me. . . . As the Father gave me commandment, even so I do. . . . My meat is to do the will of him that sent me and to accomplish his work."[2] Far above all other motives, however great, was this supreme aim. It was his heart's desire. His feeling for man comes in order of strength after this and because of it. In exhibiting this loyalty to God, Jesus supplied the world's greatest need. A recent writer has said: "The one great aim of all philosophy, ancient and modern, has been to discover in the nature of things a rational sanction for human

---

[1] Matt. x. 28.   [2] John vi. 38; xiv. 31; iv. 34.

conduct." This great question Jesus came to answer. He came to show man the standard of right, the great motive of life. He showed it by his words, and above all, by his life. To do the will of God, was the mainspring of the life and work of Jesus.

Jesus taught that there is but one self-existing God. He himself, although equal in nature, never assumes any other than a subordinate place. In Jesus we see the most profound reverence for God and the most implicit obedience to him, faith in him, and dependence upon him. None can surpass in all these, him who is "the express image of his person." He will have nothing to attract the gaze of man from God the Father. All he does he attributes to him. It has been repeatedly shown that the whole purpose of the creation of man, and all this long procession of ages, and all the strange story of sin and sorrow, is to demonstrate once for all that there must be but one Will, and that Will God's, as the law of all existence; and that anything short of this is sin, and as the certain consequence, suffering and death. So Jesus came to set this perfect example of an absolutely perfect obedience and whole-hearted yielding up to God, and living for him first of all.

The title which expressed this relationship to God was "Son." In this title and relationship we see the attitude of Jesus. It is in this relationship there appears all that class of passages which speak of the subordination of Jesus to the Father. These will not be understood unless the great purpose and attitude of Jesus is kept in mind in his incarnation, — to exhibit a perfectly devoted and obedient heart and life. It is as Son he says, "My Father is greater than I;" "the Son can do nothing of himself." Nor is this assumed for the life on earth only. In his eternal state he is seen yielding up all to the Father, and dutifully subjecting himself to God. This should be the feeling of every child of God. It is the greatest possible to man.

In it is all holiness and all happiness. To seek the will of God is that singleness of eye which fills the whole heart and life with light. It brings the soul into perfect accord with the one Source of all good. It was this which Jesus had and which brought him the word of God saying, "Thou art my beloved Son; in thee am I well pleased."

It was not devotion to man first of all, but to God which produced that perfect self-abnegation which showed itself in the self-forgetfulness and self-sacrifice of Jesus. He loved man because he loved God. He came to save man because it was the will of God. He gave himself for us because he had given himself to God. The highest subject of contemplation and the great object of affection is God the Father. This Jesus taught. He himself directed all attention to God. He presents himself as a manifestation of God and the way to God. His work is to bring man to peace with God, and ultimately to the very presence of God; and then to render up all to God the Father, that God may be all in all. Christ in all his mediatorial work must ever be viewed in this light. He does not present himself as the object of our worship, but directs us to worship God in his name. So the apostles address not Christ but God the Father in all the recorded prayers after Christ's ascension. There appears to be but one prayer addressed to Jesus, — the closing words of John in the Apocalypse, "Even so come Lord Jesus," which is, however, more a response to the previous vocal message of Christ, than a prayer.

From this attitude of the soul to God, there necessarily follows the right feeling to man. In the personal exhibition of this, as has been seen, and as the world acknowledges, Jesus surpasses all. His teachings correspond. The maxims of the world's teachers abound in good sayings as to the treatment of others. Altruism is not a newly discovered virtue nor exclusively a Christian one. The world has always loved its own and done much for the poor and commended benevolence. But the teachings of Jesus as to the treatment of others as far surpass the sayings of the world's sages as his example excels theirs. He overtops the highest, and rises in the greatness of his self-sacrifice as far above the world's humanitarianism as in his unapproachable divinity above their deities. Socrates replied, when asked how to treat one's friends: "As we would desire they should bear themselves to us." Jesus extends this rule to all others as well as friends. Confucius taught, "What you do not want done to yourself, do not do to others." Seneca says, "Expect from others what you do to others." Compare the rule of Jesus: "As ye would that men should do to you, do ye also to them likewise." The rule of Jesus is positive where that of Socrates is negative, and active where that of Seneca is merely passive. There is no such devotion to man as by those who have the Spirit of Jesus. It surpasses all patriotic self-sacrifice, all humanitarian benevolence, all natural affection. It sinks the love of self, the strongest of human feelings, and leads the one fully possessed by it to say, "For to me to live is Christ."

The ministry of Jesus is divided into three periods of about a year each, marked respectively as the periods of obscurity, popularity, and opposition. About a year was required for his fame to spread, then followed the harvest time, and from this success came the jealousy of the Jews which culminated in open opposition, ending only at the cross. The space given by the evangelists to these periods is significant. Matthew allots ten chapters to the last six months, and eighteen to all the rest, say three years. Mark gives seven chapters to the last six months, and nine to all the rest. Luke gives to these periods fourteen and ten chapters respectively, and John gives eleven and ten to them. Indeed, in the latter the last eleven chapters are devoted to the last week of the life of Jesus and the events following. The lesson of this is apparent, this is the time of great importance to us for whom they wrote. We are therefore to follow Christ as he enters upon the great work for which he came, which transcends that for Israel and the church, and is to affect the world and all eternity.

The last night of Jesus in earthly form saw the formal ending of all he came to do as Israel's Messiah, and the transfer of privileges to the church. Yet there is no break. The passover fades into the Lord's supper almost insensibly. We can scarcely tell where the account of the one ends and the other begins. In the whole we see Jehovah again preparing his people for a greater deliverance. The passover was the Old Testament picture of Calvary. Jesus was the Lamb of God, chosen to give his blood for our sprinkling and his flesh for our eating. It is significant, as is said, that the passover lamb was prepared for roasting by having a spit run through from head to tail and another from shoulder to shoulder, thus forming a cross. Every passover lamb was crucified. The supper contains in itself the whole gospel — the whole truth as to the believer and the church, her work and life and hope of the future. Its full depths of meaning have never been sounded.

The feelings of Jesus as he approached the cross were those of perfect acquiescence in this divine appointment. There was the glad consciousness that all the long, vast accumulation of sin was to be atoned for by his offering on the cross. But we must not suppose that there was an absence of painful feelings in Jesus as he contemplated this great act. His state can be seen reflected in the faces of the twelve in the following passage: "And they were in the way going up to Jerusalem: and Jesus was going before them; and they were amazed; and they that followed were afraid. And he took again the twelve and began to tell them the things that were to happen unto him."[1] This state is reflected in the Messianic Psalms. The shadow of the cross fell gradually upon the little band who followed him. His warnings of the coming tragedy are given with increasing distinctness. First he tells them he is to suffer, then to die. Then he tells that he is to be betrayed, and adds, "One of you shall betray me;" and at the table first privately to John, close to him at one side, by the sign of the sop; and at last to the traitor next him on the other side. The walk out to Gethsemane was a silent one. The circumstances of the company, surrounded by enemies and now being watched by a traitor, called for the protection of secrecy. The dark, rough, and narrow streets were no place for conversation. The disciples were oppressed by the solemn events of the evening, and his repeated warnings of approaching danger.

What personal conflicts Jesus had with Satan after his first temptation are not recorded. They were not incessant, for Satan chooses his times and opportunities. In the ending of the account of the temptation, it is recorded that Satan "departed from him for a season." That season had now expired. Now was Satan's hour and the power of darkness. Gethsemane was not a time of suffering only for Jesus. It was an ordeal of fierce temptation. The great purpose of Satan in the temptation of Jesus in Gethsemane was to prevent the cross, or mar the work of Jesus at its close, as by the first temptation he would have stopped it at the beginning. The cross was the weapon Satan feared most of all. His empire was founded on sin and guilt, and the cross swept sin and guilt away. The foundation gone, his house must fall. Calvary, then, was Satan's object of fierce attack in Gethsemane. To prevent the great

[1] Mark x. 32.

sacrifice was his purpose. He must have known the scope of the death of Jesus. He was willing to have him die, and stirred up Judas to betray him to the Jews, expecting them to kill him by their own hands; but if by this temptation he could prevent the cross, that would be better than all. His purposes often are at variance, and one instrument is set against another, he little caring which plan succeeds.

Gethsemane was also the testing of the victim for the passover sacrifice. The Lamb had to be without blemish. If fault or flaw was found, it was unfit for the sacred use. The great point on which the test was to be made was submission to the will of God, the original purpose referred to so often, and for which the whole history of man is being made. The lamb-like submission was the great essential for the passover sacrifice. There were three elements in the trial in Gethsemane which made it terrible, — the power of Darkness; the Hour; and the Cup. It was as he said to the band coming to apprehend him, "This is your hour and the power of darkness."[1] Satan was and is always present to defeat the purpose of God, but there are special marshalings of the forces of hell. "The Power of Darkness" was such. All that could be put forth of satanic energy was present then — the "principalities, the powers, the world rulers of this darkness, the spiritual hosts of wickedness in the heavenly places."[2] Further, it was their "Hour." It was their set time to do their worst. God then gave them permission to try the Son of God as he never had been tried before. Lastly, there was "the Cup." This figure is used in Scripture to represent the portion of the sinner — "the wine of the wrath of God, which is prepared unmixed in the cup of his anger." Jesus took the place of sinful man, guilty and doomed man, the worst of men deserving of this cup. He must therefore drink of their cup.

[1] Luke xxii. 53.   [2] Eph. vi. 12.

He suffered guilty man's hunger and weariness and pain and sorrow.

The attack was threefold, as the first temptation was. This points to the same threefold nature of the temptation, involving the three natures and three corresponding forms of temptation. There is indication, however, of a reverse order in the presentation. Satan would win the main issue, and failing in this, some lesser gain. The spiritual attack probably came first. It is to this phase of the ordeal the Scripture refers— "Ye have not yet resisted unto blood, striving against sin."[1] It does not seem credible that Satan could hope to overthrow Jesus here after his life of trial and corresponding gain in all spiritual strength. But we must keep in mind that Jesus was fighting our battle under our conditions; that he lived and wrought entirely by the Holy Spirit; that the most holy are the most fiercely assaulted. Awful thoughts have come into the mind of the purest and best. Doubts as to their salvation have tormented the dearest of God's children. Suspicions as to God's goodness have found a way into the minds of the most trustful. There has come over the spirits of the most firm at times a doubt of everything. All they have known and been sure of has seemed untrue or uncertain. The most precious hopes of heaven have seemed a hollow sham. All the good one has done vanishes from sight, all the usual spiritual comforts are absent. Not a promise comes to the mind with any power. All is dark and hopeless and awful. There comes a strange impulse to rush into some awful delusion or to do some wicked thing or even to abandon God and hope and heaven. This form of temptation comes later in life than that represented by the temptation in the wilderness. It comes after a trial of the life of the believer, often after much Christian work and great success. So Elijah was pressed,—"O Lord,

[1] Heb. xii. 4.

take away my life, for I am not better than my fathers."[1]

What makes this form of temptation so terrible is that these thoughts are so mingled in the mind that they seem to arise from within. The believer thinks he is conceiving all this himself, and is plunging into apostasy of his own impulse and desire. Here is the difference between this and that kind represented by the temptation in the wilderness. That was objective, this subjective. That was temptation to outward acts; this to an inward state, or act. Bunyan, in "Grace Abounding," discloses his own temptation to such an inward act of renunciation of Christ and the dark years which followed.

We can judge Jesus by ourselves for he was tempted in all points as we are, and all these are points of temptation to believers. So it is no disparagement of the divine nature of Jesus to believe that Satan pressed all of these upon his mind with superhuman power and subtlety. Not a dark or blasphemous doubt was left unsuggested. But the depths of these experiences are in proportion to the nature in which they occur. Into a nature of infinite depth we can look, although we cannot fathom it. No mind can conceive of this trial of Jesus at the very verge of his great mediatorial work. Satan's purpose was to unfit him for it or prevent it in any way. This was the struggle of Gethsemane. The danger of some interference with, or unfitness for, his great work as Redeemer, was the awful agony of Jesus in the darkness of that fearful conflict.

His recourse is to prayer. But prayer does not always at first give relief. Satan may "tremble when he sees the weakest saint upon his knees," but there is no evidence of it in Scripture, and he shows none in his conduct. On the other hand, he presses closest to the struggling, seeking one, to prevent his

[1] 1 Kings xix. 4.

access and to break his faith and to darken his view and to drive him from the place or exercise. Such times are battles. At such times "our wrestling is not against flesh and blood, but against the principalities, against the powers, against the world rulers of this darkness, against the spiritual hosts of wickedness in the heavenly places."[1] Jesus wrestled and struggled against the enshrouding darkness out of which there came not one ray of spiritual light. He comes out from the shadows of the place of prayer to the three chosen disciples to get from them some human sympathy, and to be in their presence relieved for a few moments from the awful strain of the satanic conflict. He finds them asleep. From the beginning to the end, no human help was given him. It could not be otherwise. Jesus was to drink the cup and suffer and die alone. No human voice can ever be raised to say, "I helped the Son of God in the day of his atonement."

Jesus returned alone to meet the second assault of Satan. The nature of this may be read in this passage: "My soul is exceeding sorrowful even unto death."[2] This is a soul state as distinguished from spiritual conflict. It is not confined to the believer or to spiritual beings. Our age has much of it. It affects its victim in forms of mental depression or prostration. One is conscious of its presence, yet powerless to resist. The mind is filled with strange thoughts which sweep through in a whirlwind of fury, and leave one prostrated in weakness afterward. Mental collapse often follows, and the person is left unaccountable as to his actions. In such attacks self-destruction is often suggested, and this is the inward history of many a suicide. Indeed, if the person is conscious of his state, either insanity or suicide appears to be the certain consequence of his distressing condition. There are other forms of peculiar oppression which

[1] Eph. vi. 12. [2] Matt. xxvi. 38.

are now coming to be understood, by which one mind comes to control another, and works awful consequences to the victim. All this is possible to Satan, indeed comes from him. He has used it many times. With how much of all this or other kinds of oppression he now assaults Jesus, we cannot know. Only this we are sure of: he was "tempted in all points as we are," and here is one of the most distressing forms of human affliction. To incapacitate Jesus from making a voluntary sacrifice of himself or to destroy its value as the act of one not in full possession of self-control, would accomplish Satan's object to prevent or mar the work of the cross.

Jesus was in a state favorable to the inroads of such an attack. There are in the records evidences of delicacy of temperament and nervous organization. He was at the close of a long and exhausting work which had taxed nerves and brain and mind. The exciting events of the past few days and the long hours with his disciples left him needing rest and quiet. The approach of his crucifixion, with all the attending trying events, still further wrought upon him. It was Satan's hour to assault Jesus. He bears down upon Jesus in his weakness with all the mysterious yet real power of mind over mind. Nerves and brain feel the awful pressure. That great and powerful and inexpressively malignant being presses with all his mighty power upon that sinking nature.

We can well believe all hell is present to assist in that which will give them such a prize. To so control Jesus even for a time, and have it recorded that the work of Calvary was that of one not in his senses, was a plan of surpassing subtlety. Jesus feels the awful pressure. It was the human nature which was the subject of the second temptation. Reason seems tottering. He feels as if in the mad whirl of insanity. Such a state cannot last long. Utter wreck seems the certain consequence of the fearful strain. In the darkness of the hour it might have seemed as if it was God's will to let him fall a victim. It was an awful thought. He cries out in his agony against it, begging to be spared such an awful blow. Yet under all is seen the immovable submission which is inwoven into his very nature and cannot change even in that awful vortex of mental agony. He rises to seek again the group he brought to help him on this night of his dire distress. They are stupid with sleep and scarcely wake to hear what he says to them. So he leaves them, to return to the final conflict.

This seems to have been an attack upon Jesus' physical frame. The final deliverance and the final attack is thus recorded: "Who in the days of his flesh, having offered up prayers and supplications with strong crying and tears unto him that was able to save him from death, and having been heard for his godly fear, though he was a Son, yet learned obedience by the things which he suffered."[1] Satan, unable to sway Jesus from his purpose or to incapacitate him for it, now seeks to forestall the crucifixion by forcing him to a premature death in the garden. It would not be a moral victory, as in the second temptation, or a spiritual victory as in the first; but it would prevent the great atonement. Such was Satan's thought and purpose. Nor was it wholly impossible from his standpoint. He has the power of death. Jesus was physically exhausted. His work had taxed all his not very great strength. Every miracle was a draught upon his energies. "There went virtue out of him," we read of one healing; but it was always so. In a sense more real than we know. "Himself took our infirmities and bare our diseases."[2]

The frequent wearinesses mentioned in the Gospels tell of wasting strength and receding powers. It is believed by competent medical authorities who have

Heb. v. 7. [2] Matt. viii. 17.

made a study of the state of Jesus before and in his death, that he was during all his ministry suffering from a fatal and painful disease. The bloody sweat, the water flowing from the heart with blood, all point to abnormal conditions and to some vital derangement. In all this we see the opportunity of Satan. This, then, was his last fierce onslaught on Jesus. He attacks every vital organ of Jesus' body. The blood seemed to desert its accustomed channels, to return again with such unnatural force to the frail tissues which held it as to ooze in drops from the pores of the skin. The breath seemed to stop and leave him scarcely able to recover it. The damps of death were upon him. Jesus seemed dying, and dying without the cross. It was an awful thought to him. It was the failure of all for which he had come. To reach the cross was the great desire of Jesus. For this he came, for this he was sent, for this a body was given him, for this he had prepared; of this he had prophesied. On this depended all the past, while countless types awaited this fulfilment. The innumerable private and public sacrifices all were useless without this redemption. These temptations were doubtless cumulative. The first and second were still upon him when the third and last falls with crushing force upon the sinking Jesus. Spirit, soul, and body are in the throes of the awful conflict. Humanly speaking, there can be no escape or recovery. He prayed in an agony of desire. It could not be possible God would permit this awful thing to happen. He cries, "Let this cup pass from me." Yet if it is the will of God so to humiliate him; if in God's infinite wisdom this can be and must be, "Nevertheless not as I will but as thou wilt."

The victory was won, but Jesus was left utterly exhausted. He had not strength enough to finish his work. We can see him lying prostrate for very weakness. He is thus helped: "There appeared unto him an angel from heaven strengthening him."[1] Enough strength is imparted to him to enable him to undergo the arrest and trial and scourging and smiting and to reach the cross and to finish his work. He returns to the disciples, and together they step forward into the open to meet his approaching fate.

The sting in the soul of Jesus in his last hour was that his death was to be brought about by the hand of one of his own. This also finds a place in the prediction, "Mine own familiar friend, in whom I trusted, which did eat of my bread, hath lifted up his heel against me."[2] This Jesus quotes at the table. Soon after he hands the sop to Judas who thus literally eats of Jesus' bread. Judas appears to have been on terms of special intimacy with Jesus. "Mine own familiar friend" is a term expressing something more than discipleship. He seems to have sat next to Jesus at the table and to have enjoyed his confidence. Judas was not allowed to enter the course of treason unrebuked. Seven distinct warnings can be seen given by Jesus as to his approaching death, each successive announcement more definite than the preceding. Judas hears all, and must have known whom he meant when he said, "One of you shall betray me." When all were asking, "Lord is it I?" Judas also secretly, for the disciples did not know of the reason of his going out, asks, "Lord, is it I?" and Jesus responds also secretly, "Thou hast said." He hears and goes out on his awful errand, although the words of Jesus must have rung in his ears, "Woe unto that man through whom the Son of man is betrayed. Good were it for that man if he had not been born."[3]

It is difficult to understand the conduct of Judas. How one so near to Jesus and on such terms of special intimacy and so repeatedly and plainly warned,

[1] Luke xxii. 43.   [2] Ps. xli. 9.   [3] Matt. xxvi. 24, 25.

could have deliberately sold his Lord is scarcely capable of explanation. It is true "Satan entered into him;" but there was, as is the case in all who fall, a preparation. In Judas this was of long development. We read, "He was a thief and carried the bag." There appears to have been a special purpose in Judas' mind for the sum he received for the betrayal of Jesus. The end of his guilty act and life reveals the secret. "Now this man obtained a field with the reward of his iniquity; and falling headlong, he burst asunder in the midst, and all his bowels gushed out. And it became known to all the dwellers of Jerusalem; insomuch that in their language that field was called Akeldama, that is, The field of blood. For it is written in the book of Psalms, Let his habitation be made desolate, and let no man dwell therein.[1]"

The fact of his buying this place, its character, and his purpose in it are all declared here. It was a sightly place overlooking from its precipitous location the surrounding country, perhaps the city of Jerusalem, close to which it was situated. He intended it for a habitation as indicated in the psalm, "Let his habitation be made desolate." He had bought it either by bargaining for it or by having paid part for it. The thirty pieces of silver were required to finish paying for it, and were so applied after his death. He had set his heart on this place. He has it in full possession except for thirty pieces of silver. His stealings have gone into it. His conscience is blunted to right and wrong. At this juncture he is approached by Satan. It is intimated to him he can make money by assisting to secure Jesus. He perhaps is told he might as well make it as any one else. If he does not some one else will. Perhaps he reasons, Jesus is able to save himself, and will doubtless do so. Jesus' popularity has waned. He is a suspected man; some

[1] Acts i. 18–20.

say, beside himself. It is easy to disbelieve in an unpopular religion or person. Judas has lost faith in Jesus. He knows his integrity but everybody doubts his claims. All these reasonings pass through his mind as he deliberates this thing of sin. To deliberate here is to be lost. He seeks the enemies of Jesus and sells his Lord and Master.

The traitor goes out to his self-chosen task. He knew the place, for Jesus often resorted thither with his disciples. A band of men is given to him. He places himself at their head. He guides them accurately to the garden. Many a time he had accompanied Jesus thither. Jesus advances to meet him. Judas salutes him with the kiss of friendship. Jesus replies, "Judas, betrayest thou the Son of man with a kiss?" It was the manner of the betrayal which hurt the heart of Jesus. They had often exchanged this customary salutation of love. It was the fatal act for Judas. All else was but preparatory to this and might have been repented of. Jesus was betrayed and Judas damned by that kiss. Jesus chides the people who have no grievance against him for their coming with spears and staves as if he were a thief, reminding them they could have taken him any time in the temple. He rebukes the hasty act of Peter in drawing his sword and smiting the servant, and heals the wound. Then they lead him away. Judas is confounded at seeing Jesus thus taken and bound. He must have expected Jesus to save himself as before. He is conscience-stricken. He rushes to those who paid the money to him, flings it down with expressions of intense remorse, rushes out to his coveted possession, fastens a rope around his neck, casts himself over the precipice, the rope breaks and he is crushed by the fall. The place is counted accursed thenceforth, and is used for the burial of strangers.[1]

[1] Matt. xxvii. 3-10; Acts i. 18-20.

The story of the sufferings and death of Jesus have caught the attention and touched the heart of the world. No one can read the narrative and not be at least silent from respect. He was led or rather dragged about from place to place as silent and submissive and as helpless, so far as physical strength or resistance was concerned, as the lamb to which he is compared. While waiting for the morning and the meeting of the council, he stands bound and silent. It is there occurs the incident in which Peter figures so disgracefully. He is near enough to Jesus for recognition. What a comfort he could have been and what immortality of glory he would have won by even a word of comfort addressed to Jesus, or even by faithful acknowledgment and silent sympathy! But even this is denied Jesus. He must bear it all alone. At length the day comes, and the trial and all its tortures of body and mind. His strength was exhausted by his night of struggle and watching. His pale face was stained with the bloody sweat. He stood helpless before his captors who were hungry for his blood. To all the jeering he answers not a word.

Jesus was brought successively before Annas, Caiaphas, Pilate, the sanhedrim, Pilate, Herod, Pilate again, and at last is presented to the people. In each every right and precedent were violated. Jesus was found guilty on two charges, and for these he was condemned to death. These were that he claimed to be the Son of God and the King of Israel. For the first he was condemned by the Jewish council, and the last was the official and legal accusation hung on the cross by the Roman governor Pilate. Christ admitted both charges. He was condemned and treated accordingly. He was kept bound, was smitten on the face, the hair plucked from his cheeks: he was arrayed in scarlet, and a crown of thorns placed upon his head. He was hooted and derided by the soldiery, and the angry crowd cried fiercely, "Crucify him," and asked the release of a murderer in his place.

All this being over and the necessary authority given by Pilate, he is led away to execution. It was no uncommon scene in Jerusalem. The usual crowd gathered, but there was an unusual fierceness in their yelling. There were some present who were of importance and not usually at such scenes. They were the foes of Jesus going to make sure he was crucified, and to gloat over his disgrace and sufferings. The procession files down the street and out of the gate. We may picture the scene. It was led probably by two of the soldiers, then one of the malefactors bearing his cross, Jesus bearing his cross, then the second malefactor, and then the other two soldiers. A shout tells the forward soldiers something has happened. They halt and look back. Jesus has fallen. The heavy cross has overtaxed his failing strength, and he lies prostrate on the ground. With a curse at the prisoner, one of them pulls the cross away, and then roughly drags him to his feet. He stands unsteady a moment. The cross is laid upon a stranger who happens to pass, and the procession moves forward again. A woman's voice is heard weeping, and bewailing Jesus. He addresses her a word of comfort. The place is reached. It is the common scene of such executions. The cross is laid upon the ground. Jesus stretched upon it. He speaks. "Father forgive them, they know not what they do" is his prayer. Nails are driven through each hand and foot. Then it is lifted, bearing up his body. The end is placed in a hole, one soldier guides it to its place, and the others steady it. They press the earth firm about it. The inscription is placed over his head, "This is Jesus of Nazareth the King of the Jews." The thieves are also crucified. The soldiers wipe the perspiration from their faces, and sit down to rest. The victim's clothes are their perquisites, and these they now divide among themselves. One of the garments is a woven one. It cannot be divided, so they cast lots for it. There is now nothing more to do, so they sit and watch.

In the crowd there are many who know of his power. They had seen him raise the dead. Why should he not deliver himself now, they ask. There is some expectancy that he will do so; but after some time passes and he does not, all conclude that he is not able to do so. They now begin to jeer and call upon him to come down from the cross. The malefactors, who at first called upon him to deliver himself and them, finding he does not do so, turn and rail at him. One, however, afterward repents and rebukes the other, and turning to Jesus says, "Lord remember me when thou comest in thy kingdom." To him Jesus replies, "To-day shalt thou be with me in paradise." He was the first of the blood-washed throng. The last act of Jesus — "the ruling passion strong in death" — was the saving of this poor sinner. He commends his mother to John who takes her immediately away to his home, thus sparing her the agonizing spectacle further. There is a small prophecy yet unfulfilled. It was written in the Messianic psalm,[1] "In my thirst they gave me vinegar to drink." So Jesus cried, "I thirst." A sponge dipped in vinegar is lifted to his lips: of this he tastes. All is complete. He calls aloud, "It is finished."

It is high noon. A great darkness gathers over the sky. The people are terrified, and most leave the place. No human eye rests upon the dying Christ. Then comes to him an agony he did not expect. The agony of Gethsemane was awful, but this far exceeds it. There entered into this something Jesus had never suffered before. What it was is seen in his cry, "My God, my God, why hast thou forsaken me?" Heretofore Jesus had the constant presence of

[1] Psalms lxix. 21.

the Father. In the eternal past, in creation, in the life on earth, in all the conflicts, even in Gethsemane, God was with him. Now God leaves him to die alone. It was necessary. It was the portion of the sinner's cup which Christ was draining to the dregs. This was the agony of the cross. To be separated from the Father, to cease to feel his presence, to realize that his face was averted, was the bitterness of Christ's death. It was the last stroke. It came at the ninth hour. He repeats the words of the psalm, "Into thy hands I commit my spirit," and breathes out his life, his last and highest act of perfect submission to God and faith in him. As Jesus died, the earth shook, the rocks were rent, and many of the dead rose; the vail of the Temple was rent in twain, and the darkness rolled away. At sundown the soldiers put the crucified thieves to death. They pierced the side of Jesus, and there flowed out blood and water. The earth received the contents of his heart and arteries and veins. The blood of Jesus was shed literally on earth, and its soil received it.

Next in sacredness to the custody of the infant Jesus was the care of his lifeless body. To another Joseph it was committed. The two Josephs represent the extremes of society; the one a carpenter, the other a councilor and a man of wealth. He used his influence as such to obtain the body of Jesus. Another councilor, Nicodemus, helped him. It was a hasty burial owing to the approach of the Sabbath. In Joseph's family tomb, not as yet occupied, Jesus was laid. The Jews secured a guard and sealed the sepulcher. All was over. Jesus was dead and buried. Man and Satan had done their worst.

Reading such a story for the first time, one would conclude upon his guilt without further evidence. We would say that one so universally condemned by friend and foe and by all the constituted authorities, must be very wicked. We in this day of familiarity with the gospel story have lost our feelings of horror at the knowledge that this was not only an innocent man, as proved by all these trials, but that this was the holiest man who ever lived on earth; that he spent his whole life doing good, and saved thousands from disease, and comforted thousands more; that he only desired to be permitted to continue all this indefinitely and extend it to all the earth. Besides all that he was the legal King of Israel, and entitled to the humble allegiance of every one of those who so derided him. He was their Messiah for whom they had long looked and on whom their deliverance as a nation depended. More still, he was the Son of God. All this he substantiated by proofs of every kind — Scripture, miracles, and witnesses.

This was an awful crime — the wickedest act ever done on this or any other world. It must be asked, Who was responsible? It was begun by one of Jesus' own followers, who went to the enemies of Jesus and offered to betray him. Jesus laid blame on all the apostolic band, — "One of *you* shall betray me." They followed this by all forsaking him in his hour of need, and one with oaths denied him before his enemies. Not a soul of them ever lifted a voice in his defense. Jesus was condemned to death by Israel. It was their animosity which hunted him out and finally brought him to the cross. Israel can never escape the stigma of having crucified their Messiah. Last of all, Jesus was "crucified under Pontius Pilate." Pilate represented Rome, and Rome ruled the world. The whole world, then, is guilty of the death of Jesus. The church, Israel, and the world crucified Jesus. This is the view from man's standpoint. It must however be regarded from above and from Jesus' own personal action and purpose.

Everywhere in Scripture God is represented as sending and giving Jesus, and he as coming in response to the will of God. He expressly declared his death to be voluntary. "Therefore doth the Father love me, because I lay down my life, that I may take it again. No one taketh it away from me, but I lay it down of myself. I have power to lay it down, and I have power to take it again. This commandment received I from my Father."[1] Not all the agencies could have caused Jesus' death without his own consent. The sufferings and death of Jesus affected himself also. "Though he were a Son yet learned he obedience by the things which he suffered" "It became him, for whom are all things, and by whom are all things, in bringing many sons unto glory to make the captain of their salvation perfect through sufferings. For both he that sanctifieth and they who are sanctified are all of one."[2] The course traveled by Jesus and every believing soul is the same. Jesus therefore for his own sake endured the cross. All the discipline any soul endures of suffering necessary to bring it into the condition fit for fellowship with God, Jesus also passed through.

The state and place of the Spirit of Jesus during the time between his death and resurrection is intimated by his promise to the believing malefactor, "To-day shalt thou be with me in paradise."[3] Paradise is the place where the believer is after death. There the dying beggar went. Here, then, was Jesus awaiting his resurrection as all his people are still in this happy place. He thus follows our path in this also. It is said of the saints in paradise that "they rest from their labors and their works do follow them." Rest surely Jesus needed after the fearful struggle. He was not yet in his eternal state. If the spirits of the saints need and can experience rest, so could he who was walking their path and entering into all their needs and changes and experiences. Jesus no doubt also entered into the enjoyment of the sweet fellowship of the saints pictured by the at-

[1] John x. 17, 18. [2] Heb. v. 8; ii. 10, 11. [3] Luke xxiii. 43.

titude of the beggar reclining by the side of Abraham and enjoying whatever is represented by the table which is necessary to the figure used there. Jesus also no doubt told the saints of the accomplishment of the work of the cross and the approaching completion of it in his resurrection. Paradise is not, however, the highest place of the believer. It is simply where the saints are gathering and awaiting the completed church, when in one company, all will enter into the highest and fullest glory. So this was not the exaltation of Jesus. That could not occur until he rose from the dead, and ascended to the Father.

Both human enemies and friends were asleep; neither expecting his resurrection. It was an event in which the inhabitants of the unseen worlds were the only active and interested spectators. In heaven the resurrection of Jesus was eagerly looked for, not as a doubtful thing or as a critical event, for in their minds knowing him as they did and having him in spirit with them, they knew he was as sure to become reunited to that earthly body as that he was the Son of God. But it was longed for by them. It was the victory over death they wanted to see. It was the induction of their Lord in his eternal state in which he was to become possessed of an immortal human body which he was to wear forever, and in which he was to rule in glory over them and all. Although neither the church nor the world understood or realized it, that first Lord's Day was the day of crisis in the affairs of eternity and of intensest interest to both heaven and hell. The one side full of faith and the other full of apprehension, — all were watching the outcome of that day. We do not know what Satan did to endeavor to prevent the resurrection of Jesus. He who contended with the archangel for the body of Moses we may be sure struggled with all the energy of his mighty power to prevent the resurrection of Jesus. The rising of Jesus threatened his supreme authority over man by death. Hitherto all had fallen before him.

We may look in reverent imagination upon the scene within the sepulcher. It is a low-roofed place, in which it is scarcely possible to stand erect. There lies the form we saw hanging on the cross. Loving hands have wrapped it in a clean linen cloth and fragrant spices. Limbs and head are carefully adjusted. No human body could be more truly dead than that one. Jesus died a broken-down man, and, as we have seen, was probably a sufferer from a fatal disease. By his crucifixion every vital organ must have been wrenched out of all hope of restoration. His heart was pierced by the soldier's spear, which probably emptied the entire blood from the body. He had lain since the third day in this state. The tomb is closed by a stone which required the strength of several men to move. It was sealed, and a guard of soldiers watched before it. No one of his own power had ever come out from the dead, and there was no prophet to work such a miracle. To human eyes all was hopeless. Except his own word and the predictions of Scripture, there was not a single ray of hope that Jesus would rise.

The preliminary and preparatory events of the resurrection of Jesus are thus described: "And behold, there was a great earthquake; for an angel of the Lord descended from heaven, and came and rolled away the stone, and sat upon it. His appearance was as lightning, and his raiment white as snow: and for fear of him the watchers did quake, and became as dead men."[1] But all this is not the event itself. We may with reverent minds try to picture it. The Holy Spirit had never left that precious form. He is the giver of life. Now he simply exercises his office work. Therefore life flows through that lifeless body. Lungs and brain and nerves and muscles all respond as naturally as in one in full health. The cause only

[1] Matt. xxviii. 2–4.

of that life and movement is different. Blood is the means of the life of the human body, but not so in this, for it is absent from Jesus' veins. A change, too, takes place in the body itself. It is the resurrection change. It becomes superior to natural laws; yet it was a real body. Jesus was afterward handled and felt, did eat and drink, was heard and spoken to, and recognized. It was true corporeal life but sustained by the immediate power of the Holy Spirit. All the functions of the body were in full state of perfection. It was the same yet not the same. The change is thus described: "It is sown in corruption; it is raised in incorruption: it is sown in dishonor; it is raised in glory: it is sown in weakness; it is raised in power: it is sown a natural body; it is raised a spiritual body."[1]

It is clothed also in garments of immortality. The garb Jesus wore was neither his former raiment nor the grave-clothes. There should be no difficulty in accounting for his being supplied with clothing. The angels who ministered in Gethsemane could do so now in this also. Christ entered again the tabernacle he occupied so long and is now to inhabit forever. He opened his eyes as calmly as if from a refreshing sleep, sat up and unwrapped the burial clothes, folded them up neatly and laid them aside, the napkin which was about his face in a place by itself. He rose and stepped out of the open door.

There was no human being to greet the risen Saviour. Had they had faith, all the apostles certainly would have been there to meet him. Jesus waited about the sepulcher and saw the women come and go away again in haste and excitement at finding the sepulcher open and empty. He also saw Peter and John come and look in and go away again. He kept himself unseen and was silent. He was evidently looking or waiting for something. He was looking for what he constantly longed for in life and

[1] 1 Cor. xv. 43, 44.

always — faith in himself and in his word. Nothing so delighted him on earth as to find faith in any one, and nothing so grieved him as unbelief. Now he longs to find among them some who have faith to believe in his resurrection, and to show their faith by coming to the sepulcher to meet him. But he finds none. The women come to finish the embalming, and not to see a risen Jesus. Peter and John come to the sepulcher, but only to see the thing reported by the women. All come and go but one, and she remains, not to see a living Saviour, but to find if possible where they have taken the body. It seems strange that with the empty sepulcher before them and the linen clothes and the napkin folded in proper shape and place, all showing Jesus' careful ways and not the work of robbers or of foes, and the repeated predictions of Jesus himself in mind, and the appearance of the angels and their message, "He is not here: for he is risen, even as he said. Come see the place where the Lord lay,"[1] — it is strange that with all this they did not believe he was risen. Jesus found affection for himself personally, but not faith in his word. They were yet lacking in the work of the Spirit, without which faith and every other grace and gift are impossible. Their need was set before them as ours is set before us for our self-examination, by this scene about the empty sepulcher. Having shown them their total absence of faith, he now proceeds to the revelation of himself.

The first human being to see the risen Christ and to become the bearer of the good news to the church was Mary Magdalene. Why was she selected for so great an honor, as great almost as that of the other Mary who gave him birth, to whom, in her history, she was such a contrast? She had been a great sinner and had had much forgiven and loved Jesus correspondingly. Mary Magdalene had little faith but

[1] Matt. xxviii, 6.

great love, and this covers a multitude of shortcomings. For the same reason Peter was honored above the other apostles. Jesus will overlook anything where there is true love for himself. An act of Mary shows her great love and little understanding. She lays hold on him, probably falling at his feet and clasping them, as the other women did, as if she feared he would immediately ascend and leave her. To her Jesus says, "Take not hold upon me; for I am not yet ascended to the Father."[1] As much as to say, You need not hold me; I am not leaving you immediately. He gives her a message to the disciples whom he now for the first time calls "my brethren." Having been now made perfect by suffering he is not ashamed to call them so. He follows his message by a personal appearance to two of the disciples, and by these successive means prepares the apostles gradually for the startling event of his appearance.

There is no record of the doings or state of the apostles during the time Jesus lay in the sepulcher. Jesus had said, "Ye shall be scattered every man to his own, and shall leave me alone."[2] The record tells us that at his arrest the disciples left him and fled. Peter followed into the palace afterward only to deny him thrice. John also was in the assembly but silent. They no doubt engaged with all others in the duties and services of the passover feast. Their state may be seen reflected in the account of the two Jesus met on the way to Emmaus. They said, "We hoped that it was he which should redeem Israel." The whole company of disciples no doubt shared these feelings. All were sad, disappointed, and hopeless. No doubt there was, too, the usual feelings we all have at the loss of dear ones, and especially the very common feelings of self-reproach at real or fancied neglect or wrongs done to the dear departed. They all had occasion for such thoughts

[1] John xx. 17, margin. [2] John xvi : 32.

and especially Peter. There was apprehension also. They were the followers of a condemned and executed leader. They share his odium and guilt. They may perhaps meet the same fate. They meet the third day, the doors locked for fear of the Jews. There has come startling intelligence of the open and empty sepulcher and that angels had been seen and that they had said that Jesus was alive. Some of the apostles ran to the sepulcher and found it empty. Finally, Mary Magdalene appears and tells them she has seen the Lord, and then later Peter comes and announces that he also has seen Jesus; and just at evening the two disciples come, breathless, to tell of their seeing Jesus, of their talk, and his breaking bread with them, and recognizing him as he did so.

We can imagine their condition. Intense excitement and expectancy must have filled every mind. They were nervous and strained to the keenest attention to every passing sound and step. They were questioning each other and asking and giving opinions. In the midst of this excited company the object of all their thoughts suddenly appeared. Perhaps he was there all the time and listening, as at the sepulcher, and for the same purpose. Surely now they will believe. They had every reason to cast away every doubt, but it is clear that they did not yet believe. Unbelief is a stubborn thing. Nothing but the power of the Holy Spirit will drive it out.

The first words of Jesus were, "Peace be unto you." It was a common salutation but fraught also with meaning to them in their condition. They needed peace just then. A nervous and excited state is not favorable to the work of grace. Its effects are transient and unreliable, and liable to suspicion by the subject and by others. But there was a deeper meaning, as he showed by repeating the salutation, and the significant act with which he accompanied the words and their changed feelings, "And when he had said this, he showed unto them his hands and his side. The disciples therefore were glad when they saw the Lord."[1] Here was an answer to all their self-reproaches. Doubtless they would have cast themselves at his feet in humiliating confessions of cowardice and unfaithfulness and unbelief. But with greathearted graciousness he gently stops them with these words of full forgiveness and blessing.

But there was a deeper and broader meaning yet in these simple words of Jesus and the act with which they were accompanied and the succeeding words and acts, which were as follows; "Peace be unto you: as the Father hath sent me, even so send I you. And when he had said this, he breathed on them, and said unto them, Receive ye the Holy Ghost: Whose soever sins ye forgive, they are forgiven unto them; whose soever sins ye retain, they are retained."[2] The raised hands were the proclamation of the gospel of the crucified and risen Saviour. The repeated salutation of "Peace be unto you," gives the verbal message. There is the proclamation of the three forms of peace,—peace *from* God, peace *with* God, and the peace *of* God. The latter covered peace for the past with all its sins and mistakes; peace for the present, with all its anxieties and burdens; and peace for the future, with all its hopes and fears down to the end and into eternity.

The authority Jesus conferred on the apostles is seen in these words, "As the Father hath sent me, even so send I you;" "Whose soever sins ye forgive, they are forgiven unto them; whose soever sins ye retain, they are retained." These words were spoken to the apostles alone, and this authority for them alone. This was the great commission given the apostles, in which they after spoke and wrote and acted in Christ's stead. He accompanied these words with this significant act and word— "He breathed

[1] John xx. 20.   [2] John xx. 21-23.

on them and saith unto them, Receive ye the Holy Ghost."

The apostles only were present, and it was an exclusive commission which was given them. We do not read of this being repeated or given any others. The time was forty days before the public and general giving of the Holy Ghost at Pentecost. The act was intensely personal on the part of Jesus and the apostles also. It was therefore a transferrence by Jesus of his life and work to the apostles.

The act and words are mutually explanatory. All that breath is to the body, the Holy Spirit is to the believer. It is life. Jesus said, "I came that they may have life, and may have it abundantly."[1] Now he fulfils this. He imparts to them his own life by the Spirit as there was imputed to them life by his death and resurrection. Breath means speech. They were to be witnesses for him. In this simple act we have the very thing called "inspiration." In this, then, Christ shows us not only that his apostles were to be inspired, but how. He himself breathed into them. He authorized them to speak and write as he himself. So here we have the word and act of Christ to show that the writings of his apostles are of equal inspiration with his own. All was received by simple faith. They saw nothing and felt nothing. They were to receive and to believe that he then gave the Holy Spirit to them, all on his word. The effects of this interview and experience are seen in the apostles in the absence of the disturbed feelings, in their joy at his ascension, in filling the vacant apostleship, and patient, faithful waiting and holding of the others about them in prayer until the outpouring of Pentecost.

While this was for the apostle, there is a lesson of the work of Christ in giving the Holy Spirit here for all. The believer has the same spirit as Jesus had on

[1] John x. 10.

earth. All that he had and did we may in a measure also enjoy and do. We have his life imparted as well as imputed. We are to receive all by faith. "Received ye the Spirit by the works of the law, or by the hearing of faith? ... He therefore that supplieth to you the Spirit and worketh miracles among you, doeth he it by the works of the law, or by the hearing of faith? ... That we might receive the promise of the Spirit through faith."[1] There is no need of waiting for signs or feelings. We may take Christ at his word and accept the Holy Spirit as fully and as freely as we do Christ himself, and go our way believing we have received.[2] The sight of the crucified and risen Christ and his many promises all furnish the same warrant for accepting the Holy Spirit as for accepting the salvation of which Jesus is the Finisher as well as the Author.

The forty days between the death and ascension of Jesus were a time of great activity with him. We are not to suppose that the ten appearings to his disciples were all such appearings during that time any more than the few miracles recorded were all he wrought in his life. The list given by Paul of the appearings of Christ is not inclusive. It does not enumerate half of the gospel list. It omits that to the women and the two going to Emmaus. The statement is made by Peter that he appeared "not to all the people, but unto witnesses that were chosen before of God, even to us, who did eat and drink with him after he rose from the dead."[3] The meaning of this is that he did not appear to the public but only to his own, that they might be witnesses of his actual resurrection. There were reasons for his not appearing to the world. The last seen of Jesus by the world was on the cross, which is their only sight until he comes in judgment.

[1] Gal. iii. 3, 5, 14.   [2] Mark xi. 24.   [3] Acts x. 41.

After the account of his call to Thomas to put his finger in the print of the nails and his hand into his side, John writes, "Many other signs therefore did Jesus in the presence of his disciples, which are not written in this book; but these are written that ye may believe that Jesus is the Christ, the Son of God, and that believing ye may have life through his name."[1] The reasons for believing that this statement refers to the events of the forty days and not to the entire life of Jesus are as follows: John makes a further general statement covering the life of Jesus at the close of the book, and it does not seem probable he would make two such statements. The first is the less in force and scope of the two, and evidently refers to a lesser time and sphere. Again, John often in his gospel interjects such local remarks in his narrative referring to the immediate subject in hand. Further the expression, "Other signs," refers to the one just preceding, of asking Thomas to put his finger in the print of the nails and thrust his hand into his side. Jesus did not give such signs during his life, though often asked for them by the Jews. Again, these signs were done "in the presence of the disciples" and evidently for their special benefit, all of which was true of his resurrection acts and not true of his former miracles. But the purpose of the signs shows clearly when they were wrought. "These are written that ye may believe that Jesus is the Christ, the Son of God, and that believing ye may have life through his name." As Alford states it, "The mere *miracle faith* so often reproved by our Lord, is not that intended here. This is *faith in himself* as Christ the Son of God."[2] We must remember that we here stand on resurrection ground, and it is this great fact which is now being demonstrated. It is proof of, and faith in, the risen Christ which is the subject of these words of John.

[1] John xx. 31.
[2] Alford's Greek Testament; London, 1868, Vol. 4, p. 913.

We know by the character of the ten specimen appearances and deeds of the risen Jesus what the others were. We may believe that he appeared to his assembled apostles many times, perhaps every Lord's day. This was so called because it was the Lord's day for meeting with them. Seven such meetings could have taken place. He doubtless appeared to many as he did to the two on the way to Emmaus. Many such homes doubtless enjoyed his visits. Perhaps in distant places he appeared, and to humble persons whose narratives are not recorded, and to feeble and old persons who like Simeon and Anna were waiting for the consolation of Israel.

We know he went to Galilee, and met his people there. It seems almost certain he would visit again the loved circle at Bethany, and that Martha would know a new meaning to his word, "I am the resurrection and the life;" and that Lazarus whom he loved — that sad, silent character — would have another sight of him who was more than life to him. Joseph and Nicodemus saw the form they bore to the tomb living with a new life, and the latter saw what he further meant by being born again. Mary saw once more him who was more to her than son, and the sword wound in her heart was healed. Zaccheus may have welcomed the divine guest once more to his home and the woman at the well given him drink again. By the seashore, at their tables, by the wayside, in their assemblies, on the hillsides, at night and by day, by appointment and unexpectedly, Jesus came to his loved brethren. He fulfilled his promise, "I will not leave you comfortless. I will come to you." Their joy is full. Their Lord lives to die no more.

What he did, too, we are told. He instructed those who did not know the meaning of his death. He comforted weeping ones like Mary. He convinced doubting ones like Thomas. He met and forgave faithless ones, as Peter, and met and helped some in their needs, as the seven fishermen who had caught nothing, but whom he directs to a bountiful haul of fish. In short, he ministered to body, to soul, and to spirit as he did before. He showed them he was to be an ever-present friend and helper in all their needs. They learned for themselves what they afterward taught to us, "Casting all your anxiety upon him, because he careth for you." By the lessons of the imminence of the Lord they learned the truth of his constant presence with each one of them wherever they might be or whatever their temporal or spiritual needs or states. There is this difference however between the resurrection and earthly life of Jesus. In the latter he ministered to all. In his resurrection life he confined himself to his own people.

The last appearing of Jesus was to his assembled church. It was great in significance, as was the first. The place of departure was chosen for many evident reasons. "He led them out until they were over against Bethany."[1] It was close to the little home so dear to him. It was on the road along which he had come riding in his formal approach to offer himself to Israel as their Messiah. It was as near to Jerusalem as could be and not be seen from the great city. It was on the Mount of Olives, and it was written, "His feet shall stand in that day upon the Mount of Olives," the point of departure being the place of arrival. It was the place from which he beheld the city and wept over it. Here he gathers the company about him. He had already announced to his apostles the resumption of his administrative work, saying, "All authority hath been given unto me in heaven and on earth." He had further given them their command as to the work, saying, "Go ye therefore and make disciples of all the nations, baptizing them into the name of the Father and of the Son and of the Holy Ghost: teaching them to observe

[1] Luke xxiv. 50.

all things whatsoever I commanded you: and lo, I am with you alway even unto the end of the world."[1] Now he gives them the parting promise, "Ye shall receive power, when the Holy Ghost is come upon you: and ye shall be my witnesses both in Jerusalem, and in all Judea and Samaria, and unto the uttermost part of the earth."[2] "And behold, I send forth the promise of my Father upon you: but tarry ye in the city, until ye be clothed with power from on high."[3] All has now been finished which he came to say and do.

The ascension of Jesus is thus simply described by one of the witnesses: "He lifted up his hands, and blessed them. And it came to pass, while he blessed them, he parted from them, and was carried up into heaven," and a cloud received him out of their sight."[4] He was hid from their sight, but they were not hidden from his. He looks down upon the little company at his feet. They are his flock. They heard his voice and followed him. He remembers none of their failures or faithlessness. They are inexpressibly dear to him. They were the germ of the church, the depositaries of his truth for all the world and all the age. He is leaving them as sheep among wolves. They are to face untold dangers for his sake, and to suffer joyfully and at last to die, some of them as he died, from love to him. But they are to be kept true and to finish their course in triumph and to meet him in glory. As he rises, a larger scene meets his view. Jerusalem was spread out before him. It has crucified him. But he had cried, "Father, forgive them," as his blood flowed out, and the prayer sealed with his heart's blood will be answered. It was the city of David, and he remembered his promise to David that his seed should sit on his throne. It was the site of his Father's House. Temple and city

---

[1] Matt. xxviii. 19, 20. [2] Acts i. 8.
[3] Luke xxiv. 49. [4] Luke xxiv. 50, 51; Acts i. 9.

must and will be redeemed. He rises still higher. The land of Israel is all before him. He had walked its roads and preached and healed from village to village. Under the open sky he as Jehovah promised Abraham that land in possession forever. He has sealed that covenant afresh with his blood. He remembers Israel's early love, their following him into and through the wilderness. He calls to mind all the long line of faithful men and women who had kept his truth. For a time they are to be hardened, but he knows they are to "look upon him which they have pierced," and to receive him as their Messiah.

As he ascends, a still larger scene meets his eye. The world he made and has just redeemed rolls at his feet. Surely he paused to gaze upon it. Successively its cities swarming with people and all its lands with their many tribes of men pass in review before him. To save this world he came. It is his by creation and now by redemption. It was all in his mind as he hung upon the cross. He took all its load of sin upon himself and expiated all by one sacrifice. He had left his heart's life-blood in its soil. He thinks of the coming centuries of wars and famines and gospel proclamation. He knows that out of every nation and tongue and tribe and people shall they come to sit down with him in his kingdom; and after some ages shall pass, the earth shall be full of the glory of the Lord as the waters cover the sea.

An event occurred in the history of Jesus after his death which is thus described: "Christ also suffered for sins once, the righteous for the unrighteous, that he might bring us to God; being put to death in the flesh, but quickened in the spirit; in which also he went and preached unto the spirits in prison, which aforetime were disobedient, when the longsuffering of God, waited in the days of Noah, while the ark was a preparing, wherein few, that is, eight souls, were saved through water."[1] This is a much-disputed passage. It has been interpreted as meaning only that Jesus preached through Noah who had the Spirit of Christ. Undoubtedly Jesus did by his spirit preach through Noah as through all the prophets from that day on. But this statement goes far beyond that. Alford thus writes on this passage,[2] "Jesus went to the place of custody of departed spirits, and there preached to these spirits which were formerly disobedient when God's longsuffering waited in the days of Noah. Thus far I conceive our passage stands committed; and I do not believe it possible to make it say less or other than this. Meyer states, 'This is the view of the oldest Fathers of the Greek and Latin churches as also of the greater number of the later and modern theologians.'"

The visit of Christ to this place is also referred to by both Peter and Paul in a quotation from the Psalms: "Thou wilt not leave my soul in Hades, neither wilt thou give thy Holy One to see corruption;" "He foreseeing this, spake of the resurrection of the Christ, that neither was he left in Hades, nor did his flesh see corruption."[3] It is also referred to by Paul in these words, "He that ascended, what is it but that he also descended into the lower parts of the earth?"[4]

The purpose of this preaching of the gospel to these is thus referred to by the same apostle who gives the first passage: "For unto this end was the gospel preached even to the dead, that they might be judged according to men in the flesh, but live according to God in the spirit."[5]

To these spirits Jesus preached the gospel. It was the perfect gospel only then fully prepared by the atonement for sin. The same gospel by which we and all are saved. The hearers were those who had lived

[1] 1 Peter iii. 18-20. [2] Greek Testament, 4 Vols., London, 1869.
[3] Acts ii. 27, 31. [4] Eph. iv. 9. [5] Peter iv. 6.

and died without any gospel or any law. They are thus referred to by Paul: "For until the law sin was in the world: but sin is not imputed when there is no law. Nevertheless death reigned from Adam until Moses, even over them that had not sinned after the likeness of Adam's transgression, who is a figure of him that was to come."[1] This mission of Jesus he referred to in his opening sermon describing the errands he came to fulfil: "He hath sent me to proclaim release to the captives."[2] He looked forward to this from the beginning of his mission.

The following scripture gives the account of the full success of this gospel mission of Jesus: "Wherefore he saith, when he ascended on high, he led captivity captive and gave gifts unto men. (Now this, He ascended, what is it but that he also descended into the lower parts of the earth? He that descended is the same also that ascended far above all the heavens, that he might fill all things.)"[3] The term "captivity" refers to those taken by the enemy and afterward recaptured by their own friends again. It is so applied to the captive Israelites by Deborah: "Arise, Barak, and lead thy captivity captive."[4] Rev. Elijah R. Craven, D. D., writes as follows:[5] "Christ, between the periods of his death and resurrection, delivered from Hades a captivity contained therein. . . . The fact that he did so the writer believes to be referred to in several passages."

This was a victory over Satan such as Christ described in this scripture: "No one can enter into the house of a strong man, and spoil his goods, except he first bind the strong man; and then he will spoil his house."[6] Having bound the strong man, Christ now spoiled his house.

It was Christ remembering his first human friend

---

[1] Rom. v. 13, 14.
[2] Luke iv. 18.
[3] Eph. iv. 8-10.
[4] Judges v. 12.
[5] Lange's Commentary, Revelation; New York, 1874; pp. 373, 374.
[6] Mark iii. 27.

and his children. It was Jehovah fulfilling the type of Abraham, bringing back the captive Lot and his family taken by the enemy, and David coming in triumph with his own, taken from Ziklag. It was the first gospel revival. Before Pentecost came, there was a pentecost in the nether world. They heard the good news. It was truly "news" to them. Whether they hoped for any deliverence we do not know; but if they knew, we can imagine their expectancy and delight when the Saviour came and flung the prison doors wide open.

The church is a glorious body, but we must not limit the work of Christ to it or to our agencies. We do not have a monopoly of the custody of the grace of God. He can work with us or without us, mediately or immediately, by us or by himself alone.

There is no warrant, however, from this incident, for the doctrine of a second probation for any since that time. It was a single errand of Jesus before his ascension to a single class who lived and died under exceptional circumstances. They had neither law nor gospel and were cut off suddenly as a whole world by an awful overthrow, which was necessary to bring in a new dispensation. The following passage refers to those we are considering, and declares their spiritual state and the grace of God to them: "Until the law, sin was in the world, but sin is not imputed where there is no law. . . . Where no law is there is no transgression."[1] The world has had since both law and gospel, and as the apostle teaches, has rejected the truth and is now in self-chosen darkness. There are direct statements of Scripture as to the relative positions of those in Hades and paradise, as well as the possibility of the former being delivered. In the narrative of the rich man and beggar, Abraham tells the former: "Between us and you there is a great gulf fixed, so that they which would pass from hence

[1] Rom. v. 13; iv. 15.

to you may not be able, and that none may pass over from thence to us."[1]

The time when Jesus preached to "the spirits in prison" is, by those who take this view, usually held to have been between his death and resurrection. But this does not seem possible for the following reasons: The redemption which he undoubtedly preached was the same we enjoy, and this was not finished until his resurrection. The Scriptures teach that his resurrection was the vital part of redemption. Christ was "delivered for our trespasses, and was raised for our justification." "If Christ hath not been raised; your faith is vain; ye are yet in your sins. Then they also which are fallen asleep in Christ are perished."[2] Jesus could not proclaim the finished gospel until he rose from the dead, for redemption was not finished until then. Again, it is not at all probable nor according to his own words that he would proclaim the finished gospel to these disobedient spirits before he announced it to his loved circle of chosen and intimate friends on earth.

Still further, as we shall see, the company of these spirits had a place with him in his ascension, and it does not seem probable that he would keep them waiting forty days after his proclamation of the gospel of their deliverance. Besides the account gives the impression of an immediate deliverance connected with his ascension. Further, he was in paradise during the time of his burial, as he promised the dying thief, and as the analogy of the believer's death requires us to believe. His dying words, "Into thy hands I commend my spirit," are in harmony with the view of his being in paradise. Another objection is that to preach in his disembodied spirit after having assumed his human nature, would be a retrogression which does not occur elsewhere in his work. And, most vital of all, is the objection that Jesus in his disembodied spirit is not the Christ of redemption the

[1] Luke xvi. 26.   [2] Rom. iv. 25; 1 Cor. xv. 17.

saved are to know, who consists of the eternal Christ in the glorified nature and risen body of Jesus. The words "put to death in the flesh, but quickened in the spirit" refer to his death and resurrection, and simply place in contrast his earthly and resurrection state and life in which he went and preached to the spirits in prison.

The history of the earthly life of Christ usually ends with his ascension. But this divides the narrative of his exaltation which began with his resurrection. By the aid of Scripture we can follow him further. We know where Jesus went by his words, "What then if ye should behold the Son of man ascending where he was before?"[1] A body requires a place. Christ is therefore in some place. We apply the word "heaven" to all the holy part of the unseen world. But there are localities there as here. We are not in the dark as to where Christ is. The present state of Christ is everywhere described in Scripture as "sitting on the right hand of God." The dying Stephen saw him there, and so testified. It was the prophecy in the Messianic Psalm quoted by our Lord and the apostles so often: "Sit thou on my right hand, until I make thine enemies thy footstool."[2]

The reception of the ascending Jesus is described to us. If heaven was vocal when Jesus was born, what must have been the joy and glory there when he re-entered in triumph with his attending angels and the "captivity" taken from the hand of the enemy. The sons of God shouted for joy because of the finished creation. We do not know their song, but we have the anthem of welcome to the triumphant Redeemer:—

"Lift up your heads, O ye gates, and be ye lifted up, ye everlasting doors, and the King of glory shall come in.

"Who is this King of glory?

[1] John vi. 62.   [2] Ps. cx. 1.

"The Lord strong and mighty. The Lord mighty in battle. Lift up your heads, O ye gates. Yea, lift them up, ye everlasting doors, and the King of Glory shall come in.

"Who is this King of Glory?

"The Lord of Hosts. He is the King of Glory."[1]

The great act of Christ on entering heaven was to present for us his finished work as declared in the following passage: "For Christ entered not into a holy place made with hands, like in pattern to the true; but into heaven itself, now to appear before the face of God for us."[2] This was "a once for all" act. In this act he presented himself and his blood as the evidence of his fulfilment of all the forfeits accepted by him since the world was; he fully met all the obligations assumed by him.

The work of Christ on entering heaven was applied there also; for heaven had been defiled by sin as well as earth. Angels had fallen. Satan had entered, and his work there needed that cleansing should be applied. This is referred to by the following text: "It was necessary therefore that the copies of the things in the heavens should be cleansed with these; but the heavenly things themselves with better sacrifices than these."[3] The far reaching scope of the work of redemption is here indicated. Jesus would have had to die if not a soul of man had been saved. In some way angels are or will be lifted up by the great atonement. It applies to all the creation also. For that, too, was defiled and waits for its release from the "bondage of corruption." The effects of the sacrifice on Calvary go down to the smallest animalcule and up to the highest archangel and into the remotest point of the eternal future as it sweeps back to the "beginning" in its scope.

There is also another phase of the story of redemption. Christ said before his death, "I beheld Satan

---

[1] Ps. xxiv. 7–10. [2] Heb. ix. 24. [3] Heb. ix. 23.

fallen as lightning from heaven;" "Now is the judgment of this world: now shall the prince of this world be cast out."[1] Only by force did Satan renounce his right to a place among the sons of God he had held so long. The victory was won by the blood of the Lamb. It is to be observed that this ascension victory of Christ over Satan affects Christ personally. His people are still exposed to the accusations, but, as will be seen in the next chapter, are protected by Jesus with his blood as a plea.

The vision of John completes the description of the advent of Jesus to heaven on his return from earth: "And I saw, and I heard a voice of many angels round about the throne and the living creatures and the elders; and the number of them was ten thousand times ten thousand, and thousands of thousands; saying with a great voice, Worthy is the Lamb that hath been slain to receive the power, and riches, and wisdom, and might, and honor, and glory, and blessing. And every created thing which is in the heaven, and on the earth, and under the earth, and on the sea, and all things that are in them, heard I saying, Unto him that sitteth on the throne, and unto the Lamb, be the blessing, and the honor, and the glory, and the dominion, forever and ever."[2]

The ascension of Christ involves more than the acquiring of heavenly, imputed, and unseen benefits. Its actual benefits, immediate and experimental, are of vast extent. They are thus described by Peter on the day of Pentecost: "Being therefore by the right of God exalted and having received of the Father the promise of the Holy Ghost, he hath poured forth this which ye see and hear."[3] He himself had said, "If I go, I will send him unto you."[4] He charged them to remain in Jerusalem until this promise was fulfilled.

[1] Luke x. 18; John xii. 31. [2] Rev. v. 11–14.
[3] Acts ii. 33. [4] John xvi. 7.

This was the actual fulfilment: "And when the day of Pentecost was now come, they were all together in one place. And suddenly there came from heaven a sound as of the rushing of a mighty wind, and it filled all the house where they were sitting. And there appeared unto them tongues parting asunder, like as of fire; and it sat upon each one of them. And they were all filled with the Holy Spirit, and began to speak with other tongues, as the Spirit gave them utterance."[1]

This was the universal pouring out of the Holy Spirit in all his gifts and graces upon the church for themselves and for convicting power in their preaching of the gospel. We naturally ask, Why was not this given until the day of Pentecost, fifty days after the resurrection of Jesus? The reason of the delay until the resurrection of Jesus was that all this was part of the fruits of his atoning and redemptive work. But the reason of the delay until the day of Pentecost ten days after the ascension is not so clear. We have seen he had already imparted to them the Holy Spirit when "he breathed on them and said unto them, Receive ye the Holy Ghost" on the day of his resurrection. Fifty days elapsed before the coming of the Holy Spirit as afterward promised by him.

Among the reasons of this delay in sending this gracious outpouring was the state of the disciples themselves. They needed the preparation of quiet waiting in prayer after the scenes of the forty-days' appearing of Jesus. There was also a reason in the field of their immediate work. Pentecost saw a vast gathering from many lands of devout seekers after truth who had become attached to the religion of Israel; and the outpouring, wherein they heard every man in his own tongue, sent the gospel everywhere over the earth. There was also a typical reason for the waiting until Pentecost. It was on the first day

[1] Acts ii. 1-4.

of the week. Seven weeks before there was waved before the altar a sheaf, the "first fruits" of the harvest then beginning to be ripe. On the day of Pentecost there were waved two loaves of unleavened bread from the same harvest. Most of those converted at Pentecost were Israelites, not only of Jews but of the "Dispersion," the ten tribes scattered abroad. This occasion had special reference to Israel. Paul has this in mind when he writes, "If the first fruit is holy, so is the lump."[1] But the middle wall of division no longer exists so far as gospel privileges are concerned. Jesus rose on the day the first sheaf of the harvest was waved, the outpouring occurred on the day of the waving of the two loaves. The latter represents the two churches now one in the scope of grace. Paul again refers to this in the words, "We who are many are one bread."[2] The fire which baked the loaves has its fulfilment in the Holy Spirit which Jesus said should baptize them with fire. The changed character is typified by the bread.

Comparing the two givings of the Spirit, we note that the first was given by Jesus himself to the apostles only, the latter to all by the Father through him. We also observe that the former was accompanied by no manifestations except the silent breathing of Jesus. That the first was not the full, whole giving is plain from the need of the second being given, and their waiting for it. The difference is further seen by the fact that they did no work as the church except to fill the vacant apostleship, until they received the pentecostal effusion of the Holy Spirit. The further difference is seen in the immediate and great change which the latter produced in the disciples, and the mighty effects which followed in others through their speaking and miracle-working power. Still further, the latter was repeated, while the first was not. The former may be described as the conferring of apostolic

[1] Rom. xi. 16,   [2] 1 Cor. x. 17.

authority, the latter of power for service. There is also this difference; the apostles received all the same authority, but the recipients of the pentecostal outpouring each received of a portion as Paul teaches.[1]

This finished the immediate work Jesus came to do. The world was brought into relations of grace with God, the church formed and endowed with all gifts and graces for its work. There ensued the long age in which we live. The state and work of Christ in this comes next before us.

[1] 1 Cor. xii.

CHAPTER V.

JESUS CHRIST.

CHRIST IN HIS PRESENT STATE AND WORK.

THE New Testament contains three distinct revelations. They are given respectively by Jesus himself and through Paul and John. The first is contained in the Gospels, the second in the Epistles, and the third is the Revelation. These occur successively as to time and order, and each succeeding revelation is an advance upon the previous one and contains a larger and different view of Christ. Jesus had told his disciples: "I have yet many things to say unto you, but ye cannot bear them now. Howbeit when he, the Spirit of truth, is come, he shall guide you into all the truth: for he shall not speak from himself; but what things soever he shall hear, these shall he speak: and he shall declare unto you the things that are to come. He shall glorify me: for he shall take of mine, and shall declare it unto you. All things whatsoever the Father hath are mine: therefore said I, that he taketh of mine, and shall declare it unto you."[1]

This is Christ's own statement, that his people should have a fuller revelation of himself through the Spirit than he himself gave them. These revelations of Christ are found in the Acts and Epistles, and the Apocalypse.

The special medium of the next of these revelations of Christ was Paul. All the other apostles and disciples were also taught of the Spirit, and their

[1] John xvi. 12-15.

writings are of equal inspiration with those of Paul, and teach the same truths; but Paul was, as Christ said, a chosen vessel converted by the personal appearance and word of Christ himself. He places himself before us in these words, five times repeated, and as no other ever does,—"Be ye followers of me." He thus speaks of his message: "For I make known to you, brethren, as touching the gospel which was preached by me, that it is not after man. For neither did I receive it from man, nor was I taught it, but it came to me through revelation of Jesus Christ."[1]

He wrote half the New Testament. All we have of Christianity on earth to-day, certainly the best of it, is the result of Paul's work, as the labors of the Twelve are nearly unknown to us. Here, then, in Paul's writings, we may look for that fuller revelation of Christ which he himself said the Holy Spirit should give.

In the titles applied to Christ in the epistles will be found the apostolic view of his present office, dignity, and work. The name Jesus, used in the Gospels, seldom occurs in the Epistles except in combination with other names or titles, and is less and less used as time passes. So also Jesus' own favorite title, "The Son of Man," occurs but once. Both are associated with his humiliation. In passing, there is noticeable a difference in the names applied to Christ by the different apostles. Peter alone applies the full name and title—"Our Lord and Saviour Jesus Christ." Paul alone uses the title, "Our great God and Saviour Jesus Christ." John alone speaks of "The Son." The simple title, "The Lord," was the designation used by the disciples when speaking of him among themselves. It is the title Christ himself approved of in the words, "Ye call me Master and Lord, and ye say well for so I am."[2] It is spoken of thus by Paul: "No man can say Jesus is Lord, but

---

[1] Gal. i. 11, 12.   [2] John xiii. 13.

in the Holy Spirit."[1] It is expressive of his relationship to those who receive him, and therefore the title for the church. The title "King" is not applied to Christ in the Epistles in his relationship to the believer or the church. It does not express the view of Christ in his present state presented by the apostles either to the world or the church. To speak of him as "my King" or "our King," as is customary with many devout believers, does not express the Scriptural, accurate, and close present relation Christ bears to the believer or to the church. Paul uses it only in his prophetic doxologies. "CHRIST" is the great title of the epistles. It is used without the article. The term, "the Christ," is only used by the New Testament writers when Israelites are addressed, or the Israelite relationship to Christ, or that idea in some way involved. It is equivalent to "the Messiah," which is Israel's title exclusively. Neither of these are therefore properly applied to Christ from the world or Christian standpoint. The combined name, "Jesus Christ," expresses his personality and office. It identifies Jesus of Nazareth as the Christ of Israel and Christ of the church and of the world.

Paul's peculiar title is "Christ Jesus." No other writer applies this, as will be seen from the Revised Version. He uses this when he wishes to emphasize the office of Christ, and the more common title, "Jesus Christ," when he has his personality in mind. The first looks to his present spiritual relations and word, as in this text, "We preach not ourselves but Christ Jesus as Lord."[2] The other refers more particularly to the past and his redemptive work as, "Jesus Christ and him crucified."[3] The latter describes the historical order of the work of Christ, the former the order in which we recognize and enjoy him. He must be "Christ" to us before we can love him in the more personal relationship.

[1] 1 Cor. xii. 3.   [2] 2 Cor. iv. 5.   [3] 1 Cor. ii. 2.

The apostles do not stop with these well-known names and titles. They glorify their Lord and ours by the most exalted terms. Their doxologies abound in such titles as "Lord of Glory," "Prince of Life," "Only Potentate," "King of Kings and Lord of Lords," "The King eternal, incorruptible, invisible, the only God." All these, however, have a prophetic outlook, and do not come within our present field of study, Christ of the present.

In preaching Christ the apostles kept clearly in mind three classes — The Jew, the Gentile, and the church of God. A very noticeable difference will be observed in their presentation of Christ to each of these. These three — Israel, the church, and the world — must be kept distinctly in mind in the study of Christ's present state and work. Another classification of the message as to the person and work of Christ will be considered. They viewed Christ as past, present, and future, or Christ historical, Christ living, and Christ predicted.

To Israel, Jewish proselytes, and attendants on the synagogue, they presented Christ as the one foretold in the prophecies, and showed the fulfilment in Jesus of Nazareth, and asserted that he was "The Christ," or "Messiah." The death of Christ was presented as having a special reference to Israel. It was a special redemption for them, as Caiaphas unwittingly prophesied that "Jesus should die for the nation."[1] This death of Christ for Israel is regarded from the standpoint of his taking a place among them and thereby sharing their responsibility under the Mosaic law and incurring the penalty of their violation of it. The awful curse pronounced on Israel as, sprinkled with blood, they filed into the promised land, rested upon Christ, and he died for Israel to redeem them from it. So Paul presented Christ to the Galatian Church, which was a Judaized church,

[1] John xi. 51.

and therefore to bring them back to the liberty of the gospel, he presented Christ from this standpoint. He represented Christ as "born under the law, that he might redeem them which were under the law," and that "Christ redeemed us from the curse of the law, having become a curse for us, for it is written, Cursed is every one that hangeth on a tree."[1] This is Israel's view of Christ. The curse of the law rested only on those who had the law, and no nation but Israel had it given them or was commanded to obey it. It was Israel's law only. It began, "Hear, O Israel." The curse of this violated law of Israel was that which Christ bore. The world has another plane of condemnation and another doom, but this "curse of the law" is Israel's exclusively. Paul as an Israelite had a place under this gospel preached to Israel, and could therefore include himself in this, and say, "Christ hath redeemed *us* from the curse of the law."

The Epistle to the Hebrews, which was written to Hebrews, gives us the view of Christ in his present state as presented to Israel. It is simply a spiritual exposition of the Levitical law, or rather that part of it referring to the high priest's office. It presents the Christ in his mediatorial and intercessory work in figures an Israelite would understand. The culminating point is in this passage, "But Christ having come a high priest of the good things to come, through the greater and more perfect tabernacle, not made with hands, that is to say, not of this creation, nor yet through the blood of goats and calves, but through his own blood, entered in once for all into the holy place, having obtained eternal redemption."[2] This presents the central rite in the Levitical ritual and shows its meaning. Having made this central type clear, all the rest will arrange itself in intelligible order. The mediatorial work of Christ is guarded from being set forth in a purely Israelitish light by

---
[1] Gal. iv. 5; III. 13. [2] Heb ix. 11.

the reference to Melchizedek as the type of the High Priest. The great lesson of this book is in the urgings to faith in, and faithfulness to, the unseen High Priest who is passed within the veil. His dignity is shown by comparison with prophets and angels, and his sympathy for his people by his being made like unto his brethren. The sin of rejecting Christ is shown by the figure of trampling under foot the sacred blood of the covenant. It is the strongest plea possible to make with an Israelite or any believer, to "hold fast," which word is the key-note of the Epistle.

There may be advanced against this view of the gospel for Israel, the texts: "There is no distinction between Jew and Greek, for the same Lord is Lord of all, and rich unto all that call upon him;" "There can be neither Jew nor Greek, there can be neither bond nor free, there can be no male and female; for ye are all one man in Christ Jesus."[1] These passages declare the equal salvability of all, and the same standing of all in Christ after being saved, but do not refer to the presentation of the gospel leading to their salvation or the special scope of the death of Christ as affecting the two classes.

The resurrection of Jesus is the great fact held to by the apostles as proof to Israel that he was "The Christ." They advance it and attest it personally. It did not seem to be questioned by the Jews in the days of the apostles. They were not incredulous as to the supernatural, as were the Greeks. This and the Scriptural proof of the position of Jesus as the Messiah were sufficient for those who were of sincere mind and ready to follow the truth.

A special feature of Christ as presented to Israel by the apostles was his coming as the Messiah in glory. This was the great view of Israel and their desire. In Jesus they failed to see their Messiah of glory. After his ascension his disciples expected the Messiah's kingdom of glory would immediately ap-

[1] Rom. x. 12; Gal. iii. 28.

pear. Neither Jesus nor the apostles corrected this expectation as to the fact of such a kingdom, but only as to its time, manner of appearing, nature, and the characteristics of those who should enter it. The apostles held out to Israel the coming of such a Messiah and his kingdom as they expected. Peter so presented this truth as an incentive to repentance, and makes the facts of his first coming the proof of his coming as "The Christ" or "The Messiah." "Repent ye therefore, and turn again, that your sins may be blotted out, that so there may come seasons of refreshing from the presence of the Lord ; and that he may send the Christ who hath been appointed for you, even Jesus : whom the heaven must receive until the times of restoration of all things, whereof God spake by the mouth of his holy prophets which have been since the world began."[1]

In the preaching of Christ to the world by the apostles there are noticeable very great changes of several kinds. There is first of all a studied disregard of the earthly life of Jesus. This is true also to a great extent in the presentation of Christ to the church and to Israel. In the Acts and in the Epistles especially, there is almost total omission of the story of the Four Gospels up to the events of the death of Christ. There are a few brief allusions to his birth, temptation, and transfiguration, and one or two general remarks, such as that he went about doing good and healing all that were possessed with the devil; and that is all, up to the crucifixion. Of all those mighty miracles not one is related or even mentioned specifically. Of all the parables of Jesus not one is repeated, nor do the apostles ever preach upon any word of Jesus as a text. That whole great life is passed over in a silence which is evidently intentional. Indeed, Paul says as to it all, "Wherefore we hence-

[1] Acts iii. 19-21.

forth know no man after the flesh: even though we have known Christ after the flesh, yet now we know him so no more."[1] As has been seen, even his earthly name, Jesus, is little used, and less and less as the time passes. This same passing by of the life of Jesus is noticeable in the Apostles' Creed, which passes at once from "Born of the Virgin Mary" to "Suffered under Pontius Pilate."

In answer to the inquiry as to why such disregard of all this life of Christ, it is sufficient to reply that they had a greater view to present, and they would not allow the lesser to detract attention from it. It is no disparagement to say the Christ of the Acts and Epistles is larger than the Christ of the Gospels. He himself has so increasingly revealed himself from the first. There is another reason. As has been noted, Jesus came as an Israelite to Israel only as he said, "I was not sent but unto the lost sheep of the house of Israel."[2] So Jesus came under the law; he lived under it, and kept its ordinances, and preached it and sent inquirers to it saying, "What is written in the law? . . . This do and thou shalt live."[3]

Paul writes of the earthly life of Jesus as follows: "For I say that Christ has been made a minister of the circumcision for the truth of God, that he might confirm the truth given unto the fathers."[4] Jesus lived under the old covenant. Calvary had not yet come. The law was still in force. Therefore he himself referred them to the coming teachings of the Spirit, saying, "I have yet many things to say unto you but ye cannot bear them now. Howbeit when he, the Spirit of truth, is come, he will guide you into all the truth. . . . He shall glorify me for he shall take of mine and shall declare it unto you."[5] Here is a distinct promise of a larger revelation of Christ. This greater Christ was the Christ Paul preached.

[1] 2 Cor. v. 16.   [2] Matt. xv. 24.   [3] Luke x. 26, 28.
[4] Rom. xv. 8.   [5] John xvi. 12, 13, 14.

The apostles did not preach Christ to the world as the babe of Bethlehem or the meek and lowly Nazarene or the Great Prophet or Teacher, or hold him up only as the example of a holy life, bidding the world follow him. One may so look at Christ and yet be far from being one of his. John Stuart Mill said, "Nor would it be easy for even an unbeliever to find a better translation of the rule of virtue from the abstract into the concrete than to endeavor so to live that Christ would approve our life." Yet he remained an unbeliever. Napoleon said, "Between him [Jesus] and whoever else in the world, there is no possible comparison." But he did not repent of his butcheries of thousands of human lives. Strauss wrote, "Jesus remains the highest model of religion within the reach of our thoughts," and then proceeded to reduce all the narratives of Jesus' miracles to a series of myths.

The Christ of the Gospels is more largely studied and preached to-day than any other. Indeed, some know no other Christ. They think they are preaching Christ when dwelling on some feature of his earthly nature or work or some incident in his life. Now all this is useful and is a proper field for study and preaching, and all the Gospels and their beautiful lessons are ours, but the great fact remains that *none of this nor all of this is "preaching Christ."* The world cannot be saved by the babe of Bethlehem nor the prophet of Galilee. The lowly Nazarene is not the Christ of the church, nor Christ for the world. Jesus weeping over Jerusalem did not save it and cannot save us. It is not the tears of Jesus to which we look for forgiveness and which we plead at the throne of grace. Faith in Christ as the mighty wonder-worker is not that which he seeks. Admiration for his holy life and wonderful words is not faith in Christ. Receiving Jesus as a leader, as distinguished from Buddha or Mohammed, or any other, is not coming to Christ. All this may be preliminary and preparatory to a saving faith in Christ, and lead one to consider Christ truly; but all is coming short until Christ is seen as the Crucified One.

There is a noticeable difference in the presentation of the gospel to the world from that preached to Israel. The gospel as preached to the world is found partly in the messages of the apostles to the Gentiles, as recorded in the book of Acts, particularly those of Paul; for we have scarcely any other whose addresses to the Gentiles are given. The epistles also to a certain extent show Christ as preached to the world, for the churches to whom they were addressed were drawn out from the Gentiles. Cornelius, in whose house Peter preached, was "a righteous man and one that feared God, and well reported of by all the nation of the Jews;" he was undoubtedly a proselyte and therefore was addressed as the Jews were. The sermon of Paul on Mars Hill[1] to the Athenians illustrates the presentation of the gospel to the world by Paul. It was doubtless this same view he presented to Felix, who "sent for Paul and heard him concerning the faith in Christ Jesus. And as he reasoned of righteousness, temperance, and judgment to come, Felix was terrified."[2] So also Paul preached at Lystra. These were evidently awakening messages delivered to dead souls, and would have been followed by presenting Christ more fully.

How Paul preached Christ we learn from the account he himself gives of his gospel in Corinth, which he declares was as follows: "Now I make known unto you, brethren, the gospel which I preached unto you which also ye received, wherein also ye stand, by which also ye are saved; I make known, I say, in what words I preached it unto you, if ye hold it fast except ye believed in vain. For I delivered unto you first of all that which also I received, how

---

[1] Acts xvii. [2] Acts xxiv. 24, 25.

that Christ died for our sins according to the Scriptures; and that he was buried and that he hath been raised on the third day according to the Scriptures; and that he appeared to Cephas; then to the twelve; then he appeared to about five hundred brethren at once, of whom the greater part remain until now, but some are fallen asleep; then he appeared to James; then to all the apostles; and last of all as unto one born out of due time, he appeared unto me also."[1] He wrote before as to this gospel: "I determined not to know anything among you save Jesus Christ and him crucified."[2] It will be observed that this is first of all a recital of facts. The gospel then consists first of all of a series of facts. It does not consist of opinions or speculations of a philosophical kind, or even chiefly of doctrines so called. Christ, his death, and resurrection are the vital facts of Christianity.

The proof and meaning of the death of Christ is indicated by the phrase "according to the Scriptures," the "Scriptures" being the Old Testament Scriptures. Here, then, is substantial agreement with the view given to Israel. But there is not the same fulness of detail anywhere given, either in the addresses in Acts or in the Epistles. The Epistles were written to the church, but they were churches drawn out from the Gentiles mostly, and therefore the presentation of Christ to them shows how he was also preached to the world, although, as we shall see, they give to the church a far larger view than to the world. In the Epistles to the Gentile churches there is a noticeable paucity of references to the Mosaic law or age, as proof or illustration of the person or work of Christ. Paul makes no account of it as presenting Christ. Omitting Hebrews,—which was written to the Hebrews, and therefore out of this view, and Galatians written to a Judaized church—there are but few appeals of any kind to the Mosaic law or any of its

[1] 1 Cor. xv. 1-8.   [2] 1 Cor. ii. 2.

types or ceremonies. There are a few illustrative references, such as to the passover,[1] and illustrative warnings from Israel's failures.[2] These indicate how the Scriptures were used in presenting Christ to the world; for if so little reference is made and of such a desultory kind in messages to Christian churches, we may conclude as little or less reference was made in preaching Christ to the world. We are obliged to take notice of this singular omission on the part of one so full of the Old Testament as Paul and so capable of using it.

Paul tells us that Abraham and not Moses was "the father of all them that believe," and that the gospel was first preached unto him, and that he was saved by faith, and that circumcision was given him as a seal of his faith and not as a bond or badge of the law, which did not come until four hundred years after; and that this subsequent law could not be retroactive, and besides was only temporary in its purpose, — "a schoolmaster to bring us to Christ,"— and was fulfilled and finished by Christ, "Having blotted out the bond written in ordinances that was against us, which was contrary to us: and he hath taken it out of the way, nailing it to the cross."[3] That the law never could nor did save and cannot now, is shown by this scripture: "For there is a disannulling of a foregoing commandment because of its weakness and unprofitableness (for the law made nothing perfect), and a bringing in thereupon of a better hope, through which we draw nigh unto God."[4] We are brought back again to the way of faith found by Abraham and all intervening ordinances are laid aside. In short, the apostle Paul sweeps away the whole Mosaic superstructure down to the Abrahamic foundation, and upon that erects the new edifice of Christian Doctrine, Life, and Church Polity. Now

---

[1] 1 Cor. v. 7, 8.
[2] 1 Cor. x. 1–13.
[3] Col. ii. 14.
[4] Heb. vii. 18, 19.

to base upon the Mosaic law, the teachings of the death of Christ, would confer an importance upon it by so attaching it to the gospel as to practically impose it upon the young churches, especially those accessible to the Judaizing teachers whom Paul so strenuously opposed.

All this, however, does not detract from the use of all we find in the Mosaic law to illustrate the general work of Christ; indeed it is preserved to us for this purpose, and is rightly and most profitably so used. But it requires for its understanding a Scriptural education equivalent to that of the condition of the ancient Israelite, and this often does not exist, especially in miscellaneous communities and audiences. Therefore the ceremonies and sacrifices convey no meaning of a spiritual or even religious kind to many, and even are a hindrance to understanding the gospel. The offering of a thousand oxen and the attendant dividing of the bodies and parts and washings and sprinkling of the blood and burning of parts and eating of other parts, convey no specially religious ideas to such. The hearers need previous instruction. We are presenting Christ through the ceremonies and sacrifices of the Mosaic law to those ignorant of them. We do doctrinally what the Judaizing teachers did practically, and narrow the spread of the gospel to those who are able thus to receive it.

While Paul has omitted the Mosaic law as proof or even illustration of the person and nature and work of Christ for the church and the world, he has preserved every essential and universal and eternal truth wrapped up in it. The great treatise in which Christ is set forth as the Saviour of the world is the Epistle to the Romans. The world's capital was appropriately chosen as the recipient of a systematic exposition of the world's gospel. The Epistle to the Romans begins by showing man his need of salvation. This is in contrast to the gospel to Israel, who, whatever their spiritual blindness, had some idea of sin and man's state. Conscience was alive and quickened by the ceaseless round of sacrifices and cleansings and confessions. But the world is dead to the sense of sin as well as dead in sin. Paul first makes an exposé of the state of man. The picture is true to life, as the heathen acknowledge when it is shown them. Human nature is as the Scripture shows us it, and we see it when the cover is taken from some rotting plague-spot. Unless a true idea is formed of human nature, the Scriptural accounts of the work of Christ will not be understood.

This state of man in sin is declared in Scripture to be the result and penalty of "holding down the truth in unrighteousness." The world once had the truth, and has yet God's witnesses to it. Creation is such a witness as we considered in that chapter. He further states that man has another witness in himself: "When the Gentiles which have no law do by nature the things of the law, these having no law are a law unto themselves, in that they show the work of the law written in their hearts, their conscience bearing witness therewith and their thoughts, one with another accusing or else excusing them."[1] The state of the world spiritually is thus described: "For we before laid to the charge both of Jews and Greeks, that they are all under sin; as it is written, There is none righteous, no, not one; there is none that understandeth, there is none that seeketh after God; they have all turned aside, they are together become unprofitable; there is none that doeth good, no, not so much as one."[2] The world is further described as "in darkness," "children of wrath," "living in the wicked one."

Jesus had foretold the meaning of his death for the world in these words, "a ransom for many." A ransom is that which buys back a person or thing sold or

[1] Rom. ii. 14, 15.   [2] Rom. iii. 9-12.

forfeited. Jesus was this "Ransom" or "Redemption." The effect of the death of Jesus was perfectly to fulfil and satisfy every pledge given and accepted, not only by the multitudinous sacrifices and ceremonies of the Israelitish church, but to deliver as a ransom many long before Israel, as in the antediluvian age, and up to Moses, and in the heathen nations, and all from that to the end coming under this declaration: "In every nation he that feareth him, and worketh righteousness, is acceptable to him."[1] The redemption of Christ for the world rests on a vastly wider foundation, and has a vastly wider meaning than the Israelitish or Mosaic. As noted, it was contemplated in the eternal past, and began to operate immediately after the fall.

The relationship in which Christ died for the world is thus described: "As through one trespass the judgment came unto all men to condemnation; even so through one act of righteousness the free gift came unto all men to justification of life. For as through the one man's disobedience the many were made sinners, even so through the obedience of the one shall the many be made righteous."[2] Christ is here plainly declared to have taken his place at the head of the race as Adam did, and by the one act of righteousness; namely, his death, brought the free gift of justification of life unto man.

The necessity of the death of Christ for the world comes from the fact that mankind rested under the doom pronounced at the beginning. "In the day that thou eatest thereof, thou shalt surely die."[3] This sentence went out against the whole race as the presence of death proves and as the following Scripture asserts: "Therefore as through one man sin entered into the world, and death through sin; and so death passed unto all men, for that all sinned."[4] Sin is described in Scripture as a deadly

---

[1] Acts x. 35. [2] Rom. v. 18, 19.
[3] Gen. ii. 17. [4] Rom. v. 12.

plague, as poison, as a crime against nature. It is man's worst enemy. It has ruined earth and devastated heaven. It is treason against God. By its nature, effects, its manward and Godward work, it deserves death. It is a capital crime. Therefore God has said, "The soul that sinneth, it shall die."[1] Death is God's witness to this awful truth of man's guilt as a race, and conscience testifies to each individually. Yet Adam did not die. We have seen he was saved by the intervention of Christ who became thereby responsible for his sin, and procured for him not only respite from instant death in the garden as threatened, but also the hope of eternal life. We have seen that Christ followed with the same respite for all who showed their faith by obedience. A vast accumulation of sin and guilt and obligation was thus laid on Christ. This had to be met by him. It was thus Christ became the world's Substitute and so must become the world's Sacrifice.

The redemptive world work of Christ is thus declared by Paul: "Christ Jesus, whom God hath set forth to be a propitiation through faith by his blood, to show his righteousness, because of the passing over of the sins done aforetime, in the forbearance of God; for the showing, I say, of his righteousness at this present season; that he might himself be just, and the justifier of him who hath faith in Jesus."[2] The "propitiation" does not refer to God's feelings personally, so to speak. It was offended Righteousness which must be propitiated. God could not pass by sin unnoticed or unpunished. It would not be right or just, or to put it as in the above passage, it would not be "righteousness." Now God must be righteous as well as merciful. Justice is a right quality, and in God an unchangeable one, as all his divine attributes are. We see this unchanging justice in nature, who punishes impartially the violators of her laws. We

[1] Eze. xviii. 4.   [2] Rom. iii. 25, 26.

see the necessity of it in society, where unpunished crime renders places uninhabitable, and in its last, and fullest extremity is anarchy.

God occupies a double relationship. He is a Father to his children, but there are other beings beside his children. There are angels and devils. To all these he occupies the position of Ruler. Now his attitude as Father and Ruler are very different. If God is to treat a wrongdoer as a child, it must be upon some grounds which will not impugn his justice. If God is to justify the ungodly, he must be justified in doing so. Otherwise all other beings could complain, and justly, of his partiality. Such treatment of man would be subversive of all moral government. Devils would have a right to the same immunity and could charge God with favoritism and therefore injustice. All sinners in every age and of every depth of sin could demand release from penalty. There would be no restraint either of the sinner or of sin, and the universe would become a universal hell. The just, inexorable, unchangeable justice of God is the blessed barrier between all right and holy beings and such an awful possibility.

The redemptive world work of Christ is described thus: "God was in Christ reconciling the world unto himself, not reckoning unto them their trespasses."[1] The word "reconciling" must be taken in its Scriptural and not in its conversational meaning. It means primarily not a change of feeling either in the world or in God, but a change of relationship. This is seen in this text, "That he might reconcile them both in one body unto God through the cross, having slain the enmity thereby."[2] It was not that God had to be made willing to receive sinful man, but that it had to be made right for him to do so. It is not right to pass by sin and let sinners go unpunished. As has been seen, God must do right always. There was but one

[1] 2 Cor. v. 19.   [2] Eph. ii. 16.

way to accomplish both ends. Christ must bear man's guilt and penalty or an equal or satisfactory one. This he did. Nor was it God obliging Christ to do this nor Christ being more ready than God to suffer for man. They are one in this as in all things. It was God who so loved the world as to give his only begotten Son for its salvation. It was Christ who loved us and gave himself for us.

The act of righteousness by which Christ secured for the world this state of grace was his death. It was not his holy life or his words of truth or his many miracles or spotless example. To make this definite, it is his cross which is spoken of as that by which he accomplished this. The cross of Christ is not first the cross the Christian bears, but the cross Christ himself died upon. Again, the work of reconciling is said to be effected by his blood. "Through him to reconcile all things unto himself, having made peace through the blood of his cross."[1] Blood is simply life, "the life thereof which is the blood thereof."[2] Blood-shed is therefore life given or taken. Christ having forfeited his life at the very beginning for man's life, now pays the forfeit with his blood, that is his life.

The death of Christ was a satisfactory act of righteousness and answered the ends intended thereby. It was not, as has been said, a "*quid pro quo.*" Our penal verdicts are not such. Theft and assault are not punished in kind but are adequately and satisfactorily punished. Such was Christ's death. It was satisfactory to God, to angels, to saints, and even to devils, and ought to be to sinners for whom he died. The death of one great and good man is mourned more than the death of a number of worthless or vicious persons. The one great and good life far outweighs the number of worthless ones. So, to use a still stronger figure, the life of a man, as has been

[1] Col. i. 20.   [2] Gen. ix. 4.

said, would outweigh in value the lives of a universe of insects. So one life, that of Christ, is a sufficient satisfaction for the whole of mankind and all existing beings of every kind.

Only by this great Scriptural meaning can the death of Christ be adequately accounted for. Neither as an act of self-sacrifice nor as an example does it satisfy the expectations aroused by such a character or the claims of himself or the teachings of his apostles or previous scripture. Remembering that it was wholly voluntary, there must have been a great necessity for such an act. No one has a right to so voluntarily die unless there is a fully justifying gain or end. As a mere spectacle of self-sacrifice it was akin to the exhibitions performed by heathen before their deities where they sometimes immolate themselves to win supposed merit or applause under strong excitement. If the death of Christ was only a self-permitted martyrdom for right, then it can be paralleled a thousand times by the records of the martyrs or the giving of one's self for his country or for the saving of the lives of others, of which even the records of mere heroism can show equal examples. Only in the Scriptural sense is any adequate meaning possible to the death of Jesus Christ. No one has a right to read out the Scripture meaning and read in another. This is the very heart of Scripture. To refuse to see this in Scripture is to violate every rule of literary and Scriptural interpretation. The Holy Spirit only responds to the truth. Therefore to fail to so present Christ, is to fail to have the power of the Holy Spirit. It is more; it is denying the Lord who bought us, and incurring the danger of being denied by him at the last day.

The death of Jesus brought the world into salvable relations to God. He can now be just and yet justify the ungodly. This is the meaning of that scripture, "God was in Christ reconciling the world unto himself, not reckoning unto them their trespasses."[1] It was this state and age Jesus spoke of when he announced "the acceptable year of the Lord" which he came to introduce. We call these "years of grace," and so they are. God is dealing now with the world in grace. In former ages he dealt in judgment and in law. Now all is changed. The whole world is offered the gospel of the grace of God.

The great proof the disciples advanced to the world for the truth of their message was the resurrection of Christ. It is a matter of fact and not opinion. They certify to it as eye witnesses, having seen Jesus after his resurrection. Paul gives the names of other witnesses, and mentions five hundred seeing him at once. Their testimony was not apparently denied even by enemies of Christianity in the early centuries. The four evangelists are acknowledged by even infidels to have been veritable persons, and to have been of good character, and to have written unbiased accounts free of all praise of themselves or even their Master, and also free of all comment. They give names and places and dates, and the whole bears the marks of simple narratives of actual occurrences given in unvarnished style. By every legal and literary rule of evidence these are witnesses worthy of belief. It may be asked, Why did not Jesus publicly appear to all, and not only to his own? He had before said, "If they believe not Moses and the prophets, neither will they be persuaded though one rose from the dead." They disbelieved not for want of evidence but for want of desire to give up sin and live rightly. It is useless to further convince such. The gospel is a sieve. It sifts out the true. They had seen the dead raised and did not believe. Neither then nor now does God give further evidence to those who do not obey the evidence they already have. They can reject if they please, and theirs is the loss. The last view God has given the world of his Son, is Christ on

[1] 2 Cor. v. 19.

the cross, the saving view, and this is all they shall have until he comes again in glory.

Among the evidences of the resurrection are the many predictions of the Scriptures and of Jesus himself that he would rise from the dead. These are so connected with the many other predictions regarding him which have been fulfilled as noted, that all hang together. As the rest were literally fulfilled, so it is fair to believe were these also. The simple-minded Galileans were incapable of concocting such an intricate system of fraud, and unable to carry it out among hating, watchful, and cunning enemies, to a successful and undiscovered issue.

The testimony of the Jews and the Roman soldiers who watched the sepulcher, is not the least valuable as to the resurrection of Jesus. "Some of the guard came into the city and told the chief priests all the things that were come to pass. And when they were assembled with the elders and had taken counsel, they gave large money to the soldiers, saying, Say ye, His disciples came by night, and stole him away while we slept. And if this come to the governor's ears, we will persuade him, and rid you of care. So they took the money, and did as they were taught; and this saying was spread abroad among the Jews, and continueth until this day."[1] This is full of valuable corroborative evidence. The whole plot is just what would be expected in case of a resurrection. The enemies of Jesus would have had to give out some explanation, and this was the one most likely to occur to them. The guard testified that the sepulcher was empty, the body gone.

Here is direct testimony which cannot be disputed, and indeed is not by any, even unbelievers, that the body of Jesus was not in the tomb after the third day, which was the day he had set for his resurrection. They also testify that something unusual occurred which all were in excitement about. All this is just

[1] Matt. xxviii. 11-15.

what would occur on the resurrection. They do not go to Pilate, who would have condemned them to death for sleeping at their post of duty, or for neglecting their charge. They do go, as we would expect, to those most interested. That is, some of them came into the city and told what had happened. All were either not fit to go or afraid to venture until some security was had. The statement that they were asleep corroborates the Scriptural narrative. They were asleep but not in natural slumber. They admit they did not see what happened, being asleep. This also fits the Scripture account and our sense of propriety. Jesus was seen first not by Roman soldiers but by his own friends. The improbable part of this account of the soldiers is their evidence as to what they knew happened while they were asleep; the improbability of the panic-stricken disciples' attempting such an adventure; the absence of anything to be accomplished by removing the body from one place to another; the difficulty of concealing for any time a dead body, and the certainty of its discovery, in time, by their foes, and sure punishment for such an attempt; the impossibility of moving the great stone at the door of the sepulcher and removing the body without awaking the sleeping guard,—all this stamps as false and foolish the story of the Jews. The value, however, of this account of theirs is this: it was the only other explanation of the empty sepulcher except the Scripture account of the resurrection of Jesus.

The evidences of the resurrection embrace the customs and times of the church which have continued ever since: The change of the weekly day of rest and its name, "the Lord's Day;" the almost universal observance by the professing followers of Jesus of the anniversary of the event; and, what is to those who have knowledge of it, the greatest proof of all, the Christian's spiritual recognition of him, and the benefits of prayer in his name, and countless blessings which come to them from this belief and the religion founded upon it. No religion founded upon a lie or delusion could produce such effects as the gospel of Jesus has ever since its announcement and wherever it is known and received. The wide propagation of this belief and its acceptance by the best in every community and their adhesion to it are evidences which are of weight in candid minds. Christianity is its own evidence. Christianity and Christ are mutually corroborative.

The resurrection of Jesus was a complete verification of all his claims for himself. He was thereby proved to be the Son of God. God thereby certified to himself and all his statements as true. It was God's witness to his finished and perfect work. If in anything Jesus had not fully obeyed God or failed to complete the work appointed to him in the keeping of all the law, the fulfilling of all the types, the making good of all the pledges accepted by him for men's salvation, the perfecting of the salvation of the believer, God would not have so certified to him. Finally, the resurrection of Jesus is God's warning to the world that there will be the Day of Judgment. "He hath appointed a day, in the which he will judge the world in righteousness by the man whom he hath ordained; whereof he hath given assurance unto all men, in that he hath raised him from the dead."[1] This fact is the one great proof of the hereafter and all its glories and terrors.

The resurrection is the great fact for to-day. The battle rages now along the line of the supernatural. The credibility of many supernatural or unusual narratives of Scripture is denied. Accounts such as the standing still of the sun at the word of Joshua, the accounts of creation, and the garden of Eden, all these are minor events and, as compared with this astounding event, far more credible and less impossible. The one who can admit that Jesus rose

[1] Acts xvii. 31.

from the dead, can and should have no trouble in accepting any other narrative of Scripture. Here, then, is the point of attack and defense. Here is the vital question. If Jesus rose from the dead, all his claims are true. Christianity is as firm as the existence of God, and the believer's hope as sure and blessed as the risen and glorified Christ.

On these great facts the apostles based their gospel. They proclaimed a free, world-wide salvation, and called on all to believe and repent and be saved. They declared this way was by simple faith: "If thou shalt confess with thy mouth Jesus as Lord, and shall believe in thy heart that God raised him from the dead, thou shalt be saved."[1] On the other hand, they testify that whoever refuses Christ refuses God, salvation, and heaven. Peter preached: "In none other is there salvation; for neither is there any other name under heaven, that is given among men, wherein we must be saved;"[2] and Paul writes, "If any man loveth not the Lord, let him be anathema."[3]

This gospel was with Paul an exclusive one. He wrote the church at Corinth: "I determined not to know anything among you, save Jesus Christ and him crucified."[4] He wrote to the churches in Galatia: "Though we, or an angel from heaven, should preach unto you any gospel other than that which we preached unto you, let him be anathema. As we have said before, so say I now again, If any man preacheth unto you any gospel other than that which ye received, let him be anathema."[5] He did not mean by this that he never touched upon any other subject but that of the death of Christ, for he does in his epistles to the churches refer to many other subjects. But these were to Christians for Christian life. To

---

[1] Rom. x. 9.   [2] Acts iv. 12.   [3] 1 Cor. xvi. 22.
[4] 1 Cor. ii. 2.   [5] Gal. i. 8, 9.

the world, Paul had but one gospel, that of salvation and the means of salvation — faith in the crucified and risen Christ. Paul therefore preached to the world no political or social reforms, although the world sorely needed them in every direction. Misery, poverty, ignorance, oppression, and vice prevailed as it does not to-day. Yet we do not read of any efforts by the apostles to institute reforms of any kind save in the church itself. This is significant and cannot be passed by or ignored by those who have regard for the authority of apostolic example and teachings. We must ask why this disregard of the crying evils of their time and this exclusive concentration upon the single theme for the world, of the gospel of the death and resurrection of Christ.

The call to-day, we are told, is for "a practical gospel"— "less theology and more practical Christianity." We are told of the efficacy of "the gospel of a loaf of bread." We are asked for "more treasure on earth, even if we get less in heaven." We are assured our desire of converting men will by preaching such a gospel be greatly furthered; that people will be so attracted to the church and to Christ as to reach the result aimed at; that this is preaching the gospel. All this has a very taking sound. It seems to appeal to common sense, and attracts practical people, the benevolent especially. That we are to let our light so shine there is no disputing. That the gospel is commended by its humanitarian works is also clear. That an unphilanthropic gospel would not be the gospel of Christ is also true. No one will do aught but approve of every effort to help or benefit the needy, whether in physical or social need, and the church is foremost in all benevolences, and always has been. But we are now considering the specific work of the church, and the proposal to lessen this preaching and substitute for it humanitarian efforts of various kinds.

Our reply to all this is that the gospel is the accomplishment of all reforms, by its very nature, operation, and effects. It is as expelling to all evil as light is to darkness. The method of the apostles was not to expel the darkness but to turn on the light. It is the logical and Scriptural way still. The testimony of history is conclusive as to the nature of the work of early Christianity and its effects. Guizot writes: "Christianity was in no way addressed to the social condition of man. It distinctly disclaimed all interference with it. It commanded the slave to obey his master. It attacked none of the great evils, none of the gross acts of injustice by which the social system of the day was disfigured. Yet who is there but will acknowledge that Christianity has been one of the greatest promoters of civilization? And wherefore?— Because it has changed the interior structure of man, his opinions, his sentiments; because it has regenerated his moral, his intellectual character."

Here, then, is the way to the social amelioration of man. Change his "interior structure," as Guizot terms it. This the gospel does, and nothing else ever pretends to accomplish it. The preachers of the old apostolic gospel have been the world's benefactors. This gospel has been the fountain of all blessing wherever it has been received, as history testifies. Where the gospel of the cross of Christ is proclaimed with the Holy Ghost sent down from heaven, these humanitarian and philanthropic efforts are as sure to blossom out as spring is sure to come in response to the annual return of the great solar source of light and heat. This is true of the individual, the community, and the world. We claim the gospel of the crucified Christ is the greatest humanitarian influence the world has ever had. To put any external or humanitarian or philanthropic efforts first, is to plant the tree upside down. Both roots and branches will wither. The gospel is minimized thereby. The pure gospel is withheld; the state of man is concealed and also his danger; the great sanctions of divine truth are unmentioned; the power of the Holy Spirit is withheld; conversions are few or weak; and the church is reduced to a mere organization for temporal or social or benevolent purposes, having lost the distinctive character which Christ gave his church as a witness for his truth. The salt having lost its savor, men trample it under their feet, for the world knows true from false in religion.

The church exists for a specific work — the proclamation in all the world of the gospel of the cross of Jesus Christ as declared by himself and his apostles. This we dare not neglect for any other mission, however good. Christ said, "Ye have the poor always with you, and whensoever ye will ye can do them good; but me ye have not always."[1] Our opportunities and our time are limited. The spiritual work is above all others, and we cannot turn from it for any other work, no matter how valuable. The future is far above the present, and the salvation of men for the future is in Scripture made the great thing. Doing good in a physical or social way is not necessarily saving the soul for eternity and may not even contribute to it. When Jesus found the people, poor enough too they were, following him for the loaves and fishes, he discontinued giving them. Lord Shaftsbury has left this record: "I have been connected with many forms of humanitarian and benevolent works during fifty years, but I have not observed that men were thereby brought nearer to God." The Christian believes in eternity and its tremendous issues. It will make little difference in a short time what the material condition of each has been in this life, but it will make an eternal difference what his relation to God is. This, we believe, is established by faith in Christ, and only so. Therefore it is the one business of the church to preach Christ.

[1] Mark. xiv. 7.

There is also a demand for another substitute for this gospel of the crucified and risen Christ. We are told the Sermon on the Mount and the other practical teachings of Jesus are gospel enough for the world, and to teach these to man. Undoubtedly if the world would live so, all would be well. But it has been shown that the experiment of all this has been tried. We have seen the most perfect system of ethics given to a specially prepared people by the most extraordinary agencies, accompanied by demonstrations of the supernatural to impress them, and help them observe it all, the greatest line of prophets and other ministers of its provisions. It was in a land secluded from contamination by the effects of the surrounding world; it was accompanied by temporal sanctions, which by blessings when they obeyed, and adversities when they disobeyed, made every motive of self-interest alive to its observance. All this was continued for centuries and worked out to a full and absolute demonstration. Heredity, environment, and development have done their best. Failure is written on the whole demonstration. The law was a failure in Israel even as a social experiment. Man cannot be so saved even socially, still less spiritually, as Paul plainly declares.

Now the commands of Christ are infinitely above those of Moses. They are spiritual, and deal with looks and thoughts and purposes of the heart. Moses's commands under such conditions were not, and, as Paul tells us, could not be kept because of the weakness of the flesh, that is, of human nature. How, then, can we expect the spiritual commands of Christ to be kept by the same human nature; for it is the same in every age and land. It has been shown how Christ enables man to do so, and when we follow his way, we may hope to succeed, but to work over and over the old useless experiment is worse than folly.

The order for and of Christ's work is this: "Go ye therefore and make disciples of all the nations, baptizing them into the name of the Father and of the Son and of the Holy Ghost : teaching them to observe all things whatsoever I command you."[1] Here are two orders : first, make disciples ; second, teach them the commands of Christ. The teaching is for the disciples. There is no command here or elsewhere to teach the commands of Christ to the unregenerate. There was no such teaching by the apostles, and Christ taught them himself to Israel only. But they are to be taught to the church. The Sermon on the Mount and the other teachings of Christ form the laws of the church. They are to be taught and obeyed. In this lies the purity and power of the church. To neglect these teachings is departing from Christ. This is the great lack of to-day. These teachings are even regarded as impractical. Yet the apostles and the early churches literally observed them and prospered thereby. We must return again as believers to the life laid down for us by Our Lord and Master.

To the church the apostles preached a far greater view of Christ than to Israel or the world. All he is to these he is to his people, and far more. In Christ's death for the church there is seen a choice of it, a relationship to it, an efficacy for it, and special purposes in it here and hereafter. The view of his people from the eternal past has been considered. The passage relating most pointedly to the relation of Christ in his death to the church is this : " Husbands, love your wives, even as Christ also loved the church, and gave himself up for it ; that he might sanctify it, having cleansed it by the washing of water with the word, that he might present the church to himself a glorious church, not having spot or wrinkle or any such thing ; but that it should be holy and without blemish. Even so ought husbands also to love their own wives as their own bodies. He that loveth his own wife loveth himself : for no man ever hated his

[1] Matt. xxviii. 19.

own flesh; but nourisheth and cherisheth it, even as Christ also the church; because we are members of his body."[1]

This is the husband dying for the wife. This is more than the shepherd dying for the sheep, or a man dying for his friends, or Christ dying in the place of guilty man, or even the king dying for his subjects. There is a peculiar closeness of relation and affection in the motive, and a special purpose in the object which does not exist in the other two classes.

This identity of Christ with his people has been in part shown. Aside from his being made in the likeness of sinful flesh, he was made like unto his brethren also. He had not only the common humanity, but he had what all mankind do not have,— the nature of God, of which his people are partakers. Christ bore man's penalty of death for the original curse; he bore Israel's curse of the violated law; but his substitution for his people is far more. The identity of Christ with his people brought upon him the sense of shame and guilt for his people's sins. His attitude as surety for the sins of the world did not necessarily bring upon him this sense of guilt and shame, but only of responsibility. But as one of his people, he shared the feeling of the Father in the wrong-doing of his child, or, to use the exact Scriptural figure, the shame of the husband in the sins of his wife. There is a peculiar efficiency also in the death of Christ for his people. By the death of Christ the salvation of all is made possible, and the salvation of the church is made certain. Christ had purposes also in his death for his people which he had not for the world. Another peculiarity of the Scripture accounts of the scope of the death of Christ as affecting the church, is that it is spoken of as bought or purchased by his blood. "The church of God which he purchased with his own blood;" "A people for God's

[1] Eph. v. 25-31.

own possession " (same word, purchased).[1] The idea is a redemption within a redemption, or, to use a parable of Christ, the found treasure within the purchased field.

The benefits secured to the believer by the death of Christ have been seen in the foregoing. They may be briefly seen in this Scripture: "If any man is in Christ, he is a new creature, the old things are passed away; behold they are become new."[2] God regards the believer as "in Christ." It is a place of holiness. God sees no sin in him. All has been charged to Christ, and all Christ's merits credited to him. He is "justified," that is, made right or righteous. It is a place of security. "It is God that justifieth, who is he that condemneth? . . . Who shall separate us from the love of Christ?"[3]

The resurrection of Christ was also far more to the church than to Israel or the world. The resurrection of Jesus is spoken of as a type of the Christian's state and life, "that like as Christ was raised from the dead through the glory of the Father, so we also might walk in newness of life."[4] The Christian is spiritually a resurrected person, as if the believing thief had been buried with Christ literally in Joseph's tomb, and when Jesus rose had been raised with him and sent out to live out his life on earth. So is the Christian spiritually risen with Christ. All our hopes for the future depended on the resurrection of Jesus. "But now hath Christ been raised from the dead, the firstfruits of them that are asleep."[5] His resurrection makes ours certain. The first sheaf assures the rest of the harvest and is a sample of the whole. The resurrection of Jesus is a type, or more, an example of the resurrection of his people. As he rose so will they. The descending angel, the opening graves, the quiet awakening, the rising in immortality, the

---

[1] Acts xx. 28 ; 1 Peter ii. 9.   [2] 2 Cor. v 17.
[3] Rom. viii. 33, 35.   [4] Rom. vi. 4.   [5] 1 Cor. xv. 20.

same and yet not the same, with all the powers Jesus had and all the naturalness also we saw in him, are before us.

The apostle preached also a living, personal, present Christ. They regarded him as an actual person having a body and a locality. Paul and John attest to seeing and hearing him since his ascension. This is the vital element of Christianity. It is a living and not a past and dead Christ we serve and trust in and look for. To think of Christ as a historical character only, is not enough to satisfy the claims of himself or his apostles for him. This is one phase of unbelief of to-day. Christ is regarded as one of several saviours, such as Confucius, Mohammed, Buddha, Zoroaster, and others. We repudiate the classing of Christ with any other, even as their superior. All these, if they ever lived at all, were men only, and are now dead, while Christ is a living being, and before him will Confucius and Mohammed and Zoroaster and all the so-called saviours appear in judgment, and he will assign them their places in eternity.

The terms applied by the apostles to Christ show their appreciation of him. He is to them a most glorious being. They never hold up Christ as an object of pity and to be received from sympathy. His past sufferings, even, are not so used. Christ now is beyond the need of such consideration. He is represented under visible form and even described as to his appearance. John thus describes him: "One like unto a son of man clothed with a garment down to the foot, and girt about at the breasts with a golden girdle. And his head and his hair were white as white wool, white as snow; and his eyes were as a flame of fire; and his feet like unto burnished brass, as if it had been refined in a furnace; and his voice as the voice of many waters. And he had in his right hand seven stars : and out of his mouth proceeded a sharp two-edged sword : and his countenance was as the sun shineth in his strength."[1] This agrees with the appearance seen by Paul. And there is no reason to doubt both were actual personal appearances of Christ. Paul speaks of having seen the Lord, and this was his general appearance. We see the same appearance as in Jesus in the transfiguration : "He was transfigured before them and his face did shine as the sun, and his garments became white as the light."[2] So that we may believe that this was not only the same Christ, but that he was in his own proper, eternal state.

The purpose of giving us a picture of the risen Christ is to impress us with his actual existence, identity, and personality. Christ is not a conception or a doctrine, but a person who has a bodily form and can be seen and has been handled and felt, as the apostles testify. We have no reason to believe he is any different now than he was after his resurrection during the time the apostles saw him. They speak of him as the same with whom they did eat and drink after he rose from the dead. A further reason for this picture being given us is that we may have an impression of his personality. We have no idea of what the earthly Jesus looked like. The pictures are wholly imaginative, and there is reason to believe are wide of the appearance Jesus must have had. But we are not to think of Christ as the rabbi of Judea. We shall never so see him. The view John gives is his appearance in which we shall know him in eternity. Further, this picture is that of a being of great dignity and glory. He is one to be thought of in greatest reverence and to be addressed accordingly. The sentimental terms of endearment sometimes addressed to Christ are wholly out of place. The silly songs such as might be sung by lovers to

[1] Rev. i. 13-16.   [2] Matt. xvii. 2.

each other, are seen to be worse than out of place, when compared with the dignity and reverence in such scenes as the following, a description which Jesus acknowledged as that of himself: "I saw the Lord sitting upon a throne, high and lifted up, and his train filled the temple. Above him stood the seraphim; each one had six wings; with twain he covered his face, and with twain he covered his feet, and with twain he did fly. And one cried unto another, and said, Holy, holy, holy, is the Lord of hosts: the whole earth is full of his glory."[1] In such reverence Christ is to be regarded and addressed even by his nearest and dearest disciples.

The attitude everywhere described of Christ in his ascension glory is that of sitting at the right hand of God. It is an exceedingly significant expression. It describes his attitude toward the past, his present office and work, and his and our future. It is the position of one who has finished his work. His great humiliation and its results are accomplished. There is very great joy from the satisfaction in successful effort. This Christ has. Christ is infinitely satisfied with his work as approved by the Father. His position is also an element of his present honor, power, and glory. The right hand of God is the next place in all these three to God himself. It expresses more than all else the dignity of Christ. There is also nearness to God the Father in this position. This he prayed for when he said, "Father, glorify thou me with thine own self, with the glory which I had with thee before the world was."[2] This is now fulfilled. The eternal state was "in the bosom of the Father." This may not correspond to it in all respects, but expresses more, the attitude of activity. In his present state Christ is not idle.

Christ is on the right hand of God as intercessor and advocate. The Scriptures which teach

[1] Isa. vi. 1–3.   [2] John xvii. 5.

this are many: "It is Christ Jesus that died, yea, rather that was raised from the dead, who is at the right hand of God, who also ever maketh intercession for us."[1] Christ has all the requisites of an advocate. Such a position and office require that the advocate possess the right relationship to both the parties with whom he has had to do. He must have the wants of the supplicant not only in his mind but upon his heart. He must have access to, and influence with, the upper power, to present them rightly and effectively. He must have a sufficient plea and be able to secure the favors or rights wanted. All this Christ has. The plea Christ presents for us is spoken of in Scripture, as his blood. It means, as we have seen, his own life poured out as man's ransom. It answers every accusation which might be brought against the believer, whether true or false. It can make up for all deficiencies in any case, however great, even though it be a whole life misspent, or one coming at the last moment to Christ, as the thief upon the cross. It can call for the greatest gifts from God. Its power as a plea is so great that, when joined to the feeblest petition, however unworthy the offerer, it must prevail at the throne of infinite justice and power, still more at the throne of grace; for it must be borne in mind that all Christ obtained and continues to secure for his people, while in exact accord with full justice, so great is his plea, is asked for, not as justice, but as grace. Christ is not pleading at the judgment throne of sinners but at the mercy seat of saints.

A beautiful picture is presented in the Apocalypse, of the presentation of the prayers of the people of God: "And another angel came and stood over the altar, having a golden censer; and there was given unto him much incense, that he should add it unto the prayers of all the saints upon the golden altar which

[1] Rom. viii. 34.

was before the throne. And the smoke of the incense with the prayers of the saints went up before God out of the angel's hand."[1] This is during a special future time, but represents the offering up of the prayers of all God's people at all times.

Christ's mediation is for his peoples' persons, sins, needs, prayers, and work. Their persons are his first care. The position of the believer has been considered. He is maintained in this position by and because of his identity with Christ. The believer in the sight of God is "in Christ," that is, the body of believers and Christ are one. The figures to express this are many. Christ is the corner-stone on which the church is the building. Christ is the vine, the believers being branches; Christ is the husband, the church the wife; Christ is the head, the church the body. All these express the closest identity. There is this view, however, to be taken of the mediation of Christ for his people as distinguished from their sins and prayers and needs and work individually. The first is always spoken of in Scripture as a finished work which needs no renewing.

The prayer of Christ before his death may be taken as an illustration of his advocacy and intercession in general. These are the petitions in the prayer. "I pray for them: I pray not for the world. . . . Keep them in thy name which thou hast given me, that they may be one, even as we are. . . . Keep them from the evil one. . . . Sanctify them in the truth, thy word is truth. . . . Neither for these alone do I pray, but for them also that believe on me through their word; that they may all be one; even as thou, Father, are in me, and I in thee, that they also may be in us; that the world may believe that thou didst send me. I will that where I am, they also may be with me; that they may behold my glory which thou hast given me."[2] In brief, the desire of the heart of Jesus for his people was that they may be united, sanctified,

[1] Rev. viii. 3, 4.   [2] John xvii.

made efficient, and glorified. It will be seen from this that the burden of Christ's intercession is first for their own sakes and also for the sake of the world. It is through the church he is to bless the world. He has done everything for the world which can be done. He has by his death brought it within the scope of grace, and has sent his Spirit to convince it of its need by convincing it of "sin, righteousness, and judgment," and now he leaves his people to carry his message of mercy to it. It is therefore the great care of Christ to see that his people are kept right. This he does by his intercession, the Holy Spirit, and the means of grace.

The intercession of Christ for his people is that they may be kept in his name. This is equivalent to that in his exhortation, "Abide in me." It is faith in him and faithfulness in adhesion to him. This union with Christ secures union with the Father — "one as we are." The sanctity of his people is the great subject of Christ's work and intercession. The prayer shows the great means of sanctification — "sanctifiy them through thy truth ; thy word is truth." The concern of Christ is that the word of God shall be kept before his people. The efficacy of the church depends upon its unity—"that they all may be one, that the world may believe that thou hast sent me." In life Jesus was continually urging his disciples to "love one another." Here in his intercessory prayer is the same wish. The final wish of the prayer is the presence of his people with himself in glory. The share we in these latter days have in this prayer lies in the petition for "them that shall believe on me through their word."

The intercession of Christ is also for his people individually, first for their sins : "And if any man sin, we have an Advocate with the Father, Jesus Christ the righteous."[1] The devil is called the accuser of the brethren "which accuseth them before our God

---

[1] 1 John ii. 2.

day and night."[1] "Devil" and "slanderer" are the same word in Greek. Every slanderer, especially every slanderer of the people of Christ, is voicing the feelings of the devil. The blood of Jesus is the plea which answers all charges in heaven. It can and does cleanse our consciences from condemnation. Akin to this is the intercession of Christ for the believer in his times of trial. Such was his intercession for Peter which we may take as illustrative of all: "Simon, Simon, behold, Satan asked to have you, that he might sift you as wheat: but I made supplication for thee, that thy faith fail not: and do thou, when once thou hast turned again, stablish thy brethren."[2] Here Satan asked and obtained permission to sift this chosen band; for the word "you'" is plural while "thee" is singular. Christ undoubtedly interceded for all, but out of them he makes special mention of one specially weak on a certain vaunted point, and soon to be tempted on a trying occasion; and so Christ said to Peter; "I have prayed for *thee*." He singles out special persons for special intercession and care at critical times in their lives. Christ foresees these times of sifting or searching, and knows the certain result if we are left to our own boasted consecration and love and holiness and determination to hold out and to be faithful to the end, and all this we so often utter or think. If it were not for the faithfulness of our loving, patient Intercessor, we would make awful and shameful wreck of our professions. But, "I made supplication for thee that thy faith fail not," is the anchor which holds us when all else has given way.

There is one kind of intercession our Lord said needed not to be made: "In that day ye shall ask in my name: and I say not unto you, that I will pray the Father for you; for the Father himself loveth you."[3] This is not a declaration that he will not

---
[1] Rev. xii. 10.   [2] Luke xxii. 31-34.   [3] John xvi. 26.

pray the Father for us but that the Father does not so require to be interceded with. The use of the name of Christ, however, is equivalent to his advocacy in person. The believer has two advocates. "He will give you another comforter [*paraclete*, or advocate, same word] that he may be with you forever, even the Spirit of truth."[1]

Paul refers to the office and effect of the advocacy of the Holy Spirit in the believer in these words: "And in like manner the Spirit also helpeth our infirmity: for we know not how to pray as we ought; but the Spirit himself maketh intercession for us with groanings which cannot be uttered; and he that searcheth the hearts knoweth what is the mind of the Spirit, because he maketh intercession for the saints according to the will of God."[2] The prayers which are inspired of the Holy Spirit need no further advocacy. In these two advocates, Christ and the Holy Spirit, we have the common figures of the counselor and barrister. The one advising privately and preparing for the case and inspiring the whole movement, and the other presenting publicly in court the case as thus prepared; both in communication with each other and devoted to the interests of the client. Such a case at the high court of grace is certain of success. Here, then, are four great elements of power in the believer's prayers, the inspiration of the Holy Spirit, the use of the name of Christ, the personal intercession of Christ, and the love of God himself for the believer.

The apostles not only preached a glorified Christ in heaven, but Christ present in each of his people. They express this truth in the phrase, "Christ in you." The former relationship of being "in Christ" we have considered. It relates to our standing, where we are, as seen by God — a position secured by the death of Christ. But the second

[1] John xiv. 16, 17.   [2] Rom. viii. 26.

phrase, "Christ in you," expresses something far different. It is a matter of fact so declared of every Christian — "Know ye not as to your own selves, that Jesus Christ is in you? unless indeed ye be reprobates."[1] Unless the person is a reprobate, Christ is in him. This may not be a matter of consciousness, but it follows from the fact of his being "in Christ." "Of his fulness have we all received and grace for grace."[2] It is not a part of Christ in each as in the Old Testament believers, but all of Christ in every believer. This is a great mystery as Paul declares.[3]

The natural figure is followed in the Scriptures. It is spoken of as being "born of God," "born of the Spirit," all in the sense of conception. Paul follows this by intimating a still further resemblance to the natural figure: "My little children, of whom I am again in travail until Christ be formed in you."[4] There is the infancy of the new creature, and growth, and finally the "full-grown man, the measure of the stature of the fulness of Christ." The whole is spoken of as another and a second life, which the believer lives; a person within a person, a life within a life, growing up into all his being day by day, and absorbing and controlling all his faculties, and finally as a butterfly from the chrysalis, emerging into the life of eternity.

All this is not without resistance, especially from within. Not only Satan but the flesh is the antagonist of the new life. "For the flesh lusteth against the Spirit, and the Spirit against the flesh; for these are contrary the one to the other; that ye may not do the things that ye would."[5] Here, "Christ in you," is called "the Spirit," and this is the usual name in Scripture for it. The struggle, especially in the early stages, is very great and painful. It is described by Paul in the seventh of Romans, where he admits his

[1] 2 Cor. xiii. 5. [2] John i. 16. [3] Col. i. 26, 27.
[4] Gal. iv. 19. [5] Gal. v. 17.

identity with both natures, and speaks of each as "I." If these two natures are kept in mind, the passage will be understood. The secret of victory is given us in this scripture: "Reckon ye also yourselves to be dead unto sin, but alive unto God, in Jesus Christ. Let not sin therefore reign in your mortal body, that we should obey the lusts thereof; neither present your members unto sin as instruments of unrighteousness; but present yourselves unto God, as alive from the dead, and your members as instruments of righteousness unto God. For sin shall not have dominion over you, for ye are not under law but under grace."[1]

The effect of the presence of Christ in the believer is to reproduce Christ himself so far as he is given full control. All the graces of Christ are in embryo in each believer and only need to be developed. The full state is that expressed by Paul: "I have been crucified with Christ; yet I live; and yet no longer I, but Christ liveth in me."[2] This is the ideal state of the Christian.

The whole work of God in the believer may be summed up in the three terms (misused in the natural view): heredity, environment, and development, in their spiritual application. He is born of God, that is the believer's heredity; old things are passed away, all things are become new, that is his environment; he grows up into Christ, that is his development.

The work of Christ in this age relates also to Israel, the church, and the world, collectively. Israel had a great place in the spread of the gospel in the apostles' days. Not only the Jews but also the other tribes were found everywhere. They were the seed-bed in which the first plantings of the gospel took root. They were the first visited in every place by the apostles, and to them was first offered the gospel. They accepted of it by thousands. Those thus converted to the gospel, furnished as they were like Paul

[1] Rom. vi. 11-14.   [2] Gal. ii. 20.

with the teachings of Scripture, were the fittest to do the work of the missionary of the cross. The Israelite was the merchant of the middle ages. He was the common carrier of the world. The merchant and the missionary were often one, as in the case of Lydia, a seller of purple, and Aquila and Priscilla, makers of tents. Christ foretold their fate nationally by which they were still further dispersed: "There shall be great distress upon the land, and wrath unto this people. And they shall fall by the edge of the sword and shall be led captive into all the nations; and Jerusalem shall be trodden down of the Gentiles until the times of the Gentiles be fulfilled."[1] Their spiritual state during the succeeding centuries is declared by Paul: "For I would not, brethren, have you ignorant of this mystery, lest ye be wise in your own conceits, that a hardening in part hath befallen Israel, until the fulness of the Gentiles be come in; and so all Israel shall be saved."[2] Both these prophecies have been fulfilled. The change evidently took place after the breaking up of their worship and nationality. They are to remain so until near the end. Their restoration is to be as Paul tells us, the precurser of a mighty blessing to earth. They are witnesses to the truth and of one only living and true God, the Scriptures, and Christ, and his gospel. Next to Jesus as the greatest proof of Christianity is Israel.

The work of Christ in the present age also relates to the church as a body. The establishment of the church as a family under Abraham and as a nation under Moses has been seen. The formation of the church as a great universal spiritual body is the work of Christ in the present age. The word "church" means "called out," and also "called together," as a secondary meaning. It is therefore a body called out of the mass and kept separated. Its peculiar rela-

[1] Luke xxi. 23, 24.   [2] Rom. xi. 25.

tions to Christ will be seen by the terms applied to it. It is called, the Body of Christ, the Bride of Christ, the Temple of the Holy Ghost, the Kingdom of Heaven, and the Kingdom of God. These are in a sense synonymous but not coterminous. They express enlarging spheres as given in the order named.

In the term "the Body of Christ" there is the closest possible identity expressed. It is identity of origin, nature, mission, experiences, and destiny. The term "the Bride" expresses the same identity but differently. In the former the natural relations are subjective; in the latter objective. There is, also, another difference in the use of these two terms. The former expresses the earthly relationship of the church to Christ. The feet walk the earth although the head is in heaven. There is also the idea of service connected with the figure of the body. This is seen in Paul's well-known chapter on spiritual gifts: "Now ye are the body of Christ, and severally members thereof."[1] The other term, "the Bride," expresses mutual fellowship. Lange writes thus upon this word: —

"The Bride of the Lord is in accordance with a standing Biblical view, based upon deep and essential spiritual relations, the contrast of spiritual receptivity and spiritual creative power is the Christian church."[2]

This figure has also a future meaning. It looks to the marriage and the fellowship which follows. "The Temple of the Holy Ghost" expresses the place of the church with reference to the whole body of the saved and the relation of the whole to God the Holy Spirit. "Built upon the foundation of the apostles and prophets, Christ Jesus himself being the chief corner stone; in whom each several building, fitly framed together, groweth into a holy temple in the Lord; in whom ye also are builded together for

[1] 1 Cor. xii. 27. [2] Commentary, Revelation, p. 245.

a habitation of God in the Spirit."[1] The entire body of God's people is here compared to a temple in which "the several buildings" represent the various companies of the saved. The place of the church is the most holy place, "a habitation of God." All these figures express the very highest place not only above all earth but above all beings of any world or age. Christ has but one Body, but one Bride, but one Holy of Holies.

The secret relationship of Christ to his church in this age is illustrated by this scripture: "I saw seven golden candlesticks and in the midst of the candlesticks one like unto a son of man. . . . He had in his right hand seven stars. . . . The seven stars are the angels of the seven churches, and the seven candlesticks are seven churches."[2] This is a representation of the attitude and office of Christ toward his church during the present age. By the ministries of the church and the supply of the Holy Spirit he keeps the flame of the church's graces glowing.

A noticeable feature of the Epistles is the fewness of exhortations to believers to engage in what is termed now, "Christian work." There are exhortations to give to help the needy, especially in the church. There are general directions as to "serving the Lord," "patient continuance in well-doing," "abounding in the work of the Lord," not to be weary in well-doing. The epistles to those set aside to the work, as Timothy and Titus, have also such directions, but for the church at large those quoted are about the kind given. The great urgings of all the Epistles is to knowledge of Christ and holiness of life. The apostles were most anxious to have their people holy. They were more zealous to secure true believers than a multitude of them. They cared more for quality than numbers. A pure, loving church was more to them than a large one. There is a lesson for

[1] Eph. ii. 19–22. [2] Rev. i. 13, 16, 20.

us to-day in this great fact. Purity of doctrine, the energy and life and power of the Holy Spirit, are the great sources of Christian activity. Where these are there is no lack of workers, and where these are not, urgings may induce some to work, but their work will be lifeless and fruitless. We need to return to the apostolic plan and endeavor to bring about a return of purity of faith and life in the church. From these will flow a stream of missionary and other activities which will bless the world. The greatest reason, however, for this singular omission is that the people of God are first in the heart of Christ and the apostles. The Bible is, as has been remarked, all, or nearly all, about God's people or to them. In looking back to the beginning, we see they were the great objects of divine contemplation. God's people themselves, rather than what he does by them or gains from them, are upon the heart of Christ. Not ours, but us, is his desire.

The term "kingdom," as applied to the work of Christ, designates its sphere, time, conditions, and principles, preparation for, its people, and its ruling powers. It has the same threefold application we have observed in the Gospels and Epistles, as to the work of Christ. There is a kingdom for Israel, the church, and mankind generally. It has also a past, present, and future aspect. All which shows it is a subject which requires careful study. The kingdom is spoken of as offered to Israel by Christ as their Messiah, the Son of David, in which he was the King of the Jews and the King of Israel, and for claiming which he was put to death. This is the subject of all the Old Testament prophecies, and to this Israel ever looked forward. It is spoken of in this scripture: "Many shall come from the east and the west and shall sit down with Abraham and Isaac and Jacob in the kingdom of heaven, but the sons of the kingdom shall be cast forth into the outer darkness."[1] This kingdom, we have seen, Israel lost by rejection, or rather they lost the immediate privilege of it, for it has a prophetic aspect to be considered later. The second aspect of the kingdom is that which is to come, as in this passage spoken in connection with the end of the world or age: "Then shall the righteous shine forth as the sun in the kingdom of their Father."[2] It is always the future kingdom which is meant when it is spoken of as the Father's or in connection with the Father, as in the Lord's prayer: "Our Father which art in heaven . . . Thy kingdom come." The word "kingdom" without any possessive is also applied to the future aspect of the kingdom.

The terms "kingdom of heaven" and "kingdom of God" are in a general sense synonymous, yet there is a difference. The former is applied to the earthly and visible aspect, the latter to the spiritual or eternal aspects of the kingdom. Both are applied to the church as representing the phase of the kingdom now existing. The church is part of the kingdom. It is the governing or inspiring power as distinguished from the subjects of the kingdom. It means a sovereignty. To gain the kingdom is to gain a place of honor in it. The word "kingdom" is applied to those who acquire a place in it, the principles which govern it, the right or privilege of entering it, and its coming and course. Although the kingdom is far greater and future, still as the church is composed of those who shall possess the kingdom, the same principles apply to both in a measure.

The condition and history of the church as a phase of the kingdom is declared by Christ in the seven parables of the kingdom: The Sower, The Tares, The Mustard Plant, The Leaven, The Hid Treasures, The

---

[1] Matt. viii . 11, 12. [2] Matt. xiii . 43.

Pearl, the Net.[1] These seven parables represent the kingdom in its embryonic or formative state. They must be considered together, and as covering the same period. Some of these are explained by Christ, as The Sower and The Tares and The Net. These give us the outline of the whole, of which the remaining furnish further details. We see from the three mentioned that this time is to be, in its inception, progress, and close, a mixed state of affairs. The seed sown is to be received only by part of the field, and is to be mingled with tares even where it is received, and these are to continue to the close, when the four diverse results of the sowing are found, the tares and wheat are growing together, and the net contains good fish and bad. It is a well-known principle of interpretation that obscure scriptures are to be explained by those clearly understood. With this in mind the parables of the Mustard Plant, Leaven, Hid Treasure, and Pearl, must agree with the Sower and the Tares and Net. The Mustard Plant is not a natural symbol of anything perfect. Whether it was the tree or the plant of that name, neither are conspicuous for size or beauty or longevity. That which characterizes it is a small beginning, rapid growth, and, as compared with garden plants, large size. The fowls are never used in Scripture as symbols of good, but the reverse. Here is the rapid extension of the visible church and the sheltering of forms of evil by it, or rather such forms of evil coming into it. All this agrees with history.

The symbol used in the parable of the Leaven is one of the most fully explained of any in Scripture. In the Mosaic law it was commanded not to be offered in sacrifice, and at the passover was to be put entirely away. The one instance where it is used, the wave loaves, is a type of the conditions of this very age we are discussing, as we noted. It is in-

[1] Matt. xiii.

credible that Jesus who came to fulfil the law should so disregard its teachings on such a point as to take this divinely commanded symbol of evil and make it a type of good. It is also incredible that, knowing the meaning the Israelite attached to this symbol, he should, without a word of explanation, use it, meaning thereby the opposite of what they understood and had a right to understand from the command of God. The meaning Jesus attached to leaven we have from his own words as follows: "Beware of the leaven of the Pharisees and Sadducees. Then understood they how that he bade them not beware of the leaven of bread, but of the teaching of the Pharisees and Sadducees."[1] Paul also so used this symbol: "Know ye not that a little leaven leaveneth the whole lump? Purge out the old leaven, that ye may be a new lump, even as ye are unleavened. For our passover also hath been sacrificed, even Christ: wherefore let us keep the feast, not with old leaven, neither with the leaven of malice and wickedness, but with the unleavened bread of sincerity and truth."[2]

After this explicit teaching of Christ and his apostles, and the Scripture use, as seen in the Mosaic law, sound principles of exegesis demand that we use it the same way, and interpret the leaven as meaning evil, and only evil.

The remaining three parables were spoken to the disciples apart, the others being to the multitudes as well as the disciples. The Hid Treasure is the church which Christ finds in the field, which he has before explained is the world. In spite of the failure of the sowing to be received by all, and the presence of tares among the grain, and the defective growth of the visible church, and sheltering of evil, and the gradual leavening by evil doctrine and practices, there remains the church which Christ had in mind from the beginning, and for which he planned the redemption of the

---

[1] Matt. xvi. 11, 12.   [2] 1 Cor. v. 6-8.

world, and came and died. The parable of the Pearl refers to the character which belongs to it. Such are like the merchant. They seek the best of spiritual things to which Christ applies pearls as a symbol: "Give not that which is holy unto the dogs, neither cast your pearls before the swine."[1] It is that which Christ urged when he said, "Seek ye first the kingdom of God and his righteousness."[2] The last parable confirms all the previous parables in this interpretation. The good fish and the bad are found in the net, are separated, and this in the end of the age. The gospel net has gathered a mixed haul as we see it to-day, and as all church history declares. From these seven parables of the kingdom we gather that the kingdom in the present age is to be in a state of imperfection, the good in admixture with evil, and this to continue to the end of the world, or age. This is analogous to the spiritual condition of the individual, in whom the flesh remains until the end, and wars with the spirit. It also follows the analogous course of Israel as a nation. It is also confirmed by facts. The history of the church presents this state from the beginning.

The beginnings of all this are apparent in the apostolic church. There is dissension over the distribution of the bounty of the church, and contention between Paul and Barnabas, and also Peter. We see the inroads of heresies. Later we find Paul rebuking the Gentile churches for the grossest scandals, as fornication. The same state of things is shown by the letters to the seven churches. There is declining love in Ephesus, the harboring of teachers of heresy and evil practices in Pergamum, the suffering of an adulterous prophetess in Thyatira, deadness of activity in Sardis, and lukewarmness or great worldliness in Laodicea. Only two of the seven escape reproof. Two have no words of praise. Sardis has only a few

[1] Matt. vii. 6.   [2] Matt. vi. 33.

left true to Christ, and Laodicea is condemned and threatened with rejection. Church history shows an increasing state of evil as the centuries go on, until Christianity was imperialized under Constantine, which was simply baptized heathenism, and which finally developed the monstrous papal apostasy which lasted as a system of persecution for over twelve hundred years, and continues yet to hold in ignorance and superstition a seventh of the world's population. This came from the Christian church. It was all this Christ had in mind when he spake the parables of the Mustard Plant and the Leaven, and no one who has read history, whether church or political, will hesitate to acknowledge that the prophecy has been so far fulfilled.

Besides the present spiritual and imperfect phase of the kingdom, Christ and the apostles everywhere speak of the kingdom as future, and connected with another age, and of a totally different character from the state of things now existing. Not even the universal spread of the condition of the most favored Christian lands would satisfy the descriptions of the coming kingdom. That the kingdom has not come is admitted. Indeed, this is one of the claims of destructive criticism. The Kingdom prophecies, it is claimed, have not been fulfilled in nearly two thousand years. Boastings of a coming, victorious condition of the church are merely speculations, having no Scriptural foundation. If the church, either visible or invisible, or any state of things which it controls or inspires, is the kingdom, then the Kingdom predictions have proved abortive, and we are left with a Bible whose most solemn and greatest and most vital part is by the lapse of time shown to be fallacious. But on the view that this kingdom was and is still future and supernatural, we are on sure ground, and all the assaults of this latest and most mischievous of all attempts to undermine the faith of the people of God come to naught. Indeed, it but adds to the force of the proof of the truth of Scripture ; for it is itself an evidence of the fulfilment of the predictions of Scripture which were made as to these latter days. There is good also coming even out of the evil. For this destructive criticism while attacking the foundations of faith is forcing a new examination of the Messianic kingdom, and insisting upon the meaning intended by the writers.

These two phases of the kingdom are presented in the following Scripture : "And being asked by the Pharisees when the kingdom of God cometh, he answered them and said, The kingdom of God cometh not with observation: neither shall they say, Lo, here! or, there! for lo, the kingdom of God is within you [Margin, in the midst of you]. And he said unto the disciples, The days will come, when ye shall desire to see one of the days of the Son of man, and ye shall not see it. And they shall say to you, Lo, there! Lo, here! go not away, nor follow after them: for as the lightning, when it lighteneth out of the one part under the heaven, shineth unto the other part under heaven ; so shall the Son of man be in his day."[1]

Professor Hermann Cremer thus writes of the *Basilia*, or kingdom : —

"So far as the saving designs of God have already found their realization with and in Christ, it is said, 'The kingdom of God is within you'— compare John i. 26. 'In the midst of you standeth one whom ye know not; The kingdom of God is come upon you.' But so far as this realization first becomes manifest when Christ's work is completed, the kingdom of God is spoken of as yet to be revealed, with the tacit assumption that it can only take place after the appearance of Christ. In this sense it is future for Christ also. When therefore Christ says, ' My kingdom is not of this world,' his meaning is that the present order of things does not set forth the glory and saving purpose of God."[2]

[1] Luke xvii. 20–24.
[2] Biblico-Theological Lexicon of New Testament Greek, Edinburgh, 1872, pp. 111–113.

Dr. Auberlin thus comments upon this passage : —

"It is true that it was necessary for our Lord to oppose the carnal expectations of the nation, and to insist, with double emphasis, on the spiritual internal conditions of partaking in the kingdom; namely, repentance and faith. But he by no means dissolves the kingdom into mere inwardness; but it is to him, as Schmidt expresses it,[1] the divine order of things which is realized by him, the Messiah, and which develops itself from within outwardly. Thus the kingdom of Christ has different periods; it is come in Christ; it spreads in the world by internal, spiritual, hidden processes; but as a kingdom in the strict sense of the word, in royal glory, it shall only come with the *Parousia* of Christ, even as we are, according to Christ's command, to pray, even now, day by day, Thy kingdom come."[2]

We have in the letters to the seven churches the light thrown upon the attitude of Christ in his present state toward his people. It is the same as when he used the whip of small cords in the temple. It is Jehovah with his new Israel in chastening. Here are some of his messages of this kind: "Repent and do the first works; or else I will come to thee and will move thy candlestick out of its place, except thou repent. . . . Repent, therefore, or else I come to thee quickly, and I will make war against them with the sword of my mouth. . . . I will kill her children with death; and all the churches shall know that I am he that searcheth the reins and hearts; and I will give unto each of you according to your works. . . . I will come as a thief, and thou shalt not know what hour I will come upon thee. . . . Because thou art lukewarm and neither hot nor cold, I will spue thee out of my mouth." His parting message was, "As many as I love I rebuke and chasten." Christ has not changed. He is "the same yesterday, to-day, and forever." Nor has his method changed. He has often, since the days of the apostles, punished his people terribly, to the extent of sweeping away

---

[1] Bib. Theo. N. T. I., p. 325.
[2] "Daniel and the Revelation," Edinburgh, 1856, p. 324.

entire communities and churches. We may be assured the present church, unless she repents and returns to primitive Christianity, will not escape what Israel received for her apostasy, and also the apostolic churches and the whole of Christendom since.

The Roman empire long before its overthrow was professedly Christian. In 423 A. D., a law of Theodosius II, states there were no more pagans in the empire. It was upon this professed but worldly Christianity was poured out the vials of the barbarian invasion from the north. Following the destruction of paganism came in the sixth century the worship of saints and angels and relics, and following this second stage in the apostasy was sent the invasion of the Saracens. Later, following further decline of the faith, came the invasion of the Turks. The country of the prophets and apostles alike has been under this "abomination which maketh desolate" from that time to this. Christ has many ways of chastising his people, and we must not think the church of to-day is exempt from his usual course of procedure. This chastisement could come from several sources. The uprising so often spoken of as the social revolution, may be Christ's method of dealing with the church or it may come from without, from the heathen hordes, two thirds of the world, now fast arming for war.

In considering the work of Christ in the present age as to the world, we must note the purposes, the agencies selected, and the extent of the work. We shall then be able to see the ultimate plan involved. Christ's purpose is seen by recalling the great view presented by John in his gospel of Christ as the Saviour of the world, and the world-wide command given the apostles by the ascending Saviour. Christ's direction of the work of evangelization of the world is both direct and indirect. The latter is seen in his allowing the breaking out of persecution in Jerusalem at the death of Stephen by which they were all scattered abroad except the apostles. The twelve do not seem to have grasped the idea of a world-wide evangelization until sometime after Pentecost. They reproved Peter for going to the house of the Gentile Cornelius, and on his reporting the reception of the gospel by him and his house, and the outpouring of the Holy Ghost upon this company of Gentiles, they express their surprise, saying, "Then to the Gentiles also hath God granted repentance unto life."[1] The direct work of Christ for the world is seen in the mission of Paul. He was converted directly by Christ's own voice, and so comissioned and received his commission and a new revelation of the gospel. His life reads like a sequel to the life of Jesus.

Christ himself is not represented as engaging personally in seeking, following, and beseeching sinners to be at peace with God. He does this wholly through the believers and the agencies of the church. It is the Spirit and the Bride which say, Come. The order of the gospel is God the Father by Christ through the Holy Spirit in the believer, appealing to sinners by the truth to be reconciled to God through Jesus Christ. It is worthy of note in passing, that all the calls to sinners in this age to repentance are in the singular: "Him that cometh unto me," "He that believeth," "If any man sin," "If any man hear my voice." This indicates the nature of the gospel work. It is to be man by man, an individual call rather than national. The church gathers not by nations but by individuals.

The preparation of the world for the gospel was most remarkable. Greek philosophy had made this people keen to hear any new thing, and their own schools of philosophy were now losing their power over the minds of their followers. Politically and

[1] Acts xi. 18.

physically the world was ready for the rapid propagation of the message. It was practically under one government, and in a stable and peaceful state. The great Roman roads and lines of commerce went everywhere. The Israelite's place in the world's evangelization has been seen. There is clearly discernible a divine and universal plan in the preparation of the world for the gospel. The three great peoples of the world furnished their respective parts: Rome, the physical; Greece, intellectual; and Israel, the spiritual. Thus was prepared the threefold way for the gospel. All this helps us to see how the disciples of Christ literally fulfilled his parting message—"Preach the gospel to the whole creation." Paul tells us the gospel "was preached in all creation under heaven."[1] Pliny states that there was no family of men where the praises of Jesus were not sung. The whole world was evangelized. This, if we do not misread history, has been done again and again. The world has been more than once evangelized since the days of the apostles. We are now in the midst of such a worldwide movement at home and abroad, to which attention is often and well called. The hundreds of foreign missionary societies, with thousands of missionaries in every land; the thousands of other organizations of an auxiliary kind; the movement among young men, students, young people, and children; the publication of hundreds of millions of Bibles, and uncounted millions of Christian books and papers; the thousands of Christian educational institutions,—all are remarkable and peculiar to our day. There are still greater movements before us. The gospel is to be preached to all nations, and the Spirit is to be poured forth upon all flesh. In all this we see Christ directing his work and fulfilling his promise, "I am with you alway, even unto the end of the age."[2]

[1] Col. i. 23.   [2] Matt. xxviii. 20, margin.

The view of the world since Christ, presents a very mixed picture. It is not a story of constant victory of the gospel. The world, as has been seen, has been once, and we believe several times, evangelized. But in each case the revival was followed by a falling away. Sometimes this was an almost universal apostasy as in the case of the Roman church. The north of Africa, once Christianity's stronghold, is to-day Mohammedan. The lands preached over by the apostles are to-day in a state little better than heathenism, and we are sending missionaries to them. That part of the continent of Europe traversed by Paul with such zeal and love is to-day largely wrapped in papal superstition, and worst of all two thirds of the world is in pagan darkness, and all this after nineteen hundred years of gospel work begun by apostles and followed by the best and most self-sacrificing of earth. It is sometimes charged to the church that this state of affairs exists. Doubtless the church has not done her full duty, and as a body and as individuals we must all own our failure. But the blame cannot be laid wholly at the doors of the church. There is often much unjust and cruel censure of churches and ministers and Christians for the want of more success in converting the world or special localities to Christ. There have been places and times when all has been done by the church to save the surrounding mass, and yet all have not been converted. Not even apostles, with all their mighty power and miracles, could effect the conversion of all. Paul, and even Jesus himself, turned from many places, leaving them to the course they chose.

Any true faith in Christ must believe that he has been directing the affairs of the church and especially this part of his work during these nineteen hundred years. We must also believe that his plan is working all this time. Any other view than this would strip God of his power of control and leave his actings at the mercy of whatever mishaps might spring up in the path of progress. God lives and reigns, and all is working on in his great plan whether it agrees with our ideas of what ought to be or not. It is useful constantly to remember this: "My thoughts are not your thoughts, neither are your ways my ways, saith the Lord."[1] Christ fully declared such a state of affairs as we see existing now and during the past centuries. The predictions of himself and his apostles agree with this condition. There are reasons, deep and fundamental, lying in the very nature of things why this condition exists and will exist until the end of the age. It is not merely an arbitrary edict or the result of neglect by the church or any other adverse influences. The same great causes which we have seen operating from the beginning, operate still, and will until the whole great demonstration is finished.

The first great fact we must consider is the nature of that called "the world." There are three words so translated. These mean respectively, the age, the habitable earth, and mankind. The word is used in two senses: First, as we generally use it, in a neutral sense as to moral character; and second, as meaning something evil or defective. We have already considered Christ's relation as to his death and work for the world. But besides this world there is an evil age and an evil thing called "the world," and an evil spiritual influence corresponding to these. This age or world is spoken of by Paul as "this present evil world," and he urges us to "be not conformed to this world," and speaks of Satan as "the god of this world." He refers to its character, ruler, and effect in these words: "And you did he quicken, when ye were dead through your trespasses and sins, wherein aforetime ye walked according to the course

[1] Isa. lv. 8.

of this world, according to the prince of the power of the air, of the spirit that now worketh in the sons of disobedience."[1]

The contents of this world are thus described by John, "All that is in the world, the lust of the flesh and the lust of the eyes, and the vain glory of life, is not of the Father, but is of the world."[2] The world as a body of persons is spoken of in contrast with the church, and as in antagonism to it: "If the world hateth you, ye know that it hated me before it hated you. If ye were of the world, the world would love its own; but because ye are not of the world, but I have chosen you out of the world, therefore the world hateth you."[3] This world the Christian is warned against: "Love not the world, neither the things that are in the world. If any man love the world, the love of the Father is not in him."[4] It is evident from these scriptures that the world in this sense is of the satanic trinity,— "the world, the flesh, and the devil," and can no more be converted than can the devil himself.

Another great principle announced by Christ is in these words: "Wide is the gate and broad is the way, that leadeth to destruction, and many be they that enter thereby. For narrow is the gate and straitened the way, that leadeth unto life, and few there be that find it."[5] There is no intimation in any of the after words of Christ or the apostles that the broad way was to become any narrower or the narrow way broader, or that the respective number of journeyers was to be changed. All the history of the church, and all our observation as individuals, confirm this account of the character and dimensions of these two ways and their companies. The New Testament writers always speak of the church as a little flock, sheep among wolves, wheat among tares, as pilgrims and

---

[1] Eph. ii. 1, 2. [2] 1 John ii. 16. [3] John xv. 18, 19.
[4] 1 John ii. 15. [5] Matt. vii. 13, 14.

strangers, and hold out no promise of earthly aggrandizement, either individually or as a church in numerical or political influence. They are pointed to another age and life as the time and place of reward. The course of the church in this age, Christ everywhere declares, is to be like his own. He reached the cross, so will his church. The church is to follow the Master to Calvary before it can follow him to enthronement.

There are not only reasons in the foregoing Scriptural passages for the fact of the small number converted so far in the world, but they form an irrefutable argument for the statement that the remainder of the age will show the same results. If in nineteen hundred years the world has not been all converted, it is not more probable that even another such period would show different results. The same agencies which have prevented the whole world's conversion still exist. Nor would the conversion of the present or any future generation be the conversion of the world, for the most of the world are dead. The eighteen centuries of those who lived since Christ, are beyond the gospel's reach. Nor is there any assurance that the world would remain as a world in a state of conversion. The history of the past points to great apostasies following great turnings to God. But the words of Christ and of the apostles are conclusive upon this point. There is not one word in all the promises of Christ or the New Testament writers, promising the conversion of the world in this age.

There are certain scriptures which speak of the prevalence of the gospel and righteousness. These must either be placed according to their chronological data, or if no such definite time is mentioned, then in harmony with those which are so dated. They all refer to future times. Some of those most common used are manifestly for a future age, as for example, the following well-known and often quoted passage:

"Ask of me and I will give to thee the heathen for thine inheritance and the uttermost parts of the earth for thy possession. Thou shalt break them with a rod of iron; thou shalt dash them in pieces like a potter's vessel."[1] The latter part certainly does not refer to the work of Christ in the gospel age. The promise our Lord made was: "I, if I be lifted up from the earth, will draw all men unto myself. But this he said signifying by what manner of death he should die."[2] This has not been fulfilled as yet, and the promise does not specify a time. We must therefore interpret it in accordance with other more definite promises. It could not have been intended to apply to the succeeding nineteen hundred years, for they have come and gone and the promise is not fulfilled. We look for its fulfilment in another age.

The objections raised against this view from supposed necessary conditions, as the work of the Holy Spirit, are all answered by the fact that the Spirit carries out the purposes of God. The Holy Spirit can convert the world to God, if it is God's will, just as he could have converted Paul; but he did not. Paul was converted by the appearance of Christ himself. So if it is the will of God to convert the world by other agencies than those we are seeing, we have no right or reason to object.

It is not derogatory to the work of Christ or the Holy Spirit to see in this age of the gospel only what Scripture declares is the purpose of it. Some have conceived false impressions as to the purpose of the gospel dispensation. They think it is to bring about a full and complete victory for Christ and all his cause, and that by the present agencies. There is such a victory coming as sure as God is and reigns, but not now nor by our feeble arms or means. We are not to be the means of seating Christ upon the throne of universal dominion. We are the recipients

[1] Ps. ii. 8, 9.   [2] John xii. 32.

of his bounty, saved by grace, and are "his workmanship, his tillage," a flock to be fed and guarded, the bride to be sanctified and honored. We are not to crown Christ, but he is to crown us; we are not to bring him a victory, but he is to bring us a victory. The world is not to be subdued by us, even through the gospel, but by himself or rather by God for him as the above scripture declares.

Some testimonies to this view of the Scriptural truth are given. Calvin wrote, "There is no reason why any person should expect the conversion of the world." John Knox said, "To reform the face of the whole earth, which never was, nor yet shall be till that righteous King and Judge appear for the restitution of all things." Luther said, "The older the world, the worse." Dr. Luthardt writes as follows:—

"The path of the church of Jesus Christ is like that of her Lord and Saviour — through the cross to the crown. Let her know; let her comfort herself thereby." [1]

Dr. Robert Patterson writes:—

"If we are to enjoy any period of outward peace during his absence; if his church is to be delivered from the assaults of the world; if there is to be an age of purity when the tares shall not grow among the wheat; or if at his coming he shall be welcomed by the population of an earth filled with the glory of the Lord; even if he be able to find faith on the earth, it will be to him a most welcome surpise. In all his discourses and parables there is not the least hint we are to hope for any period of peace or glory before his coming."

Bishop Ryle thus writes:—

"I believe the world will never be completely converted to Christianity by any existing agency before the end. The wheat and tares will grow together until the harvest. When the end comes, it will find the earth in much the same state it was before the flood."

Professor Chas. A. Briggs referring to the Presbyterian Standards, writes:—

[1] "Saving Truths of Christianity," p. 308.

"The current doctrine of a millennium in the future before the advent of Christ is another extra-confessional doctrine for which there is no basis in the Westminster Standards."[1]

"The conversion of the Jews and a more glorious condition of the church before the advent predicted in the New Testament has been improperly associated with the millennium. The idea of a future millennium before the advent is ruled out by the Westminster Symbols."[2]

Dorner writes as follows: —

"The New Testament does not countenance a theory which assumes merely a quiet, steady, growing interpenetration or subjugation of the whole world by Christianity in the course of history. This is the optimistic view which is unprepared for eclipses of the sun in the firmament of the church. The New Testament foretells catastrophes to the life of the church so that in this respect also it is a copy of the life of Christ."[3]

Dr. Robert J. Breckinridge writes: —

"As a question of mere doctrine, no reason can be assigned which tends to limit the period of the struggle between good and evil in this world or to determine any positive issue for it. It is only by express revelation we could know that the kingdom of God will triumph completely and possess the whole earth, and I have already said that the Scripture seems to me to teach that in order to this triumph that kingdom must assume a new form, and exist under another dispensation. Whoever will assert that the church of God, independently of some divine change in the elements of the problem which it has been working out under its gospel form for more than eighteen centuries, can have a future very materially different from her past history, or that the human race can have a future spiritual history essentially variant from that which is past, without some further and marvelous interposition of God, will in each instance, it appears to me, contradict the whole current of divine revelation, and disregard the absolute economy of the plan of salvation. The augmentation of the present saving operation of the divine spirit is not that supernatural change in the element of the problem, is not that further interposition of God which will extinguish sin and

---

[1] "Whither," New York, 1890, p. 200.
[2] "Messiah of the Apostles," New York, 1895, pp. 347, 349.
[3] "System of Christian Doctrine," Vol. 4, p. 389.

misery in the world, and give to the saints millennial glory and reign with Christ."[1]

We are now to examine the results of this mixed state of affairs which we have seen exists in the individual believer, in Israel, in the church, and in the world, and see what plan Christ has in our age, and its final outcome. We can see first of all that no better state or world could exist for the development of individual character. We have seen the fight within the believer, the struggle between the flesh and the spirit. The same struggle is met also without. The opposing elements which the Christian meets, the struggle he is called upon to make, the final and constant victory he may have, all furnish the gymnasia he needs to strengthen the gifts and the graces of the spirit. By this life of constant turning away from sin and self and to God, he is so fixed in holiness that he becomes permanently holy.

What has been said of the individual believer is true also of the church. We look back to the eternal past and see the divine plan under consideration and that the great object of Christ's care was the church. To train this body for eternal service and enjoyment, was the great purpose of all the divine plan. The statement of the forerunner of Christ, of his plan, of his work as to the church, is in these words: "Whose fan is in his hand, and he will thoroughly cleanse his threshing floor; and he will gather his wheat into the garner, but the chaff he will burn up with unquenchable fire."[2] The sifting process is going on. Everything adverse contributes to this end. Even as to the delusions of Satan, Paul writes: "For there must be also heresies [margin, factions] among you, that they which are approved may be made manifest among you."[3]

---

[1] "Knowledge of God Subjectively Considered," New York, 1869, p. 677. [2] Matt. iii. 12. [3] 1 Cor. xi. 19.

The divided state of the church seems lamentable, and yet it could exist, as the world and as human nature are, in no other state. The church was once organically one and never was it more corrupt. The days of the Church supremacy were the days of the beginning of her spiritual downfall. In those days were developed all the evils which have since existed. The prizes of power in a universal church were and would be so great, that human nature, even in the church, could not resist the temptation to self-seeking and self-aggrandizement as we see it in almost every sect and party however small. Ecclesiastical ambition and love of gain has stooped to any means of gaining its end. Therefore Christ as at Babel, has sent confusion of tongues, that this idolatrous purpose may be thwarted. The sects of to-day are a necessary means of preserving the spirituality of the invisible church. In the same way the truth has been preserved. The doctrine which one sect has ignored has been emphasized by another. Some have been raised up to bear aloft some forgotten truth. In the days of some powerful and worldly sect some humble party has been called out to preach the gospel to the masses, and has been the means of calling believers back to more pure doctrine, life, and word.

The vitality of the church on earth all this time is an amazing feature of its history. Every device of man and the devil has been exercised to exterminate it. It has been decimated by persecutions and enswathed in the smothering influence of godless secular power. It has been exposed to the ridicule of the world by the doings of false members and by the shortcomings of true ones. It has been almost destroyed by world-wide apostasies and its doctrine corrupted by the admixture of abominable heresies. It has been divided and redivided and split into hundreds of warring factions and sects, and it has been poisoned and enervated by worldliness and invaded and attacked by every form of unbelief. There has been scarcely any way of destruction it has not faced, and yet it still exists. Christ ever has had his care over it. It has come through all, and will until it emerges from this world of conflict into the kingdom of God eternal.

In respect to evangelizing the world also, we can see how the state of the world, as we have seen it, and as it is to continue, is the best condition for the offers of the gospel to secure true believers. In a state such as existed in the time of Constantine, and as exists to-day in limited localites, where religion is a matter of great repute and of gain, the converts, so-called, multiply with great rapidity, but they are of questionable quality. All this, by a state of humility and obscurity for the church, is avoided. As the quicksilver attracts the gold, so the gospel under such circumstances attracts the true believer, and the false reject it.

The world has been greatly blessed temporally by the gospel of Christ. This is a fact to which attention is often called and is self-evident. It was in the plan of Christ that this should be so. The promise to Abraham was: "In thee and in thy seed shall all the families of the world be blessed." The seed Paul tells us was Christ. One need only compare those lands and communities in which the gospel is preached in purity with those where it is perverted or where it does not exist, and the fact is clearly shown. The evils which afflict man, especially the poor, are far less than before Christ. The world is better behaved. Vice is more concealed and so far made less an example and is more under reproof. The law came to restrain transgressions, so did the gospel, only far more effectively. Great evils entrenched in centuries of life and supported by wealth and power have gone down under the silent secret power of the influence of the gospel. The world could not have existed as it was unless the restraining influences of the gospel had come. This is but a temporal and a temporary benefit it is true, but it is a benefit and was in the plan of Christ. The people of Christ have been, as he said they would be, the salt of the earth as well as the lights of the world. They have preserved and illuminated mankind.

The whole plan of Christ, as to the individual, the church, and the whole world in this and every age, is described in this parable of Christ's: "So is the kingdom of God as if a man should cast seed upon the earth; and should sleep and rise night and day, and the seed should spring up and grow he knoweth not how. The earth beareth fruit of herself; first the blade, then the ear, then the full corn in the ear. But when the fruit is ripe straightway he putteth forth the sickle, because the harvest is come."[1] The work of Christ in nature is everywhere illustrative of his work in the affairs of life and grace. The great lesson of this parable is that every age is a sowing, and that each age is left to develop its own results, and when these have come to full fruition, the results are gathered in a harvest. So it was as we have seen in the age before the flood and also in Israel. The latter were given every opportunity, and when they had accomplished all they could, the age was brought to a close, and the seed saved for a new sowing. Our age is no exception to this great law of divine action. The sowing has been made. The age is to be permitted to develop and to show its nature as all others were permitted. It is essentially different from those which preceded it as to the forms of development, although not as to nature. The great demonstration has reached another stage. The world was tried under license, and the results were seen in the age before the flood. In the Israelitish age, law was tried and the results gathered. In our age, grace is being shown, and man is being tried under a great display of the mercy and love of God. The most searching of all

[1] Mark iv. 26-29.

tests is the gospel. As has been seen, it tells by the acceptance or rejection of the hearer, whether there is true desire for salvation and to do the will of God; so for the world at large. To this age has been sent the gospel of grace. All has been done for man's salvation. He is offered free grace. It is a searching test of the nature of the world to be one day shown to the universe for their instruction.

The world will have to be brought to the end of its resources for self-saving before it will accept the gospel of Christ. It is true of the world as it is true of the individual. We come to Christ from our sense of need. So all the mooted plans for remedying the evils of life without the gospel will be given an opportunity to show what they can do. Material civilization, especially in the newer countries and communities in the flush of achievement, is the much-hoped-for means of bringing the age of universal prosperity and contentment. The improvements of living, the multiplication of means of amusement, the increase of wealth, the discovery of remedies of disease, or the prevention of them, rapid means of transportation,—these are expected to produce all that is needed to make man all he wants to be or have. All this will be given the fullest trial by being allowed to come and be actually tried.

The great hope of our age is intellectual power. With this it believes it will yet transform earth and make this world a paradise for man. Sin is to be educated out of man and the world, the influence of music, art, culture, and education are relied upon for this change. Political improvement will cooperate to this end. Great evils are to be eradicated, and with them will go temptation, and with the temptation will go sin itself. All this is to have a fair, full trial. It is needless to say to those who see things as the Scriptures delineate them, that all this must fail. Intellectual power is not the saving power. This has been abundantly demonstrated in the past. The most intellectual race who ever lived on earth, not excepting any now existing, was the Greek. Lecky writes of them as follows:—

"Within the narrow limits and scanty population of the Greek states arose men who, in almost every conceivable form of genius, in philosophy, in epic, dramatic, and lyric poetry, in written and spoken eloquence, in statesmanship, in sculpture, in painting, and probably also in music, attained almost or altogether the highest limits of human perfection."[1]

Galton has written of the same race thus:—

"The millions of all Europe, breeding as they have done for the subsequent two thousand years, have never produced the equals of Socrates and Phidias. . . . The average ability of the Athenian race is, on the lowest possible estimate, very nearly two grades higher than our own; that is about as much as our race is above that of the African negro. This estimate, which may seem prodigious to some, is confirmed by the quick intelligence of the Athenian commonality, before whom literary works were recited, and works of art exhibited, of a far more severe character, than could possibly be appreciated by the average of our race, the caliber of whose intellect is easily gauged by glancing at the contents of a railway bookstall."[2]

Yet this race with all its power did not and could not save itself. The character of the Greek is well known. Immorality was not even apologized for. Unchastity was the essential element of the religion of Greece at this very time. The priestesses of her temples were prostitutes, and sixty thousand of them were required for the temple of Venus.

All forms of government will have been tried, all social systems, all reforms, the full development of modern science will come with its material benefits in invention and appliances of every kind. All forms of religion, too, are to be given their day as many have had already. New forms of belief and worship imitating all more or less closely the religion of Christ but

---

[1] "History European Morals," London, 1877; Vol. I, p. 418.
[2] "Hereditary Genius," London, 1869, p. 320.

without the cross of Christ, will arise and are already arising. Socialism in some form will undoubtedly come and be given its opportunity to make an Eden of earth without the regenerating power of the Holy Spirit and the gospel of the crucified Christ. The great demonstration will never need to be repeated when it is over. All future ages will read the story of man's trial and failure and will profit by it. The possibilities of self-saving and self-keeping will have been exhausted.

This outlook will be perplexing unless an intelligent and Scriptural view is had of the purposes of Christ in our age. It is better to know the truth and have the right motives operating within us, than to be swayed by false views of an impossible state of things which will in the certain failure leave us disappointed.

Dr. Auberlin writes on this subject as follows:—

> "It is not good that our modern theology scarcely ever views the present time in the light of Biblical prophecy. In all historical works or philosophical remarks on the times, much is said about modern anti-christianity; and there is no instruction given the laity how to view this phenomenon in connection with divine prophecy. . . . What is bringing thousands from Christianity, and preventing others from coming to a belief in a full and true Christianity, is nothing less but a respect for these intellectual powers which rule in these days of modern science and culture. But the worst thing is that scarcely any one sees the depth of the evil. For even in the Old Testament — the Old Covenant — the chief and most active aim of the false prophets was to make the people believe that their state was not so bad, and that the judgments of God were not near. Therefore the fundamental and oft-repeated charge against them was, 'They heal the hurt of my people slightly and say it is peace, it is peace, when there is no peace.'"[1]

There must ever be kept in view the great difference between the ending of our age and the final outcome on which we are to fix our eyes. A short-

[1] "Daniel and Revelation," Edinburgh, 1856, p. 312.

sighted view is either false or discouraging. Complete victory comes only at the end.

The present age of the church has to do with the beings of the other world as the following scripture teaches: "To the intent that now unto the principalities and the powers in the heavenly places might be made known through the church the manifold wisdom of God."[1] This he writes was one purpose of the grace given him to preach the gospel. The Epistle to the Hebrews states that we are compassed about by a great cloud of witnesses. This world is a theater of grace. Paul writes he was a spectacle to men and angels. Peter tells: "Which things angels desire to look into."[2] The reference is to the preaching of the gospel. The cherubim are represented bending over the mercy seat and looking down in wonder and reverence upon the type of sprinkled blood. Daniel hears in vision a holy one asking, "How long shall be the vision concerning the continual burnt offering and the transgression that maketh desolate, to give both the sanctuary and the host to be trodden underfoot?" and again another asks, "How long shall it be to the end of these wonders?"[3] In the Apocalypse the heavenly hosts are continually represented as breaking out into songs in the accomplishment of the divine plan. All which goes to show that we are actors upon a stage about which are gathered in most intense interest the heavenly beings, looking down and learning by us and our doings, and above all, by the gospel we are given and the grace shown us of the love of God and the grace of our Lord Jesus Christ.

The apostles, as stated at the beginning of this chapter, preached a future Christ. They did not regard his work in this age as complete. They pointed to a coming age and victory. We must ever remem-

[1] Eph. iii. 10.   [2] 1 Peter i. 12.   [3] Dan viii. 13; xii. 5, 6.

ber that this age is only one of several, and its results are not a finality. Other ages preceded this and were only preparatory to it, as Peter tells us: "To whom it was announced that not unto themselves but unto you did they minister these things."[1] This view of the plan of Christ is necessary to an understanding of Christ in his present work. There is nothing more injurious in the contemplation of the purposes of God than a limited view. It narrows one's ideas, dwarfs faith, and dims hope.

This view is plainly taught in this scripture quoted or referred to eight times in the New Testament: "The Lord said unto my Lord, Sit thou at my right hand, until I make thine enemies thy footstool."[2] This does not refer to the gospel work of winning men to loving relationship to Christ. Such work is never so described. It is conquest. It is victory over enemies. Christ's attitude to the future is here described. He is expectant and waiting. He is at the right hand of God. This is the place of the heir, the King by right rather than the King by actual possession. This is the nature of Christ's present kingship. As has been shown, his title in the church is "Lord," and his view before the world is on the cross. The kingdom is a future condition as manifested. To this Christ looks forward as we do.

One of the purposes which occupied the attention of Christ in his present state is intimated in the well-known scripture: "In my Father's house are many mansions; if it were not so I would have told you; for I go to prepare a place for you."[3] The preparation of this place was part of the work of Christ in this present age. The One who wrought so in creation to prepare a place for the human race now works for a higher and dearer object,— the home of his bride. This place Christ has gone to prepare must not be identified with the so-called middle state, where the spirits of the

[1] 1 Peter i. 12.   [2] Ps. cx. 1.   [3] John xiv. 2.

departed are now and until the resurrection. It is some special place out of the many mansions in the house of God. This comes into consideration in the closing chapters.

CHAPTER VI.

THE KING OF KINGS AND LORD OF LORDS.

CHRIST IN THE DAY OF THE LORD.

ALL Scriptures tell of a coming DAY. It is the theme alike of Old Testament prophets and New Testament apostles. It is the summing up of all history and the focal point of all prophecy. It is described by the successive writers in terms of cumulative description. Each, as though he received the picture made by his predecessor, adds to it, and hands it down to his successor. The day grows from mere mention to outline, and from that to full detail, and ends in a panorama of figures and events which move along the narrative and produce upon the reader almost the effect of the original revelation.

Every event of Scripture seems to be connected directly or indirectly with the Day of the Lord. The flood is a type of its coming, and the destruction of Sodom is declared to be a foretaste of it. The plagues of Egypt are repeated in the plagues of that day, and the deliverance song of Israel is the song of larger Israel at a greater sea. The victories of Israel at Megiddo are types of still greater victories of the church at the end. Indeed, the whole of Israel's history is woven into it. The defeats of Israel's enemies and the judgments upon them are used as materials to construct the picture of the last great judgments upon the enemies of Christ. So also the glories of Israel are found within the framework of the story. Their capital city, the ritual of worship, the eldership, the tabernacle, and the temple are part of the scene. Not only Israel but all nations furnish their share of the view, and when it is analyzed, it is found to be the converging point of the world's histories.

All the prophecies seem to await their final fulfilment at that time. The first promise, "The seed of the woman shall bruise the serpent's head," is a prediction of that day. The message of the first prophet, Enoch, has this for its theme. So through all the Old Testament prophecies, whatever their other messages, all find space for some reference to the Day of the Lord. Jesus himself gave full details of it, and all his apostles who have left us writings, and all other writers of the New Testament gave space to this great theme. The Bible ends in a book wholly devoted to it. It is a mingled scene of glory and terror. All nature's beauties are exhausted to describe its glories and its awful phenomena,— clouds, storms, earthquakes, darkness, pillars of smoke, fire, are gathered into the picture. All that human life and history can furnish — voices, trumpets, thrones, great assizes, vast armies, battles, are called for to bring to the imagination a picture of surpassing grandeur.

The great characteristic of the Day of the Lord is that it is an inburst upon earth of the supernatural. The other world breaks in on this. Angels are seen. Great signs unaccountable to man appear. Voices are heard from the sky. Its supernatural character must ever be kept distinctly in mind. The supernatural will be as common as the natural. It will be constantly in some form before the world. It is not an unknown thing that this should be so. The people of Israel had such displays. The ages of law, prophets, and the gospel were introduced by supernatural outbursts, and so will be this greater age.

The coming of such a time has been a tradition or belief of all peoples and ages. The view of the peoples of the earth has been that there would come a supernatural being from the skies and call the earth to judgment and then destroy it by fire. This was the belief of Greek philosophers, particularly the Stoics. The sibylline oracles are full of it and relate substantially the Scriptural account as they no doubt received it. It was taught by Zoroaster to his followers. The Hindus and Egyptians had also such a belief. The fable of the Phœnix had reference to this. It was found among the Aztecs who expected a coming One who would put all things right. It is still almost universally looked for. Every nation has its own peculiar ideas of its nature and coming. It is spoken of as the "end of the world," the "Day of Judgment," and properly so, although not in the narrow sense in which these terms are used.

The apostles presented a double view of the Day of the Lord. They preached it as affecting the church and the world. To each they presented it as the one great motive. To the church they held it up as the great incentive to the cultivation of all graces and the reward for all services and the compensation for all sacrifices. They regarded it as something extremely desirable, and urged the saints to "look for and hasten unto the coming of the Day of God." They kept it before the minds of the churches constantly. Every Epistle is full of it. There is no subject which is more purifying and elevating than this. The study of the world above, and events to come, is set before us in the Scriptures as the stimulant to holy frames of mind and earnest life : "Seek the things that are above, where Christ is, seated on the right hand of God. Set your mind on the things that are above, not on the things that are upon the earth."[1] *Augustine* says, "The love of things temporal can only be overcome by a certain pleasurableness in things eternal."

It is the exaltation of these glories of the future which is needed in this materialistic age. The pre-

[1] Col. iii. 2, 3.

sentation of these realities will prove the corrective for the worldliness of the age of sensuousness in which we live. The church must be made to see the greatness of the future life and world as the apostles and the prophets saw it. The future now has little attractive power. This age of comfort and conveniences is characterized by unbelief in, or undesire for, the things of hereafter. We are so engaged in securing for ourselves and others a heaven here by means of our improvements of material and intellectual and social kind, that we are indifferent to any future heaven. The bright pictures of the word are neglected in our day as never before. Only at funerals are they alluded to, and at other times are listened to with heavy hearts as something for which we must forego the present. A great loss has come to the church from the neglect of this great incentive. The result is seen in so minimizing the eternal rewards, and unduly exalting the temporal benefits of religion that the gain of salvation hereafter is in some a thing almost forgotten or even despised. There is little left of hereafter but a dim idea of a mysterious state which is only accepted as a last resort and as an alternative from a worse fate. This neglect of the things of the hereafter amounts almost to a heresy or a great apostasy.

To the world the apostle preached the Day of the Lord in all its terrors. The apostles did not preach hell specifically. The word does not occur in the Acts or Epistles except incidentally. They dwell upon the coming of Christ, the resurrection, the Judgment, the wrath of God, and the destruction of the world by fire, as warnings and incentives to repentance and faith in Christ. The narrowing of all this to the special place or fact called "hell," is one cause of the misunderstanding of the nature and justice of the punishment of sin. It will be objected that this is the Christ of power and not of grace. It must not be forgotten that Christ nowhere declares himself as confining his work to the operations of grace. This is the great element in his acting in our age. But the great feature of Christ's acting in the Day of the Lord is power and justice. Wrath is as real and as holy as love. When Scripture says God is love, it does not say he is nothing else. There is a sense in which love is all inclusive, but such love is not the sentimental thing generally understood by the word to-day. "Our God is a consuming fire" is also written by inspiration of the Holy Spirit.

This whole subject, Eschatology, the Science of the Last Things,— is the most neglected department of Bible study to-day. The general view is shut up to "dying and going to heaven and after that the general judgment." Few venture beyond that bare outline. In fact the whole subject is, in the minds of many, in a state of utter confusion. Works on Eschatology of a thorough and systematic kind are few. Many do not know what to believe upon the subject, and therefore lose the comfort and the power to comfort others by it. Yet this is one of the most voluminously treated subjects in Scripture. In the New Testament one verse in twenty deals with it, and the events are described with great minuteness. It is a difficult subject when approached with preconceived opinions or systems to be affected by it. But, if studied in a simple manner with a mind willing to receive what Scripture teaches regardless of the consequences to one's favorite views *or reputation*, light will come. That it is difficult is reason for more study and not less. It is true there is great difference of opinion upon this subject, but so there is on all other subjects; and this is no good reason for neglecting this or any subject, but rather the more reason why it should be considered, and the truth found. Under the persevering study of many diligent students, the whole is assuming form, and the state of the light upon it is far greater now than ever before. In this respect the prediction of Daniel is being fulfilled: "But thou, O Daniel, shut up the words and seal the book even to the time of the end; many shall run to and fro, and knowledge shall be increased."[1] The running to and fro is investigation of the Scriptures by study as well as the general travel and enlightenment.

One reason of the failure to understand the predictions of Scripture has been the system of interpretation in vogue, which is known as spiritualizing, or, more correctly described, the interpreting of Scripture in a figurative manner. Bishop Ryle writes:—

"I believe that the literal sense of the Old Testament prophecies has been far too much neglected by the churches, and is far too much neglected in the present day, and that under the mistaken system of spiritualizing and accommodating Bible language, Christians have too often missed its meaning."

Bishop Jeremy Taylor wrote:—

"In all the interpretations of Scripture the literal sense is to be preserved and chosen, unless there is evident cause to the contrary."

Tyndall said:—

"The greatest cause of this captivity and decay of faith, and this blindness wherein we are now, sprang first from allegories; for Origen and the doctors of his time drew all Scripture into allegories insomuch that twenty doctors expounded one text twenty different ways."

Sir Isaac Newton wrote:—

"About the time of the end, in all probability, a body of men will be raised up, who will turn their attention to the prophecies, and insist upon the literal interpretation in the midst of much clamor and opposition."

This is the very issue between the evangelical and unevangelical denominations to-day. We affirm and

[1] Dan. xii. 4.

they deny the literal statements as to the divinity of Christ, his miracles, his resurrection, and ascent, and the descent of the Holy Spirit. To allow spiritualizing on these, as might be claimed with as much reason, would be to surrender all we hold dear.

Certain scriptures have been used to support this so-called spiritualizing system. One of these is, "The letter killeth, but the spirit giveth life."[1] Examination of the context of this verse will show that Paul is not dealing with systems of interpretation here. He is contrasting the law and the gospel, and by "the letter" refers to the law, and by "the spirit" to the gospel and its power. He is showing the superiority of the work of the gospel to that of the law. He shows what he elsewhere plainly teaches,—that the law kills, while the gospel gives life, because through it the Spirit works. The passage is as follows: "Our sufficiency is from God; who also made us sufficient as ministers of a new covenant: not of the letter, but of the spirit: for the letter killeth, but the spirit giveth life. But if the ministration of death, written and engraven on stones, came with glory, so that the children of Israel could not look steadfastly upon the face of Moses for the glory of his face; which glory was passing away: how shall not rather the ministration of the spirit be with glory?"[2] Here the "letter" is the same as that "written and engraven on stones," which was the law. The "new covenant" is the gospel. It is the former "letter," or law, which kills, and the gospel, or "new covenant," which gives life. The same antithesis is seen in the use of these terms by Paul again in another place: "But now we have been discharged from the law, having died to that wherein we were holden: so that we serve in newness of the spirit, and not in oldness of the letter."[3] Here he uses "letter" as referring to the law. Another text relied upon to support this system is the saying of Christ: "It is

[1] 2 Cor. iii. 6.   [2] 2 Cor. iii. 6–8.   [3] Rom. vii. 6.

the Spirit that quickeneth ; the flesh profiteth nothing ; the words that I have spoken unto you are spirit, and are life."[1] The antithesis here is between the flesh and the spirit and not words and spirit. There is no reference to interpretations of any kind. In fact a meaning the very opposite from the view antagonized could be drawn from this scripture, for it says plainly that *the words* are spirit and life.

Predictive scripture has also come to be neglected by reason of disgust at the extravagances of some who have given study to it. This reason would, if applied, also shut us out of all Bible study; for every truth has been carried to extravagant extremes by some. Nor are we to be moved by the fear of consequences. God, who gave the scripture, takes all the consequences, and so may we. The first question for an honest seeker to ask, is, "What is truth?" and follow the quest until he finds it.

Undoubtedly this attempt will, as others, show many points for criticism. The expositor of predictive prophecy subjects himself more than any other to such criticism. It is a most mysterious sphere in which we are feeling our way as with a light in a dark place, as Peter tells us. There are many conflicting views before the student. There is needed in both expounder and reader much patience. We are all eager to know, and all intensely and personally interested in the events of this great future. Only sound exegesis and the illumination of the Holy Spirit can give us light. In this spirit, feeling it is a vast and mysterious and awful subject, far beyond any of us as yet, the author would venture to add the results of many years of study of the Scriptures and examination of many authorities upon this subject, to the sum of knowledge obtained.

The great prophet of the coming age was John. He was the nearest to Jesus of the apostolic band, and

[1] John vi. 63.

probably the youngest. He was mightiest in the greatest of all graces. John was able to climb to that point which Paul declares was the summit of Christian experience — "The greatest of these is love." He apprehended the pure gospel as seen in the character of the evangel written by him. Christ in John's gospel is for the world. The view of Christ in the Apocalypse is also for the world. The Revelation is unique among the books of the Bible. It is as different from the rest of the New Testament as the New is from the Old. Lange says: "As the Bible stands alone among the books of the world, so does the Apocalypse among the books of the Bible." It is like a third testament. It has upon the one who reads it earnestly, some of the effect of the first giving of it, and this apart from the understanding of it. The book is supernatural and produces a supernatural effect. There is no book so verified as the Revelation. It is the direct communication of Jesus Christ himself, the only words dictated by him to a scribe and ordered to be committed to writing.

The Apocalypse opens with this promise: "Blessed is he that readeth and they that hear the words of the prophecy and keep the things which are written therein; for the time is at hand."[1] Christ himself closes it with these words — his last message: "I testify unto every man that heareth the words of the prophecy of this book, If any man shall add unto them, God shall add unto him the plagues which are written in this book; and if any man shall take away from the words of the book of this prophecy, God shall take away his part from the tree of life, and out of the holy city, which are written in this book."[2] This is a warning against fanaticism on the one hand, and faithlessness on the other. To "add unto them" is to give them impious and extravagant interpretations. Setting times and seasons for the end of the world and

[1] Rev. i. 3.   [2] Rev. xxii. 17, 18.

other events connected with it, or declaring utter wrath unmixed with mercy as the doom of all in this time, founding sects and parties upon it, and claiming to be the parties therein meant,—all such are adding to the things written therein, and will meet the certain fate of having added to them "the plagues which are written in this book." On the other hand, taking away from the words of this prophecy also meets its penalty. It is a taking away to disparage the study of the book, or to despise this class of subjects in the Scripture, all of which are by inspiration. To neglect such a book after such solemn promises and warnings is surely exposing oneself to the threat therein contained. To make these things in the book mean less than they are intended is also to bring oneself within the warning. Such are all systems of interpretation which lighten the solemn warnings herein, and make them mean anything or nothing according to notions or interests.

The use of the various names of Christ in the Apocalypse is significant. The personal, official title, "Jesus Christ," only occurs in the introduction by John.[1] It seems only to serve the purpose of identification of the Christ of the Day of the Lord with the historical Jesus and the Christ of the Epistles. The name "Jesus" occurs more often. It is found in the opening and closing paragraphs and in the body of the prophecy. It is always used in connection with the testimony, patience, or martyrdom of the saints, or the faith and testimony of Jesus. It is, then, the title of the time of trial. "Lord Jesus" is used by John alone in his closing prayer and benediction. It is the title as noted of the present age. The name "Christ" occurs only in connection with the triumph of the millennial kingdom.[2] This, then, is the title for the time of victory, and points forward to it.

[1] Rev. i. 1, 2.   [2] Rev. xi. 15; xii. 10; xx. 4, 6.

Christians are then by their very name, professors of the coming kingdom of Christ. "The Christ" and the Pauline title, "Christ Jesus," do not occur. The first is, as we noted, Israel's peculiar title, and the latter the evangelistic title of the present age of gospel. To none of the seven churches does Christ reveal himself by any of his proper names. The great name, "King of kings and Lord of lords," previously used by Paul in his prophetic doxology,[1] finds its significance in the Old Testament use. It was applied to Nebuchadnezzar by Daniel and Ezekiel, and to Artaxerxes, one of his successors.[2] Its significance comes from the Babylonian king's world-wide sovereignty and the place Christ takes as the successor of the world powers in the vision of the stone smiting the image, representing the long term of the reign of the world empires, of which Nebuchadnezzar was first and head. It only refers to Christ's earthly kingship, however.

The peculiar title of Christ in the Apocalypse is given by himself alone: "I am the Alpha and the Omega, saith the Lord God, which is and which was, and which is to come, the Almighty."[3] With this he opens the Revelation, and with the same he closes the last of the works of sin and opens the New Jerusalem. The alphabetical letters identify Christ as the "Word." The first and last alphabetical letters show he is the complete Word or manifestation and message of God. It also includes Christ as the Creator and the Jehovah of the Old Testament. It is not the name of Christ in the eternal future, however, nor in the eternal past. The title is the designation of Christ in his work from the beginning of creation to the end of time.

The name applied to Christ more often than all others together in the Revelation is "The Lamb."

---

[1] 1 Tim. vi. 15.   [2] Dan. ii. 37 ; Ezra xxvi; vii. 12
[3] Rev. i. 8.

This is, however, a different form of the word from that used elsewhere. It is the diminutive meaning, "the little lamb." The same word in its diminutive form is used by Christ in his word to Peter, "Feed my little lambs." It represents Christ in his personal character, and expresses the great mission of Christ both in its Godward and manward aspects. It expresses first the perfect submission of Christ in trustful yielding up of all in whole and final consecration to the will of God as a perfect sacrifice. It represents Christ as God's substitute for man upon the altar of justice. It expresses the victory of redemption. It is as the Lamb that Christ is praised by the heavenly hosts in the opening of the Apocalypse, and as the Lamb, Christ obtains the right and power to open and administer the sealed book of the future. It is "the wrath of the Lamb" which is most feared by the impenitent world on the edge of the judgment, and in the same title he is praised by the innumerable throng of the saved. By this name he is appealed to for victory by the angels in the war in heaven against Satan, and by it they overcome. It is by this name he is known when he comes in judgment, and as the Lamb he meets Satan and overcomes him. In this name he is united to the church forever as his Bride, and she is ever known as "the Bride, the Lamb's wife." It is as the Lamb that he reigns in the New Jerusalem, and the last we see of the glory of the city of God and of its God and his Christ is as "the throne of God and of the Lamb." Here, then, is the great title of Christ — "The Little Lamb." It is the opposite of man's ideals. Man chooses ferocious beasts or birds, such as the lion, bear, eagle, or dragon, for his standards. God's Little Lamb overcomes and destroys them all. Man chooses boldness and courage as his favorite virtues; God opposes with meekness and weakness and wins the victory.

There are to most, and perhaps all Scriptural predictions three interpretations; First, the spiritual; second, the figurative; and third, the literal. So in the first prediction, "The seed of the woman shall bruise the serpent's head." This is true spiritually of every believer in the sense of Christ's victory for him and in him. But it refers to the redemptive work of Christ in which the serpent's head was bruised. The third reference is to the final overthrow of Satan personally. The prophecy of Enoch was, "The Lord cometh with ten thousand of his saints." It is true at all times that Christ comes in vengeance on evil-doers. It has direct reference to the flood also. The further interpretation is the great one, as Jude tells us, which will be at the end. The seventy-second Psalm is another illustration of this principle. It describes a state of Christian experience. It was predicted directly of Solomon by his father David. But there was the final fulfilment in the reign of Christ.

So in these three senses the Apocalypse may be interpreted. It has furnished constant edification to the people of God in all ages by its spiritual meaning, whether the predictive meaning was understood or not. There has been also a figurative fulfilment all along the course of history. This Christ declared by the opening declaration: "The Revelation of Jesus Christ which God gave him to shew unto his servants, even the things which must shortly come to pass." That Christ should apprise his servants of what was coming is in accord with all the past. Always have the people of God been informed as to the future from the first to the present. To prove that this is a meaning of the Apocalypse, one need only take such a history as that of Gibbon, covering the same period, the work of an unbeliever, yet reciting sometimes in almost the same terms the events predicted by the Apocalypse. The Revelation has been a lamp in a dark place to the church all these centuries. The diligent student may still make out the shadows of coming events by the aid of this great prophecy.

But the predictions of Scripture, and especially the Apocalypse, have a future and a greater fulfilment. The historical and the spiritual fulfilments do not exhaust the language nor the figures. For example, the opening of the sixth seal, where the world of sinners call upon the rocks and mountains to fall on them and hide them from the face of him that sitteth on the throne and from the wrath of the Lamb, was fulfilled historically in the overwhelming convulsions of the downfall of the Roman empire. But any reader, looking at these sublime words and being told this was the fulfilment of them, would ask, "Is that all they mean?" The fact that many Old Testament scriptures use the same kind of language in predicting the fall of lands like Babylon, is not opposed to the view here held, for all these have, as intimated, a connection with the Day of the Lord. Scripture intimates that things of the past and of the earth are shadows of things above and of the future. This idea is embodied in such common sayings as, "History repeats itself" and, "Coming events cast their shadows before." In a higher sense than these sayings mean, the idea is correct. The Epistle to the Hebrews speaks of the ordinances of the Mosaic economy being "shadows of the heavenly things," "copies of the things in the heavens."[1] Milton says,

> "What if earth
> Be but the shadow of heaven, and things therein,
> Each to the other like, more than on earth is thought."

The law and its ordinances were shadows of the spiritual realities which came in Christ. By this historical fulfilment we may read the greater one, and

[1] Heb. viii. 5 ; ix. 23.

it is for this reason the two are given, as well as for the edification of contemporaneous believers. This future fulfilment of the Apocalypse is the history of the Day of God.

A consideration of the Christ of the future and his work, demands a review of the events of the Day of the Lord. The events of the age to come are many. The record is crowded with the outline of it. Great political systems rise and fall, and many peoples are gathered into world-wide combinations. Strange events happen among them; battles are fought and cities are overthrown. All show that time is occupied by its events. Nor is the work of that day all judgment, although it is "the Day of Judgment." There are to be offers of mercy and calls to repentance and a world-wide proclamation of the gospel. There also will be events affecting the church, and blessed raptures and glories for the believers, and a long age of universal peace and happiness for man. The sequence of events is the great matter of difficulty and of diversity among students of the word. We have before us a mass of glittering mountain peaks, and we are looking at the whole from a distance, and their relative position and relationship is not easily perceived. They are presented here in the consecutive order of the Apocalypse on the conviction that whatever other fulfilments that greatest of prophecies has, it is a history of the Day of God. We shall follow, then, its order, and add other Scriptures as they seem to fit that systematic record. The church, Israel, and the world will each be found to have a place in these events as in the previous ages.

The mistake made commonly is in shutting up each feature of the Day of the Lord in a single event, as for example, but one appearing of Christ and one rapture of the saints, a single resurrection and but one judgment, the same mistake as was made by the

Jews in regard to the coming of Christ. This conception must be gotten rid of if the predictions are to be understood at all.

From Steffan's " Das Ende : "—

" Does not the ' Day of the Lord,' since Scripture knows only one great day, comprehend both the *Parousia* and the last universal judgments? Does not even the same scripture say, 'A day with the Lord is as a thousand years'? Yea, does not John call the last time itself the 'last hour'? What hinders us to believe that the Day of the Lord begins with the *Parousia* and ends with the universal judgment. We shall look for not one or two appearances of Christ, or one or two resurrections, and but a single judgment, but a succession of each of these. Christ coming often during this age of the supernatural. So also several described resurrections and judgments. The whole is one coming of Christ, one long Judgment Day, one long Resurrection Day. All these are the normal events of the age."[1]

We quote from Lange : —

" The resurrection of the dead is exhibited as a vital process, working from within outwards, through an entire æon from the first glorious blossoms of the resurrection to the last general resurrection. The judgment is set forth as a distinct series of judgments, reaching from the war judgment at the return of Christ, through the peace judgment of the thousand years, to the judgment of damnation at the close of those years. . . . The entire æon is to be conceived of as an æon of separations and eliminations in an ethical and a cosmical sense, separations and eliminations which are such as are necessary to make manifest and to complete the ideal regulations of life."[2]

The Apocalypse opens the future by the figure of the gradual opening and slow unrolling of a sealed book or scroll.[3] The state of things accompanying this is the same as described by Christ in the Olivet discourse[4] which is a history of our gospel age, which ends at the sudden inburst of the Day of the Lord.

---

[1] "Premillennial Essays," Chicago, 1879, p. 509.
[2] Commentary, Revelation, New York, pp. 350, 403.
[3] Rev. vi. [4] Matt. xxiv. 4–14.

CHRIST IN THE DAY OF THE LORD. 301

The believer is to be apprised by premonitory signs, so as not to be taken unawares. Among these are a general world-wide proclamation of the gospel;[1] an apostasy;[2] unbelief in the coming of the Lord;[3] probably a persecution of the saints;[4] national movements among the Jews;[5] and calamities affecting the Turkish abomination and the papacy.[6] A special call of some kind is indicated by the midnight cry in the parable of the ten virgins.

Upon the world the Day of the Lord is to come as a thief, as a snare, as lightning. They are to be at their usual vocations.[7] The first intimation the world will have will be the enshrouding of the whole earth in a pall of impenetrable darkness. This is the common idea of the last day, or the end of the world, as this great event is commonly termed, and in a sense correctly so. In attempting to describe the conditions of that time we can only use the language of Scripture: "I will show wonders in the heaven above, and signs on the earth beneath, blood, and fire, and vapor of smoke; the sun shall be turned into darkness, and the moon into blood, before the Day of the Lord come, that great and notable day."[8] Christ himself mentioned these phenomena among the accompaniments of the end. Clouds and darkness are everywhere associated in the Old Testament predictions with the coming of the Day of God. The state of things on earth at this time is thus described by Christ: "There shall be signs in sun and moon and stars; and upon the earth distress of nations, in perplexity for the roaring of the sea and the billows; men fainting for fear and for expectation of the things which are coming on the world; for the powers of the heavens shall be shaken."[9]

---

[1] Matt. xxiv. 14. [2] 2 Thess. ii. 1–10. [3] 2 Peter iii. 3, 4.
[4] Matt. xxiv. 9; Rev. vi. 9, 10. [5] Matt. xxv. 32–34.
[6] Rev. xvi. 12; Rev. xvii. 16–18. [7] Luke xvii. 26–30.
[8] Acts ii. 20. [9] Luke xxi. 25, 26.

There is to be in the midst of the wonders in earth and air and sky, a special sign which will show the world it is the presence of the Day of God. "But immediately after the tribulation of those days, the sun shall be darkened, and the moon shall not give her light, and the stars shall fall from heaven, and the powers of the heavens shall be shaken: and then shall appear the sign of the Son of man in heaven."[1] Luther refers to this passage as follows: "A something strikingly awful shall forewarn that the world will come to an end and that the last day is even at the door." Alford writes upon this passage: "Such prophecies are to be understood *literally*, and indeed without such understanding would lose their truth and significance. The physical signs will happen." As to the "sign of the Son of man in heaven" he writes, "This is manifestly *some sign in the heavens*, by which all shall know that the Son of man is at hand. . . . On the whole I think no sign completely answers the conditions but that of the cross, and accordingly we find the Fathers mostly thus explaining the passage."[2]

The effect of this definite announcement of the imminent advent of Christ himself in person, is given us in the following extract from the vision of John, "The kings of the earth, and the princes, and the chief captains, and the rich, and the strong, and every bondman and freeman, hid themselves in the caves and in the rocks of the mountains; and they say to the mountains and to the rocks, Fall on us and hide us from the face of him that sitteth on the throne, and from the wrath of the Lamb: for the great day of their wrath is come; and who is able to stand?"[3]

The appearing of Christ himself is the great event of the Day of the Lord. Although there are many events connected with the age called the Day of the

---

[1] Matt. xxiv. 29, 30.   [2] Greek Testament, *In loco*.
[3] Rev. vi. 15-17.

Lord, yet so great is this event that it is often spoken of in Scripture as the beginning and end of all. Nearly every body of believers has given it a place in their expressions of belief. Whatever difference exists as to times or order of events there is practical unanimity that Christ will come and call the world to judgment. It was the hope of the apostolic and patristic churches, and has been, as Dr. David Brown says, the pole star of the church. In two great facts all evangelical believers agree as to the coming of Christ. It is personal and possible; personal as to its nature, and always possible as to its occurrence. Some expressions from learned and devout writers as to the importance of this event are here given.

Dr. Albert Barnes wrote:—

"It may be added with great force, whether Christians now have any such expectation of the appearing of the Lord Jesus, or whether they have not fallen into the dangerous error of the prevailing unbelief, so that the expectation of his coming is allowed to exert almost no influence on the soul. In the passage before us, Paul says that it was one of the distinct characteristics of the Christian, that he looked for the coming of the Saviour from heaven. Let us look for the coming of the Lord. All that we hope for depends in his appearing. Our days of triumph, and our fulness of joy, are to be when he shall return."

The Westminster Confession contains this paragraph:—

"As Christ would have us to be certain that there shall be a day of judgment, both to deter all men from sin, and for the consolation of the godly, so will he have that day unknown to men, that they may shake off all carnal security, and be always watchful; because they know not at what hour the Lord will come, and may be ever prepared to say, 'Come, Lord Jesus, come quickly.'"

Bishop Ryle wrote:—

"I believe that the second coming of our Lord Jesus Christ will be a real, literal, personal, bodily coming. That as he went away in the clouds of heaven with his body, before the eyes of men, so in like manner will he return."

Spurgeon said: —

"O Christian, do you know that your Lord is coming? In such an hour as ye think not, the man who was hung on Calvary, will descend in glory; the head that was crowned with thorns will shine with a diadem of brilliant jewels."

Matthew Henry thus comments: —

"To watch implies not only to believe that our Lord will come, but to desire that he would come, to be often thinking of his coming, and always looking for it as soon and near and the time of it uncertain. Our looking at Christ's second coming as at a distance is the cause of all those irregularities that render the thought of it terrible."

Thomas Chalmers wrote: —

"Let us await the coming of our Lord. . . . I desire to cherish a more habitual and practical faith than heretofore in that coming which even the first Christians were called to hope for with all earnestness, even though many centuries were to elapse ere the hope could be realized."

Rev. George Mueller, founder of the Orphan Houses, Bristol, England, and author of "The Life of Christ," writes: —

"The effect it produced upon me was this: From my inmost soul I was stirred up to feel for perishing sinners and for the slumbering world around me living in the wicked one, and considered, Ought I not to do what I can to win souls for the Lord Jesus while he tarries, and to rouse a slumbering church?"

Calvin wrote: —

"Not to hesitate, ardently desiring the day of Christ's coming as of all events the most auspicious."[1]

Luther said: —

"I ardently hope that amidst the internal dissensions of earth, Jesus Christ will hasten the day of his coming."

Richard Baxter said: —

[1] Book iii, chap. 9.

"The thoughts of the coming of the Lord are of all most sweet and joyful to me, so that if I were but sure that I should live to see it, and that the trumpet should sound, and the dead should arise, and the Lord appear before the period of my age, it would be the joyfulest tidings to me in the world."[1]

The coming of Christ is sometimes spoken of as the descent of the Holy Ghost, the destruction of Jerusalem, the spiritual coming to the believer, death, chastisement, and special judgments. Some of these are so termed in Scripture as the spiritual coming and chastisement and judgments, others, as death, are not; and others, as the first two, were past when the Revelation was written. None of these fully satisfy in any measure the statements of Scripture such as are quoted herein. One feature of this great event must be kept in view. As stated by Jamieson, Fausset & Brown: "Christ's second coming is not a mere point of time but a period beginning with the resurrection of the just and ending with the general judgment." In this latter advent there are many appearings of Christ. He appears again and again during the progress of that long day. He appears for his people and with them. He appears to his people alone and to the assembled world. He appears as a single dazzling center of ineffable light, and again among his people, arrayed like them and riding forward with them to victory. So we must be prepared to see all through the Day of God one great Figure frequently appearing upon the scene.

In his entrance upon the work of the day of the Lord, Christ adopts a wholly different appearance, attitude, and method of procedure. The Christ of the Revelation is a very different manifestation from the Christ of the Gospels or the Epistles. In the Gospels he is the lowly traveler, toiling, teaching, until his strength is gone. In the Epistles he is invisible. The world knows him only on evidence.

[1] Vol. 17, p. 555.

He is sitting at God's right hand in expectancy, and by his church beseeching them to be reconciled to God. He is patiently bearing man's neglect and profanity. His people are persecuted and killed, and he makes no sign of displeasure or even knowledge. They cry to him and he waits long before avenging their wrongs. His truth is denied and vilified, and he is silent. The world takes possession of the fairest portions of earth and turns them into scenes of sin and cruelty, and he appears to see it not. In the Apocalypse all is changed. Christ is no longer sitting, but in every form of activity. He is the Christ of energy. He is coming in clouds, riding on horseback, leading armies, smiting down evils, taking vengeance upon all foes, calling the dead to life, summoning the world to judgment, and dealing out justice with a high hand. He is seen leading his people in triumph, openly rewarding them, and crowning them with glory.

The work of Christ in the Day of the Lord begins with his own people. Two events relating to them are described in the following scriptures: "But we would not have you ignorant, brethren, concerning them that fall asleep; that ye sorrow not, even as the rest, which have no hope. For if we believe that Jesus died and rose again, even so them also that are fallen asleep in Jesus will God bring with him. For this we say unto you by the word of the Lord, that we that are alive, that are left unto the coming of the Lord, shall in no wise precede them that are fallen asleep. For the Lord himself shall descend from heaven, with a shout, with the voice of the archangel, and with the trump of God: and the dead in Christ shall rise first: then we that are alive, that are left, shall together with them be caught up in the clouds, to meet the Lord in the air: and so shall we ever be with the Lord. Wherefore comfort one another with these words."[1] Nothing

[1] 1 Thess. iv. 12-18.

can add to the clearness of this account, nor could comment make more plain supernatural experiences such as these, which we must await until we enjoy one or other of them, as we certainly shall.

The resurrection of the departed believer is here placed before the translation of the living. There is a longing to be among those who shall so be "caught up in the clouds," but the apostle, for our own sakes as well as for the sake of those who sorrow over the loss of dear ones, tells us the departed shall come first. Death is the enemy of the human race. This is as true of the believer as of any other. The victory over it is always associated with the resurrection. It is in a sense a victory for the believer to die in peace and joy, but this is not the victory spoken of in the scripture. The victory of Christ was won at his resurrection. The victory of his people over death is won at their resurrection, and as Satan has the power of death, it is their victory over Satan.

The above scripture also plainly teaches us that the resurrection of the believers is to precede that of all others. This is mentioned in several other places. The following scripture seems emphatic upon this point; it describes such a resurrection: "And I saw thrones, and they sat upon them, and judgment was given unto them: and I saw the souls of them that had been beheaded for the testimony of Jesus, and for the word of God, and such as worshiped not the beast, neither his image, and received not the mark upon their forehead and upon their hand; and they lived, and reigned with Christ a thousand years. The rest of the dead lived not until the thousand years should be finished. This is the first resurrection. Blessed and holy is he that hath part in the first resurrection: over these the second death hath no power; but they shall be priests of God and of Christ, and shall reign with him a thousand years."[1]

[1] Rev. xx. 4-6.

On this passage Alford writes thus : —

"I cannot consent to distort words from their plain sense and chronological place in the prophecy, on account of any considerations of difficulty, or risk of abuses which the doctrine of the millennium may bring with it. Those who lived next to the apostles and the whole church for three hundred years, understood them in the plain, literal sense; and it is a strange sight in these days to see expositors who are among the first in reverence of antiquity, complacently casting aside the most cogent instance of consensus which primitive antiquity presents. As regards the text itself no legitimate treatment of it will extort what is known as the spiritual interpretation now in fashion. . . .

"It seems to me that if in a sentence where two resurrections are spoken of, with no mark of distinction (it is otherwise in John v. 28, which is commonly alleged for the view I am combating),— in a sentence where one resurrection having been related, 'the rest of the dead' are afterward mentioned,— we are at liberty to understand the former one figuratively and spiritually, and the latter literally and materially, then there is an end of definite meaning in plain words, and the Apocalypse, or any other book, may mean anything we please. . . . I have again and again raised my earnest protest against evading the plain sense of words, and spiritualizing in the midst of plain declarations of fact."[1]

Christlieb thus writes : —

"The resurrection power coming from Christ, through the medium of his word and sacraments, tends mainly to the sanctification of and the renewing of the sinner; and thus interpenetrates first the spiritual nature of man, planting within those who are regenerate, a germ for the resurrection of the body. Then the spiritual life of Christ breaks forth into a manifestation in the visible world by revivifying the bodies of those who are sanctified in the first 'resurrection. In the succeeding general resurrection this grand and gradually progressive process of the world's renewal has its fitting consummation."[2]

As to the subject at large, the following comments are given. From Moses Stuart on The Apocalyse : —

[1] Greek New Testament, Vol. 4, pp. 731, 732.
[2] "Modern Doubt and Christian Belief," American Tract Society, pp. 451, 452.

"After investigating this subject I have doubts whether the assertion is correct that such a doctrine as that of the first resurrection is nowhere else found in the Scriptures. What can Paul mean when he represents himself as readily submitting to every kind of suffering and affliction, 'If by any means he might attain to the resurrection from the dead?' Of a figurative resurrection or regeneration, Paul cannot be speaking, for he had already attained to that on the plains of Damascus. Of the like tenor with the text seems to be the implication in Luke xiv. 14: 'Thou shalt be recompensed at the resurrection of the just.' Why the resurrection of the 'just'? This would agree entirely with the view in Rev. xx. 5. There is more reason to believe that such is the simple meaning of the words in Luke xiv. 14, inasmuch as two recent antipodes in theology, Olshausen and De Wette, both agree in this exegesis: 'The Apocalypse teaches a twofold resurrection; first, of the saints at the beginning of the millennium, the second, of all men at the final consummation.'"

Dr. Robert J. Breckinridge writes: —

"It is commonly alleged that this coming of the Lord is in his glory and all his holy angels with him, for it is repeatedly so declared in the Scriptures. Moreover that the resurrection of the dead will occur at that time, which is true, but not exactly in the sense generally understood; for it is expressly declared by the apostle John that none but such as he describes will reign with Christ a thousand years or have any part in the first resurrection, and that the rest of the dead live not again until the thousand years are finished."[1]

The first resurrection is also referred to in the following passage: "For as in Adam all die so also in Christ shall all be made alive. But each in his own order; Christ the first-fruits; then they that are Christ's at his coming. Then cometh the end when he shall deliver up the kingdom to God even the Father."[2] Jamieson, Fausset & Brown comment on this as follows: —

"Every man in his 'own order.' The Greek is not abstract but concrete; image from troops each in his own regi-

---

[1] "Knowledge of God Subjectively Considered," New York, 1869, pp. 677, 678.
[2] 1 Cor. xv. 22-24.

ment. Though all shall rise, not all shall be saved, nay, each shall have his proper place. Christ first, after him the godly who die in Christ in a separate band from the ungodly. Then the 'end,' i. e., the resurrection of the 'rest of the dead.'"[1]

The distinction between the two resurrections is seen in the names applied to each; the one is the resurrection to life, the other to judgment, to shame, and contempt. The distinction between the two resurrections is further observed by the use of the respective phrases, "the resurrection *from* the dead," and "the resurrection *of* the dead." The saints are raised out *from among* the dead. So the word "from" is always applied to the resurrection of Christ, it will be observed in the above mentioned passages. This first resurrection is also spoken of as "a better resurrection."[2] Christ speaks of they that are accounted to attain that world (age) and the resurrection from the dead."[3] It is spoken of as special, prior, and eclectic. General scriptures about the resurrections must be interpreted in accordance with these special ones.

There has been a great change from the days of the apostles in the way the resurrection of the believer has been relegated to the rear, and death brought forward as the hope of the believer. The late Dr. A. J. Gordon thus writes on this subject:—

"Indeed I may say in popular appreciation, death has very largely usurped the place that belongs to the resurrection. But death, we must remember, is an enemy. It never was and never can be anything but an enemy. It is cruel, repulsive, and humbling. But man has learned to idealize this hideous enemy into a good angel. Indeed, I think it would be no exaggeration to say that in the appreciation of many Christians, death has been thrust into the place that belongs to Christ. The crown of welcome which we should ever be waiting to put upon the head of him who will swallow up death in victory, is put upon the ghostly brow of him who is daily swallowing up life in defeat."

[1] "Critical Commentary," Chicago, 1885. [2] Heb. xi. 35.
[3] Luke xx. 35.

The poet Young writes:—

> "Death gives us more than was in Eden lost.
> The king of terrors is the Prince of Peace."

There is little said in Scripture as to the state of the departed believer in the so called "the middle state." There are a few words, enough to satisfy our longings, and to assure us it is well with them. We are told of the dying beggar being carried by the angels into Abraham's bosom, and in that we may see all our dear ones so carried, and believe we shall be so also. We read that the saints rest from their labors, and so shall we. They are with Jesus, as Paul tells us he longed to be at his departure. We have, as the dying malefactor, the same promise to be with Christ in paradise. This is about all we are told of the saints in the middle state, for it is not on this our minds or hearts are to be set. It is not to death but to victory over death we are to look for our hope.

The second great event at the coming of Christ is described in these words: "Behold, I tell you a mystery. We shall not all sleep, but we shall all be changed, in a moment, in the twinkling of an eye, at the last trump: for the trumpet shall sound, and the dead shall be raised incorruptible, and we shall be changed. For this corruptible must put on incorruption, and this mortal must put on immortality."[1] Death is not inevitable. It has not been an unknown thing that some escaped death. There has been one out of each age who so went to be with God; Enoch out of the antideluvian age, Elijah from the Israelitish, and, it is believed by some, John out of the gospel age. To never die, to miss the pain and dying and grave and the decay and all, is a consummation to be wished as we wish for nothing else except salvation and Christ. This will be the happy lot of some,— "we shall not all die."

[1] 1 Cor. xv. 51-53.

It is to this strange taking away Christ refers in this passage, "I say unto you, In that night there shall be two men on one bed; the one shall be taken, and the other shall be left. There shall be two women grinding together; the one shall be taken, and the other shall be left. And they answering, say unto him, Where, Lord? And he said unto them, Where the body is, thither will the eagles also be gathered together."[1]

This is the individual aspect of this wonderful change from life on earth to life in heaven. It will be instantaneous all over the world. In some places it will be night and will find the believer asleep; in other places it will be early morning and find a humble woman at her early toil; in other places still, it will be broad day and some are at their labor in the fields. It makes little difference to the child of God what his immediate occupations are, whether Christ calls him asleep or awake. In an instant he is gone from the presence of the companion of his labor or bed. There will be no time for partings. Some are united in life who are not so in the Lord— companions, partners in business, friends, but divided in this, the greatest of all concerns.

The above passage of scripture intimates a private and secret call, and flight to an unseen center. This is the view taken by many thorough students of this subject; that the Christian is called secretly and before any alarm has been given the world. It may be so. There does not, however, seem to be any definite statement as to such a calling, and the above is not conclusive. On the other hand, the scriptures previously quoted are clear that there is world-wide alarm: "The trumpet shall sound, and the dead shall be raised, and we shall be changed;" "The dead shall hear the voice of the Son of God;" "The Lord himself shall descend from heaven with a shout

[1] Luke xvii. 34-37.

and the voice of the archangel, and with the trump of God." It seems clear that all happens at the inburst of the Day of the Lord upon the world. It is, however, before all or perhaps any of his judgment work begins. It is probable that Christ himself is not yet revealed personally to the world, as in the conversion of Paul the company did not see Christ. The above-mentioned thoughts are confirmed by the scriptures presenting the public aspect of Christ calling his own people: "He shall send forth his angels with a great sound of a trumpet, and they shall gather together his elect from the four winds, from one end of heaven to the other."[1]

There is a line of very searching scriptures which intimate one may come up to the very day and into it and think it is well with himself and yet be mistaken, and find this out at the last. The five foolish virgins are waiting as the others, and have lamps and expect to enter in to the wedding, and are excluded. At the very table of the marriage feast the guest without the wedding garment was detected and cast out. Lot's wife escaped from Sodom, but was destroyed, while he himself and his daughters escape "as by fire." The Lord himself tells us as follows: "When once the master of the house is risen up, and hath shut to the door, and ye begin to stand without, and to knock at the door, saying, Lord, open to us; and he shall answer and say to you, I know you not whence ye are; then shall ye begin to say, We did eat and drink in thy presence, and thou didst teach in our streets; and he shall say, I tell you, I know not whence ye are; depart from me, all ye workers of iniquity."[2] There are also the warnings of the salt which has lost its savor, and the allusions to the "reprobate" and the "cast-away" and Esau who lost his birthright. There is the possibility of a tremendous loss here, and even the loss of the

[1] Matt. xxiv. 31.   [2] Luke xiii. 25–27.

soul. Bunyan pictures a trap-door to hell from the very gate of the Celestial City. Christ will then thoroughly purge his threshing-floor. He shall have no Judas this time among the holy band or any who will turn into such.

The event which appears to follow the resurrection of the believer and his gathering together with Christ is thus described: "For we must all be made manifest before the judgment-seat of Christ; that each one may receive the things done in the body, according to what he hath done, whether it be good or bad."[1] This is not the final judgment in which the world appears before the great white throne. The reasons for so concluding are as follows: First, the direct statements of Scripture: "Verily, verily, I say unto you, He that heareth my word, and believeth him that sent me, hath eternal life, and cometh not into judgment, but hath passed out of death into life."[2] It would place on trial again those who have answered for their sins in the person of their Substitute. Christ, as we have seen, has satisfied every demand for his people and kept their record clean by his intercession. After being justified, and the witness of the Spirit given to them, and being raised in glory or translated, to be again placed on trial for sins which were laid on Christ and borne by him, and the claims of divine justice fully met, and all declared sufficient, and the blood of Christ satisfactory,— after all this, it is inconceivable that there should be either any doubt of their salvation, or any other reason for their being placed on trial.

Second, the saints are to assist at the general judgment of the world: "Know ye not that the saints shall judge the world? Know ye not that we shall judge angels?"[3] If we are to sit with Christ

[1] II Cor. v. 10.   [2] John v. 24.   [3] I Cor. vi. 2, 3.

in the judgment of the world, it is wholly incongruous that we should be placed at the bar of judgment ourselves. Third, nor can we see how it is possible for the departed saint to be brought back from paradise and the presence of Jesus and placed with the abandoned and condemned of earth even to hear the verdict of "Not guilty," which they heard long ago in life or certainly knew in heaven. Fourth, the appearance of the Christian before the great white throne is not required by the account of that event. It is the "dead" who there appear, and the believer is not "dead" then. Fifth, there is no similarity between these two judgments. The word describing the sinner's "judgment" is not used of the Christian's. The issues of the great white throne are final and fatal, and some of the ones we are discussing are not. Sixth, There is no reason for interpreting this as the judgment of the world, and the further scriptures we shall consider show it is far different in the persons and things judged and the results, and in the time when it comes.

Schmidt writes on this : —

"The judgment of the church is distinguished from the universal judgment, and is thus represented in the parables of the ten virgins and the talents. The former judgment has to do in faithful conduct in Christ's kingdom."[1]

Dr. Robert J. Breckinridge writes thus : —

"The resurrection of life, the resurrection of the just, the judgment of the saints, and their reign, are altogether distinct from the resurrection of damnation, the resurrection of the unjust, and the judgment and perdition of ungodly men. The judgment of the saints is not to ascertain their salvation, but to disclose and to proclaim the special ground upon which each crown is gained, the special grounds upon which each crown was won — all to the infinite glory of the Lord and the unutterable joy of the redeemed."[2]

---

[1] "Biblico Theological New Testament," quoted in "Premillennial Essays," Chicago, 1879, p. 501.

[2] "Knowledge of God Subjectively Considered," New York, 1869, p. 680.

The matters for which the believer is to be judged are "the things done in the body," good and bad. The Scriptures are full of the promises of reward for faithful doing. The most emphatic of these, and the one further locating this judgment, is the words of Christ himself: "Behold, I come quickly; and my reward is with me, to render to each man according as his work is."[1]

Not a service done for Christ loses its reward. "For his sake," is the criterion by which everything is to be judged. The sacrifices of the believer are then shown and rewarded. It is then the Beatitudes are completely fulfilled. Then those who have laid up treasure in heaven receive it with manifold interest. All losses are made good. Then it is the promises are fulfilled, made "to him that overcometh." It is then the righteous "shine forth as the sun in the kingdom of their Father." At this time the faithful servants are rewarded for good use of their pounds and talents. At this time, too, is the promise made good — "They that be wise shall shine as the brightness of the firmament; and they that turn many to righteousness as the stars for ever and ever."[2] The rewards are of glory, power, and privilege. The glory, as has been shown by Paul, differs as one star differs from another. The power, as the ruler over ten cities is superior to the ruler over one city. Among the privileges seem to be nearness to the person of Christ. There were two who asked that they might sit on his right hand and left. Christ said this was to be given to those for whom it was prepared. The twelve he promised should "sit with me on my throne." In the distribution of rewards it is not against one that he came in at the eleventh hour.

The believer is also to be judged for the things done in the body which were bad. This also looks to services. Paul speaks of such works: "For other

[1] Rev. xxii. 12.   [2] Dan. xii. 3.

foundation can no man lay than that which is laid, which is Jesus Christ. But if any man buildeth on the foundation, gold, silver, costly stones, wood, hay, stubble; each man's work shall be made manifest: for the day shall declare it, because it is revealed in fire; and the fire itself shall prove each man's work of what sort it is. If any man's work shall abide which he built thereon, he shall receive a reward. If any man's work shall be burned, he shall suffer loss; but he himself shall be saved; yet so as through fire."[1]

There is a searching process here which will be terrible to works done from wrong motives, or works left undone. Christ said to each of the seven churches, or rather to the angel or minister of the church, for these seven letters are to the ministers of these churches first of all: "I know thy works." The judgment of Christ is of the persons as well as of their works. "Saved as by fire" intimates a searching personal examination. The Christian life will be gone into by Christ as we are told by the apostles. Every secret thing not repented of and confessed, will be exposed, to the shame and mortification of the doer. Paul writes of issues to come up in this judgment: "Wherefore judge nothing before the time, until the Lord come, who will both bring to light the hidden things of darkness, and make manifest the counsels of the hearts; and then shall each man have his praise from God."[2] All wrong estimates of men will be set right, and the result will be as Christ has said, "Many that are first will be last, and the last will be first." All idle words, as Christ said, will be accounted for at the day of this judgment. All unsettled quarrels will be brought to account.

The fact of the chastening of the unfaithful servant at the judgment of the saints, is also taught directly by Christ in this scripture: "But if that servant

---
[1] 1 Cor. iii. 11–15.   [2] 1 Cor. iv. 5.

shall say in his heart, My lord delayeth his coming; and shall begin to beat the menservants and the maidservants, and to eat and drink, and to be drunken; the lord of that servant shall come in a day when he expecteth not, and in an hour when he knoweth not, and shall cut him asunder, and appoint his portion with the unfaithful. And that servant, which knew his lord's will, and made not ready, nor did according to his will, shall be beaten with many stripes; but he that knew not, and did things worthy of stripes, shall be beaten with few stripes. And to whomsoever much is given, of him shall much be required: and to whom they commit much, of him will they ask the more."[1] Here is certain exposure, condemnation, and more, for the fruitless or faithless servant. "Beaten with many stripes" does not mean the loss of the soul, but it does mean more than has been generally taught. The "stripes" are connected with the coming of Christ. The same truth is taught in the parables of the same talents when the unprofitable servant is cast out "into the outer darkness: there shall be the weeping and gnashing of teeth."[2] Olshausen thus comments on this:—

> "The reference is not to eternal condemnation, but to exclusion from the *Basilia* [kingdom] into which the faithful enter. The Basilia is viewed as the region of light, which is encircled by darkness.
> "Concerning the children of light who are unfaithful to their vocation, it is said they are cast into the *skotos* (darkness): but as respecting the children of darkness, we are told they are consigned to the *pur aionion* (eternal fire) so that each one finds his own punishment in the opposite element."[3]

The judgment and rewarding of the saints continues as long as there are those who are Christ's to be so judged. This continues, as we will see, during the whole age of the judgments in which the gospel is

---

[1] Luke xii. 45-48.   [2] Matt. xxv. 30.
[3] "Gospels," 4 Vols., Edinburgh, 1855; Vol. 3, p. 287.

preached, and some are being saved. The number is not therefore complete until the close of the period of earth judgments; and as it seems probable that Christ himself does not appear visibly upon the scene until the close of the judgments upon earth, it is fair to assume he is occupied with his people above.

While Christ is dealing with his true followers, the unfaithful church left on earth enters into great tribulation as Israel did for her rejection of Christ. This is foretold by Christ and also by Daniel.[1] These are great afflictive dealings evidently accompanied by persecution in which the visible church is overthrown, her people scattered and rendered homeless and subjected to great hardships by the enemies of God, who by this time have recovered from their terror, and blaming the people of Christ, turn upon them in fury.

Dr. James W. Alexander wrote to a friend: —

"I was struck with these words of Chalmers to Bickersteth: 'But without slacking in the least our obligation to keep forward this great cause, I look for its conclusive establishment through a widening passage of desolating judgments, with the utter demolition of our present civil and ecclesiastical structures.'"

The character of the victors in this fearful struggle and their triumph and deliverance are described in this passage: "After these things I saw, and, behold, a great multitude, which no man could number, out of every nation and of all tribes, and peoples, and tongues, standing before the throne, and before the Lamb, arrayed in white robes and palms in their hands: and they cry with a great voice, saying, Salvation unto our God which sitteth on the throne, and unto the Lamb. . . . And one of the elders answered, saying unto me, These which are arrayed in the white robes, who are they, and whence came they? And I say unto him, My Lord, thou knowest. And he said to me, These are they which come out of

[1] Matt. xxiv. 21; Dan. xii. 1.

the great tribulation, and they washed their robes, and made them white in the blood of the Lamb. Therefore are they before the throne of God; and they serve him day and night in his temple: and he that sitteth on the throne shall spread his tabernacle over them. They shall hunger no more, neither thirst any more; neither shall the sun strike upon them, nor any heat: for the Lamb which is in the midst of the throne shall be their shepherd, and shall guide them unto fountains of waters of life: and God shall wipe away every tear from their eyes."[1] The references to hunger, thirst, exposure, and tears, indicate the character of their peculiar sufferings in the great tribulation they endure.

The judgments of the Day of God fall upon widening circles as did the giving of the gospel whose course they follow. First, as we have seen, Christ begins with his own people, then that part of the world called in the Apocalypse "the third part of earth." This we think is that called Christendom, after the removal of God's people. It occupies the same territory ruled by that strange prophetic power, Rome, and exercises the same authority over the rest of the earth. It is a peculiar part of the world when looked at in the long perspective of history. While other parts of the world have had the gospel and lost it, this part of the earth has been blessed by its preservation. It has been, so far as locality and autonomy and authority and sphere of influence are concerned, the special field of the visible Christian church. Nearly every nation of civilization is professedly Christian. The state publicly acknowledges the Christian religion, indeed the ruler of the state is in many cases the head also of the church. For centuries, indeed for the greater part of the time since the gospel came, the church has ruled the state. The popes were

[1] Rev. vii. 9-17.

princes, and their power supreme. The church still controls the state. The Christian church to-day rules as truly as it did in the supremest days of temporal power. Mr. Gladstone thus writes: —

> "Christianity is the religion in the command of whose professors is lodged a proportion of power far exceeding its superiority of numbers; and this power is both moral and material. In the area of controversy it can hardly be said to have a serious antagonist. Force, secular or physical, is accumulated in the hands of Christians in a proportion absolutely overwhelming; and the accumulation of influence is not less remarkable than that of force. This is not surprising, for all the elements of influence have their home within the Christian precinct. The art, the literature, the systematized industry, invention, and commerce — in one word, the power — of the world are almost wholly Christian. The nations of Christendom are everywhere arbiters of the fate of non-Christian nations."[1]

After the true people of God have been removed from earth, the character and record before God of this highly favored part of the earth will come into judgment. The record of all spiritual work will have gone with God's people as their part. What will be the record of Christendom? It has laid hands on the fairest regions of the world "for their good" and ostensibly to "extend civilization," really to extend national power and trade and to enrich the merchants of the dominant nations. It has taken, without compensation, from weaker nations their God-given heritage, and in doing so has turned these lands into scenes of bloodshed. The work of the missionary of the gospel has been taken advantage of, and has been followed by the trader, and he by the soldier. There has followed them the train of evils which have destroyed these peoples. Opium was forced into China by Christendom. Rum is being poured into Africa by Christendom. Where the so-called Christian civilization has appeared, the native races have gone down by its drugs, drinks, and diseases. It has put into

[1] Introduction to People's Bible History, Chicago, 1895.

the hands of these races, arms and material of most diabolically consummate perfection for the destruction of human life. It calls the arming of these peoples with these infernal weapons "advancing in progress and civilization." It lends them money for this purpose and sends them teachers who instruct them in the satanic art of wholesale butchery of human life, and sets them at war with each other, and profits by their mutual destruction.

There has been given the nations of whole continents, in place of their original paganism, a bastard Christianity more difficult to overthrow than their pagan faith. It is the scholarship of these lands of Christendom which is attacking so persistently and insidiously the foundations of faith. Infidelity, blasphemy, and profanity are sins only of Christian lands. In these lands is presented such vice as sends the heathen visitors home scandalized at the exhibition. The greatest crime of Christendom, besides her corrupting of the peoples of the earth, is her slaughter of the saints. The story of the persecutions is a well and often told tale. Suffice it to say that the blood of the saints of Christ rests upon Christendom. The pagan persecutions lasted but for a short time and destroyed few in comparison. But the so-called Christian nations, it is estimated by good authorities, have slain fifty millions of the best and purest followers of Christ. This has never been punished as yet; nor has it been repented of. As Christ said of Israel that upon that generation would fall all the blood of all the saints slain from Abel to Zacharias, the last victim of their fury, so on this Christless Christendom will fall the full and awful measure of the just reward of their destructive work in doctrine, in life, in heathen nations, and at home, — all done in the light of gospel and under the reign of grace.

The day of her visitation for all this is approaching. The God of heaven and earth is not oblivious to the awful sins of Christendom. That part of the world entrusted with the gospel continuously for nineteen hundred years, need not suppose God is so enraptured with its civilization and progress as to shut his eyes to these awful sins against the nations of the earth, against the people of God, and against Christ. As certainly as the hand of God fell upon the Israel in the destruction of their cities and their polity and their dispersion abroad over the face of the earth, so will the judgments of the same God who changes not, fall upon this greater Israel to whom he has committed a far greater wealth of material, intellectual, and, above all, spiritual privileges.

The judgments of the Day of God are represented under the symbols of seven sounding trumpets, and seven poured out vials. Each series commencing in a judgment alarm and followed by an interval of relief from the plagues, in which mercy is offered, God's people are gathered out, Satan's power put forth, and the world still further apostatizes, still greater judgments fall, until the last great conflict closes the day. The first great alarm announcing the Judgment day appears to pass away as time goes on and no immediate judgments follow. The world relapses into the former state of indifference, as we shall see is the case all along in the respites, and as we see now in the case of ungodly people aroused for the time by some alarm. Suddenly the sounding trumpets are heard.[1] These call for great afflictions affecting "a third part of earth," evidently that we call Christendom. The first four of these are calamities in nature affecting earth and sea and rivers and air.

The succeeding judgment appears to be the appearance and onslaught of myriads of satanic beings in some form. Their identity is established by the words, "They have over them as king the angel of the abyss." They spare the face of nature, but spend

[1] Rev. viii. ix.

their dreadful energy upon mankind. Nor do they kill, but only torment. It is recorded: "And in those days men shall seek death, and shall in no wise find it; and they shall desire to die, and death flieth from them."[1] The next is also Satanic but more intense; the beings are greater and more terrible in form and fury. The earth in all this time will be an awful place in which to live. Death will be far preferable, but for some reason will be impossible voluntarily.

The cessation of the Trumpet Judgments gives a respite in which the following scripture is fulfilled: "And the rest of mankind which were not killed with these plagues, repented not of the works of their hands, that they should not worship devils, and the idols of gold, and of silver, and of brass, and of stone, and of wood; which can neither see, nor hear, nor walk: and they repented not of their murders, nor of their sorceries, nor of their fornication, nor of their thefts."[2] There is to be left on earth a residuum of hard impenitence which not even the positive proof of the reality of the unseen world and the visitation of dire penalty for godlessness and idolatry and demon worship will change. It seems incredible that such a state could exist during such a time. But we must bear in mind the length of this period. There are to be long respites. During these, mankind, as Pharaoh of old, hardens its heart. We have often thought that if the world could only be convinced of the truth of religion, and perhaps feel some of the evils threatened in the Scriptures against sinners, they would repent. God will give all this to the world. There will be no effort spared to bring men to repentance and salvation. Christ had said, "If they hear not Moses and the prophets, neither will they be persuaded if one rose from the dead."[3] They have this and far more, yet are not persuaded. There are present on earth all

[1] Rev. ix. 6.   [2] Rev. ix. 20, 21.   [3] Luke xvi. 31.

this time, certain witnesses for God, who are either Moses and Elijah, or some of the same spirit and power. To these the world charges all their troubles and finally kills them and makes merry over their death, thinking they are now safe from further evils.[1]

In this time there rises a great satanic power which attains world-wide supremacy.[2] It is both political and religious. It is a church-state. The head is called in Scripture Antichrist, meaning a substitute for, and an opponent of, Christ. He is to be visible and reigning. He is to charm the world by his superhuman intelligence, graciousness, and ability. The Scripture account is as follows: "The whole earth wondered after the beast; and they worshiped the dragon, because he gave his authority unto the beast; and they worshiped the beast, saying, Who is like unto the beast? and who is able to war with him? and there was given to him a mouth speaking great things and blasphemies; and there was given to him authority to continue forty and two months. And he opened his mouth for blasphemies against God, to blaspheme his name, and his tabernacle, even them that dwell in the heaven. And it was given unto him to make war with the saints, and to overcome them: and there was given to him authority over every tribe and people and tongue and nation. And all that dwell on the earth shall worship him, every one whose name hath not been written in the book of life of the Lamb slain from the foundation of the world."[3] Under all his glory there is the beast, and Scripture so designates him. He has all the characteristics of the wild beasts whose names are attached to him. They have insisted on the beast origin of man, and glorified the animal. They have rejected God's Son and God, and have taken a beast as their supreme ruler.

Dr. Dorner writes as follows on this subject:—

[1] Rev. xi. 3–10.   [2] Revelation xiii.   [3] Rev. xiii. 4–8.

"The beast of Revelation is the world power hostile to God. The antichristian power is a union of the falsification of the divine worship with the hostile world power, the result of which is pseudo-Messiahship. Paul seems to regard the man of sin as an incarnation of the wicked antichristian power and as an individual."[1]

There is also a church for Antichrist (Revelation xvii) for he always imitates the work of God. He reigns as Christ will, and has a kingdom as Christ has, and now must have a spiritual body as Christ has in his church. This antichristian church is thus described: "I saw a woman sitting on a scarlet-colored beast, full of names of blasphemy, having seven heads and ten horns. And the woman was arrayed in purple and scarlet, and decked with gold and precious stones and pearls, having in her hand a golden cup full of abominations, even the unclean things of her fornication, and upon her forehead a name written, MYSTERY, BABYLON THE GREAT, THE MOTHER OF THE ABOMINATIONS OF THE EARTH. And I saw the woman drunken with the blood of the saints and of the martyrs of Jesus."[2] The church is in a place of earthly splendor and in full league with Satan. It is the church of Christendom in the Day of the Lord. The ecclesiastical system is called Babylon as against Jerusalem the city of God. It is a concentration of all earthly and churchly grandeur, having such temples and such worship and all which is sensuous, as the world has never seen. This hierarchy has its prophet or head who represents his master, and works prodigies.

The apostate church is represented under two figures, The harlot and Babylon. The symbol of a woman is everywhere in Scripture a figure of a church, true or apostate. The harlot represents the apostate spiritual body. She is now exalted to a state of

[1] "System of Christian Doctrine," Vol. 4, p. 388.
[2] Rev. xvii 3-6.

dignity outwardly never before enjoyed. Her place before was that of widowhood waiting for her returning Heavenly Spouse. She has given this up and rejected him, for she boasts, "I sit a queen, and am no widow, and shall see no mourning."

The following extended extract from Dr. Auberlin, describes the rise and nature of the mysterious body called the harlot : —

"The word harlot describes the essential character of the false church. She retains her human shape, remains a woman, does not become a beast: she has the form of godliness but denies the power thereof. Her rightful husband, Jehovah — Christ, and the joys and goods of his house, are no longer hers all in all, but she runs after the visible and vain things of the world, in its manifold manifestations. This whoredom appears in its proper form where the church wishes itself to be a worldly power, uses politics and diplomacy, makes flesh her arm, uses unholy means for holy ends, spreads her dominion by sword or money, fascinates the hearts of men by sensual ritualism, allows herself to become 'mistress of ceremonies' to the dignitaries of this world, and flatters prince or people, the living or the dead. Whenever the church forgets that she is in the world even as Christ was in the world, as a bearer of the cross and a pilgrim, or that the world is crucified to her and judged, such is the character of the harlot; and it is not only a church here, and a church there, it is not only the church in its individual manifestations, that is meant here, but Christendom as a whole, even as Israel as a whole had become a harlot. The true believers are hidden and dispersed; the invisible church is within the visible. It cannot be said, Here or there is the harlot, and here or there she is not, as little as it can be said, Lo, here is Christ, or there. The boundary lines which separate the harlot and woman, are not local, are not confessional."[1]

"John Michal Hahn says: 'The harlot is not the city of Rome alone, neither is it the Roman Catholic Church, to the exclusion of another, but all churches and every church, ours included; viz., all Christendom which is without the spirit and life of our Lord Jesus, which calls itself Christian, and has neither Christ's mind nor spirit. It is called Babylon, that is confusion, for false Christendom, divided into many churches and sects, is truly and strictly a con-

[1] "Daniel and Revelation," pp. 287-289, 293.

fuser. However in all churches, parties, and sects of Christendom, the true Jesus congregation lives and is hidden.'"[1]

Babylon,[2] while identical in some respects with the harlot, is larger. It is the ecclesiastical system as distinguished from the spiritual body. In this time church and state are one. Antichrist as Christ, is to be the head of both church and state. The whole forms a vast world-wide combination of political and religious power which will far outstrip anything we know of now. With superhuman intelligence and the development of faculties now lying dormant in man and nature, there will be such advances in invention and discovery as to make all we see and know as the doings of children. The world will believe it has attained to the state of perfection and security and happiness.

There is also a people of God on earth during the Day of the Lord. The Day of the Lord is not all judgment. Mercy is offered all this time. Peter in his Pentecostal discourse quotes the prophecy of Joel, giving the beginning and ending of the gospel age in which occurs this prophecy of the end: "Whosoever shall call on the name of the Lord shall be saved."[3] God is not even in the Day of Judgment willing that any shall perish, but that all shall come unto him and live. All this is another effort to awaken mankind and make men see and hear and feel and repent. It is for this reason the respites are given. There are many other hints of the presence on earth of some of the people of God, all during the Day of Judgment. The satanic kingdom makes war with the saints and overcomes them, all on the earth worship him except those written in the Lamb's book of life. At this time is written, "Here is the patience and faith of the saints." Those who do not worship the image of the beast

[1] Vol. 5, sec. 6.   [2] Revelation xviii.   [3] Acts ii. 21.

and who do not take his mark on head and hands are shut off from buying or selling.[1] It is sometimes stated that the Holy Spirit leaves the world with the translation of the people of God. There does not appear to be any Scriptural statement to this effect. It is an inference, and apparently unwarranted. Since there are people of God on earth all the time, as we have seen, the Holy Spirit must be with them. And as the gospel is preached, he remains to do his spiritual work in the gospel.

After this occurs a world-wide call to repentance. This is after the rise and ascendancy of Antichrist and his political system and the satanic church, and just before the outpouring of the vials of wrath. "And I saw another angel flying in mid heaven, having an eternal gospel to proclaim unto them that dwell on the earth, and unto every nation and tribe and tongue and people; and he saith with a great voice, Fear God, and give him glory; for the hour of his judgment is come: and worship him that made the heaven and the earth and the sea and fountains of waters."[2] This is undoubtedly a call to the heathen nations, or those to which the gospel was preached as "a witness." They now hear it certified to by this supernatural agency, and many believe and are saved. We read afterward of their state and fate: "Here is the patience of the saints, they that keep the commandments of God, and the faith of Jesus. And I heard a voice from heaven saying, Write, Blessed are the dead which die in the Lord from henceforth: yea, saith the Spirit, that they may rest from their labors; for their works follow with them."[3] Terrible persecution is implied in this, so that death is a blessed relief from their state of suffering. Those who are thus delivered from this greater Pharaoh and come across this greater Red Sea of deliverance are thus described:

[1] Rev. xiii. 7, 8, 10, 15, 17.   [2] Rev. xiv. 6, 7.
[3] Rev. xiv. 12, 13.

"And I saw as it were a glassy sea mingled with fire; and them that come victorious from the beast, and from his image, and from the number of his name, standing by the glassy sea, having harps of God. And they sing the song of Moses, the servant of God, and the song of the Lamb."[1] These are expressly described as victors in the satanic age we have described in these scriptures. And that they were translated is a fair inference from their position and the figure of the sea and their song.

It is at the climax of the triumphs of Antichrist's kingdom the new course of judgments are poured out. So it is before the beginning of the Day of God, this world is in the highest point of attainment of civilization and unbelief when the blackness of the last day falls upon it as a snare. So before the Trumpet Judgments. So now Antichrist is in the summit of his glory. The people of God have been once more almost, if not altogether, exterminated. A long time of quiet from the plagues has passed. The world comes to believe their adored ruler is equal to any emergency which may arise. They have forgotten again the plagues of the past.

The vials are poured out. These are world-wide in extent. They are described as follows: "And the first went and poured his bowl upon the earth; and it became a noisome and grievous sore upon the men which had the mark of the beast, and which worshiped his image.

"And the second poured out his bowl into the sea; and it became blood as of a dead man; and every living soul died, even the things that were in the sea.

"And the third poured out his bowl into the rivers and the fountains of the waters; and it became blood. And I heard the angel of the waters saying, Righteous art thou, which art and which wast, thou Holy One,

[1] Rev. xv. 2, 3.

because thou didst thus judge: for they poured out the blood of saints and prophets, and blood hast thou given them to drink: they are worthy. And I heard the altar saying, Yea, O Lord God, the Almighty, true and righteous are thy judgments.

"And the fourth poured out his bowl upon the sun; and it was given unto it to scorch men with fire. And men were scorched with great heat: and they blasphemed the name of the God which hath the power over these plagues; and they repented not to give him glory.

"And the fifth poured out his bowl upon the throne of the beast; and his kingdom was darkened; and they gnawed their tongues for pain, and they blasphemed the God of heaven because of their pains and their sores; and they repented not of their works.

"And the sixth poured out his bowl upon the great river, the river Euphrates; and the water thereof was dried up, that the way might be made ready for the kings that come from the sunrising. . . .

"And the seventh angel poured out his bowl upon the air, and there came forth a great voice out of the temple from the throne, saying, It is done: and there were lightnings, and voices, and thunders; and there was a great earthquake, such as was not since there were men upon the earth, so great an earthquake, so mighty. And the great city was divided into three parts, and the cities of the nations fell; and Babylon the great was remembered in the sight of God to give unto her the cup of wine of the fierceness of his wrath. And every island fled away and the mountains were not found. And a great hail, every stone about the weight of a talent, cometh down out of heaven upon men; and men blasphemed God because of the plague of the hail; for the plague thereof is exceeding great."[1]

[1] Rev. xvi. 2–21.

The course of the world under these awful judgments is noticeable as indicated by the last quotation. There is observed a gradual hardening and sinking in depravity under all this display of the supernatural and of wrath. We read that after the first warning, men were terrified and cried out in alarm, seeking a place of concealment, and calling on the rocks to cover them. But that is only fear and not repentance. After the first course of judgment, it is recorded that "they repented not of their murders, nor of their sorceries, nor of their fornications, nor of their thefts."[1] Later they kill the witnesses of God and make merry over it. Still further they are angry as they hear that the end is approaching, and later still worship Satan openly as their lord and master, and engage with his vicegerent in all his persecutions and diabolism and uncleanness. Now as the terrors of the last judgment are actually falling upon them, we read three times as follows: "They blasphemed the name of the God which hath the power over these plagues: and they repented not to give him glory." After another plague they gnawed their tongues for pain, and blasphemed the God of heaven because of their pains and their sores: and they repented not of their works. And at the last, "Men blasphemed God because of the plague of the hail."[2] All that display of the reality and terror of eternity is in vain. It produces naught but blasphemy. So Christ proceeds to bring the whole age to a close.

Christ begins with the apostate church;[3] her fate comes at the hands of the nations or powers of the earth with whom she has engaged in harlotry. She is first cast down from her high position, then stripped of her rights and privileges and property, and finally destroyed by the killing of her leaders, the ruin of her edifices, and the cessation of her worship. The historical interpretation shows such a partial treatment

---

[1] Rev. ix. 21.   [2] Rev. xvi. 9, 11, 21.   [3] Revelation xvii.

by the world of the Roman harlot and mother of harlots which is the figure and perhaps the nucleus of the coming apostate church. There is nothing left now but Antichrist as an object of worship. He sits openly in Christ's stead taking the worship of men. He is not satisfied by anything short of divine honors. Paul has him in view in these words: "The man of sin is revealed the son of perdition, he that opposeth and exalteth himself against all that is called God or that is worshiped; so that he sitteth in the temple of God, setting himself forth as God."[1] Mankind is demonized. They have so come under the influence of Satan that all are as devils, and worship the head of the satanic kingdom, as some are professedly and openly doing to-day. This is the final result of the promise, "Ye shall be as gods." They are as devils. This is the end of irreligion and so-called liberalism and antichristian science, formalism, and infidelity. This is the result of world-seeking life and ambition and turning after whatever promises success, making success rather than the will of God first, and catering on the part of the church to the world, and seeking its aid and coming to its aid in all its schemes, instead of coming out from among them and being separated.

There remains the great ecclesiatical and social system nurtured and supported by the seductive influence of the false spiritual church restraining men, and keeping the baser sort in subjection for the enrichment of the others, this comes now before God for judgment. That christless, godless civilization has by this time become world-wide. The ideal of the vain dreamers of this age has come to pass. Mankind and civilization are coterminous. Before the destruction of the chaff the last remnant of the wheat is saved. There are some of God's people on earth, for the call is sent out to those in Babylon. "Come

[1] 2 Thess. ii, 4.

forth, my people, out of her, that ye have no fellowship with her sins and that ye receive not of her plagues."[1] This is the last call of Christ. He has people then even in Babylon at the very end of the judgment. These are taken out probably by another translation.

The spiritual influence of the apostate church being gone, there is nothing to uphold the great system of Antichrist. In an instant, like the falling of a great stone into the sea, Babylon is overwhelmed.[2] The vast structure of that mightiest of civilizations and perfection of social systems, is in ruins. By what stroke this comes, whether by inward convulsion or outward invasion, we cannot now know. This will be the most awful stroke which so far has fallen on the world. All the past calamities which fell on man, produced but curses and blasphemies. But the overthrow of their glorious state and means of gain and enjoyment, breaks the world's heart. Such mourning the world never witnessed. A whole chapter is given to the world's lament.[3]

Following the overthrow of Antichrist and his host is given the scripture already quoted, which, however, it is again necessary to consider. "And I saw thrones, and they sat upon them, and judgment was given unto them ; and I saw the souls of them that had been beheaded for the testimony of Jesus, and for the word of God, and such as worshiped not the beast, neither his image, and received not the mark upon their forehead and upon their hand ; and they lived, and reigned with Christ a thousand years. The rest of the dead lived not until the thousand years should be finished. This is the first resurrection. Blessed and holy is he that hath a part in the first resurrection ; over these the second death hath no power ; but they shall be priests of God and of

[1] Rev. xviii. 4.   [2] Revelation xviii.   [3] Revelation xviii.

Christ, and shall reign with him a thousand years."[1] There are two separate companies spoken of here as reigning. Of the first it is simply said, "I saw thrones, and they sat upon them, and judgment was given unto them." This refers to the whole company of risen and reigning saints who in all the past time prior to the judgment, and during it, were either translated or resurrected in the successive resurrections or translations already spoken of. They are now enthroned and associated with Christ. The second company is specifically described as those who during the reign of Antichrist were beheaded as martyrs for Christ, because of refusing to receive the mark of Antichrist upon their heads or hands. The souls of these John saw. That is equivalent to saying he saw their martyrdom. The same expression is used in the beginning of the Apocalypse as to the first martyrs.[2] This completes the first resurrection, and it is added, "Blessed and holy is he that hath part in the first resurrection."

The common misapprehension is fallen into of applying the part concerning this martyr company to the whole company of the saints. The reasons for rejecting this interpretation are as follows: First, it wholly disregards the first clause, and assumes that it is merely a prior statement of what follows; but the connecting conjunction shows temporal sequence. It is a statement as to one great, general company followed by a more particular statement as to another special class. Second, it perverts a careful description of a specific company, who are designated as existing at a particular time, and as having died by a particular cause, and in a peculiar manner, and forgetting or disregarding this plain description, applies this to all the saints who have ever lived at any time and died by any cause and in any manner.

[1] Rev. xx. 4-6,   [2] Rev. vi. 9.

Such is not precise and careful exegesis. It is a fault of the system of interpretation protested against in this chapter, and is disastrous as to obtaining accurate results. The interpretation of this important passage which applies it to all the saints is fatal to the argument for the second or separate resurrection of the saints. If these beheaded saints are all who are to rise and reign with Christ, then the vast number of believers are shut out; for a careful and particular description of a particular class, excludes others. The expression, "This is the first resurrection," extends to the whole account, and embraces the two classes, the great previous number and the last. It is as much as to say, "This completes the first resurrection." The general plan of the resurrection of the saints declared by Paul, has been noted, "each in his own order," or rank.[1] It is the figure of a marching army. So the saints are gathered in. By generations, by companies, by classes, rank by rank, coming up from the Judgment Age to appear before their Lord, and then to be judged and rewarded by him as each is found worthy. The last company of risen saints are the martyrs of Antichrist, and the death by which they glorify God is by beheading.

This completes that special body called "The Church," "The Bride." It began in martyrdom. Its first members so went to their reward. In this company we see the last also going in the same way. Every member of this church of Christ is therefore enclosed in this blessed parenthesis of holy martyr companionship, and although in our day, we have not been called upon to suffer martyrdom, we may be in the company of those who have so suffered. "If we suffer with him, we shall also reign with him," includes any form of trial and hardship for the sake of Christ.

The event which follows the fall of the false church

[1] I Cor. xv. 22.

and the completion of the true church and its formal union to Christ, is the great ceremony so much referred to by himself on earth and even spoken of in the Old Testament. It is described as follows: "And I heard as it were the voice of a great multitude, and as the voice of many waters, and as the voice of mighty thunders, saying, Hallelujah: for the Lord our God, the Almighty, reigneth. Let us rejoice and be exceeding glad, and let us give the glory unto him: for the marriage of the Lamb is come, and his wife hath made herself ready. And it was given unto her that she should array herself in fine linen, bright and pure: for the fine linen is the righteous acts of the saints. And he saith unto me, Write, Blessed are they which are bidden to the marriage supper of the Lamb."[1] It was the marriage supper of the Lamb, Christ referred to when he said at the last supper, "But I say unto you, I will not drink henceforth of this fruit of the vine, until that day when I drink it new with you in my Father's kingdom."[2] Every celebration of the Lord's Supper is a forecast of a greater supper. The sacrament looks not only back to the last supper, but forward to this coming and greater one. This outlook is often forgotten in the memories of Calvary. But the apostle reminds us of this aspect of it in the words, "We show the Lord's death till he come."

There follows the overthrow of Babylon, the great battle of the Day of the Lord.[3] It is the culminating of all antichristianity. The contending sides are led by Christ and Antichrist in person. There has been in all the judgment so far no direct act of Christ upon the world. He has acted through angels and natural or cosmical agencies. In fact, save the calling of his people, and his first appearance, he has been all this time, so far as any record shows, unseen by the world,

---

[1] Rev. xix. 6-9.   [2] Matt. xxvi. 29.   [3] Rev. xix. 11-21.

as he is to-day. It is probably this absence of the visible Christ and the unbelief to which this gives rise, which hardens the hearts of men in the almost incredible degree we have seen. Satan has not only persuaded mankind to forsake God, but to serve himself, and finally, after the overthrow of their last resource, to array themselves in mortal conflict against Christ.

The preparations for the conflict, the "war of the great Day of God," have been long making, for we read of three emissaries of Satan going forth to prepare the forces of Satan for the conflict. They are thus described in symbolic language: "And I saw coming out of the mouth of the dragon, and out of the mouth of the beast, and out of the mouth of the false prophet, three unclean spirits, as it were frogs: for they are spirits of devils, working signs; which go forth unto the kings of the whole world, to gather them together unto the war of the great Day of God, the Almighty. (Behold, I come as a thief. Blessed is he that watcheth, and keepeth his garments, lest he walk naked, and they see his shame.) And they gathered them together into the place which is called in Hebrew Har-Magedon."[1] The number three is the number of deity and also of the natures of man. There is a reference to both; an imitation of the working of God as we have seen, and also an appeal to the threefold nature of man. The three influences which Satan will send out will probably appeal to man's physical, social, and spiritual natures. They will therefore be material, social, and religious forms of satanic influence. The figure of the creature chosen, calls attention to the low and unclean nature of these influences and their effects, and that they come in darkness and are unseen in their secret work of influencing the world against the religion and people of Christ. Some influences now existing may show what these which are to come may be. Alcohol, socialism, and Spiritualism may be taken as represent-

[1] Rev. xvi. 14-16.

ing three forms of satanic influence. Each appeals to one of man's natures. Around each of these may be grouped a circle of kindred agencies. With alcohol may be grouped all the narcotics, drugs, and drinks with which the world is now physically intoxicated, the demand for which is growing at an appalling rate. With socialism must be considered all the forms of revolutionary change now proposed, such as communism in France, nihilism in Russia, and anarchy in America. With the third should be placed all such antichristian beliefs as theosophy, Christian Science, and all the forms of occultism, hypnotism, etc.

In this conflict is seen the Son of God, who now appears personally and visibly before the assembled powers of earth who are now arrayed in open, as they have been in secret, rebellion against him. Christ's eyes flash with the fire of the wrath of God. Vengeance is in his hand. His garments are stained with blood. It is the blood of Calvary and of his saints, which this guilty world has shed. It is the blood this apostate world has trampled under foot, and counted it an accursed thing. This blood of Calvary is now the most awful witness of the guilt of man. It has never been repented of by the world. Every rejecter of Christ has thereby, as well as by his affiliation with the enemies of God, become a guilty accessory after the fact.

The titles applied to Christ in this act of divine judgment upon which he now enters are first, "The Word of God," and also "KING OF KINGS, AND LORD OF LORDS." The first is that by which he is called, the second is written on his thigh. The first is his immediate title, and expresses the thought that this is Christ in his creative power now fully resumed. All the time of the present dispensation of grace he is called "Christ," and is represented as seated on the right hand of God, who tells him, "Sit thou on my right hand, till I make thine enemies the footstool of thy feet." (Acts 11 : 34, 35.) The time for this has come. The mercy title is laid aside. He is no longer "Christ" to the world. The other title is written on his thigh, the place of the sword, the place of strength. It is his coming position which he now enters upon. So far Christ has been King *de-jure*, now he becomes King *de-facto*. He has been Lord to his church, now he becomes Lord of all. Christ is from henceforth until the consummation, KING OF KINGS, AND LORD OF LORDS.

The great Battle of the Day of God and its outcome is thus described: "And I saw the heaven opened ; and behold, a white horse, and he that sat thereon, called Faithful and True ; and in righteousness he doth judge and make war. And his eyes are a flame of fire, and upon his head are many diadems ; and he hath a name written which no one knoweth but he himself. And he is arrayed in a garment sprinkled with blood: and his name is called The Word of God. And the armies which are in heaven followed him upon white horses, clothed in fine linen, white and pure. And out of his mouth proceedeth a sharp sword, that with it he should smite the nations: and he shall rule them with a rod of iron : and he treadeth the winepress of the fierceness of the wrath of Almighty God. And he hath on his garment and on his thigh a name written, KING OF KINGS, AND LORD OF LORDS. And I saw an angel standing in the sun ; and he cried with a loud voice, saying to all the birds that fly in mid-heaven, Come and be gathered together unto the great supper of God ; that ye may eat the flesh of kings, and the flesh of captains, and the flesh of mighty men, and the flesh of horses and of them that sit thereon, and the flesh of all men, both free and bond, and small and great.

"And I saw the beast, and the kings of the earth, and their armies, gathered together to make war against him that sat upon the horse, and against his army. And the beast was taken, and with him the false prophet that wrought the signs in his sight, wherewith he deceived them that had received the mark of the beast, and them that worshiped his image: they twain were cast alive into the lake of fire that burneth with brimstone, and the rest were killed with the sword of him that sat upon the horse, even the sword which came forth out of his mouth: and all the birds were filled with their flesh. And I saw an angel coming down out of heaven, having the key of the abyss and a great chain in his hand. And he laid hold on the dragon, the old serpent, which is the devil and Satan, and bound him for a thousand years, and cast him into the abyss, and shut it, and sealed it over him, that he should deceive the nations no more, until the thousand years should be finished: after this he must be loosed for a little time."[1]

No words can add to this inspired description, nor indeed to any of the apocalyptic narratives, therefore we transcribe them entire. What all this means we can now only know in part. We know the array is Antichrist at the head of the united forces of the world completely submissive to his will, and probably so armed as to make the present armaments of the nations appear as the rude weapons of savages. It will doubtless be a fearful array of devices of satanic invention letting loose powers of destruction of wide sweeping scope and awful energy, operating from above and from below, from air and earth, and rendering conflict with any earthly foe a scene of cyclonic destruction.

The riders on the white horses are the angels who everywhere are described as coming with Christ in vengeance to the world. The saints are never spoken of as taking part in the judgments until the end. Not until victory is won is the church given a place of power. The armies of heaven are much

[1] Rev. xix. 11-21; xx. 1-3.

spoken of in Scripture. It is their greatness which gives Christ one of his grandest titles, "Lord of hosts." These vast hosts are now marshaled in dreadful array. Let no one suppose all this is figurative. There are such armies. Angels are as real as human beings. They have forms and bodies and locality and identity, and have means of movement, and exercise strength, and have occasion for all they possess; for they are not omnipotent. They are now to meet one who is equal in strength to themselves. Contests of the angels with Satan are frequently recorded in Scripture.

We can let our minds dwell upon this scene, but only as children. No doubt Christ waits to give one last opportunity to the assembled world, as they gaze upon him and his mighty hosts, to show repentance, or at least some sign of submission. So he waited until a week after Noah entered the ark. So also he delayed until Pharaoh was in pursuit of the Israelites and actually upon them, before he overwhelmed them. So also he came and saw Lot threatened and his house assaulted before he led him out and destroyed Sodom. And again, when Sennacherib besieged Jerusalem, God waited until all possible opportunity had been given before permitting the angel of death to draw and wield his sword against him. It is the divine way. So now man is warned in every way, and God waits until he is in actual array against him, and, no doubt, until he strikes the first blow. The first act of Christ is to destroy the head of the opposing host. Antichrist and his prophet are taken and cast into the lake of fire. There is here also mercy displayed in so beginning the overthrow of the enemy. If there is any willingness to repent among the rank and file, it does not appear. God is to be justified in this as in all his judgments. This first act seems to be performed by the angels, as in the final part of the conflict they are used, but not in the great act of judgment. The actual overthrow of the antichristian hosts is described by Paul: "You that are afflicted rest with us, at the revelation of the Lord Jesus Christ from heaven with the angels of his power in flaming fire, rendering vengeance unto them that know not God, and to them that obey not the gospel of our Lord Jesus; who shall suffer punishment, even eternal destruction from the face of the Lord and from the glory of his might, when he shall come to be glorified in his saints, and to be marveled at in all them that believed."[1]

Christ alone wars in that battle; none other is needed save to gather up. It is by the sword of his mouth Christ smites the hosts of Antichrist. It is as the Word of God he acts. One word from him who called all things into being is sufficient. Christ speaks the awful word, and the wrath of Almighty God leaps forth as a sword from its scabbard, and in millions of fiery points touches every soul of that human array, and as if stricken by the lightning's flash, they sink into instant death. The angels do their part. The battle is over, but another act follows: During all the ages of man's history, Satan himself has suffered no personal punishment save deprivation of his once glorious place as one of, perhaps, the highest of the angelic hosts, and subsequent expulsion from heaven. But now he feels the heavy hand of divine power, and is cast into the abyss so feared by the demons in the time of Christ, and where the apostate angels are who kept not their first estate.

During all this time Christ has not forgotten his ancient people. He has followed them in chastisement, and he will turn to them in blessing. Every nation who has oppressed them has suffered for it, and every nation who has favored them has been the richer. "They shall prosper that love

[1] 2 Thess. i. 7-10.

thee" is God's promise to such. There is nothing more clearly stated than the predictions of their restoration, first to their own land, and second to their Jehovah. They are to return as a nation into possession of their land. This is in every one of the prophets. It is spoken of the Jews and of the remaining ten tribes called Israel. It is in the prophecies given after the return from Babylon. It is in such form as to show it has never taken place. They are to return in their present state. They are to be favored by the nations in this, and to return with their wealth and become autonomous, and to rebuild their temple.

There are intimations running through the record that the ancient people of God have a great part in the Day of the Lord. These are alluded to under three figures. The first is the temple[1] which the apostle is commanded to measure, indicating appropriation and preservation. Their religious polity is to be preserved during all this time. The "outer court," probably the renegades from their ancient faith, the so-called "Reformed Israelites," are given over to the world. In the second type, the true faith is represented by two witnesses[2] who testify against the abominable worship of Antichrist into which the whole world, except the true ones of Israel, falls. Once more Israel is God's witness on earth. The third symbol shows Israel again in her spiritual and ancient position as regarded by her Jehovah. She is represented as a glorious form clothed with the sun and having a diadem of twelve stars.[3] It is Israel as her Messiah sees her now. The past apostasies are all forgotten. She is the temple of God, the witness of God, the bearer of the Son of God into this world. This latter is reviewed, and the story of redemption as if it was all for and by Israel. She has come back to her appointed place. It is by the

---

[1] Rev. xi. 1, 2.   [2] Rev. xi. 3–13.   [3] Rev. xii. 1.

death of her divine Son, Satan is cast out of heaven, and it is because of hatred to her and her seed that he rages now on earth. It is for the deliverance of herself and her seed that Christ is working now in judgment. All is Israel as if she had never fallen. Her sins and iniquities are remembered no more.

Satan will do all in his power to destroy them, knowing their place in the heart of Christ and in his purpose. He will first try by flatteries to seduce them into apostasy from God and into allegiance with himself. Failing in this, he will attack them by force. Their city will be again imperiled and by a more fearful fate than before. As they see their danger, they will repent and call upon God for his help. In their distress Christ will appear for their relief. Indeed this is the immediate occasion of his coming at this time and place. They are to be converted as a nation by this appearance of their Messiah, whom they will recognize and see him to be Jesus. Paul gives his own conversion as a type, or rather as a part, of that of the whole nation. He speaks of being converted, "as one born out of due time;" that is, prematurely; for the natural figure forbids the idea of a procrastination. They are to look on him whom they have pierced, and to mourn. The very substance of their mourning is given in the fifty-third of Isaiah, which is not only the prophet's lament over their hardness, but their own lament in that day over their own unbelief. It will break their hard hearts to think they crucified and so long refused their own Jehovah. They will receive him and be forever his.

The event upon which Christ enters next is described in the parable of the sheep and the goats.[1] This is another in the series of judgments which characterize the Day of the Lord and give it its

[1] Matt. xxv. 31-46.

general name, the Judgment Day. This must be distinguished from the judgment of the saints and also from that of the Great White Throne, usually called the general judgment. These judged are living nations, while in the latter it is "the dead, small and great." These are not synonymous terms, for the former are living, while the latter are the dead. In the former there is no reference to a resurrection. The name of the position occupied by Christ is different. "The Throne of his Glory" and "The Great White Throne" will be seen by careful, close study to be essentially dissimilar in time and character, as describing Christ's offices, as unlike as the Throne of Grace from either of them. The latter is for the church; The Throne of Glory for the regenerated earth. The Great White Throne for all mankind of every age, and probably for all existences of every world. The terms of judgment are also dissimilar. No books of record are opened, nor any conduct of the judged except on one point. Companies of the saved are here mentioned; in the later judgment none are spoken of. In this judgment the saved do not know they are to be saved. They are judged not by such faith as those now coming, but by works and a single kind of works. Those coming in our age do all for Christ's sake. This company do not know they even tried to do anything for him. In this the lost are sent to punishment before Satan, but in the last judgment they are sent after Satan's condemnation.

The "nations" referred to here, are those exclusive of Israel, the Gentiles. It is to these the word is applied specifically over a hundred times out of the hundred and thirty-two occasions of its occurrence. The fact that the parable occurs in the gospel of Matthew and nowhere else, also points to a special reference to Israel. By "my brethren" is included, doubtless, all of the people of Christ, but especially the Israelites, all of whom are the subjects first of the seductions, and then the malignity of Antichrist, and suffer untold hardships in that day. It is the treatment, good or evil, of these, which wins eternal life or eternal condemnation. The rule of procedure or judgment is as follows: "He that receiveth you receiveth me, and he that receiveth me receiveth him that sent me. He that receiveth a prophet in the name of a prophet shall receive a prophet's reward; and he that receiveth a righteous man in the name of a righteous man shall receive a righteous man's reward. And whosoever shall give to drink unto one of these little ones a cup of cold water only, in the name of a disciple, verily I say unto you, he shall in no wise lose his reward."[1]

The desolating judgments of the Day of the Lord will have greatly reduced the population of the earth. Out of the judgment of the nations will come a body of saved who will enter into the kingdom of Christ to be now established. We have seen that Christ began each dispensation with a small number. Adam, Noah, and Abraham, each respectively represent the beginnings of three ages. So now there may be comparatively a small body left with which the new earth or age begins. This is the tenor of many scriptures: "Behold, the Lord maketh the earth empty, and maketh it waste, and turneth it upside down, and scattereth the inhabitants thereof. . . . The inhabitants of the earth are burned, and few men left."[2] These few saved are the nucleus of the population of earthly inhabitants which form the millennial kingdom.

The millennium is a matter of universal belief. In some form at some time, all hope for it. This is the

---

[1] Matt. x. 40-42.   [2] Isa. xxiv. 1, 6.

belief of the Christian church universally. It is the belief also of almost the whole of mankind. It lies in "The Day of the Lord." It is therefore a state of the supernatural, but not wholly so. It is part of the Judgment Day. Christ sits in governmental judgment. It is a condition when the supernatural is to be seen and known, but not necessarily continuously. Its name indicates a period of a thousand years. The belief of the Jewish church was that there were to be six days of toil and sin, followed by a Sabbath of rest and holiness. All of which seems reasonable, and has this scripture: "If Joshua had given them rest, he would not have spoken afterward of another day. There remaineth therefore a Sabbath rest for the people of God."[1] That the period is this, called "another day" and "Sabbath rest," there seems no good reason to doubt. The following comments by noted and able students of Scripture are given. From Starke:—

"The one thousand years of the binding of the dragon and the reign of Christ and his saints, are properly years. There is no reason why we should deviate from a literal interpretation. If we explain them of the past, we involve ourselves in inextricable difficulties. Still less can they be referred to eternity, because verses 7 and 8 indicate their completion and show what will occur after the thousand years are expired. On the contrary, there are weighty reasons for abiding by a literal interpretation, (1) because it carries with it nothing absurd or incorrect; (2) because the circumstances demand it, inasmuch as these one thousand years are mentioned not merely twice in verses 2 and 5, but four times with the article prefixed (verses 3, 4, 5, 7), years to which nothing must be added, and from which nothing must be subtracted; (3) because the literal agrees best with the chief work of the divine creation and the course of all times."[2]

Alford wrote:—

"That the Lord will come in person to this our earth; that during that blessed reign, the power of evil will be bound,

[1] Heb. iv. 8, 9.
[2] Synopsis of the New Testament, quoted in Premillennial Essays, Chicago, 1879, p. 482.

and the glorious prophecies of peace and truth on earth will find their accomplishment,— this is my firm persuasion, and not mine alone, but that of multitudes of Christ's waiting people, as it was that of his primitive, apostolic church before controversy blinded the eyes of the Fathers to the light of prophecy."[1]

John Wesley said : —

"In a short time those who assert that they (the thousand years) are now at hand, will appear to have spoken the truth."

The millennium is to affect the world, Israel, and the church. There appears to be, first of all, some great change by which the state of nature is made more agreeable and safe and healthful for man and all living beings and creatures. Paul refers to this great change : "For I reckon that the sufferings of this present time are not worthy to be compared with the glory which shall be revealed to us-ward. For the earnest expectation of the creation waiteth for the revealing of the sons of God. For the creation was subjected to vanity, not of its own will, but by reason of him who subjected it, in hope that the creation itself also shall be delivered from the bondage of corruption, into the liberty of the glory of the children of God."[2] He names the time when this is to take place as that of "the redemption of our body," that is, our resurrection. This, then, comes in the great changes and convulsions of the years of judgment. The earth is freed from the evils which afflict man and beast. The millennium could be no such happy time as all expect and as the Scriptures describe, while storms, cyclones, malaria, earthquakes, and heat and cold, afflict man and make life, as it is for large regions, a struggle for existence.

Calvin wrote upon the above passage : —

"I expect, with Paul, a reparation of all the evils caused by sin, for which he represents the creation as groaning and travailing."

[1] Greek Testament, London, 1868, 4 Vols., Vol. 4, p. 232.
[2] Rom. viii. 18–21.

The existence of man upon the earth at this time will be much that Eden was, with the added accumulations of the best in invention and every branch of civilization. Mankind will live in families and increase and have the enjoyments of social life and cultivate the earth and do business and produce wealth and enjoy it. They will build cities and study and invent and grow in all noble arts and sciences. There are indications that the lifetime of man shall be greatly prolonged, perhaps to the full original age of one thousand years. So that, if this is the duration of the millennium, no one need die during that time. Death will be exceptional, and a special judgment upon sin, as the following shows: "There shall be no more thence an infant of days, nor an old man that hath not filled his days; for the child shall die an hundred years old, and the sinner an hundred years old shall be accursed."[1]

The great feature of the millennium will be the spiritual state of man. It is not said that all will be regenerated, at least down through the whole period, as will be seen, but the whole of mankind will be professedly Christian, and most, really so. All evils such as intemperance and oppression will be abolished. Christ will probably be present as he was in his resurrection state, and through his saints will govern and instruct the world. It will be a church-state such as Israel was intended to be. It will be the theocracy, with Christ acting more openly and directly than in Israel. In view of the history of the latter, a state in which the supernatural is seen and operates, ought not to be considered so very strange or incredible. Substituting the risen saints for angels, will be the same kind of operation of divine power. The seventy-second psalm is a prophecy of the reign of Christ during the millennium.

In all the prophecies of the millennium, Israel has a place. The Messianic kingdom for Israel is the key

[1] Isa, lxv. 20.

to the predictive prophecies of the Old Testament. We have no difficulty in applying the hortatory prophecies, especially the warnings and denunciations, to Israel. The predictions of a glorious state were addressed to the very same people as the former. The Old Testament prophets must be read in this light primarily. It must be borne in mind that they are Israel's messages first of all. Whatever we as Gentiles may derive of comfort from them, we must remember we are eating off the table of another. Christ so guarded this table as to say to one of us Gentiles, "It is not meet to take the children's bread, and to cast it to the dogs."[1] But we Gentiles have taken possession of bread, table, house, and all, and are denying the children any special share in it. DaCosta, an Israelite, thus writes:—

"Who has given us the right, while contemplating the literal fulfilment of the judgments on the Hebrews, to alter suddenly the principle of interpretation, where the curse is changed into a blessing? Who gives us the right, by arbitrary exegesis to apply the promises to the Christian church, to the Gentiles, when the judgments evidently could not have been intended for them. There is then a future for Israel, for the long degraded outcasts, an approaching glory. Israel and the regenerate nations will triumph together over the Gentiles who have forgotten God, and who oppose the kingdom of Christ. Israel's King will be King of all the nations."[2]

Then the promises made to Abraham as to the land and the increase of his people will be fulfilled. Israel will be the chief nation of the world. The land of Israel is the geographical center of the earth. It will undoubtedly be its spiritual center also. To it will come great convocations from all the world, and from it will go missions of spiritual influence to all the world. The scripture passages which speak of this time in Israel's history are very numerous. They fill large portions of the prophets. Indeed,

---

[1] Mark vii. 28.
[2] "Israel and the Gentiles." Quoted in Premillennial Essays, Chicago, 1879, p. 560.

every one of the prophecies closes with bright outlooks into this happy time for Israel. Zechariah is peculiarly the prophet of this time. A single verse gives the characteristic position of Israel: "And it shall come to pass that every one that is left of all the nations which came against Jerusalem shall go up from year to year to worship the King, the Lord of Hosts, and to keep the feast of tabernacles."[1] The types for Israel of the millennium are the great jubilee, representing their social state, and the reign of Solomon, representing their political glory; Solomon's being simply a continuation of the reign of David, the kingdom militant being succeeded by the kingdom triumphant.

The state of the saints in the millennium is that of Christ after his resurrection. He was a palpable personality. He was seen, heard, and handled, and exercised all the powers of life, such as walking, building a fire, eating, and drinking. There is no reason to believe that he is any different now, or that the risen saints will be. There has come to us out of paganism, the doctrine of the evil of matter, and that pure holiness requires a mere etherial state. There is nothing of all this in Scripture. Lange thus writes of this : —

> "Break this golden band between spirit and matter, between the actual fact and the symbol, and you fall back into that old accursed opposition between Spiritualism and materialism, which burdened the heathen world and will run through all your moral, esthetic, and philosophic ideas as a fatal cleft."[2]

There is nothing of the modern ghostly idea in the Scriptural representations of the resurrected saints or their abode. Not only the earth, but heaven, as will be seen, is material, and not a mere state or condition. These latter are unthinkable and impossible, and are the conceptions of an idealism which is wholly unscriptural. The state of the saints during

---

[1] Zech. xiv. 16.   [2] Commentary, Genesis, p. 74.

this time is described thus by Christ: "In the resurrection they neither marry nor are given in marriage, but are as angels in heaven."[1] Everything which has been associated with sin or the cause of sin will be left out of their lives, but we have no reason to say any innocent pleasure will be forbidden or impossible to the risen saints. If the risen Christ could and did eat and drink, it would be difficult to show why his people in the same state should not do so also. Indeed he said they should, as the following scripture states: "I appoint unto you a kingdom, even as my Father appointed unto me, that ye may eat and drink with me at my table in my kingdom; and ye shall sit on thrones judging the twelve tribes of Israel."[2] But none of the earthly conditions will be necessary to their life or welfare, and if used will be only as means of enjoyment.

That the saints shall reign on the earth is expressly stated by the heavenly beings in their song: "Worthy art thou to take the book, and to open the seals thereof: for thou wast slain, and didst purchase unto God with thy blood men of every tribe, and tongue, and people, and nation, and madest them to be unto our God a kingdom and priests; and they reign upon the earth."[3] There are numerous other passages which the concordance will show. Jamieson, Fausset & Brown comment thus:—

"Christ's coming kingdom is to be manifested at his appearing when the saints shall reign with him. His kingdom is real now, but not visible. It shall then be visible also. Now he rules in the midst of his enemies, expecting till they shall be overthrown. Then he shall reign over his adversaries. Christ will reign with his transfigured saints, over men in the flesh. The nations in the millennium will be prepared for a higher state, as Adam in paradise, supposing he had lived in an unfallen state. The millennium reign on earth does not rest on an isolated passage, but all prophecy goes upon the same view."[4]

[1] Matt. xxii. 30.   [2] Luke xxii. 30.   [3] Rev. v. 9, 10.
[4] Critical Commentary, Chicago, 1885.

From Theurer:—

"Whether Christ with his church during this kingdom of joy shall remain constantly visible, or whether after his visible appearance, he shall again become invisible, or sometimes one and then the other, as in the time of his resurrection, or whether the central seat of his dominion shall be Mount Zion, or whether this shall be literally exalted above all mountains, or whether the higher Pavilion-Cloud in the air shall, after banishment of all wicked spirits, be the place where Christ shall celebrate, with his church, the marriage supper of the Lamb, or whether the upper Jerusalem and Mount Zion shall be united in closest connection for the glorified Church,— these are questions on which the believing investigators of Scripture have returned various answers. Heaven will be nearer earth though not united. It will be the light evening, the still Sabbath of the earth, not yet its Sunday, or yet its still greater Easter-morn. The earth remains earth, though under a higher power of development, and an altogether new blessing from above. The physical life of man advances, but under the dominion of the Spirit. Among the nations shall stand preeminent, the now scattered, but then gathered people of Israel. For from Zion and Jerusalem, the clear gleam of God shall break forth, and from there shall proceed the law. At the end of the one thousand years the separation between heaven and earth shall be complete. Earth and heaven shall have passed through the grave to their eternal Easter-morn, and then shall be brought to glorious completion what was begun in the incarnation of Jesus."[1]

The millennium is therefore not the final state of man on earth. It is not the great and ultimate object of the saints' hope. It is not "the city which hath foundations, whose builder and whose maker is God." It is not "the kingdom which shall never pass away." It is not the full victory over the last enemy, for that does not come until death is cast into the lake of fire at the close of the final judgment. It is not the full restoration of humanity. It is not earth's eternal form. The millennium is but a day of a thousand years in a week of trial with which the story of redemption opens, to be succeeded by many weeks of

[1] Quoted in Premillennial Essays, Chicago, 1879, p. 488.

days as long as these, to roll out into years, and weeks of years, and jubilees, and millennial times of a thousand times such years. It is the unending succession of these which constitute the kingdom of God. We must guard against two possible errors as to the millennium, making too much of it, and, worse yet, wholly neglecting it. It has its place and a great one, but relatively limited, and, as all admit, temporary. It is far from a perfect state. It is one of the trial ages, the last indeed, but still an age of sifting. All the elements which contribute to moral trial are present except the active agency of Satan. He is not present. But human nature remains, and therefore sin is possible, indeed is present, for the death of the sinner is provided for. Death is still present although in greatly reduced scope. The whole age is a brief one. If our acceptance of the one thousand years is proper as the duration of the millennium, it is not more than half of the present gospel age.

The millennium is a demonstration by God that the world by doing the will of God is thereby made holy and happy. It is also a trial of man under the most favorable circumstances, as to his willingness to obey God. It is the belief professed by many that the present state of man in sin and misery, comes from his environment, and if all this could be changed, he would attain to a state of comparative perfection. Thus will all be given an opportunity to be tried during this age. With Satan bound and absent with all his angels from earth, and natural evils removed, and beginning with a selected seed of humanity, there is no reason, if this theory is correct, why mankind should not reach their ideal. All that the actual presence of the supernatural need do to demonstrate and instruct, will be given. In the millennium there is to be made the fullest demonstration of man's nature and ability under every condition for success. When it is over, nothing will have been left untried or untested. A thousand years will be long enough for the trial.

The millennium is to end in an apostasy. It begins at "the four corners of the earth," at the greatest distance from the seat of the divine government. The causes which explain the falling away, aside from the fact of the unregenerate state of many under cover of religion, are understood by comparing the history of past ages; as for example, the apostasy of Israel. It is altogether probable, that, like that age, the display of the supernatural gradually diminishes and finally ceases. The law and the prophets were introduced by such displays under Moses and Elijah, but these miraculous manifestations gradually ceased in each age as time went on. Israel sinking all the time into apostasy after apostasy, from which they were temporarily aroused by afflictions and the messages of the prophets. These messages also ceased, and toward the close, a time of freedom from alarms and prophetic appeals came, in which they fell into a state of final hardness. This will undoubtedly be the case in the age of the millennium. The mighty wonders of the Day of Judgment will become an old story and lose their power to alarm. The saints will strive to keep the world true to Christ by their efforts, governmental and spiritual.

It is not probable that Christ himself will be personally and visibly present all over the world or even constantly to any except a limited number, for this is not the full development, as has been intimated, of the kingdom. It is probable that as he was in his life, he will be more and more retired as the time of apostasy goes on. This is his spiritual method now. He hides his face from the backsliding soul. The saints will, perhaps, be left to carry on the work largely among themselves, and will faithfully do so. Moral suasion not proving equal to the task of holding man in check in the downward plunge, governmental measures will be tried. There will arise, as in this age, resentment at this control. The spirit of the world to-day and then, is seen in the words of the second psalm. "The kings of the earth set themselves, and the rulers take counsel together, against the Lord and against his Anointed, saying, Let us break their bands asunder, and cast away their cords from us."[1]

Satan now appears. As has been noted, there is always a preparation for him. The rebellion is not all his work. Under Satan's direction, the inward discontent with the rule of Christ assumes a state of open rebellion. The world arms once more for battle against the hosts of Christ. This time Satan leads in person. The previous battle of Har-Magedon was led by the Antichrist who appears to be a human being animated by Satan, and of surpassing genius. But he has been cast into the lake of fire, as the narrative tells us.

The close of the millennium is thus described: "And when the thousand years are finished, Satan shall be loosed out of his prison, and shall come forth to deceive the nations which are in the four corners of the earth, Gog and Magog, to gather them together to the war: the number of whom is as the sand of the sea. And they went up over the breadth of the earth, and compassed the camp of the saints about, and the beloved city: and fire came down out of heaven and devoured them. And the devil that deceived them, was cast into the lake of fire and brimstone, where are also the beast and the false prophet; and they shall be tormented by day and night forever and ever."[2] It seems incredible, that, after such terrors and blessings, any should be found ready to listen to the voice of Satan, but that such a multitude, amounting to an almost universal apostasy, should fall away from Christ, is the most astounding

[1] Ps. ii. 2, 3.   [2] Rev. xx. 7-10.

fact in the whole great record of sin. We must remember this is the record of every other age. We read of Israel apostatizing immediately after receiving the great revelation of God from the Mount Sinai, and Aaron with them making the golden calf and bowing down to it, among them the seventy elders who had received the spirit and had seen the vision of God on the mount.

The saints are besieged in their camp, doubtless, around Jerusalem. They have gradually retired before the rising tide of the rebellion, doubtless by Christ's secret command. They are in fearful peril as well as the people of Israel. It is the most terrible of created beings who approaches to destroy them, knowing it is his last opportunity. He is a spiritual being, otherwise he would have no terror for risen beings in spiritual bodies. It is not a mere display of hopeless resentment on Satan's part. They are committed to defense of their charge,—the beloved city. They cannot save themselves by flight, that would be victory for Satan and destruction for helpless Israel. It must not be supposed these great conflicts coming at the close of man's history are mere theatrical displays. There are none such of any kind in the Scripture. It is dreadful reality, as the world will one day know. This last conflict between good and evil, between Christ and Satan, is the most appalling display of evil the universe ever will see. It is Christ, as heretofore, attacked in his people.

The destruction of the forces of Satan is by fire from heaven. It seems to be the direct act of Almighty God. It is the last overthrow recorded. Satan is sent to his final place, the lake of fire, where his vicegerent and the false prophet are. Their fate is to be "tormented day and night forever and ever." He has caused infinite torment to the race of man, has ruined God's Eden, and devastated heaven. He has dared to lift his hand against God himself in the person of his Son, whom he has tempted, persecuted, slain, and whose work he has persistently opposed and frustrated, and now after all warnings, at the last shows no sign of repentance, but again after a thousand years of foretaste of his fate, comes forth to attack the work and people of God. Satan is an awful instance and proof of the unchangeableness of character. Whether for good or evil, the character of any being is established unalterably by his attitude toward God.

Christ now enters upon his last great work of judgment. The Scriptural account is the greatest and most sublime language and imagery which man possesses: "And I saw a great white throne, and him that sat upon it, from whose face the earth and the heaven fled away; and there was found no place for them. And I saw the dead, the great and the small, standing before the throne; and books were opened; and another book was opened, which is the book of life; and the dead were judged out of those things which were written in the books, according to their works. And the sea gave up the dead which were in it; and death and Hades gave up the dead which were in them; and they were judged every man according to their works."[1] This awful scene is pictured, as is all the history of the Day of God, to fix our attention by its sublimity and fearful grandeur. It has employed the artist and poet, but no words or colors can add to this simple account. It pictures the greatest thought which can enter man's mind,— accountability to his Maker.

Daniel gives an almost equal description of the last judgment: "I beheld till thrones were placed, and one that was ancient of days did sit: his raiment was white as snow, and the hair of his head like pure wool; his throne was fiery flames and the wheels thereof burning fire. A fiery stream issued and came forth from before him; thousand thousands minis-

[1] Rev. xx. 11-13.

tered unto him and ten thousand times ten thousand stood before him ; the judgment was set and the books were opened."[1] Here is the great fact added that there are other thrones with Christ's. The saints are associated with Christ in this judgment: "Know ye not that the saints shall judge the world? . . . Know ye not that we shall judge angels?"[2] "He that overcometh I will give to him to sit down with me in my throne, as I also overcame and sat down with my Father in his throne."[3] The scene calls for a vast array of thrones surrounding the great white throne. The picture presented to the mind is this vast array centering around the dazzling center and rising tier above tier. The angels are present in their countless hosts, to assist in this awful last assize. It is probable every living intelligent being in heaven and earth is a witness to the doings of the day.

This is the Day of Judgment proper as distinguished from all which has gone before. It is the gathering of all not heretofore raised, and their presentation before the throne. Only the dead are spoken of. It is evident all the sinful race are slain before the call to judgment. The great distinction made between the saved and others, is that of "the quick and dead." It is not said in what form the sinner appears before the judgment. The saints are described as robed in white garments. There is intimation of the sinner's appearing in shame and nakedness. Everywhere exposure is a penalty of the judgment. Exposure physically would suitably accompany exposure morally. The lost angels also appear at the judgment of the last day: "And angels which kept not their own principality, but left their proper habitation, he hath kept in everlasting bonds under darkness under the judgment of the great day."[4]

The Judge is Christ. As we have seen, all judg-

[1] Dan. vii. 9, 10.   [2] 1 Cor. vi. 2, 3.
[3] Rev. iii. 21.   [4] Jude 6.

ment is committed unto him. He appears in his glorified human form. It is he who was born of the Virgin Mary, and walked the roads of Galilee, and was crucified, and was buried, and rose from the dead, and ascended up to heaven. Many will see in him the one who was offered to them and pressed upon them so persistently, and whom they refused for the love of sin, or earthly gain, or pleasure, or ambition; or from fear of man, or shame, or unbelief, or hatred, and prejudice toward the people of God.

The judgment proceeds upon three distinct lines of evidence: Faith, Works, and the Book of Life. There is first of all shown the evidence of faith or want of it. This is and ever will be the only way of salvation. All the promises of the gospel are based on faith, and, as we have seen, the salvation of all from Adam down, has been by faith. The evidence as to the faith of the saved is shown by their resurrection and their presence with Christ in their glorified bodies. Jesus had said: "For this is the will of my Father, that every one that beholdeth the Son, and believeth on him, should have eternal life; and I will raise him up at the last day."[1] Undoubtedly he meant the previous resurrections of the saints, among whom now are all the believers, not one missing. Their faith is proven, and they are saved thereby. The rest not being so raised are shown not to have had faith. The verdict of this evidence is, "He that believeth not hath been judged already."[2]

The second evidence is that of works: "The dead were judged out of the things which were written in the books, according to their works." The only evidence of faith is works. It is true as James said, "We are saved by works;" for if these are missing, it shows there is no living faith. So now in the last Judgment and in all previous judgments, works are the test. The world has always made claim to sal-

[1] John vi. 40   [2] John iii. 18.

vation by works, and claimed merit on this account. So now they are to be tried upon their own grounds. The books are opened. The books of memory and the law and the conscience will be opened. "As many as have sinned without law shall also perish without law; and as many as have sinned under law shall be judged by law; . . . for when the Gentiles which have no law, do by nature the things of the law, these having no law are a law unto themselves; in that they show the work of the law written in their hearts, their conscience bearing witness therewith, and their thoughts one with another accusing or else excusing them: in the day when God shall judge the secrets of men according to my gospel by Jesus Christ."[1] Here are three books mentioned — law, conscience, and gospel. By one of these all will be judged. The result of this second stage in the trial is thus described: "The fearful, and the unbelieving, and abominable, and murderers, and fornicators, and sorcerers, and idolators, and all liars, their part shall be in the lake which burneth with fire and brimstone: which is the second death."[2]

The third great evidence upon which the destinies of mankind are decided is "the Book of Life." This is previously spoken of in the Scripture. Christ said to his disciples, "Rejoice that your names are written in heaven."[3] Further, and here is a great mystery, there are those whose names were always in this book, and some whose names never were there. The scriptures are as follows: "And all that dwell on the earth shall worship him [Antichrist] every one whose name hath not been written in the Book of Life of the Lamb that hath been slain from the foundation of the world. . . . They whose name hath not been written in the book of life from the foundation of the world."[4] We are not at a loss to know the fact

[1] Rom. ii. 12–16.   [2] Rev. xxi. 8.
[3] Luke x. 20.   [4] Rev. xiii. 8; xvii. 8.

that this was true of such as Judas, and of those of whom Jude spake: "These are they who are hidden rocks in your love-feasts when they feast with you, shepherds that without fear feed themselves; clouds without water, carried along by winds; autumn trees without fruit, twice dead, plucked up by the roots; wild waves of the sea, foaming out their own shame; wandering stars, for whom the blackness of darkness hath been reserved forever."[1] Our Lord also spoke of some of them, "Ye serpents, ye offspring of vipers, how shall ye escape the judgment of hell?"[2] The Book of Life is a transcript of God's secret will. It is absolute righteousness as well as the last verdict as to the destiny of every created being. It is a great comfort for every child of God that this book will be opened. It is an infallible guard against any being cast away who belong to God. Whatever the record of the life, whatever the smallness of faith, whatever the condemnation of conscience or the accusations of the world, if the name is in the Book of Life, all is well. The result of the third great test is this: "If any was not found written in the book of life, he was cast into the lake of fire."[3]

At the very beginning, upon the appearance of the great white throne and Him that sat upon it, it is written, "The earth and the heaven fled away and there was found no place for them." This is an event much spoken of in Scripture. Peter gives the fullest account of it: "The heavens that now are, and the earth, by the same word have been stored up for fire, being reserved against the day of judgment and destruction of ungodly men." "The day of the Lord will come as a thief; in the which the heavens shall pass away with a great noise, and the elements shall be dissolved with fervent heat, and the earth and the works that are therein shall be burned up. Seeing that these things are thus all to be dissolved, what

[1] Jude 12, 13.   [2] Matt. xxiii. 33.   [3] Rev. xx. 15.

manner of persons ought ye to be in all holy living and godliness, looking for and earnestly desiring the coming of the day of God, by reason of which the heavens being on fire shall be dissolved, and the elements shall melt with fervent heat."[1] This takes place apparently at the very beginning of the judgment, for it is from the face of Christ they pass away, and by his presence they are dissolved. So that the judgment is probably in the midst of these awful terrors.

The belief in such an ending of earth is common to man. Gibbon writes: —

"In the opinion of a general conflagration, the faith of the Christians coincided with the traditions of the East.

The fact that the earth, as Peter says, is "stored with fire," is known to all mankind. The suggested fate is therefore drawn from this well-known fact. Pliny states: —

"It exceeds all miracles in my opinion that any day should pass without setting the world all on fire."

The world is a vast reservoir of coal, oils, gas, all most inflammable, and lying upon, and adjacent to, the mass of fire with which the earth is filled. Air and water are composed of the most combustible gases. It requires, therefore, but a slight change of very small proportions in the constituency of either of these or to bring any of these into direct contact with the mass of fire, or the slightest change in the inclination of the earth's axis, or the addition of heat to the sun by the precipitation of some wandering star into its fires, to produce the conflagration of air and sea and earth and all they contain. This may constitute "the lake of fire." It is thus described: "Which burneth with fire and brimstone."[2] It is also written that it is the place in which was cast the beast and the false prophet and Satan. It is called the "sec-

[1] 2 Peter iii. 7, 10–12.   [2] Rev. xxi. 8.

ond death." Every terrible thought is associated with death. The pain and parting and loss and the dark hereafter for the sinner, all are aggravated many fold in the "second death." As we do not know what death is until we enter it, so none can estimate what this is until then. We may be assured it is no mere figure of speech. There is a dreadful reality in all this awful description.

The fate of the lost is the most awful, as it is the most difficult problem of religion. But for this, there would be but little question as to the whole subject of religion. The whole controversy revolves around this sometimes invisible center. There are many open and secret protests against this doctrine. It is the voice of Christ which pronounces doom upon the lost, and therefore, his work and character are in question. We have seen his work in retributive justice upon the old world, upon Pharaoh, and Sodom, and the Canaanites, and during the Day of the Lord. But all this was punishment which was temporary. This sentence of the Great White Throne remands to a fate from which there is no promise of deliverance. This is the testimony of the church in all ages as to the meaning of the scriptures on this subject. Christ himself taught distinctly this doctrine. He said, "Fear him who is able to destroy both soul and body in hell [margin, Gehenna]."[1] It is to be remembered that this is the teaching of the Scripture, and that these Scriptures of the Christian church have not only the brightest outlook into the future, of any human conceptions, but the only such outlook. It is to the Bible all poets and painters turn for bright pictures of hereafter.

The nature and conduct of man must be considered in this question. We have seen the dealings of Christ with those to whom the truth was given.

[1] Matt. x. 28.

They heard the gospel and refused it, and remained impenitent under every call of the gospel, and loved darkness rather than light. The world crucified Christ, and persecuted the people of God. As the story of the Day of the Lord shows, they will refuse Christ even under the wonders of that day, and will turn to Satan, and will lift arms against the very person of Christ himself, and attempt to destroy the very Creator of them all, and turn the rule of earth over to Satan. All this shows a depth of wickedness under all circumstances, which is amazing. We ask who and what kind of beings these are. There is not in Scripture that indiscriminate sentimental designation of sinners we hear so commonly to-day. They are called by such names as "chaff" and "tares" as distinguished from the pure grain. They are called "goats" and "wolves" and "dogs" as distinguished from the sheep of the flock. Peter calls them "mere animals to be taken and destroyed."[1] Paul styles them "vessels of wrath fitted unto destruction."[2] Christ called them "offspring of vipers," and one of them, Judas Iscariot, he said was a devil. To some he said, "Ye are of your father the devil."[3]

All this intimates some radical reason why they are not saved, and explains why they so persistently refused the grace of God. We may be sure there is some reason which God has not fully revealed, why any created being should meet with such a fate. There are analogies in nature and in human life which are of the same kind. The existence of one extreme implies the opposite. Where there is a top there is a bottom. There are cast blossoms which perish. There are stalks which never reach the garner. There are dregs in every cup. There is débris from every structure. There is the refuse of the mine from which the precious metal and jewels are taken. Society has its outcasts, its criminals,

[1] 2 Peter ii. 12.   [2] Rom. ix. 22.   [3] John viii. 44.

and its finally incorrigible. It also has its penalties and even unending punishments, so far as life is concerned. The imprisonment for life, sometimes in solitary confinement or hard labor, is of the same kind in human scale as the eternal punishment of the Bible. History is full of judgment crises. Nations and races have perished forever. As we come to scan the extent of the ultimate work of Christ, we will see that the number of the lost bears but a small proportion to the vast numbers saved. It will appear as small as the number of free and right-living citizens is to those imprisoned for their crimes. The proportion will be less and less as the ages go by.

It is a ground of faith and comfort to know all is in the power of Christ. We must trust Christ here, for it is all his work. He is the same yesterday, to-day, and forever, and we know what he was "yesterday" in his earthly life. So he will be in the Day of Judgment. His aspect will change, but he changes not. So we may feel sure he will do not only right and justice, but will leave no work of mercy untried to save rebellious man; as in Jerusalem, when he could do no more, he wept over the doomed city, so he will feel sorrow as no mortal can over the loss of every created being. Some profess to find a hopeful outlook to this darkest view possible to man. If there should be such, none will rejoice more than those who, believing this dark doctrine, have striven to call the world to Christ. If Christ in the ages of eternity should find a way to save every created being, it is his own secret. He has revealed no such doctrine to us. We can only declare what he has said. From our present light there appears no hope for those who die impenitent. Lange writes on this as follows:—

"So far as it is admissible to speak of an *intermediate state* between the last judgment and the ideal goal of all things, such a state manifestly appears to be for the wicked a series of æons to which the eye can discover no limit. Whither the river of paradise goes as it flows out of the city of God, is not declared. The mediæval conception of the endless torment of all who died out of the church, infringes on the liberty of God; the systems of the absolute restoration of all men infringe on the liberty of man ; both occupy too positive a position in regard to the hidden secrets of the æons, behind which the mountains of absolute eternity stand radiant with the glory of God."

We may dismiss the whole subject with the words of Abraham in view of the destruction of Sodom : "Shall not the Judge of all the earth do right?"

The work of Christ in the Day of the Lord ends with the judgment, and also the history of what we call "time." There has been seen Christ working through it all, conducting the great plan of God from beginning to conclusion. The great demonstration ends here. It will have been shown by every possible test that under all circumstances, in every emergency or condition, the will of God is the only rule of life for created beings. All other means of making them happy or holy will have been tried and proved wanting. The great problem of all the ages will have been solved once for all. Under license as at the first, under law as with the prepared people of Israel, under the gospel, and later still in the millennium with the demonstrated presence of the supernatural, man has failed, save as he obeyed the will of God. Any other race would have failed also. Man is but a representative of created beings, any of whom would act in the same way.

Christ came and gave the universe a perfect example of perfect submission to the will of God, and his people, so far as they followed in his steps, gave the same example. The benefits of obedience were shown in the individual, in the community, and in the whole world. The awful effects of disobedience to the will of God, called sin, were also fully shown.

The record will be made up and kept for the study of the ages to come. It will be, as was intimated, the Bible of the future. The worlds to come will read the story of sin and grace. They will therefrom learn, and fear to sin, and cleave to God. The whole history is a short one. What are seven thousand years or even thousands more, to the endless æons of eternity? It will be seen that the results well pay for all involved. It is but the preparation for the kingdom of God which now begins.

CHAPTER VII.

CHRIST IN THE ETERNAL FUTURE.

THE eternal future begins where time ends. From the Great White Throne issue the ages of eternity. These are often spoken of in Scripture. Paul writes of them and gives the grand outline in these words, "Unto him be the glory in the church and in Christ Jesus unto all generations forever and ever" [margin, "unto all the generations of the age of the ages]."[1] The word rendered "worlds" is often more properly "ages." "Through whom also he made the worlds" may be rendered "through whom also he framed the ages." These ages were framed by Christ. In the eternal past he arranged the whole eternal future. Christ was the Great Architect of the ages as well as the manifestation of the person and nature of God, and his great executive.

It is difficult to separate the prophecies which apply to the eternal state from those which refer to the millennium only. The two form one picture in the minds of the prophets looking down the long perspective of the distance. The prophecies of the millennium may be taken as were those referring to historical events, as having a typical meaning or a second fulfilment in the greater age. Dr. Craven writes on this subject : —

"Although the New Jerusalem state is not to be confounded with the millennial kingdom, nor to be regarded as a simple continuance thereof, it is to be looked upon as the antitype of that kingdom. In a sense it is that kingdom raised to

[1] Eph. iii. 21.

a higher plane — completely freed in its territory, and its subjects from all remains of the curse. The millennial kingdom is the reign of the saints over a race and earth freed indeed from the assaults of Satan, but still in measure in sin and under the curse. The New Jerusalem period is that of the reign of the saints over a race and earth perfectly purified."[1]

As another writer observes, in the millennium, righteousness *reigns*, in the eternal state it *dwells* with man.

Some general principles may be considered by which the special application of scriptures to the two states may be discerned. The predictions which speak of the presence of sin or death refer to the millennium only, for these are absent from the eternal state. So also all which intimate the existence of the sea, for this too is absent. Also all which speak of any termination are to be applied to the short time of the millennium. It is probable also that all predictions which here present geographical or ethnographical names or boundaries refer to the millennium only. The last two chapters of the Apocalypse apply to the eternal state, following as they do without intimation of chronological break, the accounts of the general judgment and the destruction of the world, and leading up to the perfect state, as far as revealed to man. So therefore all other predictions must be judged, as to their place, by this great outline. The presence of the heavenly city and the visible presence of God the Father are the great marks of the eternal state. The central point in the eternal future is the throne of God and the Lamb. Around this appears the New Jerusalem, and in a wider circle the new earth. This in turn is encircled by the new heavens. This then will be our course of study, beginning at the center with Christ, with whom by previous study and acquaintance we are familiar, and considering the successive circles by which he is surrounded.

[1] Lange's Commentary, Revelation, New York, p. 392.

We ask what Christ is or has in himself for all his work and suffering and accomplishment. That he did look forward to something for himself seems clear. "Who for the joy that was set before him endured the cross, despising the shame, and hath sat down on the right hand of the throne of God."[1] What was the joy set before him? We can see that there was, as at the ascension, the joy of accomplished endeavor. Redemption is fully accomplished. He has brought about a state of existence which can continue as long as eternity, without failing in any point by reason of weakness and sin. He has made possible the extension of the holy, happy state universally. But for himself Christ has gains also. He has a threefold human nature,—body, soul, and spirit. This human nature has been trained and schooled in the vicissitudes and sufferings of human life. He in it "learned obedience by the things which he suffered." He was made perfect through suffering. He has all that a thoroughly schooled human being could have. All that experience is to us, it is to Christ. All that character is to us, it is to him,—all this in his human nature which he has and will have forever. Christ has the possibility of a kind of fellowship with created beings, especially the church, with this human nature, so schooled, which he could not otherwise have. It is the fellowship of equals of which he spake: "No longer do I call you servants; for the servant knoweth not what his lord doeth; but I have called you friends: for all things that I heard of my Father I have made known unto you."[2] This indicates the kind of fellowship and the subjects of it. It will be the intercourse of equals as to the great designs of the eternal ages to come. All this Christ did not have before the world was.

There is the conferring of a name upon Christ often and mysteriously spoken of. It was con-

[1] Heb. xii. 2.   [2] John xv. 15.

ferred upon him at his ascension: "Wherefore also God highly exalted him, and gave unto him the name which is above every name; that in the name of Jesus every knee should bow, of things in heaven and things on earth and things under the earth."[1] This is not any of the names we now know, for it is spoken of by himself as, "My new name;" and again, "He hath a name written, that no man knoweth but he himself."[2] It is that name which he promises to write upon him that overcometh, and no doubt, which they bear who have the Father's name written upon their foreheads. This name will sum up in itself all we have known of Christ, and will declare to us in a word a revelation of Christ now utterly beyond us. The new name of Christ will no doubt embody all the many titles and offices Christ has worn. It will have not only a public and general meaning, but also a special significance to each one who knows it. This is indicated by his promise to write it upon the one who overcomes. It will probably express to each his own special view of Christ or the secret relationship which he holds individually to him. It will, like the many-faced jewel, reflect Christ's grace and glory in many forms, and to each believer his own needed or prized view of Christ. It is the name by which he is now known in heaven and which exalts him above every creature and draws praise from every beholder. Next to seeing his face will be the joy of hearing for the first time the great name which is above every name, by which he whom we have called Christ will be known forever.

There are frequent references to an orderly arrangement of the kingdom of God. That "order is heaven's first law" needs no asserting. It is true of nature, and the church also so far as it has conformed to the divine commands. It is probable the different

[1] Phil. ii. 9, 10.   [2] Rev. xix. 12.

figures for the church describe different parts of the great company. Some passages describe a complexity of organization, as the following: "Being built upon the foundation of the apostles and prophets, Christ Jesus himself being the chief corner stone; in whom each several building, fitly framed together, groweth unto a holy temple in the Lord: in whom ye also are builded together for a habitation of God in the spirit."[1] In this scripture quoted, there is presented a picture of many buildings, each representing a separate company, and all so adjusted to each other and to the central place of the throne as to form one temple for the habitation of God. The figure of the temple explains this orderly and yet varying arrangement of the city of God. The temple had its enclosing wall, its court, its inner court, its temple proper, and inside, the holy place, and the inmost, holiest of all. We can discern some of these several buildings. The great company of the antediluvians who were saved, are not of the spiritual descendants of Abraham, "the father of all them that believe" to whom the gospel was first preached, as Paul tells us, yet they have a place in the house of God. So Israel is not the Christian church by whom indeed for a time they were supplanted. But Israel has a place, and a special place too. They are seen in their tribes, and are recognized as such. We have already considered the term and figure of the bride as applied to the people of God. Israel was so called, and is in the eternal future united with the New Testament church in this figure. The names of the twelve tribes of Israel are on the gates, while the names of the twelve apostles are on the foundations of the walls. The scripture in like manner says, "Ye are fellow-citizens with the saints and of the household of God, being built upon the foundation of the apostles and prophets, Jesus Christ himself being the chief corner stone."[2]

[1] Eph. ii. 20–22. [2] Eph. ii. 20.

There are also those of every land and family of men who in all the ages have known and obeyed the truth. Many of these are the results of the world-wide work of Jehovah during the Old Testament age in many nations, as we noted in the review of the work of Christ then. The thousands of Nineveh who repented at the preaching of Jonah, and doubtless others from many cities and lands in like manner saved. So also the Queen of Sheba, and doubtless many of her subjects whom Jesus said would stand up in the judgment having repented in life. So also Nebuchadnezzar, who issued his royal proclamation confessing Christ, as he knew him, after God's afflictive dealings, and no doubt many of the subjects of this ruler over the whole earth.

The Christian church of this age has undoubtedly a superiority over all who have gone before and all who will come after. Christ teaches a distinction between the believer of the Old Testament church and those of the New: "Among them that are born of women there hath not arisen a greater than John the Baptist: yet he that is but little in the kingdom of heaven, is greater than he."[1] There is undoubtedly far more in believing on Christ now, when we have no supernatural events or a visible Saviour, than in the coming day when the supernatural is everywhere present. Christ taught this principle in showing Thomas his hands and his side; he said, "Because thou hast seen me, thou hast believed: blessed are they that have not seen and yet have believed."[2] We know that many will be saved after the coming of the Day of the Lord, as was noted. They will lose something which others will gain. This is indeed part of the reward, and a great part, for being ready for the coming of that day, and it is so held out in Scripture. That some lose their part in it does not however show that they are lost.

[1] Matt. xi. 11. [2] John xx. 29.

So also a difference is intimated to exist among those being saved in the gospel age and commonly called The Church. There are special terms applied to some, such as, "The Bride," "The first-fruits," "The Church of the First Born." We must not apply these indiscriminately to the saved. Scripture does not use terms in that loose manner. Every difference is significant of special meaning. There is a vast difference between being "saved as by fire," and having "richly supplied unto you the entrance into the eternal kingdom of our Lord and Saviour Jesus Christ." Coming into the number of "The Church of the First-Born" is far more than escaping hell. The Bride of Christ is far more than a servant or a subject. There are undoubtedly differences in the constituency of these respective bodies.

There will be also some chosen companies. One is thus described: "These are they which were not defiled with women: for they are virgins. These are they which follow the Lamb whithersoever he goeth. These were purchased from among men, to be the first-fruits unto God and unto the Lamb. And in their mouth was found no lie; they are without blemish."[1] The account tells us they act as a constant escort to the Son of God. We noticed in the life of Jesus that some were constantly with him.

Christ and his people enter the eternal future together, a completed body. The last sheaves were gathered before the last judgment, and now not one is missing, as is found by the opening of the Book of Life. The act which will give Christ as well as his people joy, is described in these words: "That he might present the church to himself a glorious church, not having spot or wrinkle or any such thing; but that it should be holy and without blemish."[2] For Christ himself this is the time of reward. His prayer on earth was, "I will that where I am they also may

[1] Rev. xiv. 4, 5.   [2] Eph. v. 27.

be with me ; that they may behold my glory which thou has given me."[1] But there is a higher pleasure for them and him. It is written that no man hath seen God at any time. Human eye cannot gaze upon him. But in the glorified state this is possible. "The pure in heart shall see God." It is written, "They shall see his face." The time for this is when all are gathered, and sin is no more. This is described as a definite act and time and experience. The presentation of the completed church before the presence of God the Father is thus described: "To present you holy and without blemish and unreprovable before him;" "To set you before the presence of his glory without blemish in exceeding joy."[2]

The object of the Christian's contemplation during the present age is Christ. In the millennium Christ will be visible to all. But in the eternal ages, the object of the Christian's contemplation and vision will be God the Father, the Eternal and Infinite. It is the summit of bliss for the people of God. We will be able as Christ does, not only to see, but, as we advance in the learning of that higher state of life, to be able to enter into the thoughts of God and his purposes, and enjoy the same kind of fellowship as with Christ himself. The mind of God will exist in all his people as it does in Christ. God will be in them as he is in Christ.

For the church there will be growth and advance in all which makes glory and character. The ideal of the Christian is "the measure of the stature of the fulness of Christ." It is further and perhaps more highly expressed in these words: "Filled unto all the fulness of God."[3] We can scarcely say all this is attained by any in its greatest sense, in this life, but it will be by all in the life to come. The believer is to become like Christ. He is to be "conformed to the image of his Son, that he might be the first-born

[1] John xvii. 24. [2] Col. i. 22 ; Jude 24. [3] Eph. iii. 19; iv. 13.

among many brethren."[1] This will be such an exaltation of the believer as will make him as like Christ as the younger son is to the older. "We shall be like him, for we shall see him even as he is."[2] The process begun upon earth will go on in increasing power. "We all with unveiled face reflecting as a mirror the glory of the Lord, are transformed into the same image from glory to glory, even as from the Lord the Spirit."[3]

All this the apostle has in mind when he prays, "That ye may know what is the hope of his calling, what the riches of the glory of his inheritance in the saints, and what the exceeding greatness of his power to us-ward who believe."[4] The promise as to these ages is, "That in the ages to come he might show the exceeding riches of his grace in kindness toward us in Christ Jesus."[5]

The Scriptural accounts of the future of God's people are all associated with material places and conditions. There is no such idea in Scripture as the ghostly condition and unsubstantial state now commonly held as to heaven, and which contemplates a mere condition or state apart from place or locality, or makes little of locality. This comes as has been said, from the leaven of doctrine absorbed from heathenism, that evil exists in matter, or that matter is in antagonism to spirituality and holiness, and that the right idea of heaven demands pure etherealism. It also comes partly from the effusions of poets not Scripturally informed, and partly from exaggerated importance being given to the middle state, the great realities of the resurrection and the resurrection state being correspondingly neglected. All this has filled the minds of people with views of heaven which are not only unscriptural but also damaging to the faith of believers. A heaven is presented which few dare to conceive

---

[1] Rom. viii. 29.   [2] 1 John iii. 2.   [3] 2 Cor. iii. 18.
[4] Eph. i. 18, 19.   [5] Eph. ii. 7.

of or even to acknowledge a location for. It is filled with ghostly beings whom we are assured we will become like, and so in some more or less imaginary state, live on and on without any definite place or purpose or outcome. Such a heaven has no attractive power. It is not the heaven of the Bible.

Among the last promises of Christ was this: "In my Father's house are many mansions ; if it were not so I would have told you ; for I go to prepare a place for you. And if I go I will come again and receive you to myself ; that where I am there ye may be also."[1] Here is as definite proof as could be given. First the naming of a place and the assertion that it is where Christ himself is. Dr. Craven writes upon this as follows : —

"A material dwelling place is as necessary for resurrected saints as was Eden for Adam, or Canaan for Israel. It should occasion no surprise, for the same loving care that will raise and glorify the body should prepare a fitting and glorious abode for it.[2]

The place of the abode of God's people is called the New Jerusalem. We are taught that it is a definite place having locality, name, and description. This is the place Jesus went to prepare. It forms the subject of the closing chapters of the Apocalypse.

"And he carried me away in the Spirit to a mountain great and high, and shewed me the holy city Jerusalem, coming down out of heaven from God, having the glory of God : her light was like unto a stone most precious, as it were a jasper stone, clear as crystal: having a wall great and high ; having twelve gates, and at the gates twelve angels; and names written thereon, which are the names of the twelve tribes of the children of Israel : on the east were three gates ; and on the north three gates ; and

[1] John xiv. 2, 3.
[2] Lange's Commentary, Revelation, New York, p. 391.

on the south three gates; and on the west three gates. And the wall of the city had twelve foundations, and on them twelve names of the twelve apostles of the Lamb. And he that spake with me had for a measure a golden reed to measure the city, and the gates thereof, and the wall thereof. And the city lieth foursquare, and the length thereof is as great as the breadth: and he measured the city with the reed, twelve thousand furlongs: the length and the breadth and the height thereof are equal. And he measured the wall thereof, a hundred and forty and four cubits, according to the measure of a man, that is, of an angel. And the building of the wall thereof was jasper: and the city was pure gold, like unto pure glass. The foundations of the wall of the city were adorned with all manner of precious stones. The first foundation was jasper; the second, sapphire; the third, chalcedony; the fourth, emerald; the fifth, sardonyx; the sixth, sardius; the seventh, chrysolite; the eighth, beryl; the ninth, topaz; the tenth, chrysoprase; the eleventh, jacinth; the twelfth, amethyst. And the twelve gates were twelve pearls; each one of the several gates was of one pearl: and the street of the city was pure gold, as it were transparent glass. And I saw no temple therein: for the Lord God the Almighty, and the Lamb, are the temple thereof. And the city hath no need of the sun, neither of the moon, to shine upon it: for the glory of God did lighten it, and the lamp thereof is the Lamb. And the nations shall walk amidst the light thereof: and the kings of the earth do bring their glory into it. And the gates thereof shall in no wise be shut by day (for there shall be no night there): and they shall bring the glory and the honor of the nations into it: and there shall in no wise enter into it anything unclean, or he that maketh an abomination and a lie; but only they which are written in the Lamb's book of life.

"And he shewed me a river of water of life, bright as crystal, proceeding out of the throne of God and of the Lamb, in the midst of the street thereof. And on this side of the river and on that was the tree of life, bearing twelve manner of fruits, yielding its fruit every month : and the leaves of the tree were for the healing of the nations. And there shall be no curse any more: and the throne of God and of the Lamb shall be therein : and his servants shall do him service ; and they shall see his face ; and his name shall be on their foreheads. And there shall be night no more : and they need no light of lamp, neither light of sun ; for the Lord God shall give them light : and they shall reign for ever and ever."[1]

The figure of the city is that of a square. This corresponds to the Scriptural figure for universality as applied to the earth and man. The other dimension, height, suggests its heavenly aspect. We must not suppose that it is a cube. The three dimensions apply as well to the figure of the mountain or pyramid which is the perfected form of the mountain. Old Jerusalem was called Mount Zion and was built upon a mountain. The dimensions given, are no doubt, all surface measurements. The height is probably not the vertical height but the slope of the mountain. The area given is more than a million times that of ancient Jerusalem, and if populated as the least crowded residence parts of any modern city, would give homes to a hundred times the present population of earth. In this vision of the home of the church are gathered all the beauties of nature, human life, and heaven. Specimens of each are named. From nature, precious stones, pearls, gold, rivers, and trees ; from human life a single figure, the bride ; from heaven, angels and light. But each of these are but specimens of the whole vast glorious aggregation of all that is beautiful in each of the spheres of nature, man, and heaven.

[1] Rev. xxi. 10-27, xxii. 1-5.

This then is the city John sees. It is a shining mountain. Around the base a wall of diamond. Three portals opening on each side. The gates of solid pearl. From each gate an avenue of gold ascends to the summit. Down the sides of each street pours a stream of the River of Life watering the trees which line each golden avenue. The figure suggests the sides of the mountain terraced to the summit, and upon these terraces the mansions of the saints. The throne of God crowns the whole. From the throne flows light eternal which radiates through every part of the transparent city. The dimensions and the description suggest the city combined with all of rural beauty and enjoyments. When John sees the vision of the New Jerusalem, the saints are in possession of their eternal home. The whole is called, "The Bride, the Lamb's wife." It is the vision of the saints in this glorious city which fills the apostle with rapture. He beholds the completed work of Christ for his church. We may be sure Christ himself is with them; indeed the record so says. To bring his church to their eternal resting place was the work of Christ in person even as the bridegroom brings the loved one to his home. This probably takes place soon after the completion of the church.

The view which John saw of the New Jerusalem presented it descending from God out of heaven. The whole context indicates that it was descending to earth where the apostle was. The mention of earth afterward with the city established, shows this to be the right view of the location of this glorious city. It is heaven coming to earth. This, we must bear in mind, was the course of the preceding ages. The Scripture narrative shows first a rupture of the relationship between God and man. Then follows a long age ending at the flood, when there seems to have been little communication between heaven and earth. In the age following, God comes to many, and all Israel see the glory of God. Angels come and go and are seen and heard. In the gospel age God in his Son appears, and many more, a worldwide body, know personally of the reality of heaven. In the millennium there is a greater disclosure still, as we have seen. The supernatural becomes well-known phenomena. The angels and risen saints and the glorified Christ himself appears. But in the eternal state, "Behold the tabernacle of God is with men, and he shall dwell with them." The peculiarity of the New Jerusalem will be "no temple therein, for the Lord God Almighty and the Lamb are the temple thereof." Dr. Craven writes upon this:—

"In the old Jerusalem the temple was at once the dwelling place and the concealer of Jehovah. Though present, he was not visibly present — in presence he was sheltered by the temple. The New Jerusalem shall have no place for the sheltering of the Lord; for she shall be sheltered by him. He shall tabernacle over her. Her inhabitants shall dwell under his manifest and sheltering light. He shall be her temple." [1]

The inspired account of the place of the New Jerusalem is as follows: "I saw a new heaven and a new earth, for the first heaven and the first earth are passed away, and the sea is no more." [2] This we believe refers to the present earth. We have every reason to believe that this planet is meant, and that the re-creation of it is the work of Christ. We are led to this conclusion from considering the types of the great conflagration. The flood was such. The effect of this was the destruction not of the planet, but only the human works and beings upon its surface. So in the fiery flood of which the former was a type, we need not see more than the destruction of the surface and the works of man upon it. Further, the words, "The sea was no more," imply the same

[1] Lange's Commentary, Revelation, New York, 1874, p. 387.
[2] Rev. xxi. 1.

earth where the sea was, otherwise the statement would have no relevancy. Still further, the statement, "The tabernacle of God is with men," implies God coming to men rather than their removal to some other place. The restoration or regeneration of the earth is in full accord with the analogy of all which has gone before, in the creative, spiritual, and resurrective work of Christ.

To merely adandon the earth as a fiery mass to burn itself out, would scarcely be in line with the predictions of complete victory. It leaves the battlefield in possession of the enemy, as Dr. George Junkin says:—

"Whereas on the supposition of its purification, and of redeemed men, and his glorious Redeemer returning and abiding upon it, in a state of felicity superior to that which Satan at first disturbed, the triumph of God, the Saviour, over the powers of hell has here an everlasting monument."[1]

Dr. Charles Hodge writes thus :—

"The destruction here foretold is not annihilation. The world is to be burnt up, but combustion is not a destruction of substance. It is merely a change of condition or state. . . . The earth, according to the common opinion, that is, this renovated earth, is to be the final seat of Christ's kingdom."[2]

There are many scriptures which teach this. Abraham is to have the land of promise "for an everlasting possession." Zion is to be "an eternal excellency." The earth is "to be inhabited forever."

The work of Christ in this preparation of the earth for its eternal use, we call the new creation. He himself speaks of it in these words: "Behold I make all things new." This is far more than "the restoration of all things." That means the return to the Edenic condition which took place in the millennium. But a repaired world is far from the idea of this greater

[1] "Lectures on Prophecy," p. 312.
[2] Systematic Theology, New York, 1873, Vol. 3, p. 854.

state and work. It is a regeneration, being born again. The earth must pass through the same process as ourselves, and become a new creation. The earth would be left by its fiery baptism very much in its original state. Indeed Jeremiah in his view of the earth given him in this time, describes it in the same language as that of Genesis. "I beheld the earth and, lo, it was waste and void, and the heavens and they gave no light."[1] The statement, "There was no more sea," tells us a very different state of earth is to exist not only on the surface of the earth but above it. The fires of the last day will vaporize the waters of the oceans, and unless removed elsewhere, these vapors would be suspended as a canopy over the earth or in rings or circles, as is the case with some of the stars; Saturn for example. This will undoubtedly produce very different climatic conditions. The result of the earth's fiery baptism will be the entire destruction of every form of evil, physical as well as moral. The countless forms of disease and the germs by which they are propagated, will be completely destroyed. It will be earth's purification. Its baptism of water will be followed by its baptism of fire. Through these, the earth will come into fellowship with the great company of unfallen worlds.

In the new creation, Christ will simply follow the process begun in the old, and manifested in every phase of cosmical and spiritual acting all along the ages. Christlieb thus states this principle of divine acting:—

"The spiritual life of Christ breaks forth in a manifestation in the visible world, by revivifying the bodies of those that are sanctified, in the "first resurrection." In the succeeding general resurrection, an act of Christ's power which extends to the whole of the corporeal world, and introduces the great mundane catastrophe, as well as in the formation of a new heaven and earth, this grand and gradual process of the world's renewal has its fitting consummation."[2]

[1] Jer. iv. 23; Gen. i. 1.
[2] Modern Doubt and Christian Belief."

We may expect to see a world filled with the products of creative work in the animal and plant spheres. They were not out of place in Eden, nor will they be here. There is no sin in organic things, nor does it come from them. All nature, as in our first chapter has been seen, is holy to the Lord. The efforts of every spot left free to the operation of nature, to become filled with life and verdure, to obliterate the ravages of man, and to restore all things, tells us a little of what we may expect when God gives the word for a perfect work. There will not be a barren spot, not a noxious weed or insect.

The descent of the New Jerusalem from heaven to earth is accompanied by the words of a voice from the Throne, which is within the city, saying, "Behold, the tabernacle of God is with men, and he shall dwell with them, and they shall be his peoples, and God himself shall be with them, and be their God; and he shall wipe away every tear from their eyes; and death shall be no more; neither shall there be mourning nor crying, nor pain any more; the first things are passed away. And he that sitteth on the throne said, Behold, I make all things new."[1] The first plain teaching of this divine message direct from the throne of God is that when the New Jerusalem descends to the new earth, it finds people already there. It is an inhabited earth to which it comes. It does not bring this population with it. They are evidently not a part of the great body who are in the city. Indeed, the fact that the city comes to them and that this coming of the city and God is to them the great event, shows plainly that they are on earth. It is stated they are not to inhabit the city, but to live in the light of it. When we remember that the city comes from heaven, while this company is of the earth, there is in connection with all before said, a plain inference that they are different in nature

[1] Rev. xxi. 3-5.

CHRIST IN THE ETERNAL FUTURE.

also. This conclusion is more certain from the statements made concerning them.

The terms applied to these residents of the new earth are peculiar and very different from those applied to the residents in the city itself. The inhabitants of the earth to whom the city comes, and to whom God comes with it, are spoken of as "men" and "peoples," and they are spoken of in connection with tears and death and mourning and crying and pain, all of which it is said are now to cease. The tears are to be wiped from their eyes. If these are resurrected persons, these allusions and declarations seem very strange. Wiping away all tears from the faces of risen saints is something wholly irreconcilable with their nature and state. The promise of banishing death from those who have gotten the victory over death by resurrection, is also incongruous, and so is the promise of no mourning, crying, or pain. The further state of these is indicated by the expression, "The kings of the earth." The risen saints would scarcely be so spoken of either by this title, or as bringing their glory into the city where they constantly abide. It is further said, "They shall bring the glory and honor of the nations into it."[1]

Dr. Elijah R. Craven writes on this as follows:—

"We should distinguish between the citizens of the city and the nations. The former are risen and glorified saints who constitute the Bride, the governors of the new creation. The latter are probably men in the flesh who 'walk in the light of the city,' who 'bring their glory and honor into it,' and who are healed (or kept in health) by the leaves of the Tree of Life,[2] i. e., who are under its instruction. . . . The nations will consist of men in the flesh, freed from sin and the curse, begetting a holy seed and dwelling in blessedness under the government of the New Jerusalem. They will not be the offspring of the glorified saints, who 'neither marry nor are given in marriage,' but the descendants of those who live in the period of the millennial kingdom. . . . The same

[1] Rev. xxi. 26.   [2] Rev. xxi. 24–27; xxii. 2.

almighty power that conveyed Noah and his family across the waters of the first deluge, can bear other families across the fiery floods of the second. It may be retorted that there is no promise of such a miracle. That there is no expressed promise is admitted, but the divine prediction of an event ever implies the promise of a sufficient cause."[1]

Part of the original curse on man was reversed after the flood, as we noted in the covenant made with Noah: "I will not again curse the ground any more for man's sake."[2] The curse upon creation is removed at the millennium as Paul says: "The Creation itself also shall be delivered from the bondage of corruption into the liberty of the glory of the children of God."[3] But the curse of a sinful nature remained upon man. This is now removed in the beginning of the eternal ages by the edict from the Throne: "Behold, the tabernacle of God is with men, and he shall dwell with them, and they shall be his peoples, and God himself shall be with them, and be their God; and he shall wipe away every tear from their eyes, and death shall be no more; neither shall there be mourning, nor crying, nor pain any more; the first things are passed away. And he that sitteth on the throne said, Behold, I make all things new."[4] In this there is a complete reversal of the original curse in all its relations. First, the communion and presence of God is restored. Second, sorrow and suffering are removed, and death is banished. The final sentence shows the completeness of the restoration: "*The first things are passed away;*" "Behold I make all things new." The original curse is now completely abolished. Humanity is at last free from sorrow, suffering, and sin. In each individual the spirit dominates soul and body, and both are glorified thereby, and brought by this control of the spiritual nature into unity with all other

---

[1] Lange's Commentary, Revelation, p. 391. [2] Gen. viii. 21.
[3] Rom. viii. 21 [4] Rev. xxi. 3-5.

beings, all of whom, because of this spiritual nature and its supremacy, and through it as the channel of communication and life are brought into immediate and full connection with God through the flow of the Holy Spirit. In this state every physical act is faultless and every exercise of the mind is holy. All are filled with the fulness of God.

These are then *restored humanity* entering the new earth. They are what Adam was before he fell, and therefore are fit for the presence of God, who can now resume the original fellowship of Eden so long interrupted. This will be the perfect restoration of humanity never before secured. It will be a victory not to be secured otherwise. The resurrection is victory over death, but man must die in order to rise. The translation of living believers saves man by lifting him above mortality into another sphere. The great restoration of the race gives him spirituality and immortality in his own sphere. It makes natural man superior to the power of death and sin. There is bestowed upon the restored race more than Adam enjoyed. By the death of Christ the spiritual power of sin was destroyed. In the millennium the social dominion of sin is removed. By the eternal edict from the Throne, that in man which responds to the attack of temptation, is removed. Man will be physically, psychically, and spiritually perfect. The first man was of the earth, earthy, but he is so no longer. By the edict from the Throne, he is made new. If God is to be glorified in the eternal state by material creatures and beauties in nature, why not by the crowning work of creation, perfected man? To lay man aside in the hour of final victory, would be to acknowledge a mistake in his creation or a defeat in his redemption. The perfection of the new earth will require the perfection of man in all his relationships and faculties.

There are some objections to this view which we

should consider here. The first is the scripture which says, "Flesh and blood cannot inherit the kingdom of God, neither doth corruption inherit incorruption."[1] Paul is speaking here of unregenerate man and the necessity of a resurrection for the admittance of such into the kingdom of God. The persons we speak of are regenerate, and they are not " corruption " in any sense. The body of Adam was not "corruption." It was in the kingdom of God also. The place in the kingdom to which Paul refers above, however, is that of sovereignty in the kingdom, which is not the place of the restored race. They are not rulers but subjects. They are no doubt the millennial population which must under the conditions of peace, plenty, health, and holiness have assumed immense proportions. These are not after spoken of as either killed or translated. The vast population of earth did not all join the last apostasy, we may feel sure. No account of their subsequent history is given us. All that were sinful were no doubt slain, and joined the dead who appeared for judgment. But these others were not dead, and doubtless passed over into the new earth as living.

There seems at first something incongruous in the idea of there being a race of human beings living as now, and increasing in the eternal ages. This comes partly from preconceived opinions as to the future state. There is nothing in Scripture forbidding the idea of material beings in the eternal ages. It is the leaven of heathenism in our Christianity, which deprecates the material as inherently sinful, and that true holiness can only be obtained by abstraction from all this, and in a state of etherialism hereafter. A mystical state has come to be considered as the necessary condition for purity. Another reason comes from considering the fall as having consisted in, or having led to, the introduction of marital relations.

[1] 1 Cor. xv. 50.

This we have seen has no foundation in Scripture. Such relations and the propagation of the race were contemplated in the creation of man, as the following scripture states: "And God created man in his own image, in the image of God created he him; male and female created he them. And God blessed them; and God said unto them, Be fruitful, and multiply, and replenish the earth."[1] Here is express command before the fall for the propagation of the race. What was right and fitting in the original Eden, is also fitting in the new earth. There was here contemplated the holy increase of the race of man, and their gradual filling of the earth.

There is another essential reason, however, why we must consider these to be earthly people. There is called for by the whole plan of God as we have seen it, and by numerous passages, the idea of constant increase in the numbers of the people of Christ during the ages of eternity. The Scriptures declare, "Of the increase of his government and of peace there shall be no end."[2] We cannot conceive of the work of God coming to a stand as to the number of his people, no matter what the extent of their individual advancement might be. The whole law of God in nature and in grace is increase. We have followed this progress from the beginning, and seen not only advance in the character of the individuals, and the manifestations of God's character and grace, but the spread of the work of God numerically among men. It is wholly irreconcilable with the apparent plan of divine action, to suppose this increase will stop when the full victory of Christ over sin is gained. It leaves the great scheme of redemption narrowed to those gathered out of mankind who remain thereafter a fixed number. Christ could create new beings, but these would not be the race which he purchased with his blood. The same scriptures which speak

[1] Gen. i. 27, 28.   [2] Isa. ix. 7.

of the perpetuity of the earth also speak of the continuance of the ordinances and people of the earth. The covenant was made for "perpetual generations."

The new earth is described in this state by Bickersteth : —

> "And easily we found
> Each haunt to memory dear of pilgrim days,
> Each hill and valley; for the flood of fire
> Which wrapped the earth in its baptismal robe,
> Had purged, not changed its lineaments; as once
> The deluge of great waters overwhelmed
> All life, except the cradled church, but left
> Creation's landmarks and the river beds
> Coasting the land of Shinar undisturbed.
> The wastes of ocean only were no more,
> Nor wastes of sand, nor aught of barrenness;
> And yet the earth through all her vast expanse
> Of golden plains and rich umbrageous hills
> Already seemed too narrow for the growth
> Of her great family; so quick
> The virtue of her Maker's law, when once
> Sin's crushing interdict was disannulled,
> That primal law, 'Be fruitful; multiply
> Your joys; replenish and subdue the earth.'"[1]

There is diversity in the population of the new earth. We read in the account of the descent of the New Jerusalem to earth: "They shall be his peoples." The plural in the form of the latter word is very significant. Not a single people, but many families of peoples. The same is also expressed by the plural form of the word "nations." There is governmental life in the new earth. The Scripture speaks of the "kings of the earth." This gives us the idea of self-government to some degree. These kings are not the saints who occupy the higher relations to the earth, but their own rulers in subordination to the rule of Christ and his assistants. There is diversity of gifts and place in the new earth. There is no such idea in the Scriptures as a common level of character or position or ability in the descriptions of the eternal state. Such ideas of leveling come from below

[1] "Yesterday, To-day, and For Ever," book xii., line 1482.

and not from above. A state of pure communism is impossible and impracticable anywhere.

The whole picture is that of an orderly kingdom having its capital city, and reigning king with his immediate family and court, and others who occupy positions of power and honor, and still a greater number who assist in many ways, and still larger numbers who have no such special honors, but have the privileges of the capital city, and a vast number of subjects, happy in being under such a king. It is a wholly natural life and state altogether different from the unnatural and unscriptural idea of heaven, which is a mixture of heathenism, spiritualism, poetry, and rationalistic theology.

A great fact is brought to our attention by astronomy. Besides the elementary unity of the universe, it has also an organized unity. It is one in its whole construction and motion. It is one vast mechanism. We can understand this by beginning at the unit, for us, of the stellar universe. Our earth is the center of a system consisting of itself and a single satellite — the moon. This is a type of the whole existing universe, as the latest conclusions of astromony seem to indicate. This earth system is itself related as a satellite to a greater orb, the sun, around which earth revolves, drawing its satellite with it. But the sun is only a member of a greater system of which it is but a single sun of many others, all revolving around a greater sun. This whole sun system is, it is believed, also involved in a vast system of such sun systems, all revolving about some distant center to us, unknowable in the present state of knowledge. We have every reason to believe that the whole existing universe of worlds, however far it extends, is one great mechanism revolving about the throne of God, from whence they get the power we call gravity, and other forces, and by which all is kept in being.

This suggests a view as to the meaning of the expression, "the new heavens," which are to accompany the new earth. We read of there being no longer need of the sun, and the inference is that this familiar orb is no longer present. The sun in Scripture is associated with earthly things. In Ecclesiastes, "under the sun" is wholly the earthly view. The sun is the source of the calamities in two of the plagues poured upon the earth in judgment. It would be then fitting if earth were to be released from its grasp. We know this earth is not the center of the universe, but on the contrary very far from it, in a corner of the universe, in fact, where stars are comparatively few and far between. Yet it is to be the site of the city and throne of God. John beholds the latter coming down from heaven. The same effect would be produced if the earth was caught up to heaven. It would be seen then as if coming down from God. Will this be the case? Will this poor, little, sinful, dark earth itself be taken into the bosom of God? To be caught away from the scenes of its suffering and sin in a physical rapture, would be following out the spiritual method in the translation of the saints. There are cosmical reasons, too, which seem as if some such change would be required. It would give to the new earth the new heavens mentioned. This would make the scene of Calvary the center of the universe. No longer would any wonder at the small and distant earth as the sphere of such tremendous events. The center of the universe would be earth, the site of the throne of God. This would complete the work of Christ for earth as well as for man. To see every particle of the world he died upon, lifted up into the regions of eternal bliss, and given up to God forever, would complete redemption.

The closing scene of the work and age of redemption is thus described: "Then cometh the end, when he shall deliver up the kingdom to God, even the Father; when he shall have abolished all rule and all authority and power. For he must reign, till he hath put all his enemies under his feet. The last enemy that shall be abolished is death. For, He put all things in subjection under his feet. But when he saith, All things are put in subjection, it is evident that he is excepted who did subject all things unto him. And when all things have been subjected unto him, then shall the Son also himself be subjected unto him, that God may be all in all."[1] Christ ever acknowledged this relation of himself to God: "The Father is greater than I;" "The Son can do nothing of himself, but what he seeth the Father doing; for what things soever he doeth, these the Son also doeth in like manner."[2] All this is explained by the relationship of Father and Son. It is at once a position of equality and yet subordination; equality in nature, subordination in action and office. There is given here by Christ the last and full and eternal example in his hour of complete triumph, of absolute submission to God over all. We have looked at great public scenes in the life of Christ: when he finished creation; when he relinquished primeval glory and stepped down and into human life and was born into the world; when he hung on the cross, and when he ascended and was received on high; when he came in wrath against the enemies of God and man, when he led his church to the throne of the Majesty on high; but this final scene when he lays at the feet of the Father the complete results of the full work for man, heaven, and nature is the climax of his greatness. In taking his place at the feet of the Father, he leads all in earth and heaven to the same place of submission and blessing.

[1] 1 Cor. xv. 24-28. [2] John xiv. 28; v. 19.

But the submission of all things to the Father is not the cessation of his work. It is not enough, even to satisfy our small minds, that sin and its effects should be banished and all restored as at first to be even more beautiful and holy than in Eden. We think and desire to know and see more. What after heaven is fully established? How shall we spend eternity? What will be the work of Christ during the endless æons? Our knowledge of the past work of Christ leads us to know that it will be an advance in extent and kind. The climax of the work of God is not reached. Indeed we have reason to believe there can be no climax either in the work of God or in a Christian's experience. But where is the field for a greater work than saving a world? What can be greater than redemption? Where will Christ find a field for the display of the vast powers of his divine nature? We are prepared for surprises in heaven, and there will be many such. There is some light possible to a thoughtful mind which will give itself to the consideration of this in a believing and desiring frame of mind. Scripture, Nature, and Christian reason help us to some hints. We may be mistaken in our attempts to picture the future, but we cannot exaggerate. We are at liberty to think about the matters of the other world, and urged to do so, and to set our affections upon them.

In studying Christ in the eternal past, we considered two infinite conceptions. One of these was the great fact of *limitless space*. There is no possible or conceivable end or boundary to space. We cannot think of a point, no matter how remote, where there is not farther extension. The science of astronomy tells us that wherever space extends, there stars exist, beyond our farthest point of observation. These stars are worlds. The fixed stars are suns like our own, only most of them are far larger. These suns are doubtless surrounded as ours is, with planets like our earth. The spectroscope shows the same elements to exist in the sun and stars as in our earth, showing not only a common origin, but a similar constitution, and doubtless similar conditions. The numbers of stars or suns identified and counted are far up in the hundreds of millions. But these are only a fraction of those within range of our vision, but so distant as to appear only as clouds. Single points have, under more powerful glasses, separated into clusters of stars, and the clouds have proved to be universes.

M. Camille Flammarion thus describes the view of the heavens: —

"Let us imagine that we thus sail a million years with the velocity of light, 186,000 miles a second. Are we at the confines of the visible universe? See the black immensities we must cross! But yonder new stars are lit up in the depths of the heavens. We push on toward them. We reach them. Again a million years; new revelations; new starry splendors; new universes; new worlds; new earths. What, never an end? We are at the vestibule of the infinite. We have advanced but a single step. We are always at the same point, — the center everywhere, the circumference nowhere. We see before us the infinite of which the study is not yet begun. We have seen nothing. We recoil in terror. We might fall in a straight line during a whole eternity nor ever reach the bottom. It is infinite in all directions."[1]

All this is the work of Christ, and part of his great plan, whatever it is. We must believe in the unity of the divine plan. We must believe in purpose in all this vast creation. We must also believe that it is, or is to be, the scene of life. It is true of every place on earth. Earth, air, and sea swarm with life. So must that vast material universe in the coming ages, if not now. This is the plan of God as seen in all nature. These stars, however beautiful they may be to sight as a spectacle, do not fulfil the demands of reasonable consideration as such. The

[1] "Popular Astronomy," New York, 1894.

most of them are not seen by man at all, and few more than dimly seen at best. While it is true that many a flower blooms and fades unseen, and many a gem lies unknown to man, yet the worlds of the heavens are so great, so many, that knowing God as the God of design and life and purpose, we are irresistibly led to feel these great and innumerable worlds are to be the scene of life and activity. Further, the same arguments lead us to believe they must be intended as the spheres of intelligent life, of beings who can enjoy all this, and think, and reason, and glorify the Creator of all. Here, then, is the field worthy of the powers of Christ, boundless space the scene of the work of Christ, and eternity the duration of his operation. To fill these worlds with life and beauty, to people them with living, happy beings as the new earth, is a work worthy of Christ, and which will be work for eternity, for space and duration run on interminably together. The prediction was, "Of the increase of his government there shall be no end." Increase, then, is the work of Christ, and here is its sphere.

We ask what beings will inhabit these new worlds? Christ could create races for each as he did man for earth. He could also repeat the work of redemption upon each. But both of these suppositions seem incredible. Either, as said before, would be a break in the continuity of the divine plan. It would be a departure from the plan as we have seen it unrolled before us, in which each age grows out of the preceding and leads up to another, and each advances upon a forecasted plan. Besides, if other races were created, sin might come to them, and other and greater falls take place. The whole outlook seems to comprehend extension of the work already commenced.

Looking back to the beginning, we conceived the plan of God to be the production of a race of beings of a character established in holiness, whom he could trust under all circumstances, and to whom he could commit the carrying out of his great designs. We noted the repeated sowings and siftings by which such a race was produced, the care to exclude all tares at the last great sifting. We are irresistibly led to believe God has some great purpose in man, aside from the peopling of this little world. It has often been a source of wonder that God should choose so small a world as the scene of Calvary,— that in a universe so vast, the Almighty God should pass by all those great worlds and come to this small, distant, and inferior earth, and here display his power and personality as the story of the Bible declares. As a finality, it is wholly inexplicable, but as a means to some vast purpose, we can understand it. The purpose has been intimated. The care in selecting the seed, the time in preparation, the place at the beginning of the eternal future, all attest the connection of earth with this great ultimate purpose. Earth is but a seed-bed from which God will people the heavens. This purified race are to be the progenitors of worlds of such holy, happy creatures.

If our view of the preservation of a human race from the last destruction of the world, in their earthly bodies, is correct, some sphere for the accommodation of the increase of the race will be required. In a thousand years they would so increase as to fill the earth far beyond the present most crowded parts. From whatever point we view the future of the eternal age, we are led to see that there must be increase, and room for it. We can see plainly the room for the spread of the increase and the increase itself, and there seems to be no Scriptural or reasonable objection to this. Indeed, the Scripture tells us plainly the church is to be but "a kind of first-fruits of his creatures."[1] If sin had not come to man, some provision for the accommodation of the race in the cer-

[1] James i. 18.

tain event of their finally filling the earth, would have been necessary; and their removal to some other world would have been undoubtedly effected. In short, the plan here proposed as the possible design of God in the preparation of the universe, seems to have been the plan from eternity.

One of God's great promises will be fulfilled literally by such a work in the universe as we have described. The promise made to Abraham was five times repeated. The first giving was this: "I will make thy seed as the dust of the earth; so that if a man can number the dust of the earth, then shall thy seed also be numbered." Again the promise was thus given: "And he brought him forth abroad, and said, Look now toward heaven, and tell the stars, if thou be able to tell them; and he said unto him, So shall thy seed be." It was his faith in this last which brought him salvation. It was again repeated: "In blessing I will bless thee, and in multiplying I will multiply thy seed as the sand which is upon the sea shore." God again repeats it near the end of his life: "I will multiply thy seed as the stars of heaven." To Jacob the same promise is given: "Thy seed shall be as the dust of the earth;"[1] of this promise Jacob reminds God in his day of trouble. This applying to the seed of Jacob alone, vastly increases the proportions of the promise. This was figuratively fulfilled in the age of Solomon when, as the scripture says, the children of Israel were as the sand of the sea, and later when Paul tells us the same. But here in this eternal view is the literal fulfilment of the promise upon which the covenant to Abraham was based. It is not rhetoric. It is not hyperbole. It is actual certitude that if the worlds, innumerable as astronomy tells us they are, should be peopled as the earth is and will be in the time of blessedness, the actual number of the population of the universe would be as in-

[1] Gen. xiii. 16; xv. 5; xxii. 17; xxvi. 4; xxviii. 14; xxxii. 12.

numerable, on any system of human computation, as the sand of the sea or the dust of the earth.

The mission of the church is indicated by the recurrence and use and composition of the number twelve. It is typical of the completeness of God in man. It is the multiple of three, the number of divine personality, and four, the number everywhere indicating humanity and universal extension and completion. So the number of the tribes of Israel and of the apostles is twelve, and the foundations of the city and the gates are twelve, and the dimensions are measured by twelve. In the previous age the number of perfection was seven, three added to four, — God added to man, indicating the work upon the church as distinguished from the work with the church. In the eternal state the progress of the church will be multiplied by the divine ratio. The open gates opening to all quarters, indicate further the universal mission of the church in eternity. These directions, east, west, north, and south, are sidereal as well as geographical. They indicate universality as to other worlds as well as earth. We can conceive of the saints endowed with divine or angelic power of flight, going upon missions to distant worlds. We can believe their responsibilities will extend to these worlds. They will occupy relations of superiority as well as of love and mercy. Those who saw the age of sin and were combatants in that age and struggled and overcame, will be to these worlds as veterans are to us. Their numbers cannot be added to, for the story of sin will never be repeated, we feel sure. Such will occupy a position unique among the myriads of the universe. They may become world rulers, well trained for the great responsibility by their lives of struggle.

This view opens up a realm for vast possibilities of attainment as well as accomplishment. These thoughts will show us that eternity is not the vague and empty sphere some imagine, that the other life and world may be so full of histories of peoples, nations, worlds, and events, as will make our earth story seem brief and small. So not only limitless extension but endless variety are in the prospect. There will be the rise of problems for solution, emergences to meet, great designs to plan, conditions to provide for. To the three infinities,—God, duration, and space,—we must add another,—infinite possibilities.

The work of the church in the eternal ages is thus described by Bickersteth:—

> "Ceaseless, indeed, our ministry, and limitless
> The increase of that government and peace,
> Messiah's heritage and ours. For as
> Our native orb ere long too strait became
> For its blest habitants, not only some
> Translated without death, for death was not,
> As Enoch joined the glorified in light;
> But at the voice of God, the stars, which rolled
> Innumerous in the azure firmament,
> By thousands and ten thousands, as he spake
> Six words of power, the seventh, it was done,
> Were mantled and prepared as seats of life;
> And it was ours to bear from earth and plant,
> Like Adam, in some paradise of fruits
> The ancestors of many a newborn world,
> Like Adam, but far different issue now,
> Sin and the curse and death forever crushed.
> And thus from planet on to planet spread
> The living light. As when some white-robed priest
> Himself, surrounded by his acoylites,
> In some vast minster, from the altar fire
> Lighting his torch, walks through the slumbrous aisles,
> And kindles, one by one, the brazen lamps
> That on the fluted columns cast their shade,
> Or from the frescoed ceiling hang suspense,
> Until the startled sanctuary is bathed
> In glory, and the evening chant of praise
> Floats in the radiance; so it was in heaven;
> God's temple, the expectant firmament,
> Hung with its lamps, innumerable stars;
> The Priest, Messiah; earth, the altar flame;

Angels and saints, the wingèd messengers;
And that great choral eucharist, the hymn
Of all creation's everlasting praise." [1]

The nature of the perfected relationship of all things to each other and to God is intimated in this scripture: "For this cause I bow my knees unto the Father, from whom every fatherhood in heaven and earth is named."[2] The term "Fatherhood" is descriptive of all relationships from that of the Godhead down through all things. Every family is a reproduction of the Godhead. All its persons are represented there. The family is made in the image of God. It is a copy of the heavenly family. This plan of organization is universal. It is the divine plan for this and all worlds. We see the organization of all things on the paternal plan. Emperors, kings, presidents, are but fathers in their office, and should be in their action. They are but successors of the patriarch, who was but the tribe father. The apostle intimates the heavenly hosts are arranged upon the same great divine plan of the family. Indeed, we read of the heavenly Eldership, and we know of superior rulers among the angels. Still lower in the scale is the innumerable fatherhoods of nature. All plants, insects, and animals are arranged in fatherhoods. Every parent bird or creature with its circle of dependent little ones is but a transcript of the great Fatherhood over all. The very inorganic things show the same arrangement. The solar system is but a fatherhood of worlds. The whole universe of material things is arranged upon the one plan.

The first reference of the apostle in this use of the term of fatherhood is to the church. It is arranged on earth after the fashion of a family. The church is still patriarchal. The more closely the church conforms to the model of the family, the more closely it

---

[1] "Yesterday, To-day, and For Ever," book xii, line 600.
[2] Eph. iii. 14, 15, marginal reading.

conforms to the ideal form as well as state. This arrangement of the church in fatherhoods is to continue in the eternal state. We must not suppose the church to be in heaven one undivided, unarranged mass. It will have its subdivisions and lesser and greater parts. There will be rule among the saints as well as by them. There must be such order for the perfect state as well as for this present condition. Abraham is the head of such a fatherhood. Many of his seed will thus address him. Paul has such a position to us Gentiles. We are his spiritual children. Doubtless he will be considered worthy of headship over those who followed him as he did Christ. This is the relationship of the apostles declared by Christ when he promised they should sit on thrones judging the twelve tribes of Israel. The position is that of a fatherhood rather than that of mere authority of superior position. So on down the line of the church, we can see an orderly system established by the bonds of affectionate allegiance to those appointed in the wisdom of God to have the duties and position of the fatherhoods of the heavenly church.

These many fatherhoods are to be brought into perfect condition as to each other, and into unity with the Father over all. The perfection of nature, man, and heaven is contemplated in the consummation of all things. Every fatherhood having been made complete in itself will then be made part of the one Fatherhood. It implies not only the authority of God over all, but the right relation of all things to God. This is the work of Christ. To effect this he came and died and lives and is coming again. This will be the effect of the whole work of redemption. The title, Father, expresses God's nature and rule and work as no other does. It was brought to us by Christ. It was the name for God constantly on the lips of Christ. It expressed not only his own relationship, but the ideal state he had in mind and for which he strove. It is all inclusive of the attributes and offices of God. He is therein Creator, Preserver, Ruler, and final Judge.

In the Fatherhood of God there will be established the perfect theocracy,—God reigning absolutely and directly over all. The relationship is described in the preceding scriptures. The order is God the Father, Christ, the glorified saints arranged in closer or wider circles in the New Jerusalem, then the angelic hosts of many and varying offices, then the myriads of humanity and innumerable worlds of organic and inorganic nature, all permeated by the Spirit of God, and living, moving, and having their being by the life of God through the Holy Spirit and directed by the will of God, in perfect unison, every thought and act responsive to the mind of God. This is the goal of all things. It was in the mind of the apostle when he wrote: "That God may be all in all." To have a part in this infinity of existence, happiness, holiness, and achievment is the possibility, yea, the certainty, on divine conditions of this life we live.

Eternity, as we have noted, consists of successive ages. If the belief of the Jewish church and of the ancient Christian church is right, the whole history of man is but a week of which the millennium is the Sabbath. "A thousand years are with the Lord as one day." If this is the case, there may come in the great weeks of eternity, the Sabbaths of universal rest and worship, when by some means, even now beginning to be understood, by the mutual relation of light and sound, all the universe may come into one accord in great anthems of praise, and the "music of the spheres" be more than a figure of speech.

God gave his ancient people the model social state and worship. The worship of Israel may yet be repeated on a universal scale. The yearly feasts may be but figures of the great feasts of eternity, when representatives of worlds will gather to the new Jerusalem to celebrate a Saviour's dying love and reigning power and glory. There may be great years of rest, when even the bliss of eternity will be multiplied. There may come great jubilees in the eternal cycles, when even greater gifts shall be given, and perhaps myriads raised from lower to higher places of glory and power, and even millenniums of greater glory. Eternity is not one long unbroken period, but is arranged in ages or periods as the time we have known, and we may believe that they are distinguished by peculiarities as those we have known. We have seen in the succession of the ages of earth and man, development. One age prepares for another, and this opens up into one still more advanced. One age is to another as seed to plant and this to flower and this to harvest. But harvest only means a new sowing and a still greater growing and harvests unceasing. The same operation we have every reason to believe will continue. God's plan is one. Great ages will come and go. New purposes will dawn upon the universes. The resources of the Almighty are inexhaustible. There will be no climax with its inevitable retrogression. It will be progress ever upward, onward, nearer and still nearer to God, the infinite and eternal.

We may now see what great things lay upon the heart of Christ as he came to earth and suffered and died. All eternity depended on the outcome of his conflict. The future of other worlds than ours hung in the balance. All the universe had an interest in the great conflict. Success or failure were universal in their sweep. We see also in this great view of the work of Christ and its possibilities, the meaning of the promise, "He shall see of the travail of his soul and shall be satisfied." It must be an infinite aim which shall satisfy the heart of Christ. But it will be satisfied when he sees the myriads of worlds filled with holy, happy beings, circling in perfect harmony about the throne of God, each being growing in grace, and by some system of spiritual promotion, drawing nearer to the state of perfection of the risen saints, perhaps attaining as a great prize, that state as the reward of faithful effort. Instruction and development are part of the work of eternity. The great part Christ fills is that of the Shepherd. This will be as necessary in eternity as here. His flock will have increased by many million fold. All these will need to be fed spiritually and materially. Then will be fulfilled his prophecy, "There shall be one fold and one Shepherd."

CONCLUSION.

THE subject of this book stands before two classes, — those who are the people of Christ, and those who are not. To the first, the message of the book is, that all Christ is described here, he is to you. This is *your* Creator, Saviour, Comforter, Intercessor, Judge, King, and Eternal Companion. If you believe this, act accordingly. Every motive of love, gratitude, or even self-interest, bids you hasten to come to the decision to say, "For to me to live is Christ, to die is gain." Surely such gains are worth striving for. It is your privilege to enter into the acceptance and possession of all this by full submission to the will of God and acceptance of God's purpose in all its fulness for you. "All things are yours; whether Paul, or Apollos, or Cephas, or the world, or life, or death, or things present, or things to come; all are yours; and ye are Christ's and Christ is God's."

This book may be read by some who are not yet the people of God. You have read this with some wonder, perhaps incredulity, perhaps with personal indifference. Be assured you may have a part in the blessings of the future. You may have all that is promised to any one in the Scripture. The Bible is given us for our sakes to save and bless us. It is by its appeals we are persuaded to come to Christ. Everything in Scripture, to the very highest attainment of perfection of character or glory, is included in the attainment of the place spoken of as "in Christ." Within this sphere lie all the blessings of the Christian for this life, and that to come. It is a matter first of place, that is, where you stand as to Christ, a relationship established when one takes Christ as his personal Saviour, and commits the keeping of himself for time and eternity to Christ. This is coming to Christ. It is generally a definite act and is best so, that we may remember it and get comfort from the memory of the step.

Have you come to Christ so? If not, will you do so before you close this book, by saying to yourself and God, " I will this moment take Christ to be my Lord and Saviour, and begin to serve and follow him"? If you will heartily do so, you may know by his own word in a thousand places, he does then and there receive you, and will keep you. To refuse to do this is to refuse to come to Christ, and thereby refuse eternal life, for "he that believeth on the Son hath eternal life; but he that obeyeth not the Son shall not see life, but the wrath of God abideth on him." Here are the two issues, there are no others. "The Spirit and the Bride say, Come!"

www.ingramcontent.com/pod-product-compliance
Lightning Source LLC
Chambersburg PA
CBHW022119290426
44112CB00008B/733